SONAR 2
POWER!

Scott R. Garrigus

SONAR 2 Power!

Credits: Senior Editor, Mark Garvey; Production Editor, Rodney A. Wilson; Cover Design, Chad Planner, *Pop Design Works*; Interior Design and Layout, *GEX Publishing Services*; Indexer, Kevin Broccoli, *Broccoli Information Management*.

Publisher: Andy Shafran

Library of Congress Catalog Number: 2002107567

ISBN 1-929685-63-7

5 4 3 2

MUSKA & LIPMAN

Muska & Lipman Publishing

2645 Erie Avenue, Suite 41

Cincinnati, Ohio 45208

www.muskalipman.com

publisher@muskalipman.com

About the Author

Scott R. Garrigus
www.garrigus.com

Scott R. Garrigus has been involved with music and computers since he was 12 years old. After graduating from high school, he went on to earn a B.A. in music performance with an emphasis in sound recording technology at UMass, Lowell. In 1993, he released his first instrumental album on cassette, entitled *Pieces Of Imagination*. In 1995, he began his professional writing career when his first article appeared in *Electronic Musician* magazine. In 2000, he authored his first book, *Cakewalk Power!* This was the first book to deal exclusively with the Cakewalk Pro Audio, Guitar Studio, and Home Studio software applications. In 2001, his second book, *Sound Forge Power!*, which was the first book to deal exclusively with Sonic Foundry's Sound Forge audio editing software, was published. Also in 2001, his third book, *Sonar Power!*, which was the first book to deal exclusively with Cakewalk's Sonar software, was published. Today, Garrigus continues to contribute articles to *Electronic Musician*, in addition to a number of other print and online publications. He also publishes his own music technology e-zine, called DigiFreq (**www.digifreq.com**), which provides free news, reviews, tips, and techniques for music technology users.

Dedication

To Mom, Dad, Babci, Dziadzi, Grandma, Grandpa, Mark, and Steve. Thanks for all your love and support. And to Ron, Claire, Ellie, Vinny, and Ron Jr. for being there and making me feel like a part of your family. Also, to my cat, Figaro, who recently turned 15 years old.

Acknowledgments

Thanks to all my music technology friends who take the time to visit my Web site and to read my ramblings in the DigiFreq newsletter each month. The DigiFreq family is now over 9,000 strong!

Thanks to all the SONAR users who's dedication and support helped to make this book possible.

Thanks to all my friends over at Cakewalk (Chris Rice, Jerry Antl, Morten Saether, Carl Jacobson, Steve Thomas, and others).

Thanks also to the Muska & Lipman publishing team.

And as ever, thank you, God for everything.

Appendix C—Producing for Multimedia and the Web . . .539

Appendix D—SONAR Resources on the Web 557

Introduction

This is the first book on the market that deals exclusively with Cakewalk's SONAR 2. You can find other Cakewalk-related and generic books about using computers to create and record music that may provide a small amount of information about SONAR 2, but none of them provides complete coverage of the product. Of course, SONAR 2 comes with an excellent manual, but like most other manuals, it is meant only as a feature guide.

Instead of just describing the features of the program and how they work, I'm going to dig deep down into the software and show you exactly how to use the product with step-by-step examples and exercises that will help make your composing and recording sessions run more smoothly. I'll explain all of the features available, and I'll do it in a manner you can understand and use, right away.

So why should you listen to me? Well, I've been using SONAR (and its predecessor, Pro Audio) for many years. I've written two Cakewalk-related books before this one—*Cakewalk Power!* and *SONAR Power!* I've also written about Cakewalk products in numerous review articles for magazines such as *Electronic Musician*, *Keyboard*, and *Recording*. In addition, I've been working with the people at Cakewalk for quite some time now, learning all there is to know about SONAR 2, as well as testing the product during the beta process. And the people at Cakewalk have helped me develop much of the information in this book, making sure that everything is "officially" technically accurate. How's that for a seal of approval? Suffice it to say, I know my way around the product, and now I would like to share that knowledge with you.

I'm going to assume that SONAR 2 is installed on your computer and that you know how to start the program. In addition, you should have at least skimmed through the manual that comes with the software and have all your external audio and MIDI gear set up already. I'm also going to assume that you know how to use your mouse for clicking, dragging, double-clicking, right-clicking, and so on. You should also know how to work with basic Windows features such as Windows Explorer and the Windows Control Panel. And you should have access to the World Wide Web or perhaps a friend who does. Otherwise, all you need is a strong interest in learning how to get the most out of SONAR 2.

Just leave the rest up to me, and I promise that you'll be working with SONAR 2 like you never have before. You might even have some fun with it, too.

How This Book is Organized

You'll find that, although I've tried to avoid overlapping content between this book and the manual that comes with SONAR 2, in some instances, this overlap just can't be avoided. I wanted to be sure to help you understand all the important features of the program, and doing so means including some basic explanations to begin with. For the most part, though, the information included in this book is more "how to" rather than "this feature does so-and-so."

Chapter 1, "MIDI and Digital Audio Basics," and Chapter 2, "Getting Started with SONAR," provide an introduction to computer music and the software. These chapters explain the importance of registration and how to find help, as well as the major features and more obscure parts of the software, and how they work together. You'll also find a brief description of the differences between SONAR 2, Plasma, and Home Studio 2002.

Chapter 3, "Customizing SONAR," shows you how to make SONAR 2 work the way you want it to. This chapter explains program preferences and workspace customization, as well as how to find the optimal settings for MIDI and audio functionality.

In Chapter 4, "Working with Projects," you'll learn how to work with Projects. This chapter includes step-by-step instructions for opening, closing, and saving existing Projects. You'll also learn how to create new Projects and how to make your own Project Templates.

Chapter 5, "Getting Around in SONAR," and Chapter 6, "Recording and Playback," describe how to navigate within SONAR 2 and how to record and play back your Projects. You'll find instructions on how to record and play MIDI, as well as audio, and you'll learn about recording multiple tracks at once. I'll explain the importance of the Now Time and show you how to use the Go menu, Search, and Markers, as well as the Zoom features. After you read these chapters, you'll be making your way through SONAR 2 like a pro.In Chapter 7, "Editing Basics," and Chapter 8, "Exploring the Editing Tools," you're ready to dive into editing. First, I'll explain the basics to you, including Tracks and Clips, the Event Editor, and Piano Roll. Then you can investigate the editing tools in more detail.

Similar to the VST synth features that you find in Steinberg's Cubase software, SONAR gives you access to virtual synthesizer plug-ins. These plug-ins let you compose music with MIDI using software-based synthesizers rather than the synth in your sound card or your external MIDI keyboard. Chapter 9, "Software Synthesis," explores these features.

Chapter 10, "Composing with Loops," will show you how to use the looping features and Loop Construction View found in SONAR 2. With these features you can compose songs using nothing more than audio sample loops. The looping features add similar functionality to SONAR 2 as you would find in Sonic Foundry's ACID software.

Chapter 11, "Exploring Effects" explains one of my favorite parts of SONAR 2. The things you can do with these tools are amazing. I'll cover both the MIDI and audio effects, and I'll show you how to use them in offline and real-time situations. I'll even share some cool Presets I've developed, so you can use them in your own recording projects.

Chapter 12, "Mixing It Down," takes a look at mixing. I know that mixing music via software can be confusing sometimes. Nothing beats being able to just grab a fader on a hardware-based mixer, but after you read this chapter, you may find that with all the functionality that SONAR 2 provides, mixing is actually easier, and you have more control when using an on-screen software mixer.

I've received many questions as to SONAR's capabilities in terms of music notation, so that's the topic I'll cover in Chapter 13, "Making Sheet Music." I'll explain all the tools you have at your disposal, as well as what you can and cannot do. Although SONAR doesn't provide full-fledged music notation features, you might be surprised at what you find here.

Chapter 14, "Studio Control with StudioWare and Sysx"; Chapter 15, "Advanced StudioWare Techniques"; Chapter 16, "CAL 101"; and Chapter 17, "Advanced CAL Techniques," jump into some of the more complicated features that SONAR 2 offers. Don't worry if you think that StudioWare and CAL are out of your reach as a beginning user. Actually, you can use these features in plenty of ways even if you decide not to explore them fully. But just in case you're interested in learning more, I'm going to show you how to develop your own Panels in StudioWare and your own programs in CAL. By the time you finish reading, you won't know how you lived without them.

Finally, in Chapter 18, "Take Your SONAR Project to CD," I'll show you how to prepare your SONAR 2 Project and burn it onto CD.

My hope is that, by reading this book, you will learn how to master SONAR 2. And, along the way, if you have a little fun while you're at it, that's all the better.

Conventions Used in This Book

As you begin to read, you'll see that most of the information in this book is solid and useful. It contains very little fluff. I won't bore you with unrelated anecdotes or repetitious data. But to help guide you through all this material, I'll use several different conventions that highlight specific types of information that you should keep an eye out for.

TIP

Tips are extra information that you should know related to the current topic being discussed and, in some cases, include personal experiences and/or specific techniques not covered elsewhere.

CAUTION

Cautions highlight actions or commands that can make irreversible changes to your files or potentially cause problems in the future. Read them carefully because they may contain important information that can make the difference between keeping your files, software, and hardware safe, and you from losing a huge amount of work.

NOTE

Of course, sometimes you might like to know, but don't necessarily need to know, certain points about the current topic. Notes provide additional material to help you avoid problems or shed light on a feature or technology, and they also offer related advice.

1

MIDI and
Digital Audio Basics

If you're anything like me, you want to get started right away learning all about SONAR. But if you don't understand the basic concepts and terms associated with computer music, you might have a hard time working your way through this book. So, just to give you a quick overview of the most significant aspects of music technology, this chapter will do the following:

> ▶ Define MIDI and explain how it works
>
> ▶ Define digital audio and explain how it works
>
> ▶ Explain the difference between MIDI and digital audio

Of course, this one chapter can't replace an entire book about the subject. If you want to learn more about MIDI and digital audio, plenty of extended resources are available. For example, there is an e-book called the Desktop Music Handbook available for free reading on the Web. You can find it at **http://www.cakewalk.com/Tips/Desktop.htm.**

What Is MIDI?

MIDI (which stands for Musical Instrument Digital Interface) is a special kind of computer language that lets electronic musical instruments (such as synthesizer keyboards) "talk" to computers. It works like this: Say you use a synthesizer keyboard as your musical instrument. Every key on the keyboard of your synthesizer has a corresponding electronic switch. When you press a key, its corresponding switch is activated and sends a signal to the computer chip inside your keyboard. The chip then sends the signal to the MIDI interface in your keyboard, which translates the signal into MIDI messages and sends those messages to the MIDI interface in your computer system.

NOTE

A *MIDI interface* is a device that is plugged into your computer allowing it to understand the MIDI language. Basically, you can think of the interface as a translator. When your electronic musical instrument sends out MIDI messages to your computer, the MIDI interface takes those messages and converts them into signals that your computer can understand.

The MIDI messages contain information telling your computer that a key was pressed (called a Note On message), which key it was (the name of the note represented by a number), along with how hard you hit the key (called the MIDI velocity). For example, if you press Middle C on your keyboard, a Note On message is sent to your computer telling it that you pressed a key. Another message containing the number 60 is sent telling the computer that you pressed Middle C. And a final message is sent containing a number from 1 to 127 (1 being very soft and 127 being very loud), which tells your computer how hard you hit the key.

Different MIDI messages represent all the performance controls on your keyboard. In addition to each key, MIDI messages represent the modulation wheel, pitch bend wheel, and other features. Your computer can store all the MIDI messages that are sent to it as you play your keyboard. The timing of your performance (how long it takes you to hit one key after another and how long you hold down each key) can be stored as well. Your computer can then send those MIDI messages back to your keyboard with the same timing, so that it seems like you are playing the music, but without touching the keys. The basic concept goes like this: You play a piece of music on your keyboard. Your performance is stored as instructions in your computer. Then those instructions are sent back to your keyboard from the computer, and you hear the piece of music played back exactly the same way you performed it, mistakes and all (see Figure 1.1).

Figure 1.1
This diagram shows how MIDI messages are recorded and played back with a computer

What Is Digital Audio?

Digital audio is the representation of sound as numbers. Recording sound as digital audio is similar to recording sound using a tape recorder, but slightly different. Let's say you have a microphone connected to your computer system. When you make a sound (such as singing a tune, playing a musical instrument, or even simply clapping your hands), the microphone "hears" it and converts the sound into an electronic signal. The microphone then sends the signal to the sound card in your computer, which translates the signal into numbers. These numbers are called *samples*.

NOTE

A *sound card* is a device that is plugged into your computer, allowing it to understand the electronic signals of any audio device. Basically, you can think of the sound card as a translator. When an audio device (such as a microphone, electronic music instrument, CD player, or anything else that can output an audio signal) sends out signals to your computer, the sound card takes those signals and converts them into numbers that your computer can understand.

The samples contain information telling your computer how the recorded signal sounded at certain instants in time. The more samples used to represent the signal, the better the quality of the recorded sound. For example, to make a digital audio recording that has the same quality as audio on a CD, the computer needs to receive 44,100 samples for every second of sound that's recorded. The number of samples received per second is called the *sampling rate*.

The size of each individual sample also makes a difference in the quality of the recorded sound. This size is called the *bit depth*. The more bits used to represent a sample, the better the sound quality. For example, to make a digital audio recording with the same quality as audio on a CD, each sample has to be 16 bits in size.

NOTE

Computers use binary numerals to represent numbers. These binary numerals are called *bits*, and each bit can represent one of two numbers: 1 or 0. By combining more than one bit, computers can represent larger numbers. For instance, any number from 0 to 255 can be represented with 8 bits. With 16 bits, the range becomes 0 to 65,535.

Your computer can store all the samples that are sent to it. The timing of each sample is stored as well. Your computer can then send those samples back to the sound card with the same timing so that what you hear sounds exactly the same as what was recorded. The basic concept goes like this: Your sound card records an electronic signal from an audio device (such as a microphone or CD player). The sound card converts the signal into numbers called samples, which are stored in your computer. Then those samples are sent back to the sound card, which converts them back into an electronic signal. The signal is sent to your speakers (or other audio device), and you hear the sound exactly as it was recorded (see Figure 1.2).

Figure 1.2
This diagram shows how audio is converted into numbers so that it can be recorded and played back with a computer

So, What's Really the Difference?

After reading the explanations of MIDI and digital audio, you might still be wondering what the difference is between them. Both processes involve signals being sent to the computer to be recorded and then the computer sending those signals back out to be played, right? Well, the point that you have to keep in mind is that, when you're recording MIDI data, you're not recording actual sound. You are recording only performance instructions. This concept is similar to a musician reading sheet music, with the sheet music representing MIDI data and the musician representing a computer. The musician (or computer) reads the sheet music (or MIDI data) and then stores it in memory. The musician then plays the music back via a musical instrument. Now what if the musician uses a different instrument to play back the music? The musical performance remains the same, but the sound changes. The same thing happens with MIDI data. A synthesizer keyboard can make all kinds of different sounds, but playing the same MIDI data back with the keyboard yields the exact same performance, no matter what.

When you're recording digital audio, you *are* recording actual sound. If you record a musical performance as digital audio, you cannot change the sound of that performance, as described earlier. And because of these differences, MIDI and digital audio have their advantages and disadvantages. Because MIDI is recorded as performance data and not actual sound, you can manipulate it much more easily than you can manipulate digital audio. For example, you can easily fix mistakes in your performance by simply changing the pitch of a note. And MIDI data can be translated into standard musical notation. Digital audio can't. On the other hand, MIDI can't be used to record anything that requires actual audio, such as sound effects or vocals. With digital audio, you can record any kind of sound whatsoever. And you can always be sure that your recording will sound exactly the same every time you play it back. With MIDI, you can't be sure of that because, although the MIDI data remains the same, the playback device or sound can be changed.

I hope that this description clears up some of the confusion you may have about MIDI and digital audio. You need to be familiar with a number of other related terms, but I will cover them in different areas of the book as I go along. For now, as long as you understand the difference between MIDI and digital audio, I can begin talking about the real reason you bought this book—how to use SONAR.

CHAPTER 1

2

Getting Started with SONAR

Now that you have a basic understanding of the technology involved in making music with computers, I think you'll find working with SONAR more enjoyable. Ready to get started? This chapter will do the following:

▶ Tell you how to obtain the latest product update

▶ Explain the importance of registering your software

▶ Give you a quick tour of SONAR's major features

▶ Briefly cover the new features in SONAR 2

▶ Explain the differences between SONAR, Plasma, and Home Studio 2002

▶ Describe a basic SONAR studio environment

▶ Let you know where to look for help, if problems arise

CHAPTER 2

What Version of SONAR Do You Have?

Even though you're using SONAR 2, it still may not be latest version. Cakewalk is constantly fixing and improving the software. Any problems that you may experience might easily be remedied with an update. To find out exactly what version you're using, start SONAR, and click Help > About SONAR. A dialog box similar to Figure 2.1 then appears, displaying your exact version number. You should then check to see whether a more recent update is available.

Figure 2.1
The About SONAR
dialog box shows the
program's current
version number

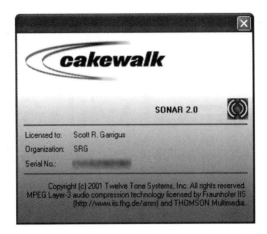

Get the Latest Product Update

Although automatically receiving new product updates would be nice, most companies
(except maybe Microsoft) can't afford to send out CDs to all their users every time they
create updates. That's one of the reasons the Internet has become such a wonderful tool.
Sometimes the answer to your problem is just a download away. Cakewalk provides a
support area on its Web site where you can get the latest updates for SONAR. Just follow
these steps to get the updates:

1. Log on to the Internet.

2. Start SONAR and choose Help > Sonar On The Web. This will automatically
    open your web browser and take you to the SONAR Owners page. Click on
    the Updates And Patches link to go to the SONAR Downloads page as
    shown in Figure 2.2.

Figure 2.2
You can download
SONAR updates from
the SONAR
Downloads page

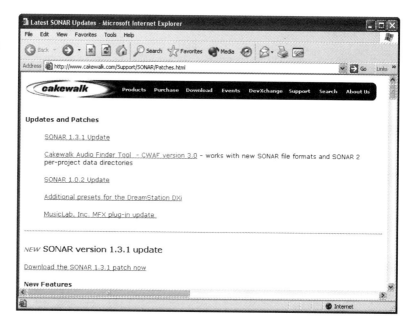

2. From the list of links, click the name of the update that you need.

3. If more than one update is available, simply compare your current version with the updates listed and select the appropriate one. For instance, if you have SONAR 2.0, you'll want the update that upgrades version 2.0 to the current version.

4. Click the Download link for the update, and then follow the instructions to download the update patch.

5. Create a temporary folder on your Windows desktop and download the update file to that folder.

6. Run the file, and your software is upgraded. That's all there is to upgrading.

CHAPTER 2

NOTE
Think you've found a bug? Just because a software product is released to the public doesn't mean it's perfect. Improvements are always being made. That's why updates become available. If you have a problem with SONAR on a regular basis and you can reproduce that problem by performing the same steps each time, you may have found a bug in the software. Before you go spreading any rumors, first tell a friend about it and see whether he or she can reproduce the problem on his or her computer system. If so, then you should drop an e-mail to Cakewalk at **support@cakewalk.com** and let the people there know about the problem. The staff may already be aware of the bug and be working on a fix for it. But then again, they may not, and although your diligence won't make you famous, you'll feel good to know that you may have saved your fellow SONAR users from a lot of frustration. Really, you will.

Register Your Software

Do you think registering your software is important? If not, think again. First and foremost, if you don't register your software, Cakewalk won't provide you with technical support. You'll be sorry if you run into a problem that causes you to lose some of your precious work, and the only thing between you and your sanity is the people at Cakewalk. If you're a techno-wizard, and this situation doesn't worry you, that's great. But there's something else you may not have thought about. What if your hard drive crashes, and you need to reinstall all your software applications, including SONAR? And at the same time, what if you can't find the jewel case that your SONAR CD came in? Yes, the jewel case, not the CD. Why is it significant? Because the jewel case has a little sticker with a very important number printed on it—your serial number. Without that number, you can't install SONAR. So, now who you gonna call? Yeah, that's right. By the way, your product serial number is important, too. Remember to send in that registration card! And, just to be safe, you might want to check with Cakewalk to make sure your information is on file. You just do the following:

1. Find your CD jewel case and look on the back to make sure your CD-KEY is printed there.

2. Log on to the Internet and start SONAR (if you haven't already).

3. Choose Help > Register Online. This will automatically open your web browser and take you to the Cakewalk Registration Form page.

4. Fill in the form and click the Register button.

Now you can rest easy, knowing that help is just a phone call or e-mail away.

TIP

To prevent yourself from losing your serial number, you might want to write it on your SONAR CD. Be sure to use an indelible pen and write the number on the top (the side with the printed material) of the CD. Don't write on the shiny side. You also might want to write down the number in a second location, just in case. I like to keep track of all the serial numbers for my software applications in a simple text file. I have a list containing the names and serial numbers of all the important software installed on my computer system. I also include the current version number and company contact information for each product. Then, if I ever run into a problem, I just refer to the list. By the way, you might also want to print the text file each time you update it. If your hard drive crashes, the text file won't do you any good since you won't be able to access it.

Take a Quick Tour of SONAR

Because SONAR is such a powerful application, you can use it for a variety of different tasks. They include composing music, developing computer game music and sounds, producing compact discs, creating audio for the World Wide Web, and even scoring films and videos. SONAR provides a number of features to support all these endeavors and more. As a matter of fact, you can use SONAR as the central piece of "equipment" in your studio because it allows you to control all your music gear from your computer via on-screen control panels. However you decide to use SONAR, you'll find plenty of flexibility and power in the tools provided.

Projects

In SONAR, all your music data for a single body of work is organized as a *project*. A project can be anything from a Top 40 song or a 30-second radio spot to a full-length symphonic score, such as a movie soundtrack. Along with the music data, all of SONAR's settings for a single work are stored in the project as well. A project is saved on disk as a single file with a .CWP or .CWB file name extension. The difference between the two file types is that a work (CWP) file stores only MIDI data and project settings, whereas a bundle (CWB) file also includes any audio data within a project. (For more information, see Chapter 4.)

Tracks, Clips, and Events

The music data within a project is organized into units called *tracks*, *clips*, and *events*. Events, which are the smallest units, consist of single pieces of data, such as one note played on a MIDI keyboard. Clips are groups of events. They can be anything from a simple MIDI melody to an entire vocal performance recorded as audio. And tracks are used to store clips. For example, a pop song project might contain seven tracks of music data—six for the instruments and one for the vocal performance. Each track can contain any number of clips that might represent one long performance or different parts of a performance. And SONAR gives you unlimited tracks. The only limitations are the speed of your CPU, the speed of your hard drive, and the amount of memory (RAM) you have in your computer. I'll talk more about tracks, clips, and events in Chapter 7.

Track View

To work with the data in a project, you have to use the tools called *views* in SONAR. Views are like windows that let you see and manipulate the data in a project in a variety of ways. The most important is the Track view, shown in Figure 2.3.

Figure 2.3
The Track view is the main window used to work with a project in SONAR

In this window, you can see all the tracks that are available in a project. You also can view and edit all the basic track settings, as well as all the clips contained in each track. I'll talk about the Track view extensively in a number of different chapters in the book.

NOTE

If you have used Cakewalk software in the past, particularly if you upgraded to SONAR from Pro Audio, Guitar Studio, or Home Studio, then you'll notice that the Audio view is no longer available. Actually, the Audio view features are still provided in SONAR, but now the Track view doubles as the Audio view.

Staff View

In the Staff view, you can work with the MIDI data in your project as standard music notation. By selecting one or more MIDI tracks in the Track view and opening the Staff view, you can see your music just as if it were notes on a printed page, as in Figure 2.4.

Figure 2.4
In the Staff view, you can see and edit your MIDI data as standard music notation

Using the Staff view, you also can edit your music as notation by adding, changing, or deleting notes. Special notation functions such as dynamics markings, percussion parts, and guitar chord symbols are included, too. You can notate anything from a single one-staff melody to an entire 24-part musical score. I'll talk about using the Staff view in Chapter 13.

Piano Roll View

Although the Staff view is great for traditional music editing, it doesn't allow you to access expressive MIDI data, such as note velocity or pitch bend controller messages. For that data, you can use the Piano Roll view. This view displays notes as they might appear on a player-piano roll, as shown in Figure 2.5.

CHAPTER 2

Figure 2.5
The Piano Roll view gives you access to both note and MIDI controller messages

You can change note pitch and duration by simply dragging on the rectangular representations. But more importantly, you can view and edit MIDI controller messages graphically with the mouse instead of having to deal with raw numbers. For more details about the Piano Roll view, see Chapter 7.

Event List View

If you really want precise control over the data in your project, the Event List view is the tool for the job. The Event List view shows each individual event in a track (or the entire project) as special keywords and numbers in a list, as shown in Figure 2.6.

Figure 2.6
For really precise editing tasks, the Event List view gives you access to the individual events in a project

Trk	HMSF	MBT	Ch	Kind	Data		
4	00:00:00:17	2:01:081	12	Note	D 6	64	468
4	00:00:00:25	2:02:084	12	Note	E 6	69	466
4	00:00:01:02	3:01:090	12	Note	F#6	71	250
4	00:00:01:06	3:01:280	12	Note	G 6	55	273
4	00:00:01:09	3:01:467	12	Note	F#6	65	1:020
4	00:00:01:12	3:02:199	12	Wheel	256		
4	00:00:01:12	3:02:204	12	Wheel	640		
4	00:00:01:12	3:02:208	12	Wheel	768		
4	00:00:01:12	3:02:211	12	Wheel	1152		
4	00:00:01:12	3:02:216	12	Wheel	1536		
4	00:00:01:12	3:02:221	12	Wheel	1664		
4	00:00:01:12	3:02:223	12	Wheel	2048		
4	00:00:01:12	3:02:227	12	Wheel	2432		
4	00:00:01:12	3:02:233	12	Wheel	2688		
4	00:00:01:13	3:02:237	12	Wheel	3072		
4	00:00:01:13	3:02:239	12	Wheel	3328		
4	00:00:01:13	3:02:245	12	Wheel	3584		
4	00:00:01:13	3:02:249	12	Wheel	4224		

Using this view is similar to looking at the raw MIDI data that is recorded from your MIDI keyboard or controller. You can edit the characteristics of single notes and MIDI controller messages by typing in data. You'll probably use the Piano Roll view more often, but it's nice to know the Event List view is available if you need it. I'll talk more about the Event List view in Chapter 7.

Loop Construction View

The Loop Construction view gives you an easy way to create your own sample loops. These loops, which are digital audio clips designed to be played over and over again, can be used to construct entire songs. While you're working with the Loop Construction view, you see the sound wave of your loop, as in Figure 2.7.

Figure 2.7
The Loop Construction view is a special editing tool for creating sample loops

Not only does the Loop Construction view allow you to create your own sample loops, but you can even use ACID-compatible loops, like the loops found in Sonic Foundry's ACID software. In Chapter 9, I'll get into more detail about the Loop Construction view.

Console View

When you're ready to mix all your MIDI and audio tracks down to a single stereo file, you can use the Console view. This tool is made to look and function like a real recording studio mixing console, as you can see in Figure 2.8.

CHAPTER 2

Figure 2.8
The Console view
looks and functions
similar to a real
recording studio
mixing console

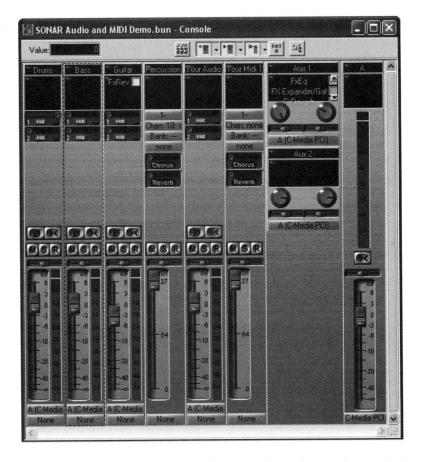

You can use the Console view to adjust the panning and volume for each track in a project. As a matter of fact, you can use the Console view in place of the Track view for adjusting track settings and recording new tracks. And just like on a real mixing console, you can monitor volume levels via on-screen meters and mute and solo individual or groups of tracks. I'll talk more about the Console view in Chapter 6, Chapter 11, and Chapter 12.

StudioWare and CAL

Two of the most advanced features provided by SONAR are StudioWare and CAL (Cakewalk Application Language). Even though these features seem complicated, they're actually quite easy to use. Sure, if you really want to dive in and master these features, they can get complex, but, for the most part, they are accessible to even the most timid user. What's more, when you start using StudioWare and CAL, you won't want to stop. Separately, StudioWare allows you to design on-screen panels to manipulate MIDI data and control your MIDI gear, and CAL allows you to create macros or small programs so that you can automate the different tasks you perform within SONAR. You can use StudioWare and CAL together to build your own editing tools within SONAR. You can even create programs that will make music automatically for you. These two features alone have quite a bit of power, so I'll talk a lot more about them in Chapter 14, Chapter 15, Chapter 16, and Chapter 17.

What's New in SONAR 2?

SONAR has changed quite a bit from version 1.0. In the interim, Cakewalk provided a free update (version 1.3), which included bug fixes, but also alterations in terms of features. Here's a brief list:

▶ New File Formats—SONAR now uses new file formats that are not compatible with older versions. This change was made to provide a decrease in file size and load times. I'll cover this topic in Chapter 4.

▶ Dual Mode Gain and Pan Controls—These allow you to control volume and panning even if you have envelopes assigned to your tracks. I'll provide more information on this in Chapter 12.

▶ Slow and Fast Curves—You can now add linear, slow, and fast curves to clip fades and crossfades. Check out Chapter 8 for more information.

▶ View Toolbar—A new set of show/hide and fit commands make it easier for you to manage your tracks in the Track View. I'll cover this topic in Chapter 7.

▶ Split Tool—The sorely missed Scissors tool from Pro Audio 9 (which was removed in Sonar 1.0) is now back (by popular demand) as the Split Tool. Check Chapter 7 to learn about this feature.

▶ Extract Timing—Another feature from Pro Audio 9 (which was removed in Sonar 1.0) is back in Sonar 2. Chapter 8 provides more detailed information.

SONAR 2 also introduces many changes in terms of features, most of which were suggested by users. These features include the following:

▶ Cyclone DXi—A new groove sampler DXi that comes standard with SONAR 2, which allows you to manipulate Groove Clips in a variety of fun and interesting ways. I'll go into detail in Chapter 10.

▶ ReWire 2.0 Support—You can now run any ReWire-compatible software synth (including Reason and ReBirth) from within SONAR. I'll tell you more about this in Chapter 10 as well.

▶ Multi-port Graphical Drum Editor—Users have been asking for this feature for quite a while. Now SONAR lets you create MIDI drum patterns quickly and easily by "painting" notes on a grid. I'll show you how in Chapter 7.

▶ Advanced Project File Management—No need to deal with cryptic file names in the WaveData folder. SONAR 2 provides a number of new tools that let you manage your Project data the way you want. Check out Chapter 3 for more information.

▶ Improved Soft Synth Integration—DXi's are much easier to manage in SONAR 2 using the new Synth Rack. I'll tell you all about it in Chapter 10.

▶ ACID File Exporting—A definite oversight of version 1, in SONAR 2 you can now export any Groove Clips you create. I'll show you how in Chapter 9.

Like version 1, SONAR 2 comes in two flavors: SONAR 2 and SONAR 2 XL. The only difference between the two are that SONAR 2 XL includes the following extras:

▶ Fxpansion DR-008 DXi—An advanced DXi drum synthesizer that provides a wide array of features. I'll talk about this in Chapter 10.

▶ Sonic Timeworks CompressorX—A very high-quality compressor effect that can be automated. I'll cover this in Chapter 11.

▶ Sonic Timeworks Equalizer—A very high-quality equalization effect, which includes spectrum analysis and can also be automated. I'll talk about this in Chapter 11 as well.

The Differences Between SONAR, Home Studio 2002, and Plasma

In addition to SONAR, Cakewalk offers two other products that are based on the same technology: Home Studio 2002 and Plasma. These products are basically scaled-down versions of SONAR, which means they work the same but provide fewer features. Cakewalk provides these additional products so that users who can't afford to purchase the full-blown

SONAR product can still have access to some of the advanced music making technology. The main points to consider when comparing Home Studio 2002 to SONAR are that Home Studio 2002 sports the following limitations:

▶ Doesn't provide audio file sampling rate higher than 48Khz.

▶ No support for SMPTE/MTC sync or MMC control.

▶ MIDI sync is provided, but only when Home Studio 2002 is used as the master.

▶ Supports only 16 simultaneous audio plug-ins (effects and DXi combined).

▶ Supports only 16 simultaneous MIDI plug-ins.

▶ No multi-channel support for audio cards.

Also, the main points to consider when comparing Plasma to SONAR are that Plasma sports the following limitations:

▶ Doesn't provide audio file bit-depth higher than 16-bits.

▶ No support for SMPTE/MTC sync, MIDI sync, or MMC control.

▶ Supports only 8 simultaneous audio plug-ins (effects and DXi combined).

▶ Supports only 4 simultaneous MIDI plug-ins.

▶ No multi-channel support for audio cards.

▶ Only one virtual main (impossible to create subgroups for advanced mixing).

▶ Only 2 aux busses.

So, if you are reading this book and using either Home Studio 2002 or Plasma, please keep the aforementioned points in mind if you find that certain features mentioned won't work with your particular software.

A Basic SONAR Studio Setup

Over the years, I've built up quite an arsenal of tools that currently reside in my home studio. But you don't need a ton of gizmos and gadgets to produce great music. If I were to scale down my setup to include only the basics, I'd be left with everything needed to compose and record my tunes with SONAR.

Other than SONAR itself, a basic studio revolves around one main component: your PC. If you already have a PC, be sure to check it against Cakewalk's system requirements for SONAR. Your best bet is to check it against the recommended system requirements rather than the minimum, because the minimum requirements won't give you very good performance.

NOTE

Cakewalk's system requirements for SONAR are as follows:

Minimum system requirements:
Operating System: Windows 98SE/Me/2000/XP
Processor Speed: 500 MHz
RAM: 64 MB
Hard disk space: 100 MB for full program installation
Hard disk type: Any
Graphics (resolution; color depth): 800×600; 256 colors
* MIDI Interface: Windows compatible
** Sound Card: Windows compatible WDM compatible ***

Recommended system requirements:
Operating System: 2000/XP
Processor Speed: 1.2 GHz
RAM: 256 MB
Hard disk space: 100 MB for full program installation
Hard disk type: EIDE/Ultra DMA (7200 RPM) or SCSI Hard Drive
Graphics (resolution; color depth): 1024×768; 24 bit color
* MIDI Interface: Windows compatible
** Sound Card: Windows compatible WDM compatible ***

* Required to connect to external MIDI devices.
** Required for audio playback.
*** Requires Windows Me/2000/XP.

If your system matches (or exceeds) the recommended system requirements, then you should be all set to run SONAR. If not, then you should seriously consider either an upgrade or purchasing a brand new system. If you decide to go with a new system, you might want to think about building it yourself or picking out the components and having it built for you. It's not that a generic Gateway or Dell PC won't do, but they are not really optimized for audio work, which is the main reason I decided to put my own system together. I cheated a little, though, and had a company called Aberdeen, Inc. (**www.aberdeeninc.com**) build the base system for me. The components I selected for my current system are as follows:

- ▶ ABIT BE6-II Pentium III ATX motherboard
- ▶ Intel Pentium III processor 700 MHz w/256 K L2
- ▶ Pentium III heatsink with cooling fan
- ▶ 384 MEG SDRAM 168-pin DIMM PC100 memory
- ▶ Promise Ultra66 PCI IDE Controller
- ▶ Teac 3.5 1.44 MB floppy drive
- ▶ 2 WD Expert WD205BA hard drives 20.5 GB 9ms 7200rpm Ultra/66

▶ Addtronics Super Tower ATX 8×5.25 / 3×3.5 300W ATX

▶ Creative Encore 6X PC-DVD drive

▶ Ricoh MP7060A CD-RW drive

▶ Diamond Stealth III S540 video card

Of course, by today's standards, my PC is a bit outdated, but you don't need a top of the line system to get good performance. This computer serves me very well, and when it comes time to get a new one, I'll continue to use this system for other tasks like dedicated software synth playback, etc. But if you have the money, by all means get the most powerful system you can afford. You won't be sorry.

TIP

One of the reasons I'm able to still get away with using an outdated system is because I have optimized it for audio work. There are a number of things you can do to your PC that will make it run more efficiently for the purpose of making music. These include adjustments to the system itself as well as to the Windows OS. If you'd like more information about how to optimize your audio PC, check out my feature article in Issue 14 of DigiFreq. You can download the issue for free at:

http://www.digifreq.com/digifreq/issues.asp

Sound Card

The most important thing to consider when purchasing a sound card for use with SONAR is if there are WDM drivers available for the card. You'll need to get in touch with the manufacturer of the card to verify this. Why is it so important? Because SONAR supports a Microsoft technology called WDM (Windows Driver Model). If you have a sound card that has WDM drivers, SONAR will give you much better performance in terms of audio latency. Basically, latency is a form of audio delay that occurs when a software program like SONAR can't "communicate" with your sound card fast enough while processing audio data, which results in an audible delay. This is usually only noticeable with features that use real-time processing. In SONAR, these include input monitoring and real-time DXi performance. I'll talk more about latency in Chapter 3, input monitoring in Chapter 6, and DXi's in Chapter 10.

You should also be aware that Windows 2000 and Windows XP are the only operating systems truly compatible with WDM drivers, which is why 2000 and XP are listed in the recommended system requirements. Windows 98 SE also provides limited support for WDM drivers, but most manufacturers are not supporting it. And as far as Windows ME is concerned, well, let's just say it's more trouble than it's worth. Some people use Windows ME without any problems, but I've heard from too many people having trouble with the OS to be able to recommend it.

TIP

For a list of audio cards recommended by Cakewalk, go to:
http://www.cakewalk.com/Tips/audiohw.htm

Of course, there are many other things to consider when choosing a particular card. You should look for a PCI-based sound card (one that is installed inside of your computer) rather than a USB-based sound card. USB audio interfaces don't really provide enough bandwidth to transfer audio data fast enough for sufficient use. A PCI sound card works much better. However, with the new USB 2.0 spec, that shouldn't present a problem once manufacturers update their products in the near future. You should also be aware of the types of connections that sound cards supply. The typical sound card provides a number of different audio inputs and outputs including line level, microphone level, and speaker. Line level inputs and outputs are used to transfer sound from cassette decks, radios, electronic keyboards, or any other standard audio device. Microphones generate a very small audio level by themselves, so they need a special input of their own, which is connected to an internal preamplifier on the sound card. Speakers also need their own special connector with a built-in amplifier in order to produce a decent amount of volume. Some high-end sound cards also offer digital inputs and outputs. These special connectors let you attach the sound card directly to compatible devices such as some CD players and DAT (digital audio tape) decks. Using these connections gives you the best possible sound, because audio signals stay in the digital domain and don't need to be converted into analog signals. You should also be aware that connectors come in a variety of forms. Low-cost cards usually provide the same 1/8-inch jacks used for head-phones on boom boxes. For better quality, there are 1/4-inch, RCA, or XLR jacks. Connections can also be balanced or unbalanced. Balanced connections provide shielding to protect the audio signal against RFI (radio frequency interference). Unbalanced connections don't provide any type of protection.

If you want to be able to record more than one audio Track at once, you'll need a card with multiple audio connections. Most average sound cards internally mix all of their audio sources down to one stereo signal, but other, higher-end (more expensive) cards let you record each device separately on its own discreet stereo channel. This capability is much more desirable in a music recording studio, but not everyone needs it. A good quality audio signal is something that everybody desires. During recording, the sampling rate (which I talked about in Chapter 1) plays a big part in the quality of the audio signal. Suffice it to say, the higher the sampling rate that a sound card can handle, the better the sound quality. The sampling rate of a CD is 44.1 kHz (44,100 samples per second) and all sound cards on the market support this. Professional cards can hit 48 kHz or higher. Bit resolution (which I also talked about in Chapter 1) is a factor in determining digital sound quality as well. The more bits you have to represent your signal, the better it will sound. The CD standard is 16-bits, which is supported by all sound cards. Some cards (again, mostly high-end) go up to 20-, 22-, or even 24-bits.

Two other measurements you need to look out for are signal-to-noise ratio and frequency response. As with the other measurements mentioned earlier, the higher the better. Since all electronic devices produce some amount of noise, the signal-to-noise ratio of a sound card tells you how much higher the signal strength is compared to the amount of internal noise made by the sound card. The bigger the number, the quieter the card. A good signal-to-noise measurement is about 90 dB or higher. Frequency response is actually a range of numbers, which is based on the capabilities of human hearing. The frequency response of human hearing is approximately 20 Hz to 20 kHz. A good sound card will encompass at least that range, maybe even more.

What do I use? I decided to go with the Mona from Echo Audio. You'll notice that it is on Cakewalk's recommended list, and for good reason. The Mona provides a wide variety of professional features, and the sound quality is great. My main reasons for choosing it, however, were good WDM drivers, built-in preamps, and multiple connections. If you get a card with built-in preamps, you can eliminate the need for yet another component in the signal chain, which can potentially add noise. And if you get a card with multiple connections, you can usually do away with having to use a mixing board, which can also be a source of additional noise. I love being able to just plug my microphone and instruments directly into my sound card, knowing that I'm getting the cleanest signal possible. The Mona does come with a hefty price tag, though, but you can find lower-priced cards with fewer, but similar, features. I usually recommend checking out the products available from Echo Audio (**www.echoaudio.com**), M-Audio (**www.midiman.com**), and Aardvark (**www.aardvark-pro.com**).

MIDI Interface

If you have any external MIDI devices (like a MIDI keyboard), then you'll need a MIDI interface for your computer. I've already explained MIDI interfaces back in Chapter 1, but I didn't really go into what you should know when looking to buy one. If you have a simple setup with only one MIDI keyboard, then you can easily get away with a simple single- or double-port MIDI interface. The best way to go here is to get a USB-based interface. This means it will be easy to install (just plug it in) and it won't take up an IRQ or PCI slot inside your computer. Also be sure that the interface has Windows 2000 or Windows XP compatible drivers (depending on what OS you are using). Bad drivers can cause problems. Other than that, the only major differences between interfaces are the number of ports they provide. If you have a lot of external MIDI devices, it's best to connect each device to its own dedicated MIDI port. I'm currently using a Midiman MidiSport 2×2 USB interface under Windows XP. It works great and does just what I need it to. I usually recommend checking out the products available from Midiman (**www.midiman.com**) when people ask me about MIDI interfaces.

Microphone

If you plan on doing any acoustic recording (vocals, acoustic guitar, etc.), you'll need a good microphone. There are literally hundreds of mics on the market and entire books have been written on the subject, so I won't go into great detail here. Basically, the microphone you choose depends on the application. For me, I needed a good vocal mic but not something that was going to put me in the poor house. While I would love to get a Neumann U87 (one of the best), there's no way I could afford one. So, luckily, Shure came to my rescue with their KSM27. It's a great vocal mic that isn't too expensive. You can find more information about it at: **http://www.shure.com/microphones/models/ksm27.asp?PN=Selection%20Guides**. I like that it can also be used for other applications in a pinch. But what's right for me may not be right for you, so I've rounded up a number of online resources that will allow you to educate yourself on the subject of microphones:

▶ A Beginners Guide to Microphones—**http://www.recordingwebsite.com/articles/microphones.html**

▶ Microphone University—**http://www.dpamicrophones.com/uni.htm**

▶ Shure Performance and Recording Microphone Selection Guide— **http://www.shure.com/selectionguides/sel-perfrecmics.html**

▶ The Microphone FAQ—**http://www.harmony-central.com/Other/mic-faq.txt**

▶ Microphone Manufacturers List—**http://www.harmony-central.com/Recording/manufact.html#mic**

Speakers

Of course you also need to be able to hear the music that you're recording, so you'll need a good set of speakers (or monitors as they're called in the professional audio world). Like microphones, there are literally hundreds of different monitors on the market. For home studio purposes, you'll probably want to get yourself a good pair of active, nearfield monitors. They're called active because they come with a built-in amplifier, which saves you the trouble of having to buy an external amp and try to match it up to your monitors. And they're called nearfield because you listen to them at a fairly close distance (about 4 feet). This lets you set up your home studio in just about any space you can find because you don't have to acoustically treat the room—at least not professionally.

There are a wide variety of monitors available, but I'm currently having fun with the V4's from KRK Systems. These are a great pair of active, nearfield monitors that really deliver great sound. I also love that they've been designed for small workstation areas, and they're shielded, which means you can sit them close to your computer screen without problems. Of course, as with microphones, what I like may not be what you like, so I've compiled a number of online resources that will help you learn about and choose the right monitors for you:

▶ Ten Powered Nearfields Reviewed—**http://www.prorec.com/prorec/ articles.nsf/files/0B7FAE7ED3205D3C86256AE100044F41**

▶ Audio FAQ (Speakers)—**http://www.tm.tue.nl/vakgr/ok/vos/audio-faq/ faq-09.htm**

▶ eCoustics.com Speaker Articles—**http://www.ecoustics.com/Home/ Home_Audio/Speakers/Speaker_Articles/**

▶ Speakers Manufacturer List—**http://www.harmony-central.com/Recording/ manufact.html#speak**

Find Help When You Need It

Cakewalk provides a number of ways for you to find help when you're having a problem with SONAR. The two most obvious places to look are the user's guide and the SONAR Help file. Actually, these two sources contain basically the same information, but, with the Help file, you can perform a search to find something really specific. At the first signs of trouble, you should go through the included troubleshooting information. If you can't find an answer to your problem there, then you can pay a visit to the Cakewalk Web site.

The support page of the Cakewalk Web site (**http://www.cakewalk.com/Support/**) contains a ton of helpful information, including FAQs (lists of frequently asked questions and their answers) and technical documents that provide details on a number of Cakewalk-related topics. You should check them first. If you still can't find an answer to your problem, the next place to look is in the Cakewalk newsgroups (**http://www.cakewalk.com/Support/ newsgroups.html**). In the newsgroups, you can trade tips, advice, and information with other Cakewalk product users. And many times, you'll find that someone has had the same problem you're having, and he or she has already found a solution. Isn't sharing great? For even more helpful information, check out Appendix D at the end of this book.

TIP

Also be sure to sign up for a free subscription to my DigiFreq music technology newsletter. DigiFreq is a monthly e-mail newsletter that helps you learn more about music technology. It provides free news, reviews, tips, and techniques for music technology users. By applying for your own free subscription, you can learn all about the latest music product releases, read straight-forward reviews, explore related Web resources, and have the chance to win free products from brand-name manufacturers. To get your own free subscription, go to:
http://www.digifreq.com/digifreq/

Of course, you can also contact Cakewalk Technical Support directly. You can either e-mail your questions to **support@cakewalk.com**, or you can call 617-423-9021 (USA). Currently, the hours are Monday through Friday from 10 a.m. to 6 p.m. Eastern time. But remember, to receive technical support, you have to be a registered user. If you call or send e-mail, you'll be asked for your serial number. As I said before, remember to send in that registration card! You'll be a much happier camper, er… Cakewalker.

3

Customizing SONAR

Although we all may be SONAR users, it doesn't mean we like to work with the product in the same exact way. I have my way of doing things, and you probably have your own way. Luckily, SONAR provides a number of settings so that you can make the program conform to your own way of working. In this chapter, you'll learn the following:

▶ How to organize all the different files associated with SONAR

▶ How to customize the program's workspace, including colors, toolbars, window layouts, and key bindings

▶ How to set up all the MIDI parameters

▶ How to find the optimal audio settings

Organizing Files

As you work with SONAR, you'll be dealing with many different types of files. These include project files, audio files, StudioWare files, CAL files, and so on. To keep things organized, SONAR allows you to specify different disk locations at which you would like to store each file type. Initially, SONAR stores most of these files in the C:\Program Files\Cakewalk\SONAR 2\Sample Content folder on your hard drive, but that doesn't mean they have to stay there.

Change File Locations

To specify your own file locations, do the following:

1. In SONAR, choose Options > Global to open the Global Options dialog box and click the Folders tab (see Figure 3.1).

Figure 3.1
Use the Global Options
dialog box to specify
your file storage
locations

2. In the Project Files parameter, specify where you would like to store all
    your SONAR projects by typing in a new folder location. This includes
    .CWP and .WRK (Work), .CWB and .BUN (Bundle), and .MID (MIDI) files.
    When you specify a folder location for this parameter, it affects the loca-
    tion to which the File > Open and File > Save As dialog boxes will
    initially open. I'll talk more about working with project files in Chapter 4.

TIP

For an easier way to specify a folder location, click the button located to the right
of each parameter, which has three dots shown on it. This will open the Browse
For Folder dialog box, which will let you specify a folder location by clicking
and selecting through your computer's file directory with your mouse.

Also, if your computer is connected to a network, you can specify a folder location
on the network rather than on your computer's hard drive. This can be useful if
you want to share your project data with other musicians in your studio.

After you have selected a new file location, click OK.

3. In the Templates parameter, specify where you would like to store all your SONAR project templates by typing in a new folder location. This includes .CWT and .TPL files. I'll talk more about project templates in chapter 4.

4. In the CAL Files parameter, specify where you would like to store all your Cakewalk Application Language (CAL) files by typing in a new folder location. This includes .CAL files. I'll talk more about CAL files in chapters 16 and 17.

5. In the Window Layouts parameter, specify where you would like to store all your window layouts by typing in a new folder location. This includes .CakewalkWindowLayout files. I'll talk more about window layouts later on in this chapter.

6. In the Wave Files parameter, specify where you would like SONAR to look for any external audio files (such as sample loops) for importing into your projects. This includes Wave, Apple AIFF, MPEG, Windows Media, and Next/Sun files. When you specify a folder location for this parameter, it affects the location to which the File > Import Audio dialog box will initially open. I'll talk more about importing audio files in chapter 6 and sample loops in chapter 9.

TIP

If you have a large sample loop collection that spans a number of different CDs, it can be cumbersome trying to find the right loop when you have to keep loading and unloading different discs from your CD-ROM drive. Instead, you might want to consider copying all your loops to a folder on your hard drive. Then specify that folder location for the Wave Files parameter. From then on, whenever you need to import an audio loop into a project, you have instant access to all the loops in your collection.

7. In the Video Files parameter, specify where you would like SONAR to look for any external video files for importing into your projects. This includes .AVI, .MPG, and .MOV files. When you specify a folder location for this parameter, it affects the location to which the File > Import Video File dialog box will initially open. I'll talk more about importing video files in Appendix C.

8. In the Sysx Files parameter, specify where you would like to store all your system exclusive files by typing in a new folder location. This includes .SYX files. When you specify a folder location for this parameter, it affects the location to which the Load Bank From File and Save Bank To File dialog boxes in the Sysx view will initially open. I'll talk more about system exclusive files and the Sysx view in chapter 14.

CHAPTER 3

9. In the Play List parameter, specify where you would like to store all your Play List files by typing in a new folder location. This includes .SET files. You can find more information about Play Lists on pages 122 and 123 of the SONAR User's Guide.

10. In the Groove Quantize parameter, specify where you would like to store all your Groove Quantize files by typing in a new folder location. This includes .GRV files. When you specify a folder location for this parameter, it affects the location to which the Open Groove File dialog box from the Groove Quantize function will initially open. I'll talk more about the Groove Quantize function in chapter 8.

11. In the StudioWare parameter, specify where you would like to store all your StudioWare files by typing in a new folder location. This includes .CakewalkStudioWare files. I'll talk more about StudioWare in chapters 14 and 15.

12. In the Patterns parameter, specify where you would like SONAR to look for any Pattern files for the Pattern Brush feature by typing in a new folder location. This includes .MID (MIDI) files. When you specify a folder location for this parameter, it affects what patterns will appear in the Pattern Brush menu in the Piano Roll view. I'll talk more about the Pattern Brush feature and the Piano Roll view in chapter 7.

13. In the Drum Maps parameter, specify where you would like to store all your Drum Map files by typing in a new folder location. This includes .MAP files. I'll talk more about Drum Maps in chapter 7.

14. When you're finished assigning new folder locations for your files, click OK.

Put Everything in Its Place

If you've decided to change the location of any of the file types mentioned earlier, be sure to also move all your existing files to their new locations. This includes all the files that ship with SONAR. Follow these steps to do so:

1. Open the Windows Explorer. Then locate and open the C:\Program Files\Cakewalk\SONAR 2\Sample Content folder on your hard drive.

2. SONAR ships with a few sample project files whose names end in .CWP and .CWB. Move those files to the same folder you specified in the Project Files parameter of the Global Options > Folders dialog box.

3. A large number of templates are included with SONAR as well. Their names end in .CWT. Move those files to the same folder you specified in the Templates parameter.

4. There are 13 CAL files shipped with SONAR whose names end in .CAL. Move those files to the same folder you specified in the CAL Files parameter.

5. SONAR doesn't provide any default window layouts, so there are no files to move in this case. But if you've created some of your own, look for files whose names end in .CakewalkWindowLayout and move them to the same folder you specified in the Window Layouts parameter.

6. Even though, when you install SONAR on your hard drive, no audio sample loops are installed along with it, SONAR still includes a collection of loops for your use. They are located on the SONAR CD. Pop the CD into your drive and choose Explore CD from the menu that appears. Now navigate to the Audio Loops folder. Copy the contents of the Audio Loops folder to the same folder you specified in the Wave Files parameter of the Global Options > Folders dialog box. This will take up space on your hard drive, but it will also give you quick and easy access to your loops if you ever want to import them into a project.

7. SONAR doesn't include any sample video files, so there are no files to move in this case. But if you have a collection of your own, look for files whose names end in .AVI, .MPG, and .MOV and move them to the same folder you specified in the Video Files parameter.

8. SONAR includes three sample system exclusive files: GMSYSTEM.SYX, GS-RESET.SYX, and XG-RESET.SYX. These are located in the C:\Program Files\Cakewalk\SONAR 2 folder. Move those files to the same folder you specified in the Sysx Files parameter of the Global Options > Folders dialog box.

9. SONAR doesn't include any sample play list files, so there are no files to move in this case. But if you've created some of your own, look for files whose names end in .SET and move them to the same folder you specified in the Play List parameter.

10. SONAR includes one sample groove quantize file: CAKEWALK DNA GROOVES.GRV. This file is located in the C:\Program Files\Cakewalk\ SONAR 2\Sample Content folder. Move this file to the same folder you specified in the Groove Quantize parameter.

11. Also in the Sample Content folder are a large number of StudioWare files that ship with SONAR. These files have names that end in .CakewalkStudioWare. Move these files to the same folder you specified in the StudioWare parameter.

12. SONAR also ships with a number of pattern brush files. These files are located in the C:\Program Files\Cakewalk\SONAR 2\Pattern Brush Patterns folder. Move these files to the same folder you specified in the Patterns parameter.

13. Finally, SONAR ships with a number of sample drum map files. These files are located in the C:\Program Files\Cakewalk\SONAR 2\Drum Maps folder. Move these files to the same folder you specified in the Drum Maps parameter.

That's it. Any other files you see in the folder locations I mentioned should be left alone. Do not move them. Only move files that have the file extensions I talked about. Of course, you don't really have to move all of SONAR's included sample files, but, personally, I enjoy having all my files properly organized. It makes finding what I need easier and working with SONAR much more efficient.

Audio Folders

Although I've already talked about sample loops and audio files that can be imported into your projects, there are additional audio files that SONAR has to deal with. These are the files that represent the audio tracks that you record directly into SONAR. SONAR stores the data for these audio tracks in a special folder on your hard drive. By default, this folder is located at C:\Cakewalk Projects\Audio Data. But of course, like all the other folders mentioned earlier, you can change the location of this folder if you'd like. One of the main reasons for doing so is if you are using two hard drives in your computer—one hard drive for the installation of all your software, and another drive for storing only your SONAR audio data. This improves SONAR efficiency during playback and recording tremendously, and I highly recommend it.

If you'd like to change the location of your audio data folder, do the following:

1. In SONAR, choose Options > Global > Audio Data to open the Global Options > Audio Data dialog box (see Figure 3.2).

Figure 3.2
Use the Global
Options > Audio Data
dialog box to change
your audio data
folder location

2. In the Global Audio Folder parameter, type the new location for your audio data folder. You can also click the triple-dot button to the right of the parameter to browse for a new location instead of typing one.

3. By default, whenever you import an audio file into a project, SONAR will automatically make a copy of that file and place it in your audio data folder. If you don't want SONAR to do this, then deactivate the Always Copy Imported Audio Files option.

TIP

If your audio folder is located on the same hard drive as the audio you are importing, you can save drive space by deactivating the Always Copy Imported Audio Files option. But if your audio folder is located on a different drive (such as a second drive as I mentioned earlier), then I recommend keeping this option activated. I recommend this because if you are using a second hard drive to store your audio data, you don't want SONAR to have to look for your imported audio in a different location on a different drive. This will decrease playback and recording efficiency. Also worth knowing is that if you import audio in a format other than WAV, then the audio will be copied whether or not you have this option activated.

4. Click OK.

Per-Project Audio Folders

Instead of storing all the audio data from all your projects in the same folder, you can use a different folder for each project if you'd like. These are called *Per-Project Audio Folders*. The advantage of using per-project audio folders is that all the data for each project is stored in its own separate location and if you want to have access to the audio files associated with a project (perhaps for editing in a different software application), it's easy to find them. To set up SONAR for per-project audio folders, do the following:

1. Choose Options > Global > Audio Data to open the Global Options > Audio Data dialog box.

2. Activate the Use Per-Project Audio Folders options.

3. Click OK.

Now when you go to create a new project, you will be able to specify a folder name for the project. I'll talk more about creating projects in chapter 4.

The Picture Folder

Whenever you record audio data using SONAR, the program creates temporary picture files for the audio data in your project, which hold "drawings" of the audio waveforms. Initially, these picture files are stored in the C:\Cakewalk Projects\Picture Cache folder on your hard drive. You can change this location by doing the following:

1. Choose Options > Global > Audio Data to open the Global Options > Audio Data dialog box.

2. Type in a new location for your picture files into the Picture Folder parameter. You can also click the triple-dot button to the right of the parameter to browse for a new location instead of typing one.

CAUTION

If you are using a second hard drive for your audio data, do *not* put your picture folder on the second hard drive with the audio data. This can decrease SONAR's performance. Instead, keep the picture folder on the same hard drive on which the SONAR software is installed.

3. Click OK.

Now SONAR will look for your picture files in the new picture folder location. Don't worry about moving any existing picture files. SONAR will automatically create new ones when you open your projects again. You can just delete the old picture folder and all the files in it if you'd like.

The Workspace

Not only can you change the way SONAR handles files, but you also can change the way SONAR looks and the way it responds to your commands. By customizing the SONAR workspace, you can increase your efficiency with the program and make it more comfortable to work with. Some of the adjustments you can make are to the colors, toolbars, window layouts, and key bindings.

Colors

SONAR allows you to change the colors of almost every element on the screen within the program. I haven't found much use for making color changes, though. The default colors that the program ships with work just fine for me. However, you might find a different set of colors more pleasant to work with, or maybe you can see some colors better than others. Changing the colors SONAR uses is simple—follow these steps:

1. In SONAR, select Options > Colors. The Colors dialog box then appears, as shown in Figure 3.3.

Figure 3.3
In the Colors dialog box, you can change the appearance of SONAR to your liking

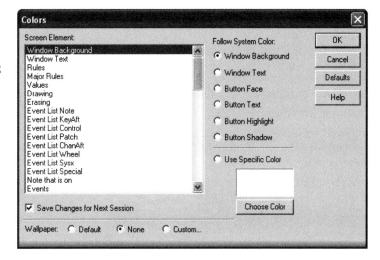

2. On the left side of the dialog box is a list of all the screen elements you can change. To change the color of an element, select it.

3. Select how you want that screen element to look by choosing a color from the right side of the dialog box. You can have the color of the element follow the color of some of the default Windows element colors, or you can use a specific color.

4. You can also change the background wallpaper of the SONAR workspace by choosing one of the options at the bottom of the Colors dialog box. If you choose the Custom option, you can even load your own Windows bitmap (.BMP) file for display. Loading your own file is not very useful, but it can be fun.

5. If you want SONAR to use the same color settings every time you run the program, make sure the Save Changes For Next Session option is activated.

6. When you've completed your changes, just click the OK button.

Toolbars

To increase your productivity, SONAR provides a number of toolbars for quick access to many of its major functions. So, instead of having to click through a series of menus, you can simply click a single toolbar button. Toolbars are available for standard file access functions, recording and playback controls, and so on.

SONAR allows you to change the look and position of its toolbars, as well as determine whether they are visible. Why wouldn't you want to have all the toolbars on the screen all the time? Because they can clutter up the workspace and get in the way while you're working on a project.

Change Their Position

Just as with most toolbars in other Windows programs, you can dock these toolbars to the top, bottom, or sides of the SONAR workspace by dragging and dropping them with the mouse. If you drop a toolbar anywhere within the workspace, it becomes a little floating window, as shown in Figure 3.4.

Figure 3.4
Toolbars can be docked
at the top or bottom of
the SONAR workspace.
They can also reside
anywhere else within
the workspace as small
floating windows

Change Their Appearance

To change the appearance of the toolbars, you need to access the Toolbars dialog box. Just choose View > Toolbars, and the Toolbars dialog box will appear, as shown in Figure 3.5.

Figure 3.5
Using the Toolbars
dialog box, you can
change the appearance
of SONAR's toolbars

By placing or removing the check mark next to each selection, you control whether the associated toolbar will be visible. For example, if you remove the check mark in the box next to the Standard selection, the Standard File Functions toolbar will disappear. You can also have the buttons in the toolbars either appear flat or similar to 3D by changing the Flat Style selection at the bottom of the Toolbars dialog box.

NOTE

The only thing that disappoints me about SONAR's toolbars is that you can't customize them in any other ways. For instance, you can't change which buttons appear in each toolbar, and you can't create your own specialized toolbars for rapid access to the features you use most often. Plus, no toolbars are available for any of the editing functions within the program. Well, guess what? I found a way around this little dilemma by utilizing StudioWare. I'll tell you all about it in Chapter 15.

Window Layouts

As you're working on a project in SONAR, you need to use many of the views described in Chapter 2. When you want to save the project, the size and position of the view windows are saved along with it. This capability is nice, because you can pick up exactly where you left off the next time you open the project. As you get more experienced with SONAR, you'll probably find that having the views set up in certain configurations helps your recording sessions go more smoothly. For instance, you might like having the Track view positioned at the top of the workspace, with the Staff view and the Piano Roll view positioned underneath it, as shown in Figure 3.6.

CHAPTER 3

Figure 3.6
The size and position
of all views are saved
along with a Project

What if you come up with a few favorite configurations that you like to use during different
stages of the same project? Or what if you want to use those configurations on a different
project? That's where window layouts come in. Using window layouts, you can save the
current size and position of the view windows as a layout file. Then you can later load the
saved layout and apply it to any open project. You can also update a saved layout, delete it,
or rename it. You do so by using the Window Layouts dialog box.

Create a Layout

You create a window layout like this:

1. Arrange the views in the workspace in the positions and sizes that you
   would like them to be saved. You also must decide whether you want
   certain views to be open.

2. Select View > Layouts to open the Window Layouts dialog box, as shown
   in Figure 3.7.

Figure 3.7
You can create new
layouts by using the
Window Layouts
dialog box

3. Click the Add button and type a name for the new layout in the New Global Layout dialog box that appears.

TIP

I've found that giving a descriptive name to each layout helps me when I want to load them. For example, I include the names of each open View in the name of the layout. If I have the Track, Staff, and Piano Roll views open in the layout, I name it "Track-Staff-Piano_Roll."

4. Click the OK button, and your new layout is then listed in the Window Layouts dialog box.

5. From here, you can rename or delete a layout in the list. You can also load a layout by selecting it from the list and clicking on the Load button.

6. When you're finished, click the Close button.

Layout Options

The Window Layouts dialog box contains two optional settings that let you control how layouts are loaded. The Close Old Windows Before Loading New Ones option determines whether any views you have currently open in the workspace will be closed when you load a new layout. The When Opening a File, Load its Layout option determines whether SONAR will load the accompanying layout when a project is opened. I like to keep both of these options activated.

Key Bindings

One of the most useful customization features that SONAR provides is key bindings. Like toolbars, they give you quick access to most of SONAR's features. Instead of having to click through a series of menus, you can simply press a key combination on your computer's keyboard. Initially, SONAR ships with a few default key bindings for opening and saving a project, for example. These bindings are displayed next to their assigned menu functions, as in the File menu shown in Figure 3.8.

Figure 3.8
Initially, the key binding for opening a project is Ctrl+O

The wonderful thing about key bindings is that if you don't like them, you can change them. You also can create new ones for functions that don't already have them preassigned. There's only one limitation: a maximum of 134 key bindings. You can work around this limitation, however; I'll talk about that later in this chapter. The available computer keyboard combinations include the following:

▶ The Ctrl key in combination with any letter of the alphabet, any number, or any function key (except F10)

▶ The Shift key in combination with any function key (except F10)

▶ Any function key (except F1 and F10)

▶ The Ctrl+Shift keys in combination with any letter of the alphabet, any number, or any function key (except F10)

▶ The Ctrl+Alt keys in combination with any letter of the alphabet, any number, or any function key (except F10)

Create Your Own Key Bindings

You can easily create your own key bindings and change existing ones. Here's how:

1. Select Options > Key Bindings to open the Key Bindings dialog box, as shown in Figure 3.9.

Figure 3.9
You can set key combinations in the Key Bindings dialog box

2. In the Key list under the Bindings section of the dialog box, select the key combination that you want to bind to a function.

3. In the Function list, select the SONAR function that you want to bind to the selected key combination.

4. Click the Bind button. You then see a connection created, as shown in Figure 3.10.

Figure 3.10
A connection between a function and key combination is made when you click the Bind button

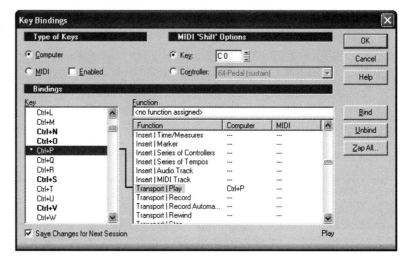

5. As I mentioned before, you can create up to 134 key bindings. You can also remove single key bindings by using the Unbind button. And if you want to get rid of them all, just click the Zap All button.

6. When you're done, click the OK button.

CAUTION

Near the bottom of the Key Bindings dialog box is the Save Changes for Next Session option. When you select it, any key bindings you create will be saved so that you can use them every time you run SONAR. If this option is not selected, you will lose any changes you make when you exit the program. By default, this option is selected. I suggest you keep it that way, unless for some reason you just need a few temporary Key Bindings during a recording session.

After you've created (or changed) some key bindings, you'll notice the changes in SONAR's menus. As I mentioned earlier, the key bindings are displayed next to their assigned menu functions.

MIDI Key Bindings

Remember when I mentioned that you can get around the limit of the 134 available key bindings? This is it: MIDI key bindings. You can assign the keys on your MIDI keyboard synthesizer or controller as key bindings to execute functions within SONAR. (Cool, huh?) For example, you can assign the File > New function in SONAR to the Middle C key on your keyboard. Then, when you press Middle C, SONAR opens the New Project File dialog box.

TIP

If your studio is set up so that your computer isn't located next to your MIDI keyboard or controller, using MIDI Key Bindings is a great way to still have access to SONAR. For example, if you want to be able to start and stop recording of SONAR via your MIDI keyboard, you can just assign one MIDI Key Binding along with the "shift" key or controller to the Realtime > Play function and another MIDI Key Binding along with the "shift" key or controller to the Realtime > Stop function.

You create MIDI key bindings the same way you create computer keyboard bindings, as discussed earlier. The only difference is that you have to select MIDI as the Type of Keys option in the Key Bindings dialog box and make sure to activate MIDI key bindings by selecting the Enabled option, as shown in Figure 3.11. Also, when you select a key combination in the Key list, you select musical keys rather than computer keyboard keys.

Figure 3.11
You select MIDI as the Type of Keys option to active MIDI key bindings

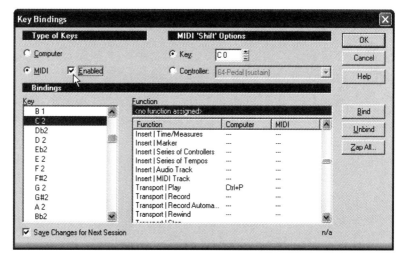

In addition, to prevent the MIDI key bindings from activating while you're performing, you need to set up a "shift" key or controller to turn the MIDI key bindings on and off. Under MIDI Shift Options in the Key Bindings dialog box, you can assign a MIDI key or controller message to act as a sort of "on/off switch." When you want to use a MIDI key binding, activate the "shift" key or controller first to tell SONAR you're about to use a MIDI key binding.

TIP

Remember earlier when I talked about window layouts? Well, normally, to load a layout you need to choose View > Layouts, select a layout, and click Load just to call up a window layout. For a much quicker way of doing this, you can assign key bindings to any or all of the layout files you create. After you've created your window layouts, you will find them listed under the Global Layout Files section of the Function list in the Key Bindings dialog box. Just assign key bindings as described earlier, and then you can instantly switch between window layouts at the press of a computer key.

MIDI Settings

Even though SONAR does a good job of setting up all its MIDI options during installation, it's still a good idea for you to go through them to make sure everything is the way you want it to be. You might be surprised at how much control you have over how SONAR handles MIDI data. Not only can you designate which MIDI devices the program will use, you can also determine what types of MIDI data will be recorded or not and optimize MIDI playback.

MIDI Devices

The first time you run SONAR, it scans your computer system to see whether you have a MIDI interface installed. SONAR prompts you to select the available MIDI ports that you want to use, but you can always change your selections later.

NOTE

As explained in Chapter 1, a *MIDI interface* is a device that is plugged into your computer allowing it to understand the MIDI language. Every MIDI interface has at least two connections on it, called *MIDI ports*. One is the MIDI In port, which is used to receive MIDI data. The other is the MIDI Out port, which is used to send MIDI data. Some of the more sophisticated MIDI interfaces on the market have multiple pairs of MIDI ports. For instance, one of the MIDI interfaces I use (a Music Quest 8Port/SE) provides eight MIDI In and Out ports. Having all these ports allows me to connect more than one MIDI instrument to my computer.

To see what MIDI ports SONAR is using and to designate which ports you want to use, do the following:

1. Select Options > MIDI Devices to open the MIDI Devices dialog box. This dialog box contains lists of all the input MIDI ports and output MIDI ports that you have available. For an example, see Figure 3.12.

Figure 3.12
The MIDI Devices dialog box lists all the available input and output MIDI ports

2. Simply select the input and output ports that you want to be able to access for use within SONAR.
3. When you're finished, click the OK button.

All the ports selected here will be available in the Track Properties dialog box, which I'll talk about in Chapter 4.

Global MIDI Options

SONAR provides a number of different MIDI options, some of which are global, and others that are project-oriented. The project-oriented options (which I'll talk about in Chapter 4) are saved and loaded along with project files. The global options remain the same no matter which project is currently open.

Filter out MIDI Messages

The global MIDI options allow you to select the types of MIDI messages that you want to record in SONAR. Sometimes you might not want certain MIDI data to be included in your recordings. For example, if your MIDI keyboard sends channel aftertouch messages or key aftertouch messages, you might want to filter them out. These types of messages are very resource-intensive and can sometimes bog down your synthesizer with too much data.

CHAPTER 3

NOTE

There are seven types of MIDI messages, each providing different kinds of functionality within the MIDI language. These categories include notes, key aftertouch, channel aftertouch, controllers, program changes, pitch bend, and system exclusive.

The notes category pertains to MIDI Note On and MIDI Note Off messages. Whenever you press a key on your MIDI keyboard, a MIDI Note On message is sent. When you let the key go, a MIDI Note Off message is sent.

On some MIDI keyboards, in addition to hitting the keys, you can press and hold them down to apply varying degrees of pressure. This pressure is called aftertouch. Depending on how the synthesizer is programmed, aftertouch lets you control how loud it is or even how it sounds. Aftertouch comes in both key and channel varieties. Key aftertouch allows you to have different pressure levels for each individual key on the keyboard. Channel aftertouch restricts you to a single pressure level over the entire range of the keyboard.

A wide range of controller MIDI messages is available. Basically, these messages give you control over different aspects of your MIDI synthesizer or device. Some controller messages let you control volume, whereas others let you control the position of a synthesizer sound in the stereo field. However, far too many are available to discuss them all here.

Program changes (also called patch changes) let you select from the many different sounds available in a MIDI synthesizer. For example, a program change #1 MIDI message might activate a piano sound in your synthesizer, and program change #10 might activate a glockenspiel sound.

Pitch bend messages allow you to temporarily alter the tuning of your MIDI instrument. Many MIDI keyboards have a lever or a wheel that lets you control pitch bend. Moving this wheel makes the instrument send out pitch bend (also called pitch wheel) messages.

System exclusive messages pertain to special MIDI data that is (as the name implies) exclusive to the instrument sending and receiving it. For instance, the manufacturer of a MIDI synthesizer might include special functions in the product that can't be controlled via standard MIDI messages. By using system exclusive messages, the manufacturer gives you access to these special functions but still keeps the product compatible with the MIDI language.

For more in-depth information about MIDI and the different types of messages available, check out the *Desktop Music Handbook*, which is available for free on the Cakewalk web site: **http://www.cakewalk.com/Tips/Desktop.htm**. Also read the section of the SONAR help file entitled *Beginner's Guide to Cakewalk Software*.

By default, SONAR has notes, controllers, program changes, pitch bend, and system exclusive messages activated, and it has key aftertouch and channel aftertouch deactivated. If you want to change these settings, though, you can do the following:

1. Select Options > Global to open the Global Options dialog box.
2. Click the MIDI tab at the top of the dialog box.

3. Under the Record section, select the types of MIDI messages that you want to allow SONAR to record, as shown in Figure 3.13.

Figure 3.13
You can determine the types of MIDI messages SONAR will be allowed to record

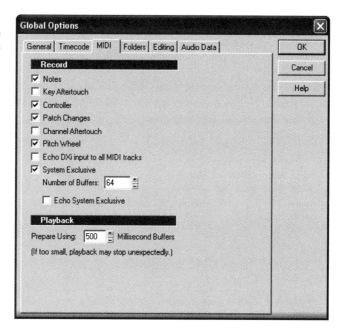

4. Click the OK button when you're finished.

Optimize MIDI Playback

To get smooth and consistent playback of MIDI data, SONAR uses a buffer (a temporary storage area) to hold the data before it gets sent out through the MIDI interface. This buffer keeps the data from getting backed up, which can cause erratic playback or even stop playback altogether. The buffer also helps to control playback latency. Whenever you change a parameter in SONAR while a project is playing, a slight delay always occurs between the time you make the adjustment and when you hear the results. That's called *latency*.

The Global Options dialog box contains a setting that allows you to adjust the size of SONAR's MIDI playback buffer. If the buffer is set too low, it can cause erratic playback, and if it is set too high, it can cause noticeable latency. By default, the buffer size is set to 500 milliseconds. This setting should be fine in most cases. However, you might want to experiment to find an even better setting. The trick is to find the lowest setting without affecting playback. I've been able to get away with a setting of 100 (on a Pentium II/300 computer system), so depending on the speed of your computer system, you might want to try that. You can change the buffer size like this:

1. Select Options > Global to open the Global Options dialog box.
2. Click the MIDI tab at the top of the dialog box.

3. Under the Playback section, type the new buffer size.

4. Click the OK button when you're finished.

Instrument Definitions

Most MIDI instruments today provide a bank of sounds compatible with the General MIDI standard. At the same time, most instruments also provide additional sounds as well as other features that aren't defined by General MIDI. Some older MIDI instruments don't support General MIDI at all. To let you work more efficiently with these instruments, SONAR provides instrument definitions.

NOTE
Sounds in a MIDI instrument are stored as a group of parameter settings called a *patch*, and patches are stored in groups called *banks*. A MIDI instrument can have up to 16,384 banks of 128 patches each. This means that a MIDI instrument can theoretically contain up to 2,097,152 different sounds, although most don't.

With such a large potential for diversity, MIDI instruments from one manufacturer usually don't provide the same functionality as instruments from another manufacturer. This point is important, because MIDI data is ambiguous. The same data can be played back using any MIDI instrument, but that doesn't mean it will sound the same. Different instruments contain different sounds, and they interpret MIDI differently as well.

To remedy the problem, General MIDI was created. *General MIDI (GM)* is a set of rules applied to the MIDI language that standardizes the types of sounds contained in a MIDI instrument (along with their patch numbers) and how different MIDI controller messages are interpreted. Most modern MIDI instruments provide a special bank of GM sounds and a GM operating mode. When running in GM mode, different MIDI instruments respond to the same MIDI data in the same way. So, MIDI data played back on one instrument is guaranteed to sound the same when played on any other instrument.

Using instrument definitions, you can "tell" SONAR all about the features and capabilities provided by each of the MIDI instruments in your studio. This information includes the name of each patch, the range of notes supported by each patch, the MIDI controller messages that are supported, which registered parameter numbers (RPNs) and non-registered parameter numbers (NRPNs) are supported, and the bank select method used. Basically, instrument definitions allow you to refer to the patches in your MIDI instruments by name rather than number when you're assigning sounds to tracks in SONAR. (I'll talk more about this subject in Chapter 4.) The same applies for musical note names and MIDI controller message names.

Set Up Your Instruments

SONAR includes a number of predefined instrument definitions so that you can simply assign them without having to go through the process of creating your own. You can assign instrument definitions to each of the MIDI ports on your MIDI interface. You can also assign them to the individual MIDI channels (1 through 16).

NOTE

The MIDI language provides sixteen different channels of performance data over a single MIDI port connection. MIDI instruments can be set to receive MIDI data on a single channel, if need be. This means you can control up to sixteen different MIDI instruments (each with its own unique sound) even if they are all connected to the same MIDI port on your MIDI interface. In addition, most MIDI instruments are capable of playing more than one sound at a time. This means the instrument is *multitimbral*. If you assign a different sound to each of the sixteen MIDI channels, a single MIDI instrument can play sixteen different sounds simultaneously.

To assign instrument definitions to each of the MIDI ports and channels in your setup, follow these steps:

1. Select Options > Instruments to open the Assign Instruments dialog box, as shown in Figure 3.14.

Figure 3.14
You can assign instrument definitions in the Assign Instruments dialog box

2. From the list on the left, select the MIDI port(s) and/or MIDI channel(s) to which you want to assign definitions.

3. From the list on the right, select the Instrument Definition you want to use. For example, if you're going to use the MIDI instrument that's connected to the selected port in General MIDI mode, choose the General MIDI Instrument Definition.

CAUTION

Near the bottom of the Assign Instruments dialog box is the Save Changes for Next Session option. When you select it, any assignments you create will be saved so that you can use them every time you run SONAR. If this option is not selected, you will lose any changes you make when you exit the program. I suggest you select this option, unless for some reason you change the configuration of your studio for each new recording session.

4.   Click the OK button when you're finished.

Now SONAR will know the capabilities of your MIDI instrument or instruments and act appropriately when you access different features, such as editing MIDI controller messages (which I'll talk about in Chapter 7.).

Take the Easy Way Out

If you don't see a specific instrument definition for your MIDI instrument listed in the Assign Instruments dialog box, SONAR allows you to import more of them. The program ships with a large collection of additional instrument definitions that cover many of the MIDI instruments on the market from manufacturers, such as Alesis, E-mu, Ensoniq, General Music, Korg, Kurzweil, Roland, and Yamaha. The instrument definitions are stored in files with .INS extensions. For example, the Yamaha instrument definitions are stored in the file YAMAHA.INS. Importing these files is simple; just do the following:

1.   Select Options > Instruments to open the Assign Instruments dialog box.

2.   Click the Define button to open the Define Instruments and Names dialog box, as shown in Figure 3.15.

Figure 3.15
The Define Instruments and Names dialog box allows you to import additional instrument definitions

Define Instruments and Names

Instruments
  General MIDI
  General MIDI Drums
  Generic (Patches 0..127)
  Generic (Patches 1..128)
  Roland GS
  Roland GS Drumsets
  SoundFont Device
  Yamaha XG
  Yamaha XG Drum Kits

Patch Names
Note Names
Controller Names
RPN Names
NRPN Names
Bank Select Methods

Close
Import...
Help

3. Click the Import button to open the Import Instrument Definitions dialog box and select the .INS file that you want to import. For example, if your MIDI instrument is manufactured by Roland, select the ROLAND.INS file. Then click Open.

4. When SONAR displays a list of the instrument definitions contained in that file, select the one(s) you want and click the OK button. Your selections are then listed under Instruments in the Define Instruments and Names dialog box.

5. Click the Close button, and you then see your selections listed under Uses Instrument in the Assign Instruments dialog box. From here you can assign the Instrument Definitions as described earlier.

6. Click the OK button when you're finished.

If you still can't find an instrument definition for your MIDI instrument from the extensive collection included with SONAR, you can download even more from the Internet. Cakewalk provides a download section on its Web site (**http://www.cakewalk.com/download/**) where you can pick up additional instrument definition files. Other sites on the Web supply them, too. For more details, take a look at Appendix D.

Create Your Own

More than likely, you'll find instrument definitions for all your MIDI equipment either included with SONAR or available for download from the Internet. On the off chance that you don't, though, SONAR allows you to create your own. Creating your own instrument definitions can be a bit complicated, because you must have a good knowledge of the MIDI language and you need to be able to read the MIDI implementation charts that come with your instruments.

NOTE

The MIDI language contains more than one hundred different messages for conveying musical information, and a MIDI instrument isn't required to be able to send or recognize all of them. A MIDI instrument needs to transmit and receive only the messages that are relevant to the features it provides. It can ignore all the other messages. Therefore, manufacturers include MIDI implementation charts with all their products.

A MIDI implementation chart lists all the types of MIDI messages that are transmitted and recognized by its accompanying MIDI instrument. The chart includes the note range of the instrument, what MIDI controller messages it supports, whether it supports system exclusive messages, and more.

CHAPTER 3

To give you an idea of how to read a simple MIDI implementation chart and how to create a basic instrument definition, let's go through the process step-by-step:

1. Select Options > Instruments to open the Assign Instruments dialog box.
2. Click the Define button to open the Define Instruments and Names dialog box.
3. Take a look at Table 3.1, which shows the MIDI implementation chart for an E-mu PROformance Plus Stereo Piano MIDI instrument.

Table 3.1
E-mu PROformance Plus MIDI Implementation Chart

MIDI Command	Transmitted	Received	Comments
Note On	No	Yes	
Note Off	No	Yes	
Pitch Wheel	No	Yes	
Program Change	No	Yes	0-31
Overflow Mode	Yes	Yes	
Channel Pressure	No	No	
Poly Key Pressure	No	No	
Control Change	No	Yes	PWH, #1, #7
Sustain Footswitch	No	Yes	#64
Sostenuto Footswitch	No	Yes	#66
Soft Footswitch	No	Yes	#67
Split Footswitch	No	Yes	#70
All Notes Off	No	Yes	
Omni Mode	No	No	

Table 3.1 (continued)
E-mu PROformance Plus MIDI Implementation Chart

MIDI Command	Transmitted	Received	Comments
Poly Mode	No	No	
Mono Mode	No	No	
System Exclusives	No	No	

4. Right-click Instruments on the left side of the Define Instruments and Names dialog box, and select Add Instrument from the pop-up menu.

5. Type a name for the new instrument. For this example, type "E-mu PROformance Plus."

6. Open the new instrument by double-clicking on it to display its data, as shown in Figure 3.16.

Figure 3.16
This dialog box shows a new instrument definition

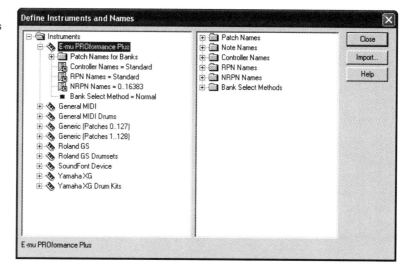

7. Take a look at what the new instrument contains. SONAR automatically creates the standard settings needed. Because the E-mu PROformance Plus doesn't support bank select messages, RPNs, or NRPNs, you don't need to change them. The PROformance supports the standard MIDI controllers, too, so you don't have to change them either. You do need to change the patch names, though.

CHAPTER 3

8. Open the Patch Names for Banks folder in the E-mu PROformance Plus instrument by double-clicking it. You should see General MIDI listed there. Because this instrument doesn't support GM, you need to change that name.

9. To change the General MIDI patch names list, you first need to create a new patch names list specifically for the PROformance by right-clicking on the Patch Names folder on the right side of the Define Instruments and Names dialog box.

10. Select Add Patch Names List from the pop-up menu, and type a name for the new list. In this case, type "E-mu PROformance Plus."

11. The PROformance manual shows all the patch names for the instrument (numbers 0 to 31). To add those names to the new patch name list, right-click the list and select Add Patch Name from the pop-up menu.

12. Type a name for the first patch (in this case, "Dark Grand") and press the Enter key on your computer keyboard. Because this is just an example, you can leave the list as is, but if you were to add more names to the list, it would look something like Figure 3.17.

Figure 3.17
This dialog box shows a patch name list for the E-mu PROformance Plus

13. Drag and drop the E-mu PROformance Plus patch names list on to the General MIDI list in the E-mu PROformance Plus Instrument Definition.

14. In the Bank Number dialog box, enter the number of the bank that you want to be used for this set of patch names. Click OK. The patch names list for the instrument is then changed.

15. Click the Close button and then click the OK button to finish.

This set of steps was actually a very simplified demonstration on how to create your own instrument definition. If the controller names needed to be changed or the instrument supported RPNs or NRPNs, you would create and edit those lists in the same way you do a patch name list. It's doubtful that you'll ever need to create your own instrument definitions, because SONAR comes with a large number of them (as well as more being available for download on the Internet), but, just in case, you can find more details in the SONAR User's Guide.

Optimal Audio Settings

When SONAR plays back digital audio on your computer, it puts a lot of stress on the system. Remember when I talked about digital audio in Chapter 1? A CD-quality digital audio recording requires 44,100 numbers (samples) to be processed every second. During playback, most of your computer's processing power is used solely for that purpose. Depending on the power of your system, this processing can make the response of some of SONAR's controls a bit sluggish, in particular the Console view controls. For example, if you adjust the volume of a digital audio track in the Console view during playback, you might experience a slight delay between the time you make the adjustment and the time you hear the results. As I mentioned above, this period is called latency, and you'll want as little of it as possible occurring during your sessions.

SONAR provides a number of different advanced settings that enable you to reduce latency. The first time you start the program, it attempts to make some educated guesses as to what these settings should be, and, although these settings usually work just fine, you might still be able to squeeze better performance out of your computer system. However, adjusting these settings can be tricky, and, unfortunately, there are no set rules. There are, however, some general guidelines you can follow to optimize your audio settings for the best possible performance.

The Latency Slider

The single most important adjustment you can make is to the Latency slider, and it's pretty simple to use. The lower you set it, the lower the latency; the higher you set it, the higher the latency. It can't be that simple though, can it? No, I'm afraid not. By lowering the Latency slider, you also run the risk of making playback unstable. If you set the Latency slider too low, you might hear dropouts or glitches or playback may even stop altogether. And the lower you set the Latency slider, the fewer digital audio tracks you can play at the same time.

To find the right setting, you have to experiment with a number of different projects. For those projects with only a small number of digital audio Tracks, you might be able to get away with a very low Latency slider setting. For projects with a large number of digital audio tracks, you might have to raise the Latency slider and put up with a bit of latency while you work. This also depends on whether you are using WDM drivers for your sound card, which I talked about in chapter 2. If you are using WDM drivers, then SONAR runs much more efficiently and you should be able to set the latency slider to a very low value. To set the Latency slider, follow these steps:

1. Select Options > Audio to open the Audio Options dialog box.

2. Click the General tab. The Latency slider is located in the Mixing Latency section, as shown in Figure 3.18.

Figure 3.18
In the Audio Options dialog box, you can adjust the Latency slider

3. Click and drag the Latency slider to the left to lower latency. Click and drag the Latency slider to the right to raise latency.

TIP
A good rule of thumb for setting the latency slider is if you are recording using Input Monitoring (see chapter 6) or playing DX Instruments live via your MIDI keyboard, set your latency to a low value—maybe as low as 2 to 4 milliseconds when using WDM sound card drivers. If you are playing a lot of audio tracks and using a lot of real-time effects (see chapter 11) while mixing down (see chapter 12), set your latency to higher value to relieve the strain on your computer system— maybe a value of around 20 milliseconds (or higher if needed) when using WDM sound card drivers.

4. Click the OK button when you're finished.

Queue Buffers and Buffer Size

Two other settings that affect latency and audio performance are the number of buffers in the playback queue and the I/O (input/output) buffer size. Like the Latency slider, if they are set too low, you can experience dropouts or glitches during playback. And higher settings mean more latency. Again, you need to experiment with the settings. I've found that values of between 2 and 4 for the number of Buffers In Playback Queue and around 64 for the I/O Buffer Size work quite well. If you want to change them, you can do the following:

1. Select Options > Audio to open the Audio Options dialog box.

2. Click the General tab. The Buffers In Playback Queue setting is located in the Mixing Latency section, as shown in Figure 3.19.

Figure 3.19
In this dialog box, you can set the Buffers In Playback Queue setting

3. Type the new value.

4. Click the Advanced tab. The I/O Buffer Size setting is located in the File System section, as shown in Figure 3.20.

Figure 3.20
In this dialog box, you can set the I/O Buffer Size setting

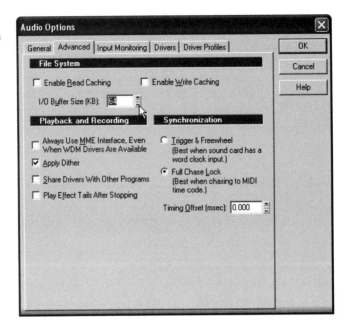

5.   Type the new value.

6.   Click the OK button when you're finished.

Read and Write Caching

When your computer sets aside a part of its memory to hold recently read or written information from a disk drive, this process is known as *disk caching*. Windows uses disk caching to help speed up read and write operations to your disk drives. When data is read or written to disk as a continuous stream (like with digital audio), disk caching can actually slow things down.

SONAR has two options that let you either enable or disable disk caching while the program is running. By default, SONAR keeps disk caching disabled. If you have a large amount of memory in your computer (such as 128MB or more), disk caching may actually improve performance. If you would like to see whether enabling this option makes any difference with your computer system, follow these steps:

1.   Select Options > Audio to open the Audio Options dialog box.

2.   Click the Advanced tab. The Enable Read Caching and Enable Write Caching settings are located in the File System section, as shown in Figure 3.21.

Figure 3.21
In this dialog box, you can set the Enable Read Caching and Enable Write Caching settings

3. Click each setting to activate it.
4. Click the OK button when you're finished.

DMA and the Wave Profiler

A device that can read your computer's memory directly without getting the CPU involved is said to support direct memory access (DMA). A sound card is such a device. SONAR uses the DMA settings of your sound card to ensure that MIDI and digital audio tracks within a project play in synchronization with one another. When you first run SONAR, it scans your sound card to automatically determine the DMA settings. These settings are listed in the Audio Options dialog box under the Driver Profiles tab. Leave these settings alone! In all but the most extreme cases, it won't do you any good to change them. And if you're having excessive problems with MIDI and audio playback, you should contact Cakewalk Technical Support.

If you accidentally change the DMA settings (or just can't help yourself from seeing what will happen if you do), you can easily have SONAR scan your sound card again to bring the original settings back. Here's how to do so:

1. Select Options > Audio to open the Audio Options dialog box.

2. Click the General tab.

3. Click the Wave Profiler button at the bottom of the dialog box. SONAR then scans your sound card and resets its DMA settings.

4. Click the OK button to close the Audio Options dialog box.

TIP

For more information about optimizing SONAR, be sure to read the SONAR help file section entitled *Improving Audio Performance*.

Also, if you'd like more information about how to optimize your audio PC, check out my feature article in Issue 14 of DigiFreq. You can download the issue for free at:

http://www.digifreq.com/digifreq/issues.asp

4

Working with Projects

As I mentioned in Chapter 2, a project is SONAR's way of representing a song or any other musical body of work. A project holds all your music data, including MIDI and/or audio, along with a number of program settings. You can't do anything in SONAR without first creating a new project or opening an existing one. So, in this chapter, I'm going to talk all about projects, including the following topics:

▶ How to open an existing project

▶ How to create a new project

▶ How to create your own templates

▶ How to save a project

Opening Projects

Every time you start SONAR, it presents you with the SONAR Quick Start dialog box (see Figure 4.1). From here, you have the choice of opening an existing project, opening a project that you recently worked with, or creating a new one.

Figure 4.1
The SONAR Quick
Start dialog box
appears when you
start SONAR

If you choose to open an existing project, SONAR displays a standard file selection dialog box so you can select the project you want to load. If you've changed the disk location of your project files as described in Chapter 3, the file dialog will initially display the contents of the folder specified in the Project Files parameter of the Global Options > Folders dialog box. Of course, you can examine other disk locations just as you would when loading a file in any other Windows application.

By choosing the Open A Recent Project option in the SONAR Quick Start dialog box, you can open a project that you've previously worked with. You simply select the project from the drop-down list and then click the folder button next to the list. SONAR keeps track of the last eight projects you've worked with. When you open a ninth, the project on the bottom of the list is bumped off—not killed or deleted, just removed from the list.

You also can open an existing or recent project by using SONAR's standard menu functions. To open an existing project, just select File > Open. To open a recent project, select the File menu and then click the name of the project you want to open from the list on the bottom half of the menu (see Figure 4.2).

Figure 4.2
You can use the File
menu to open an
existing or recent
project

CHAPTER 4

TIP
Personally, I find it easier to use the standard menu functions to open a project.
To keep the SONAR Quick Start dialog from popping up every time you start
SONAR, make sure the Show This At Startup check box at the bottom of the box
is not selected (see Figure 4.1). You can do the same thing with the Tip of the
Day dialog box.

Opening in Safe Mode

If you've used Microsoft Windows for any length of time, you've no doubt come across its notorious "Safe Mode," which allows you to start the OS in a somewhat crippled state if you're having trouble booting up your PC. Basically, Safe Mode lets you start Windows with only the bare essentials needed to run the OS. For instance, all unnecessary device drivers are disabled. This allows you to troubleshoot Windows and attempt to find the source of your faulty start-up.

SONAR provides a similar feature (also called "Safe Mode") for use when opening project files. On occasion, like any computer data, project files can become corrupt, preventing you from opening them. This can be caused by computer resource limitations or bad DirectX (audio effect), MFX (MIDI effect), or DXi (DirectX Instrument) plug-ins (I'll talk more about these plug-ins in chapter 11). Using Safe Mode, SONAR allows you to load a project file where only the Track view (in its default layout) will open. If you had any other open views in the project, they will not open in Safe Mode. You are also prompted for each and every plug-in that you have assigned to your tracks in the project. This lets you determine if a particular plug-in is preventing you from opening your project. Here is how Safe Mode works:

1. While opening a project using one of the methods described earlier, hold down the Shift key on your computer keyboard. This tells SONAR to open the project in Safe Mode and displays the File Open—Safe Mode dialog box (see Figure 4.3).

Figure 4.3
Use SONAR's Safe
Mode to open corrupt
project files

2. If your project contains any plug-ins assigned to your tracks, the Safe Mode dialog box will ask you if you want to load the plug-ins or not. You are given four choices: Yes, Yes To All, No, and No To All. Choosing Yes will load the currently displayed plug-in. Choosing No will not load the currently displayed plug-in. Choosing Yes To All will close the dialog and load all plug-ins. Choosing No To All will close the dialog box and open the project without any plug-ins.

3. If you don't choose either Yes To All or No To All, the Safe Mode dialog box will ask you about each individual plug-in contained in the project, and you will have to answer either Yes or No to each plug-in. Using this method allows you to determine if a certain plug-in is causing trouble, and which plug-in it is.

CAUTION

If you load a project in Safe Mode with some or all of the plug-ins disabled, be careful when saving the project to disk. You should save the project using a different name so that the original file remains intact. If you save the file using the same name, this will overwrite the original file and all your plug-in assignments will be lost.

Personally, I've found the best way to use Safe Mode is to load a project and individually determine whether or not each plug-in should be loaded. This lets me narrow down the problem to a specific plug-in. So I may lose the settings for that troublesome plug-in, but I can keep all the settings for any other plug-ins I have assigned to my tracks in the project.

Finding Missing Audio Files

Another problem that can occur when opening projects that contain audio data is that SONAR might be unable to determine the location of the data for that project on your disk. This can happen if you decide to move the location of your Audio Data folder (discussed in chapter 3) and you forget to specify the new location in the SONAR folder settings. You can also run into this problem if you use individual folders for each project (described in chapter 3). Your best bet is to let SONAR handle your audio data chores and save any projects containing audio data as Bundle files, which I'll talk about later in this chapter. But if you would rather handle your own audio data chores and your data gets misplaced, you can use SONAR's Find Missing Audio function:

1. When you open a project in which SONAR cannot find the associated audio data for the audio tracks, the Find Missing Audio dialog box is displayed (see Figure 4.4).

Figure 4.4
Use the Find Missing
Audio function to
locate misplaced
audio data

2. To locate the missing audio data, you can do one of two things: manually navigate through the folders on your hard drive using the Look In drop-down list, or use Search. The Look In drop-down list is self-explanatory. To use Search, click the Search button. SONAR will automatically search your entire hard drive for the audio file currently displayed in the File Name parameter of the Find Missing Audio dialog box. During the search, the Search For Missing Audio dialog box is shown (see Figure 4.5). If the file is found, select it and click OK. If the file isn't found, click Cancel and search for it manually.

Figure 4.5
Use Search to
automatically locate
audio files

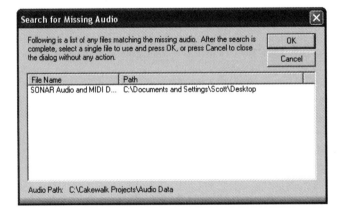

3. After you've found the missing file, you can do one of three things: move it to your project's audio data folder, copy it to your project's audio data folder (which also leaves a copy of the file in its current location), or have the project point to the file in its current location. You do this by choosing one of the options in the After Locating Missing Audio section of the dialog box: Move File To Project Audio Folder, Copy File To Project Audio Folder, or Reference File From Present Location, respectively.

4. To finish the operation, click the Open button. But if you no longer want to use the file in your project, you can click the Skip button. And to discard all audio data for a project, click Skip All.

5. If your project contains data from more than one audio file, you will need to go through steps 2 to 4 for each missing file.

Any files that you couldn't find or just skipped over will be replaced with silence within your projects. The clips will still appear in the tracks, but the clips will be empty.

Create a New Project

To create a new project, you can select the appropriate option in the SONAR Quick Start dialog box, or you can choose File > New from SONAR's menu. Whichever method you use, SONAR then displays the New Project File dialog box (see Figure 4.6).

Figure 4.6
You choose from the New Project File dialog box to start a new project

From here, you need to choose a template upon which to base your new project. After you make your selection, SONAR creates a new project complete with predefined settings that reflect the template you selected.

What's a Template?

A template is a special type of file upon which new projects are based. You can think of templates as sort of predefined projects. Templates contain the settings for all the parameters in a project. Templates enable you to quickly and easily set up a new project for a particular type of musical session. For example, if you need to record a rock song with guitar, organ, bass, and drums, you could get a head start on your project by using SONAR's Rock Quartet template. You can also use templates to set up SONAR for different kinds of studio configurations or if you need to work with a particular MIDI instrument.

SONAR ships with more than thirty different templates that represent a wide range of recording situations. You can use a template called Normal to start a new project totally from scratch. And if you don't find what you need from the templates included with SONAR, you can always create your own.

Create Your Own Template

Any parameters that are saved in a project can also be saved as a template. To create your own template, you simply do the following:

1. Select File > New, and choose the Normal template. Choosing this template creates a new, blank project for you, ready to be filled.

2. Set SONAR's parameters to reflect the type of template you want to create. This includes track configurations.

3. Select File > Save As to display the Save As dialog box (see Figure 4.7).

Figure 4.7
You can give your new template a name in the Save As dialog box

4. Choose Template from the Save As Type drop-down list.

5. Enter a name for your new template in the File Name field and click the Save button.

The next time you want to create a new project, your template will be listed along with the rest in the New Project File dialog box.

TIP

If you bypass the SONAR Quick Start dialog box—either by disabling it (as I mentioned earlier) or by clicking on its Close button, SONAR automatically creates a new project for you every time you start the program. This project is based on the Normal template, which is saved as the NORMAL.CWT file. If you would like to have SONAR configured in a particular way every time you run the program, simply create a new template and save it as the NORMAL.CWT file. Now SONAR will automatically load your special template during startup. Be sure to make a copy of the NORMAL.CWT file and rename it to something like BLANK.CWT, in case you ever want to create an empty new project.

But what parameters do you need to set when you're creating a new template? Let's go through them one at a time, shall we?

Track Configuration and Parameters

Before you start recording any MIDI or audio data in SONAR, you have to set up your tracks in the Track view. You need to add tracks and tell SONAR the types of tracks (MIDI or audio) they are going to be by right-clicking within the Track pane of the Track view and choosing either Insert Audio Track or Insert MIDI Track from the pop-up menu (see Figure 4.8). You can continue doing this until you have all the tracks you need for your template.

TIP

You can also press Insert on your computer keyboard to add new tracks. If the project is blank, a dialog box will ask which track type (audio or MIDI) you wish to create. If tracks already exist, pressing the Insert key will insert the same track type as the currently active track.

Figure 4.8
Add new tracks to your
template using the
Track pane of the
Track view

In addition to adding new tracks, you also need to set up the accompanying parameters for
each. These parameters include the name, channel, bank, patch, volume, pan, key offset,
velocity offset, time offset, input, and output.

NOTE
When you look in the Track view, you'll notice there are some additional
parameters available for adjustment. These parameters are not usually set up
when creating a template, so I will cover them later in the book.

All of these parameters can be changed directly within the Track view (see Figure 4.9), but
you can also access some of them via the Track Properties dialog box (see Figure 4.10).
Because you can change all of the parameters within the Track view, just using that method
most of the time is easiest. The only time you might need to use the Track Properties dialog
box is if you want to add a descriptive comment to a track or when you want to access the
Patch browser (I'll talk more about this later). To access the Track Properties dialog box,
right-click the track you want to change and select Track Properties from the pop-up menu.

Figure 4.9
All track parameters
can be changed within
the Track view

Figure 4.10
Some track parameters
are available within
the Track Properties
dialog box

Name

To name a track, double-click within its Name field in the Track view. Then type something and press the Enter key on your computer keyboard when you're done. That's all there is to it. A track name can be anything from a short, simple word like *Drums* to a longer, more descriptive phrase such as *Background Vocals (Left Channel)*.

Channel (Ch)

This parameter is for MIDI tracks only. It tells SONAR what MIDI channel you want it to use to play back the data in a track. To change this parameter, just click the *Ch* drop-down list and choose a channel.

Bank (Bnk)

Also for MIDI tracks only, the bank parameter tells SONAR which bank of sounds you want to use in your MIDI instrument. To change this parameter, just click the *Bnk* drop-down list and choose a bank, or press Enter on your computer keyboard and type in a bank number.

Patch (Pch)

Also for MIDI tracks only, the patch parameter tells SONAR which patch (or sound) you want to use from the bank in your MIDI instrument. To choose a patch, click the *Pch* drop-down list. If you've set up your instrument definitions as described in Chapter 3, you should see the names of the patches for your MIDI instrument in the *Pch* drop-down list.

TIP

You can also choose patches for a track using the Patch browser. Just right-click the Pch or Bank parameter of a MIDI track to open the Patch browser dialog box (see Figure 4.11). You will see a list of all the patches available from the instrument definitions you set up earlier. To search for a particular patch, type some text into the Show Patches Containing The Text parameter. To choose a patch, select it from the list. Then click OK.

Figure 4.11
Use the Patch browser
as an alternative for
assigning patches to
a track

CHAPTER 4

Volume (Vol)

The volume parameter sets the initial loudness level of a track. That's basically all there
is to it. You can set the volume by clicking and dragging within the *Vol* parameter. Drag to
the left to lower the volume. Drag to the right to raise the volume. You can also change
the volume numerically by clicking the *Vol* parameter to highlight it, pressing F2 on your
computer keyboard, typing in a new value, and pressing Enter. The value can range from
0 (off) to 127 (maximum) for MIDI tracks, and –INF to +6 dB for audio tracks.

Pan (Pan)

The pan parameter determines where the sound of a track will be heard in the sound field between two stereo speakers. You can make it so the sound will play out of the left speaker, the right speaker, or anywhere in between. That is called *panning*. You can set the pan by clicking and dragging within the *Pan* parameter. Drag to the left to pan the track to the left. Drag to the right to pan the track to the right. You can also change the pan numerically by clicking the *Pan* parameter to highlight it, pressing F2 on your computer keyboard, typing in a new value, and pressing Enter. The value can range from −127 (100 percent left) to +127 (100 percent right). A value of 0 is dead center. Pan works on both MIDI and audio tracks.

Key Offset (Key+)

The key offset parameter (which works only with MIDI tracks) lets you transpose the MIDI notes in a track during playback. It doesn't change the data that's actually recorded into the track. If you know that you're going to want the notes in a track transposed after they've been recorded though, setting up this parameter in your template can be useful. To set the key offset, double-click the *Key+* parameter to activate it. Then type in a new value and press Enter. The *Key+* value can range from −127 to +127, with each number representing a semitone (or half-step). For example, a value of −12 would transpose the notes down an octave, and a value of +12 would transpose them up an octave. A value of 0 means no transposition will be applied.

Velocity Offset (Vel+)

The velocity offset parameter (which works only with MIDI tracks) is similar to the key offset parameter, except instead of transposing MIDI notes during playback, it raises or lowers the MIDI velocity of each note in a track by adding or subtracting a number from −127 to +127. Again, the data that's actually recorded into the track isn't changed. You can set the velocity offset by clicking and dragging within the *Vel+* parameter. Drag left to lower the value. Drag right to raise the value. You can also change the velocity offset numerically by clicking the *Vel+* parameter to highlight it, pressing F2 on your computer keyboard, typing in a new value, and pressing Enter.

Time Offset (Tme+)

When you record a MIDI performance in SONAR, the timing of your performance is recorded along with the notes, and so on. Each MIDI event is "stamped" with an exact start time, which is measured in measures, beats, and clock ticks. The time offset parameter is similar to key offset and velocity offset, except that it adds or subtracts an offset value to the start time of the events in a MIDI track. Just as with key offset and velocity offset, the data that's actually recorded into the track isn't changed. The offset occurs only during playback, and you can set it back to zero to hear your original performance.

The time offset is useful if you want to make a track play a little faster or slower than the rest of the tracks, in case the performance is rushed or late. To change it, just double-click the *Tme+* parameter to activate it. Then type in the number of clock ticks by which you want the events in the track to be offset and press Enter.

TIP

To quickly set a Volume, Pan, or Velocity Offset parameter back to its default value, double-click the parameter.

Input (In)

The input parameter lets SONAR know where the data for that track is going to be recorded from, whether it be an audio track or a MIDI track. To set the Input for an audio track, choose one of the inputs from your sound card in the *In* drop-down list. For example, if you have a Sound Blaster Live card, your choices would be Left SB Live Wave In, Right SB Live Wave In, or Stereo SB Live Wave In. If you pick either the left or right choices, that means the track would record audio from either the left or right input on your sound card. If you pick the Stereo choice, the track would record audio from both inputs at the same time, making it a stereo audio track.

Setting the input parameter for a MIDI track is a bit different. Because MIDI has sixteen different channels, you can choose to record data using any one of those channels. Just make sure that your MIDI instrument is set to the same channel that you choose as your input, or your performance won't be recorded. You can also use the MIDI Omni setting. This setting allows SONAR to record data on all sixteen channels at the same time, so no matter what channel your MIDI instrument is set on, the data coming from it will be recorded. But if you're using multiple instruments with each set to a different channel, you're better off just setting the correct channel in each of the tracks right from the start.

Output (Out)

The output parameter tells SONAR which MIDI port or sound card output you want it to use to play back the data in a track. If the track is MIDI, you can select a MIDI port from the *Out* drop-down list. If the track is audio, you can select a sound card output from the *Out* drop-down list.

TIP

You can also change the properties for multiple tracks simultaneously. Just select the tracks you would like to adjust by Ctrl-clicking or Shift-clicking the appropriate Track numbers in the Track View. Then choose Track > Property > and the property you would like to change.

Timebase

Just like all sequencing software, SONAR uses clock ticks to keep track of the timing of your MIDI performance. Most of the time, you see them as measures and beats, because the program translates the clock ticks automatically. For each measure or beat, hundreds of clock ticks occur. The number of clock ticks that happen within a beat are called *pulses per quarter note* (*PPQ*) or the *timebase*. The timebase determines the resolution or accuracy of your MIDI timing data.

For example, if you want to use eighth-note septuplets (seven eighth notes per quarter note) in your performance, you have to use a Timebase that is divisible by 7 (such as 168 PPQ); otherwise, SONAR cannot record the septuplets accurately. By default, SONAR uses a timebase of 960 PPQ, which means every quarter note is represented by 960 clock ticks. The timebase can be set anywhere from 48 to 960 PPQ. To set the timebase, follow these steps:

1. Select Options > Project to open the Project Options dialog box (see Figure 4.12).

Figure 4.12
You can set the timebase in the Project Options dialog box

2. Click the Clock tab.
3. Choose the timebase you would like to use from the selections in the Ticks Per Quarter-Note section.
4. Click the OK button.

System Exclusive Banks

SONAR includes a System Exclusive (Sysx) librarian, which lets you store MIDI System Exclusive messages in up to 8,192 banks (or storage areas). All the data in the librarian is saved along with a project. This means that each project can hold its own unique library of Sysx data. This capability can be very useful when you're putting together templates for special MIDI recording situations. Because the Sysx librarian is a significant part of SONAR, I'm going to talk about it in more detail in Chapter 14. I just wanted to be sure to mention it here so that you know that data contained in the librarian is saved along with your Template.

File Information and Comments

SONAR allows you to save description information in a project, including title, subtitle, instructions, author, copyright, keywords, and comments. This information can be useful—especially when you're creating a template—to remind yourself exactly what is contained in the file. To add information to a project, do the following:

1. Select File > Info to open the File Info window (see Figure 4.13).

Figure 4.13
You can use the File Info window to add description information to your project or template

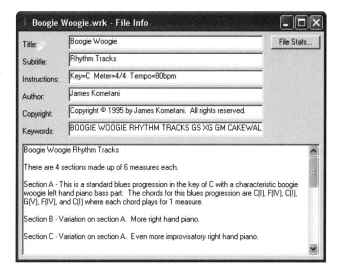

2. Type the appropriate information in each of the fields. By the way, the information you enter in the Title, Subtitle, Instructions, Author, and Copyright fields will appear in the Print Preview window and on your music notation printouts (see Chapter 13).
3. Close the File Info window when you're finished.

The information that you entered is then included in the project or template file when you save it.

TIP

If you plan to share your project or template files with others, and you want them to follow special instructions you've included in the File Info window (or you just want to be sure they see your copyright notice), you can have the File Info window displayed automatically when the file is opened. Just save the project or template while the File Info window is still open.

Tempo, Meter, and Key

Every piece of music needs to have a tempo, meter (time signature), and key, so of course SONAR allows you to set and save these parameters within a project or template.

Set the Tempo

You can set the tempo for your piece like this:

1. Select View > Toolbars to make sure the Tempo Toolbar is visible (see Figure 4.14).

Figure 4.14
To set the tempo for a project, you need to use the Tempo toolbar

2. Click the Tempo display on the Tempo toolbar. The Tempo is then highlighted.

3. Type a new value for the tempo. The value ranges from 8.00 to 250.00. You can also use the + and – spin controls to adjust the tempo with the mouse.

4. Press the Enter key on your computer keyboard to set the tempo.

NOTE
For more information about changing the tempo in an existing project, see Chapter 7.

Set the Meter (Time Signature) and Key (Key Signature)

Because a piece of music can have multiple time signatures and key signatures throughout, SONAR allows you to add multiple meters and keys to a project. For the purpose of creating a template, though, you'll more than likely just want to set the initial meter and key. To do so, follow these steps:

1. Select View > Meter/Key to open the Meter/Key view (see Figure 4.15).

Figure 4.15
You can add multiple time and key signatures to a project in the Meter/Key view

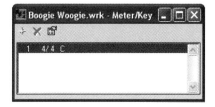

2. Double-click the first (and for purposes of this example, the only one that should be there) Meter/Key change in the list to open the Meter/Key Signature dialog box (see Figure 4.16).

Figure 4.16
In the Meter/Key Signature dialog box, you can edit individual meter/key changes in the Meter/Key view

3. Enter the Beats Per Measure and the Beat Value you want to use. For example, if your song is in 6/8 time, you would change the Beats Per Measure to 6 and the Beat Value to 8.

4. Choose a key from the Key Signature drop-down list. For example, if your song is in the key of A, choose 3 Sharps (A).

5. Click OK, and then close the Meter/Key view.

Other Parameters

A few other parameters are saved along with projects and templates, including synchronization settings, MIDI echo, metronome, record mode, and punch in/out times. But you'll usually set these parameters while you're working on a project, not beforehand. So, I'll talk more about them later in chapter 6. For the purpose of creating a template, you can just let them be saved at their default values.

TIP
A template can also contain MIDI data and audio data. This data can be useful, for instance, if you have some favorite drum grooves or melodic phrases that you like to use frequently in your projects. Simply store these tidbits as clips in one of the tracks. When you save the template, the MIDI and/or audio data is saved along with it. Then, whenever you create a new project with that template, the MIDI and/or audio data will be ready and waiting for you to use.

TIP

When inspiration hits, you don't want to waste your time fiddling with sequencer setup parameters. You want to be able to start your software and get right to work. If you create a template file that contains everything set just the way you like it, you'll have a much better chance of getting that cool lick down before you forget it. For instructions on how to set up the ultimate template, check out my Sequencer Techniques feature article in issue 11 of DigiFreq. You can download the issue for free at:

http://www.digifreq.com/digifreq/issues.asp

Save Your Project

When it comes time to save your SONAR project, do the following:

1. Select File > Save As to open the Save As dialog box.
2. Choose the type of project file you want to save from the Save As Type drop-down list.
3. Enter a name for the file and click the Save button.

The only thing you really have to decide (besides the name of the file) is the type of the file.

Project File Types

Projects can be saved as three different types of files: MIDI (.MID), Work (.CWP), and Bundle (.CWB).

MIDI Files

If you ever need to collaborate on a project with someone who owns a sequencing application other than SONAR, you should save your project as a MIDI (.MID) file. A MIDI file is a standard type of file that can be used to transfer musical data between different music software applications. Most music programs on the market today can load and save MIDI files. The problem with MIDI files, however, is that they can store only MIDI data; they can't hold audio data. And none of SONAR's settings are saved within a MIDI file either. So, if you're working on a project alone, or everyone else in your song-writing group uses SONAR, you don't need to deal with MIDI files. Of course, MIDI files can be useful in other circumstances, such as composing music for multimedia or sharing your music with others via the Internet.

Work Files

If you're working on a project that contains only MIDI data and no audio data, then you should save the project as a work (.CWP) file. Work files store all the MIDI data in a project, plus all the parameter settings (which you learned about earlier in this chapter) for the project. Work files do not store audio data.

NOTE

If you decide to manage your project audio files manually (as mentioned in chapter 3), then you should save your audio projects as work files. In this case the audio data is stored separately from the project file.

Bundle Files

For those projects that contain both MIDI and audio data, you should save them as bundle (.CWB) files. If you use a bundle file, you can store all the data in a project (MIDI data, audio data, and project parameter settings) into a single file. Having a single file makes it very easy to keep track of all the data in a project plus make a backup of the project for easy recovery in case something goes wrong. I'll talk more about backing up your project files in Appendix B.

NOTE

If you have recently upgraded from Pro Audio 9 or SONAR version 1.0, you will notice that SONAR 2 uses new file formats. Old work and bundle files had WRK and BUN extensions, while the new files have CWP and CWB extensions, respectively. This means that if you save a project in SONAR 2, you will not be able to load that project in SONAR 1.0 (although you can in SONAR 1.3) or Pro Audio 9. However, if you have old WRK and BUN files that were saved in previous versions, you can load and convert these in SONAR 2.

TIP

SONAR has an Auto Save feature that automatically saves your data to a special backup file at fixed time intervals or every time a certain number of changes have been made to the project. Using this feature is a great way to keep your data safe in case a power outage occurs or you make a huge mistake that you can't undo. To activate Auto Save, do the following:

1. Select Options > Global to open the Global Options dialog box. Then click the General tab.

2. For the option Auto-save Every 0 Minutes or 0 Changes, set either the number of minutes or the number of changes that need to occur between each time SONAR will do an automatic save of your project.

3. If you want to disable Auto Save, set both the minute and changes values back to zero.

4. Click the OK button.

During an automatic save, SONAR saves your project in a special file with a different name. If your project is named "myproject.cwp," for example, SONAR does an automatic save to a file named "auto save version of myproject.cwp." If you ever need to recover your project, you can just open the special Auto Save file and then save it under the original filename.

5

Getting Around in SONAR

To record, play, and edit your music in SONAR, you have to know how to navigate your way through the data in your project. As you learned in Chapter 2, SONAR includes a number of tools that allow you to examine and manipulate your data. They are the Track, Piano Roll, Staff, and Event views. Although each of these views provides a different way to edit your data, they all share some common means of control. In other words, even though your data appears (and is edited) differently in each view, you access the data in a similar manner no matter what view you use. A little confused? Don't worry, you'll understand exactly what I mean after I finish describing the following topics:

▶ How to use the Now time

▶ How to use the Go menu

▶ How to set place marks in your project

▶ How to search for specific music data in your project

CHAPTER 5

The Now Time

You learned a little about timing in Chapter 1 and Chapter 3. Essentially, you learned that in addition to the musical data itself, the timing of your performance is stored during recording. What this means is that SONAR keeps track of exactly when you play each note on your MIDI keyboard during a performance, and it stores those notes along with a *timestamp* (a timing value) containing the measure, beat, and clock tick when each note occurred.

To give you access to your data in a project, SONAR provides a feature known as the *Now time*. The Now time is essentially a pointer that indicates your current time location within a project. For example, the beginning of a project has a Now time of 1:01:000 (measure, beat, tick), which is the first beat of the first measure. If you want to view the data at the second beat of the tenth measure, for example, you have to set the Now time to 10:02:000. And, of course, you can get more precise by specifying clock ticks, such as in a Now time of 5:03:045, which would be the forty-fifth clock tick of the third beat in the fifth measure.

The Now time is also updated in real-time, which means that it changes constantly during recording or playback of a project. So, for example, as you play your project, the Now time counts along and shows you the current measure, beat, and tick while you listen to your music.

Show Me the Now Time

You can view the Now time in several different ways. Numerically, the Now time is displayed in the Position toolbar (see Figure 5.1).

Figure 5.1
You can view the
Now time in the
Position toolbar

You can also use the Transport toolbar to view the Now time (see Figure 5.2). For more information about toolbars, see Chapter 3.

Figure 5.2
The Now time is
displayed in the
Transport toolbar
as well

In either toolbar, you'll notice that the Now time is shown as measures, beats, and ticks. But each toolbar has an additional numeric display. This display is also the Now time, shown as hours, minutes, seconds, and frames (known as SMPTE).

NOTE
SMPTE (which stands for the Society of Motion Picture and Television Engineers) is a special timing code used for synchronizing audio and video data, although it can be used for other purposes, too. The technology was originally developed by NASA because it needed a really accurate way to keep track of space mission data. In SONAR, you can use SMPTE to keep track of the timing of your project. SONAR automatically converts the measures, beats, and ticks in a project to the hours, minutes, seconds, and frames format used by SMPTE. The frames parameter comes from the fact that SMPTE is used extensively with video, film, and television. Video is created by recording a series of still picture frames very quickly. When these frames are played back, you see them as a moving picture. SMPTE can be used to time video data accurately right down to a single frame. Every second of video data usually has 30 frames, but the number depends on the format of the data. You'll learn more details about using SMPTE in Chapter 6. For now, just know that you can view and set the Now time of your project either in measures, beats, and ticks or in hours, minutes, seconds, and frames.

TIP

If you're like me, and you have some of your MIDI instruments set up in your home studio a fair distance away from your computer, you might have trouble reading the very tiny Now time display in either of the Position or Transport toolbars. To remedy this situation, Cakewalk has included the Big Time view in SONAR. Basically, it displays the Now time as large numbers on your computer screen (see Figure 5.3). The Big Time view has its own window, so you can position it anywhere within the SONAR workspace. You can change the size of the Big Time view by dragging any of its corners, just like you would with any window in Windows. To toggle the time format between measures, beats, ticks, and SMPTE, just click inside the Big Time view window. You can also change the font and the color of the display by right-clicking in the window and then making your selections in the standard Windows Font dialog box.

Figure 5.3
Using the Big Time view, you can display the Now time in varying fonts and sizes on your computer screen

In addition to being displayed numerically, the Now time is displayed graphically within any of SONAR's view windows. In the Track, Piano Roll, and Staff views, the Now time is displayed as a vertical line cursor that extends from the top to the bottom of the view. As the Now time changes—either from being set manually or in real-time during playback or recording—the cursor in each of the views follows along in perfect sync and indicates graphically the place in the project the Now time is currently pointing. To demonstrate what I mean, try the following:

1. Select File > Open and load one of the sample project files that comes included with SONAR. For this example, choose Latin.cwp (see Figure 5.4).

Figure 5.4
This screen shows the
layout of the Latin.cwp
sample project

2. Close all the windows except for the Track view and then select Realtime > Play or just click the Play button in the Transport toolbar to start playing the project.

3. Look at the Track view. See the Now time cursor moving across the track display as the music plays?

4. Choose View > Piano Roll and look at the Piano Roll view. The same thing is happening, right? Notice the row of numbers just above the place where the Now time cursor is moving; this is the Time Ruler. Every view has one (except the Event view, which I'll talk about later). The Time Ruler displays the measure numbers in the current project. By lining up the top of the Now time cursor with the Time Ruler in any of the views, you can get a quick estimate of the current Now time.

TIP

If you right-click the Time Ruler in the Track view and choose Time Ruler Format, you can change the format of the measurements shown. So instead of keeping track of the Now time as measures, beats, and ticks, you can do so using hours, minutes, seconds, and frames. The samples measurement setting comes in handy when editing audio data, which I'll discuss in chapter 7 and 8.

5. Choose View > Event List and look at the Event view. It's different from all the other views because it shows the data as one long list instead of displaying data from left to right. And instead of a vertical line, it shows the Now time cursor as a small red box. While a project plays, the Now time cursor in the Event view moves down the list, and it marks the same exact place in the project as all the other view cursors do. Everything is synchronized to the Now time.

Set the Now Time

As you've just seen, the Now time changes automatically as a project is played, but you can also set the Now time manually while a project isn't playing. SONAR gives you this capability so that you can access different parts of your project for editing, which I'll talk about in Chapter 7.

Numerically

Changing the Now time is easy. If you would like to set the Now time to a precise numerical value, you can simply type it into the display on the Position toolbar. Here's how:

1. If you want to set the Now time using measures, beats, and ticks, click the measures, beats, and ticks display in the Position toolbar. The display becomes highlighted (see Figure 5.5).

Figure 5.5
You can change the Now time by clicking on the display to highlight it

2. Type the measures, beats, and ticks value you want to use, and press Enter on your computer keyboard.

TIP
If you want to quickly set the Now time to a particular measure or beat, you don't have to enter all the numerical values. For example, to set the Now time to measure two, type 2. That's it. Or to set the Now time to measure five, beat three, type 5:3 or 5 spacebar 3. To specify ticks, you must enter something for all the values.

3. If you want to set the Now time using hours, minutes, seconds, and frames, click the SMPTE display in the Position toolbar. The display then becomes highlighted (see Figure 5.6).

Figure 5.6
You can change the
Now time by
specifying SMPTE time
code values, too

4. Type the hours, minutes, seconds, and frames value you want to use and press Enter on your computer keyboard.

TIP

Just as with the measures, beats, and ticks, if you want to quickly set the Now time to a particular hour, minute, or second, you don't have to enter all the numerical values. For example, to set the Now time to two minutes, type 0:2. That's it. Or to set the Now time to five minutes, three seconds, type 0:5:3. To specify frames, you must enter something for all the values.

Graphically

Remember when I described the Time Rulers in each of the views in the "The Now Time Cursor" section? Well, you can quickly change the Now time by simply clicking on any of the Time Rulers. For example, you can do the following:

1. As you did earlier, select File > Open and load one of the sample project files that comes included with SONAR. For this example, choose Latin.cwp.

2. Close all the windows except for the Track view and then click the Time Ruler in the Track view. See how the Now time changes?

3. Choose View > Piano Roll and then click the Time Ruler in the Piano Roll view. Same result, right? Depending on where you click the Time Ruler, the Now time changes to the appropriate value within the measure that you click.

TIP

You might notice that when you click the Time Ruler in any of the views, the Now time is automatically set to the first beat of the nearest measure. This happens because of SONAR's Snap to Grid feature. Snap to Grid automatically snaps the Now time cursor to the nearest predefined value when you try to set it via a Time Ruler. This feature makes it easy to do quick and precise settings. Without Snap to Grid, setting the Now time accurately using a Time Ruler can be difficult.

Continued

Each view (except the Event view) in SONAR has its own separate Snap to Grid, but the feature is set in the same manner no matter which view you're using. To activate or deactivate the Snap to Grid in a view, just click the Snap to Grid button (see Figure 5.7). To set a Snap to Grid interval, right-click the Snap to Grid button (or in the Track view, click the downward arrow next to the Snap to Grid button) to display the Snap to Grid dialog box (see Figure 5.8). Now select a resolution by choosing a note duration from the list, typing a time value to use, or selecting a standard resolution such as events, markers, or clip boundaries. After you're finished setting the Snap to Grid, click the Time Ruler, and you'll notice that the Now time cursor snaps to the resolution that you've chosen.

Figure 5.7
The Snap to Grid button controls whether the Snap to Grid feature is on or off

Figure 5.8
You can set the Snap to Grid via the Snap to Grid dialog box

CHAPTER 5

4. As before, the Event view works a little differently. Here, you can simply click any event in the list, and the Now time changes to the exact timing value of that event.

The Position Slider

Another quick way to set the Now time graphically is to use the Position slider. The slider is part of the Position toolbar (see Figure 5.9). To use the slider, just click and drag it. Also, if you click to the left or right of the slider, the Now Time updates one measure at a time. That's it.

Figure 5.9
You can drag the Position Slider left or right to decrease or increase the Now time, respectively

The Go Menu

In addition to allowing you to set the Now time numerically and graphically, SONAR provides a few special functions that let you quickly change the Now time to some musically related points in a project. All these functions are a part of the Go menu. To activate them, simply select the Go menu and choose the appropriate function. Following is a list of the functions along with explanations for each of them:

Go-Time

Go-Time allows you to change the Now time numerically by entering a measure, beat, and tick value. It works in exactly the same way as the measure, beat, and tick display in the Position toolbar. The only difference is that Go-Time opens a dialog box.

Go-From and Go-Thru

When editing data in SONAR, you first need to select the data that you want to work with. It's the same as in any computer program that lets you work with data. For instance, if you want to delete some text in a word processor, you first select the data to highlight it, and then you delete it.

Well, if you have some data in your project currently selected, you can quickly set the Now time to the time that corresponds with the beginning (called the From time) or the end (called the Thru time) of the selection using the Go-From and Go-Thru functions, respectively. You'll learn more details about selecting data in Chapter 7.

Go-Beginning and Go-End

The Go-Beginning and Go-End functions are pretty self-explanatory. Simply put, they allow you to set the Now time to the time that corresponds with the beginning or the end of a project.

Go-Previous Measure and Go-Next Measure

As with Go-Beginning and Go-End, Go-Previous Measure and Go-Next Measure are self-explanatory. They let you quickly set the Now time to the time that corresponds to the first beat of the previous measure or the first beat of the next measure relative to the current Now time. In other words, if the Now time is set at 5:01:000 (beat one of measure five), selecting Go-Previous Measure changes it to 4:01:000 (beat one of measure four), and selecting Go-Next Measure changes it to 6:01:000 (beat one of measure six).

NOTE
If the Now time is set to something like 5:01:050, Go-Previous Measure actually changes it to the first beat of the current measure, which in this case would be 5:01:000. This happens because SONAR is programmed to go to the nearest measure boundary, which in this case is 5:01:000.

Go-Previous Marker and Go-Next Marker

The Go-Previous Marker and Go-Next Marker functions work in a similar manner as the Go-Previous Measure and Go-Next Measure functions. Go-Previous Marker and Go-Next Marker let you quickly set the Now time to the time that corresponds to the closest previous marker or next marker relative to the current Now time. Of course, because I haven't told you about markers yet, you're probably wondering what I mean. So, let's talk about markers, shall we?

Markers, Oh My!

All the methods for setting the Now time that I've described so far have either been based on numbers or predefined musical designations such as measures, beats, or the beginning and ending of a project. These methods are all fine when you already have the music for your project written out so you know exactly where everything occurs ahead of time, but what if you're creating a song from scratch simply by recording the parts on the fly? In a case like that, being able to put names to certain locations within a project would be very helpful, and that's exactly what markers allow you to do.

With markers, you can assign a name to any exact point in time (in either measures, beats, and ticks or SMPTE) in a project. They're great for designating the places where the verses and choruses start and end within a song. And they make it very easy for you to jump to any point within a project that you specify simply by name.

CHAPTER 5

Make Your Mark(ers)

Creating markers is a simple process. Essentially, you just need to set the Now time to the measure, beat, and tick at which you want to place the marker in the project, activate the marker dialog box, and type in a name. Activating the marker dialog box is the key here, because you can do so in a number of different ways. To create a marker, you just do the following:

1. Set the Now time to the measure, beat, and tick or the SMPTE time at which you want to place the marker in the project. As you learned earlier, you can set it either numerically or graphically.

2. Select Insert > Marker to open the Marker dialog box (see Figure 5.10). You can also open the Marker dialog box by pressing F11 on your computer keyboard; holding the Ctrl key on your computer keyboard and clicking just above the Time Ruler (the Marker section) in the Track, Staff, or Piano Roll views; right-clicking in a Time Ruler; clicking on the Insert Marker button in the Markers toolbar; or clicking on the Insert Marker button in the Markers view. (I'll describe the Markers toolbar and view later in this chapter.)

Figure 5.10
Using the Marker dialog box, you can create a marker

3. Type a name for the marker.

4. If you want the marker to be assigned to a measure/beat/tick value, you don't need to do anything more. The measure/beat/tick time of the marker is shown in the middle of the Marker dialog box.

5. If you want the marker to be assigned to a SMPTE time, activate the Lock To SMPTE (Real World) Time option.

NOTE

If you use the Lock To SMPTE (Real World) Time value, your marker is assigned an exact hour/minute/second/frame value. It retains that value no matter what. So, even if you change the tempo of the project, the marker keeps the same time value, although its measure/beat/tick location may change because of the tempo. This feature is especially handy when you're putting music and sound to video, when you need to have queues that always happen at an exact moment within the project.

By leaving a marker assigned to a measure/beat/tick value, however, you can be sure that it will always occur at that measure, beat, and tick even if you change the tempo of the project.

6. Click OK.

When you're finished, your marker (with its name) is added to the marker section, just above the Time Ruler in the Track, Staff, and Piano Roll views.

TIP

Usually, you add markers to a project while no real-time activity is going on, but you can also add markers while a project is playing. Simply press the F11 key on your computer keyboard, and SONAR creates a marker at the current Now time. The new marker is automatically assigned a temporary name, which you can later change.

Edit the Markers

Editing existing markers is just as easy as creating new ones. You can change their names and times, make copies of them, and delete them.

Name Change

To change the name of a marker, follow these steps:

1. Right-click the marker in the Marker section of the Time Ruler in one of the views to open the Marker dialog box. Alternatively, select View > Markers to open the Markers view (see Figure 5.11) and double-click the marker in the list to open the Marker dialog box.

Figure 5.11
The Markers View
displays a list of all the
Markers in a Project

2. Type a new name for the marker.
3. Click OK.

Time Change

Follow these steps to change the time value of a marker numerically:

1. Right-click the marker in the Marker section of the Time Ruler in one of the views to open the Marker dialog box. Alternatively, select View > Markers to open the Markers View and double-click the marker in the list to open the Marker dialog box.

2. Type a new measure/beat/tick value for the marker. If you want to use an SMPTE value, activate the Lock To SMPTE (Real World) Time option and then type a new hour/minute/second frame value for the marker.

3. Click OK.

You can also change the time value of a marker graphically by simply dragging the marker within the Marker section of the Time Ruler in one of the views with your mouse. Drag the marker to the left to decrease its time value or drag it to the right to increase its time value. Simple, no?

Make a Copy

To make a copy of a marker, follow these steps:

1. Hold down the Ctrl key on your computer keyboard.

2. Click and drag a marker in the Marker section of the Time Ruler in one of the views to a new time location.

3. Release the Ctrl key and mouse button. SONAR displays the marker dialog box.

4. Enter a name for the marker. You can also change the time by typing a new value, if you'd like. The time value is initially set to the time corresponding to the location on the Time Ruler to which you dragged the marker.

5. Click OK.

Delete a Marker

You can delete a marker in one of two ways, either directly in the Track, Staff, or Piano Roll views or via the Marker view. Here's the exact procedure:

1. If you want to use the Track, Staff, or Piano Roll views, click and hold the left mouse button on the marker that you want to delete.

2. If you want to use the Markers view, select View > Markers to open the Markers view. Then select the marker that you want to delete from the list.

3. Press the Delete key on your computer keyboard.

Navigate with Markers

Of course, what good would creating markers do you if you couldn't use them to navigate through the data in your project? What's more, all you need to do is select the name of a marker, and the Now time is automatically set to the exact time of that marker. You can jump to a specific marker in a project in two different ways: either by using the Markers view or the Markers toolbar.

Use the Markers View

To jump to a specific marker using the Markers view, do the following:

1. Select View > Markers to open the Markers view.

2. Select the marker that you want to jump to from the list. SONAR then sets the Now time to the time corresponding to that marker, and the Track, Staff, Piano Roll, and Event views jump to that time.

Use the Markers toolbar

To jump to a specific marker using the Markers toolbar, just select the marker from the Markers toolbar drop-down list (see Figure 5.12).

Figure 5.12
Using the Markers toolbar, you can quickly set the Now time to any marker by simply selecting a name from a list

SONAR sets the Now time to the time corresponding to that marker, and the Track, Staff, Piano Roll, and Event views jump to that time.

TIP
One other quick way to jump to a specific marker in a project is to select the Now time in the Position toolbar and then press the F5 key on your computer keyboard to bring up a list of all the markers in the current project. Select a marker from the list and click OK. The Now time is automatically set to the time corresponding to that marker.

Where, Oh Where?

Until now, I have been describing how to navigate through the data in a project by some-how specifying the Now time, with the result being that you go to a specific point within the project. Well, what happens when you don't know the exact position in a project you want to move to? For instance, out of all the data in all the tracks in your project, suppose you need to set the Now time to the first occurrence of the note Middle C? Instead of playing the project and trying to listen for the note, or looking through each and every track manually, you can use SONAR's Go-Search function.

CHAPTER 5

Go-Search allows you to automatically examine all the data in your project and find any MIDI events that have certain attributes that you specify. Upon finding the first event of the specified type, Go-Search sets the Now time to the time corresponding with that event. This function is very useful for finding significant points within a project and placing markers there or for precision editing tasks, which (as you've probably guessed by now) you'll learn more about later in Chapter 8. In the meantime, you can find specific MIDI events using the Go-Search function like this:

1.   Select Go > Beginning to set the Now time to the beginning of the project. If you don't take this step, Go-Search begins looking at your data starting at the current Now time, not at the beginning of the project. This means that if the Now time is currently set to 10:01:000, Go-Search does not look at any of the data contained in the first nine measures.

2.   Select Go > Search to open the Event Filter - Search dialog box (see Figure 5.13).

Figure 5.13
In the Event Filter - Search dialog box, you specify the criteria for your search

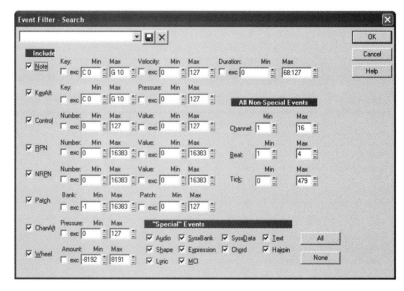

3.   Select the criteria for your search. Don't let all the settings in the Event Filter - Search dialog box intimidate you. They aren't very complicated to use. Basically, all you need to do is select the types of MIDI events that you would like to include in your search. For instance, if you want to look for MIDI note and pitch wheel events (but nothing else), deselect all the event types except for note and wheel.

TIP

By the way, whenever you open the Event Filter - Search dialog box, it automatically has all event types selected. To quickly deselect all event types, click the None button. The All button does the exact opposite.

After you select all your event types, you need to set the ranges for each of the parameters. For example, say you want to look for any MIDI note events between the pitches of C5 and G7 and with a velocity between 50 and 80. To do so, simply set the Note Key Minimum parameter to C5, the Note Key Maximum parameter to G7, the Note Velocity Minimum parameter to 50, and the Note Velocity Maximum parameter to 80. You can also specify a range of durations (note length) if you'd like. Each event type has its own unique set of parameter ranges: Key aftertouch has key and pressure parameters, patch change has bank and patch number parameters, and so on. You can also set up searches that are a little more complicated by excluding ranges of parameters. If you select the Exclude option next to any of the parameter range settings, the search excludes event types with that specific parameter range. For example, if you want to search for MIDI note events that do not fall within the range of C5 and G7, you set up the Minimum and Maximum parameters, as in the earlier example, and you activate the Key Exclude option.

Using the Event Filter - Search dialog box, you can specify "Special" Events, too, such as Audio, SysxData, Text, and Chord events. These "Special" Events don't include any additional parameter settings, though, so Go-Search simply finds any events of that kind within the data of your project. And lastly, you can choose to set a range of MIDI channels, beats, or ticks to search within. They are called Non-Special Events.

TIP

Because setting these search criteria every time you need to find specific data in a project can be tedious, it would be nice if you could save the settings for future use, wouldn't it? Well, you can. Just type a name in the Preset box at the top of the Event Filter - Search dialog box and click the Save button (the button with the little disk icon on it). All your current search criteria settings are then saved under that name. The next time you use Go-Search, you can simply select the name from the Preset box drop-down list, and all your previous settings will be loaded. You can save as many Presets as you'd like, and if you ever want to delete one, just select it from the list and click the Delete button (the button with the red X on it).

CHAPTER 5

4. Click OK.

SONAR searches through the data in your project, finds the first event that falls under the search parameters that you specified, and then sets the Now time to the time that corresponds to that event. If you want to quickly apply that same search again to find the next event with the same criteria, select Go > Search Next. SONAR continues the search (beginning at the current Now time), finds the next event that falls under the search parameters you specified, and then sets the Now time to the time that corresponds to that event, and so on. Here's another fact you should be aware of: If you first select some of the data in your project, the search is conducted only on that selected data, not all the data in the project.

The Go-Search Challenge

So, do you think that you now have a good understanding of how the Go-Search function works? To test you on what you've learned, I've put together a little search challenge. First, read the challenge, and then see whether you can set up the Event Filter - Search dialog options appropriately. When you think you've got it, take a look at the answer to see how you did.

A Simple Search

Find the first MIDI note event in the project that falls between the pitches of F4 and D7 and that has a velocity between 40 and 70. Also, restrict the search to MIDI Channel 2 only.

Here's the answer:

1. Select Go > Beginning to set the Now time to the beginning of the project.
2. Select Go > Search to open the Event Filter - Search dialog box.
3. Click the None button to clear all settings.
4. Select the MIDI note event type.
5. Set the Note Key minimum parameter to F4.
6. Set the Note Key maximum parameter to D7.
7. Set the Note Velocity minimum parameter to 40.
8. Set the Note Velocity maximum parameter to 70.
9. Set the Non-Special Event Channel minimum parameter to 2.
10. Set the Non-Special Event Channel maximum parameter to 2.
11. Click OK.

Did you get it right? If so, congratulations! I threw that MIDI channel restriction in there to make it a little more confusing. Setting both the minimum and maximum Channel parameters to the same number restricts the search to that MIDI channel. In this case, it was 2. If you didn't get quite the right settings, don't worry. With a little practice, you'll be able to easily master this feature.

6

Recording and Playback

Being able to record and play your music with SONAR turns your computer into a full-fledged recording studio. Without these features, SONAR would just be a glorified music data editor/processor. So, if you're going to memorize one chapter in the book, this should be it. You'll probably use the recording and playback features of SONAR most often. Therefore, I'm going to devote separate sections of the chapter to each way you can possibly record data in SONAR. The topics include the following:

▶ Reviewing the parameters that need to be set prior to recording

▶ Learning how to record and play MIDI tracks

▶ Learning how to record and play audio tracks

▶ Learning how to record multiple tracks at once

▶ Recording new tracks automatically using looping

▶ Correcting mistakes using punch in and punch out

▶ Recording MIDI one note at a time

▶ Using importing instead of recording

▶ Learning what synchronization is and how to use it

Preliminary Parameters

In Chapter 4, you learned about a number of parameters you can save to define a project template. Some of those parameters are related to recording, including track parameters, timebase, tempo, meter, and key. I'll mention these parameters throughout this chapter, but I won't go into detail on how to change them. If you need to refresh your memory, take a look at Chapter 4 again.

CHAPTER 6

In addition to these parameters, you need to be aware of a few others before doing any recording in SONAR. I didn't describe them in Chapter 4 because you usually set these parameters while working on a project, not beforehand when creating a template.

Metronome

If you've ever taken music lessons, you know what a *metronome* is. It's a device that makes a sound for each beat in each measure of a piece of music. You simply set the tempo you want, and the metronome sounds each beat accurately and precisely. You use this device to help you play in time with the correct rhythm. In SONAR, the metronome feature helps you to keep the right time so that your music data is stored at the right measure and beat within the project.

The metronome feature in SONAR is electronic (of course), and it's a bit more sophisticated than what you might find in a handheld unit. First of all, the tempo for the metronome is the same as the tempo setting for the project, so when you set the project tempo, you're also setting the metronome tempo. Normally, you would just have to turn the metronome on and off, but in SONAR you need to set several other parameters before using the metronome feature. You can access these parameters by selecting Options > Project to open the Project Options dialog box and then clicking on the Metronome tab (see Figure 6.1).

Figure 6.1
In the Project Options dialog box, you can access the metronome parameters

General

In the General section of the Project Options dialog box, you can determine whether the metronome will sound during playback, recording, or both by activating the Playback and Recording options. The Accent First Beat option determines whether the metronome will sound the first beat of each measure a little louder than the others. You can also select whether the metronome will use your computer's built-in speaker or one of your MIDI instruments to make its sound by activating the Use PC Speaker or Use MIDI Note options (I'll talk more about this last option shortly). You have to activate one of them; otherwise, the metronome won't make any sound at all.

Count-in

Using the Count-in option in the General section, you can get the feel of the tempo before SONAR starts recording your performance. Depending on how you set it, the metronome will sound a number of beats or measures before recording begins. For example, if your project is set for a 4/4 meter, and you set the Count-in option to 1 Measures, the metronome will sound four beats before SONAR begins recording.

MIDI Note

If you select the Use MIDI Note option in the General section of the Project Options dialog box, the settings in the MIDI Note section determine which MIDI instrument is used to make the metronome sound and which note is used for the first beat and remaining beats of each measure. The settings are reasonably self-explanatory. Using Port and Channel, you can set the MIDI port and channel that your MIDI instrument uses. Duration determines how long each metronome "beep" will sound. The duration is measured in ticks, so if you use the default timebase of 120 ticks per quarter note, a duration of 15 would be equivalent to a thirty-second note.

You can set the pitch (key) and loudness (velocity) of the first beat and remaining beats in each measure by using the First Beat and Other Beats options. If you want the first beat of each measure to be accented, you should set the velocity a little higher in the First Beat Velocity option. For example, you could set it to 127 and set the Other Beats Velocity to 110. Also, if your MIDI instrument is General MIDI-compatible and you set the Channel option to 10, you can use a percussion instrument for the metronome sound. I like to use a rimshot sound.

MIDI Echo

Some MIDI instruments do not provide any way for you to play them (such as a built-in keyboard) except by sending them MIDI messages. These instruments are called modules. To play a module, you need to trigger the module's sounds by playing another instrument, such as a MIDI keyboard. By connecting the MIDI Out from the MIDI keyboard to the MIDI In of the module, you can play the sounds in the module by performing on the keyboard.

But what if you want to record your performance using SONAR? In this case, you would have to connect the MIDI Out from the keyboard to the MIDI In of your computer. This means you would no longer be sending MIDI messages from the keyboard to the module, so how would you hear your performance? You could connect the MIDI Out from your computer to the MIDI In of the module, but the MIDI messages from the keyboard would still go directly to the computer and not the module. To remedy this situation, SONAR includes a feature called MIDI echo.

Basically, MIDI echo takes the MIDI messages from your computer's MIDI input(s) and sends the messages back out to your computer's MIDI output(s). You can control which MIDI channels the data is echoed from and which ports and channels the data is echoed to. You can access these parameters by selecting Options > Project to open the Project Options dialog box and then clicking on the MIDI Input tab (see Figure 6.2).

Figure 6.2
In the Project Options dialog box, you also can access the MIDI echo parameters

Record and Echo MIDI Channels

In the Record and Echo MIDI Channels section of the Project Options dialog box, you can choose which MIDI channels data will be echoed from. You usually should just keep all the channels activated, because these options also control which MIDI channels you can record data from. For example, if you deactivate option 1, you cannot record data from MIDI Channel 1.

Echo Mode and Echo Mapping

If you don't want to use MIDI echo, select None in the Echo Mode section of the dialog box. If you want to specify which port and channel the incoming data will be echoed to, select Manual and then make your settings in the Echo Mapping section. More than likely, you'll want to leave the Echo Mode set to Auto, though. In this mode, the port and channel to which the currently selected Track in the Track view are set determine which port and channel the MIDI data is echoed to. Using Auto works out to be easier, because you might have a number of different modules in your studio. Instead of manually changing the MIDI echo settings each time you want to work with a different module, you can have them changed automatically simply by setting up a new track in the Track view.

NOTE

One other MIDI echo option is rarely needed, but you should be aware of it. It's the Local On Port option. When you use one MIDI instrument (master) to play another (slave), pressing a key on the master instrument not only plays a sound on the slave, but also on the master. Most of the time, you'll want only the slave instrument to make sounds. To remedy this situation, you can turn off the sounds in the master instrument by using the Local On feature. All modern instruments have it. SONAR attempts to automatically set this feature every time you start it up, but sometimes it might not work (especially if you have an older instrument). If your instrument doesn't support the Local On feature, you can set the Local On Port option to block MIDI echo for a specified MIDI Port. I doubt that you'll have to use this option, so you can just keep it set to zero, unless you run across the double-note problem.

Sampling Rate and Bit Depth

You learned about the meanings of the terms *sampling rate* and *bit depth* in Chapter 1. SONAR lets you set the sampling rate and bit depth used for the audio data that you record. Depending on the sophistication of your sound card, you can set the sampling rate up to 96,000 Hz and the bit depth up to 24-bit.

So what settings should you use? Well, the higher the sampling rate and bit depth, the better the quality of your recorded audio. Higher settings also put more strain on your computer system, however, and the data takes up more memory and hard disk space. Plus, if your input signal is already bad (if you use a low-end microphone to record your vocals, for instance), higher settings won't make it sound any better.

In my opinion, if your computer has enough power, memory, and hard disk space, then you should use the highest settings your sound card will support. Using these settings will ensure that you get the best-quality recording. The only problem to watch out for is if you plan to put your music on CD. In that case, the audio needs to have a sampling rate of 44,100 Hz and a bit depth of 16-bit.

NOTE

In order to store music on a CD, the audio data is required to have a sampling rate of 44,100 Hz and a bit depth of 16. These values cannot be higher or lower. They must be exact. Of course, you can start off by recording your audio with different settings. For example, if your computer has a limited amount of memory or hard disk space, you may want to use smaller values. I wouldn't recommend this, though, unless it's absolutely necessary, because lower values mean lower quality audio. You can also record using higher values, which actually raises the quality of your audio data. When it comes time to put the audio on CD, however, you must convert the sampling rate and bit depth to the values mentioned above.

Using SONAR's Change Audio Format feature, you can convert the bit depth of the audio in your project. Just select Tools > Change Audio Format to access it. Unfortunately, the Change Audio Format feature only lets you convert between 16- and 24-bit. For any other bit depth values (and to convert the sampling rate) you will need to use a separate digital audio editing application, such as Sonic Foundry's Sound Forge (**www.sonicfoundry.com**), Syntrillium's Cool Edit (**www.syntrillium.com**), or Steinberg's WaveLab (**www.steinberg.net**).

To access these parameters, select Options > Audio to open the Audio Options dialog box and then click the General tab (see Figure 6.3).

Figure 6.3
In the Audio Options dialog box, you can access the sampling rate and file bit depth parameters

Audio Options	☒

General | Advanced | Input Monitoring | Drivers | Driver Profiles

Playback Timing Master: 1: C-Media PCI

Record Timing Master: 1: C-Media PCI

Number of Aux Buses: 2

Number of Virtual Mains: 1

Audio Driver Bit Depth: 16

Default Settings for New Projects

Sampling Rate: 44100 Hz   File Bit Depth: 16

11025 Hz
22050 Hz
44100 Hz
48000 Hz
96000 Hz

Mixing Laten

Buffers in Playba

Buffer Size: 100.0 msec

        Fast   Safe

Effective latency at 44kHz/stereo: 100.0 msec

Wave Profiler...

OK

Cancel

Help

In the Default Settings For New Projects section, you can make your selections in the Sampling Rate and File Bit Depth drop-down lists.

Input Monitoring

When recording an audio track, you usually want to listen to your performance as it's being recorded. In the past, due to the limitations of sound card drivers, you would be able to listen only to the "dry" version of your performance. This means that you would have to listen to your performance without any effects applied. With the input monitoring feature, however, SONAR allows you to listen to your performance with effects applied as it's being recorded, although the effects are not actually recorded. This can be especially useful, for example, when recording vocals where it's customary to let the singer hear a little echo or reverberation during his or her performance. If you're not sure what I'm talking about, don't worry. I'll cover effects in more detail in Chapter 11.

To activate input monitoring for your sound card, choose Options > Audio to open the Audio Options dialog box. Then click the Input Monitoring tab (see Figure 6.4).

Figure 6.4
In the Audio Options dialog box, you can activate input monitoring for your sound card

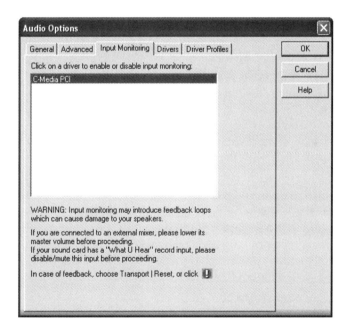

To activate input monitoring for your sound card(s), just select the driver(s) in the list. Then click OK.

CAUTION

Input monitoring may cause a feedback loop between your sound card input(s) and output(s). This happens, for example, when the signal coming out of a speaker is fed back into a microphone and the sound keeps looping and building up into a very loud signal. This feedback looping can damage your speakers. To be safe, you might want to turn the volume down on your speaker system before you activate input monitoring. If you hear feedback, deactivate input monitoring by clicking Input Monitoring tab in the Audio Options box and then clicking on the driver.

For a possible solution to your feedback problem, check the Windows Mixer settings for your sound card. Some sound cards have a monitoring feature that should be turned off when you are using input monitoring. For instance, if you have a Sound Blaster Live card, open the Record Controls in the Windows Mixer and make sure you are not using the "What U Hear" option as your recording input.

Record Mode

When you record MIDI or audio data into an empty track, SONAR simply places that data into the Track within a new Clip. (In Chapter 2, you learned how SONAR stores data as Events, which are stored within Clips, which in turn are stored within Tracks.) When you record data into a Track that already contains data, what happens to that existing data?

SONAR provides two different recording modes (actually, there are three, but I'll talk about Auto Punch later in the chapter), both of which provide a different means of dealing with existing data. The Sound On Sound mode mixes the new data with the existing data. So, for example, if you record a vocal part into a Track that already contains music, you hear both the vocal and the music when you play back that Track. The Overwrite mode replaces the existing data with the new data. So, in this example, the music is erased, and the vocal takes its place. Then, when you try to play the Track, you hear only the vocal.

Keep in mind that you need to deal with recording modes only when you're recording data into a Track that already contains data. More than likely, you won't be doing that very much because SONAR allows you to record an unlimited number of Tracks, and you can easily place each part of your song on a separate Track. If you do need to set the recording mode, however, just select Transport > Record Options to open the Record Options dialog box (see Figure 6.5).

Figure 6.5
In the Record Options
dialog box, you can set
the recording mode

In the Recording Mode section, select either Sound On Sound or Overwrite and click OK.

MIDI Track Recording and Playback

Believe it or not, you now have the knowledge needed to start recording in SONAR. Nothing is really complicated about the process, but you should follow a number of steps to make sure that everything occurs smoothly. Here and in the following sections, I'll show you step by step how to record MIDI tracks, audio tracks, and multiple tracks at once. First, let's tackle MIDI tracks. To get started, do the following:

1. Create a new project or open an existing one. If you use a template to create a new project, you might be able to skip some of the following steps, but you should probably run through them anyway, just in case.

2. Set the meter and key signature for the project. The default settings are 4/4 and the key of C Major.

3. Set the metronome and tempo parameters. The default tempo for a new project is 100 beats per minute.

4. Set the timebase for the project. The default setting is 960 PPQ (pulses per quarter note). More often than not, you won't have to change this setting.

5. Set the recording mode. Unless you plan to record data to a track that already contains data, you can skip this step. The default recording mode is Sound on Sound.

6. Add a new MIDI track to the Track view and adjust the track's properties. For more information about track properties and how to set them, refer to Chapter 4.

7. Arm the track for recording to let SONAR know that you want to record data on the track. Right after the name parameter in the Track view, you'll see three buttons labeled M, S, and R. Click the R button to arm the track for recording (see Figure 6.6).

Figure 6.6
You arm a track for recording by clicking on its associated R button in the Track view

8. Set the Now time to the point in the project where you would like the recording to begin. Most of the time, it will be the very beginning of the project, but SONAR provides the flexibility of letting you record data to a track starting at any measure, beat, or tick within a project.

9. Select Transport > Record to start recording. (You can also press the R key on your computer keyboard or click the Record button in the Transport toolbar.) If you set a Count-in, the metronome will first count the number of beats you entered, and then SONAR will begin recording.

10. Perform the material you want to record.

11. After you finish performing, select Transport > Stop to stop recording. (You can also press the spacebar on your computer keyboard or click the Stop button in the Transport toolbar.) SONAR creates a new clip in the track containing the MIDI data you just recorded (see Figure 6.7).

Figure 6.7
After you've finished recording, SONAR creates a new clip in the track representing the MIDI data

12. Listen to your performance by setting the Now time back to its original position and selecting Transport > Play. (You can also press the spacebar on your computer keyboard or click the Play button in the Transport toolbar.) If you don't like the performance, you can erase it by selecting Edit > Undo Recording. Then go back to Step 8, and try recording again.

NOTE
SONAR provides an Undo feature that allows you to reverse any action that you take while working on a project. You're probably familiar with this feature, because it can be found in most applications that allow you to manipulate data, such as word processing software and so on. SONAR goes a bit further, however, by providing an Undo History feature. This feature logs every step you take while working on a project and allows you to undo each step all the way back to the beginning of your current session. The Undo History is not saved, though, so as soon as you close a project, you lose the ability to undo any changes. To access the Undo History, just select Edit > History to open the Undo History dialog box (see Figure 6.8). You then see a list of all the tasks you've done during the current session. To go back to a certain point in the session, just select a task in the list and click OK. SONAR undoes any tasks performed after the task you selected. SONAR can keep track of as many as 2,147,483,647 tasks (although the default setting is 128 tasks), the maximum number of which you can set in the Maximum Undo Levels parameter of the Undo History dialog box. Remember, though, the more tasks SONAR keeps track of, the more memory and hard disk space it needs.

Figure 6.8
Using the Undo
History dialog box,
you can reverse
your actions

TIP

If you find that your performance for the most part is good except for only a few trouble spots, you might want to try fixing the mistakes by editing the MIDI notes rather than using Undo and then performing the whole thing all over again. You'll learn how to edit MIDI data in Chapter 7.

13.   After you've recorded a performance you like, disarm the track by clicking on its R button again. By disarming the track, you won't accidentally record over the data while you're recording any additional tracks.

14.   Go back to Step 6, and record any additional tracks that you would like to add to the project. While you're recording the new track(s), you will hear the previously recorded track(s) being played back. Because you can hear these tracks, you might want to turn off the metronome and just follow the music of the previous tracks as you perform the material for the new ones.

CAUTION

Be sure to save your project after each successful track recording. This step isn't really mandatory, but it's a good precautionary measure, because you never know when your computer may decide to crash on you. Rather than lose that really great performance you just recorded, quickly select File > Save (or press Ctrl+S on your computer keyboard) so you can rest easy in knowing that your data is safe.

Audio Track Recording and Playback

Recording audio tracks in SONAR is very similar to recording MIDI tracks, but, of course, because the nature of the data is different, you need to take a few additional steps. Here's the step-by-step process for recording audio tracks:

1. Create a new project or open an existing one. If you use a template to create a new project, you might be able to skip some of the following steps, but you should probably run through them anyway, just in case.

2. Set the meter and key signature for the project. The default settings are 4/4 and the key of C Major.

3. Set the metronome and tempo parameters. The default tempo for a new project is 100 beats per minute.

4. Set the timebase for the project. The default setting is 960 PPQ (pulses per quarter note). More often than not, you won't have to change this setting.

5. Set the recording mode. Unless you plan to record data to a track that already contains data, you can skip this step. The default recording mode is Sound on Sound.

6. Set the sampling rate and the file bit depth for the project.

7. Add a new audio track to the Track view and adjust the track's properties. For more information about these properties and how to set them, refer to Chapter 4.

8. If you want to hear effects added to your performance while you're recording, activate input monitoring for your sound card. Then add effects to your track by right-clicking on the *Fx* parameter (located in the Track pane along with all the other track parameters) and choosing Audio Effects > Cakewalk > (the effect you would like to add). I'll talk more about effects in Chapter 11.

9. Arm the track for recording to let SONAR know that you want to record data on the track. Right after the name parameter in the Track view, you'll see three buttons labeled M, S, and R. Click the R button to arm the track for recording.

10. After you arm the track, you'll notice the meter (shown right below all the other track parameters) light up (see Figure 6.9). This meter displays the level of the audio input for your sound card in decibels.

Figure 6.9
Each audio track has
a meter showing its
input signal level in
decibels

NOTE

Decibel is a very complicated term to describe. The most basic explanation
would be that a decibel is a unit of measurement used to determine the loudness
of sound. In SONAR, the audio meters can range from –90 dB (soft) to 0 dB
(loud). To change the display range of a meter, right-click it and choose a new
setting from the pop-up menu. For now, that's really all you need to know.

11. Set the audio input level for your sound card so that it's not too loud but
    also not too soft. To do so, you have to use the software mixer that came
    with your sound card. In the Windows taskbar, you should see a small
    speaker icon. Double-click the speaker icon to open your sound card
    mixer. Then select Options > Properties to open the sound card mixer
    Properties dialog box. In the Adjust Volume For section, select Recording,
    make sure all boxes below are checked, and click OK to display the
    recording controls for your sound card mixer (see Figure 6.10).

Figure 6.10
You use your sound
card mixer to adjust the
input levels for your
sound card

12. For the set of controls labeled Line-In, either activate the Select option or deactivate the Mute option (depending on your mixer configuration). This option tells your sound card that you want to record audio using its line-input connection. If you want to use a different connection (such as microphone or internal CD player), you need to use the set of controls associated with that connection.

NOTE

These steps show how to use a standard Windows sound card for recording. You may have a sound card that uses a different method for setting audio input levels. In that case, you need to read the documentation for your sound card to find out how to use it correctly.

13. When you have access to the input level controls for your sound card, begin your performance, playing at the loudest level at which you plan to record. As you play, the meter for the track will light up, displaying the sound level of your performance. You should adjust the input level so that, when you play the loudest part of your performance, the meter does *not* turn red. If it turns red, you have overloaded the input, and if you record at that level, your audio signal will be distorted. When you play the loudest part of your performance, if the meter lights up anywhere between −6dB and −3dB, then you have a good input level setting.

14. After you finish setting your input level, close the sound card mixer. Next, set the Now time to the point in the project where you would like the recording to begin. Most of the time, it will be the very beginning of the project, but SONAR provides the flexibility of letting you record data to a track starting at any measure, beat, or tick within a project.

15. Select Transport > Record to start recording. (You can also press the R key on your computer keyboard or click the Record button in the Transport toolbar.) If you set a Count-in, the metronome will first count the number of beats you entered, and then SONAR will begin recording.

16. Perform the material that you want to record.

17. After you finish performing, select Transport > Stop to stop recording. (You can also press the spacebar on your computer keyboard or click the Stop button in the Transport toolbar.) SONAR creates a new clip in the track containing the audio data you just recorded (see Figure 6.11).

Figure 6.11
After you've finished recording, SONAR creates a new clip in the track representing the audio data

18.   Listen to your performance by setting the Now time back to its original position and selecting Transport > Play to start playback. (You can also press the spacebar on your computer keyboard or click the Play button in the Transport toolbar.) If you don't like the performance, erase it by selecting Edit > Undo Recording. Then go back to Step 14 and try recording again.

19.   After you've recorded a performance you like, disarm the track by clicking on its R button again. By disarming the track, you won't accidentally record over the data while you're recording any additional tracks.

20.   Go back to Step 7 and record any additional tracks that you would like to add to the project. While you're recording the new track(s), you will hear the previously recorded track(s) playing back. Therefore, you might want to turn off the metronome and just follow the music of the previous tracks as you perform the material for the new ones.

TIP

If you have your home studio set up within a single room containing all your equipment (including your computer) and you are recording audio tracks using a microphone, the microphone will pick up the background noise made by your electronic devices (including the fan inside your computer). To remedy this situation, you might want to set up your microphone and one of your MIDI instruments in a different room, while keeping them connected to your computer via longer cables. Then you can set up some MIDI key bindings (you learned about them in Chapter 3) so that you can control SONAR remotely. This way, when you record the audio from your microphone, it won't pick up all that background noise.

Multiple Track Recording and Playback

If you have more than one MIDI input on your MIDI interface or more than one audio input on your sound card, you can record to multiple tracks simultaneously. Recording multiple tracks works well when you need to record a whole band of musicians. Instead of having each musician play individually (which can sometimes ruin the "groove"), you can record everyone's part at once (which usually makes the song flow much better).

To record multiple tracks, just follow the same instructions I outlined earlier for recording MIDI and audio tracks. The only difference is that you must set up and arm more than one track. When you start recording, the MIDI or audio data from each musician will be recorded to separate tracks simultaneously.

NOTE

When setting the input property for multiple MIDI tracks, SONAR doesn't allow you to select specific MIDI input ports. If you want to record more than one MIDI track at once, you must set the input property of each track to a different MIDI channel. You also have to be sure that each MIDI instrument is set to send data on a specific MIDI channel. If you have more than one instrument sending data on the same channel, the data from both instruments will be recorded on the same track.

TIP

Even if you're using a basic sound card to record audio, you can still record two different audio tracks at once. You can do so because your sound card has a stereo input. This means you can use the left and right audio channels separately to record two individual tracks. When you set up the tracks prior to recording, just select the Input for one track to be the left audio channel of your sound card and the input for the other track to be the right audio channel of your sound card. You also might need a special audio cable. Most basic sound cards provide only one stereo input connection at a 1/8-inch size. The cable you will need is called a Y-adapter audio cable with a stereo 1/8-inch mini plug to phono plugs (or connections). You should be able to find the cable at your local Radio Shack.

Loop Recording

If you plan to add a vocal track or an instrumental track (such as a guitar solo) to your project—something that may require more than one try to get right—you might want to use *loop recording* instead of recording and undoing a single track over and over again manually. Loop recording allows you to record several tracks, one right after the other, without having to stop in between each one. Here's how it works:

1. If you want to record MIDI tracks, follow steps 1 through 7 in the "MIDI Track Recording and Playback" section presented earlier in this chapter. If you want to record audio tracks, follow steps 1 through 13 in the "Audio Track Recording and Playback" section earlier in this chapter.

2. Set the Now time to the point in the project where you want looping to begin. Then select Transport > Loop And Auto Shuttle to open the Loop/Auto Shuttle dialog box (see Figure 6.12). Press F5 on your computer keyboard to bring up the Markers dialog box. Select the Marker named <Now> from the list and click OK to set the Start time where the looping will begin.

Figure 6.12
In the Loop/Auto Shuttle dialog box, you can set the loop recording parameters for SONAR

3. Type an End time for the loop using measure, beat, and tick values. Then activate the Stop at the End Time and Loop Continuously options and click OK. Setting these options tells SONAR that, when you start recording, it will begin at the Loop Start Time, continue to the Loop End Time, and then loop back to the Start time to cycle through the loop over and over again, until you stop it.

TIP

For a quick way to set the Start and End times, just click and drag in the Time Ruler of the Track View to make a data selection, then right-click in Time Ruler and choose Set Loop Points from the pop-up menu. For more information on selecting data, read chapters 7 and 8.

TIP

You can also use the Loop/Auto Shuttle toolbar to set the parameters for looping. Refer to Chapter 3 for more information about toolbars.

4. Select Transport > Record Options to open the Record Options dialog box. In the Loop Recording section, select either Store Takes in a Single Track or Store Takes in Separate Tracks. The first option stores each performance in the same track but in different clips stacked on top of each other. The second option stores each performance in a different track, automatically setting the same track parameters as the one you began with. I like to use the second option because it's more flexible, especially when I want to edit the data I just recorded. So, for this example, choose the Store Takes in Separate Tracks option. You can experiment with the other option later if you'd like.

5. Select Transport > Record to start recording. (You can also press the R key on your computer keyboard or click the Record button in the Transport toolbar.) If you set a Count-in, the metronome will first count the number of beats you entered, and then SONAR will begin recording.

6. Perform the material you want to record as many times as you require to get a good take.

7. After you finish performing, select Transport > Stop to stop recording. (You can also press the spacebar on your computer keyboard or click the Stop button in the Transport toolbar.) SONAR creates a new track containing the data you just recorded for every loop you cycled through (see Figure 6.13).

CHAPTER 6

Figure 6.13
For every loop you
record, SONAR creates
a new track containing
each individual
performance

8. Each track (except for the original one) is disarmed. To listen to any of your
    performances, turn off looping by selecting Transport > Loop And Auto
    Shuttle to open the Loop/Auto Shuttle dialog box. Deactivate the Stop at
    the End Time option and click OK. Set the Now time back to its original
    position and select Transport > Play to start playback. (You can also press
    the spacebar on your computer keyboard or click the Play button in the
    Transport toolbar.) To listen to one of the recorded tracks, solo it by clicking
    on the S button next to its name parameter in the Track view.

9. After you've found a performance that you like and want to keep, delete
    the others by selecting the track (click the appropriate track number on the
    left side of the Track view) and then select Track > Delete. If you want to
    select more than one track at once, just hold down the Ctrl key on your
    computer keyboard while you're selecting track numbers.

TIP

Instead of deleting all the extra tracks you created during looping, you might
want to keep them for use later. You can do so by using SONAR's Archive
feature. By archiving tracks, you store them within the current project, but they
become "invisible" to SONAR. This means that when you play your Project,
the archived tracks will not play. As a matter of fact, archiving tracks helps to
increase SONAR's performance because it doesn't process the tracks at all when
they are archived. To archive a track, just right-click its track number and select
Archive from the pop-up menu. You'll notice that the track's Mute button turns
into an A (Archive) button. This change in the button name shows that the track
is archived. You can still make changes to the track (and the data in it), but
SONAR will not play the track.

Punch Recording

When you make a mistake while recording MIDI data, it's usually no big deal, because you can easily make corrections (such as changing the pitch of a note) with SONAR's various editing tools (see Chapter 7). But what about when you're recording audio? Sure, you can edit the data by cutting and pasting sections or processing it with effects, but you can't edit the pitch of a single note or make any other precision corrections like you can with MIDI data. So, with audio, you have to record your performance all over again. By using SONAR's punch recording feature, however, you have to rerecord only the part of the performance you messed up, leaving the good parts alone.

Using punch recording, you can set up SONAR to automatically start recording and stop recording at precise times during a project. You therefore can record over certain parts of your performance without having to redo the whole thing. Punching is very similar to regular audio track recording, but with a few differences. Here's the step-by-step procedure:

1. Say you want to correct some mistakes on an audio track you just recorded. To get started, make sure the track is still armed for recording (its R button is red).

2. Activate punch recording by selecting Transport > Record Options to open the Record Options dialog box (see Figure 6.14). In the Recording Mode section, select Auto Punch. Then, for the Punch In Time, type the measure, beat, and tick at which you want SONAR to begin recording. For the Punch Out Time, type the measure, beat, and tick at which you want SONAR to stop recording. The section of the track that falls between the Punch In Time and the Punch Out Time should contain the part of your performance in which you made the mistakes.

TIP

For a quick way to set the Punch In and Out Times, just click and drag in the Time Ruler of the Track View to make a data selection, then right-click in Time Ruler and choose Set Punch Points from the pop-up menu. For more information on selecting data, read chapters 7 and 8.

Figure 6.14
You use the Record
Options dialog box to
set the recording mode
to Auto Punch and to
set the Punch In and
Punch Out Times

3. Set the Now time to the point in the project before the Punch In Time where you would like playback to begin. You might want to start from the very beginning of the project or just a few measures before the Punch In Time. However long it takes you to get into the groove of the performance is how far ahead of the Punch In Time you should set the Now time.

4. Select Transport > Record to start recording. (You can also press the R key on your computer keyboard or click the Record button in the Transport toolbar.) If you set a Count-in, the metronome will first count the number of beats you entered, and then SONAR will begin playback.

5. Play along with the existing material, exactly as you did before when you first recorded the track. When SONAR reaches the Punch-In Time, it will automatically start recording the new part of your performance.

6. When the Now time has passed the Punch Out Time, SONAR will stop recording, and you can select Transport > Stop to stop SONAR. (You can also press the spacebar on your computer keyboard or click the Stop button in the Transport toolbar.) SONAR replaces any existing material between the Punch In Time and the Punch Out Time with the new material you just played. As long as you didn't make any mistakes this time, your track will now be fixed.

7. Listen to your performance by setting the Now time back to its original position and selecting Transport > Play to start playback. (You can also press the spacebar on your computer keyboard or click the Play button in the Transport toolbar.) If you don't like the performance, you can erase it by selecting Edit > Undo Recording. Then go back to Step 3 and try recording again.

Step Recording

Even though you may be an accomplished musician, more than likely, you have one main instrument you're good at playing. If that instrument is the keyboard, that skill puts you ahead of some other musicians, because the keyboard is one of the easiest instruments to use to record a MIDI performance. You can use other MIDI instruments, such as MIDI woodwind instruments, MIDI drums, and MIDI guitars, but those instruments tend to be very expensive. And if you learn to play a wind instrument or the drums or a guitar, you probably have a real instrument of that kind, not a MIDI one. This puts you at a bit of a disadvantage when you're trying to record MIDI tracks. However, SONAR provides a feature called step recording that allows you to record a MIDI track one note at a time without your having to worry about the timing of your performance.

In other words, you select the type of note you want to enter (such as a quarter note or a sixteenth note), and then you press one or more keys on your MIDI keyboard. SONAR then records those notes into the track with the timing you selected. You can also enter the measure, beat, and tick at which you want the notes to occur. Here's how the step recording feature works:

1. Follow steps 1 through 8 in the "MIDI Track Recording and Playback" section, earlier in this chapter.

2. Select Transport > Step Record to open the Step Record dialog box (see Figure 6.15).

Figure 6.15
Using the Step Record dialog box, you can record MIDI data to a track without having to worry about the timing of your performance

3. In the Step Size section, enter the size of the note you want to record. For example, if you want to record a quarter note, select Quarter.

4. In the Duration section, you can set the length of the note independent of the step size. More often than not, though, you'll want the duration to be the same as the step size. To make things easier, you can set the Duration to Follow Step Size, so that both values will be the same and you won't have to bother selecting a duration.

5. To record the note, press a key on your MIDI instrument. For example, if you want to record a Middle C to the Track, press Middle C on your MIDI instrument. By the way, you can also press more than one key at a time if you want to record a chord. For example, if you want to record a C Major chord, press the C, E, and G keys on your MIDI instrument at the same time.

6. SONAR records the data to the track and (if the Auto Advance option is activated, which it is by default) moves the Now time forward by the step size amount (which is a quarter note in this example). If the Auto Advance option isn't activated, you have to click the Advance button to move the Now time manually. Also, if you want to record a rest instead of a note, you have to click the Advance button. This way, SONAR will move the Now time ahead by the step size amount without recording anything.

7. To change the Now time manually, just enter a new value into the field shown below the Auto Advance option. To move forward or backward by a step, click the arrows on the scroll bar shown next to the Now time. Also, if you want to delete the most recent step, click the Delete button.

TIP

If you need to record many repeating patterns, you might want to use the Pattern option in the Step Record dialog box. In the Pattern box, you can enter a pattern of beats that SONAR will follow automatically so that you don't have to click the Advance button at all, even for rests. For example, if you need to record a pattern with notes on the first two beats, a rest on the third beat, and another note on the fourth beat, you enter 12R4 in the Pattern box. Now, when you start to record the pattern, you simply press keys on your MIDI instrument for beats 1 and 2, SONAR advances past beat 3 because it is a rest, and then you press another key for beat 4. Then you keep repeating the same routine over and over again until you get to the point in your music where you no longer need to repeat the same rhythmic pattern. I know this process sounds a bit complicated, but if you play with it for a while, you'll get the hang of it.

8. When you're finished recording, click the Keep button to keep the data and have SONAR add it to the track. Alternatively, you can click the Close button to discard the data you just recorded.

9. Listen to your performance by setting the Now time back to its original position and selecting Transport > Play to start playback. (You can also press the spacebar on your computer keyboard or click the Play button in the Transport toolbar.) If you don't like the performance, you can erase it by selecting Edit > Undo Recording. Then go back to Step 2 and try recording again.

TIP

As an alternative to the step recording feature, you might want to try using the Staff view. With the Staff view, you can still enter your MIDI data one note at a time without worrying about performance timing. Plus, the Staff view allows you to enter and edit your data using standard music notation. I'll describe this feature in more detail in Chapter 13.

Importing

One other way you can get MIDI and audio data into a project is to import it rather than record it. SONAR allows you to import data from audio files, MIDI files, and other project files. Why would you want to import files? Well, you may have a great drum track in a project or a MIDI file that you would like to use in another project. You might also want to use sample loops for some of the material in your audio tracks (I'll talk about sample loops in Chapter 9). Importing material is actually very easy.

Importing from Project and MIDI Files

Importing data from a Project or a MIDI file into another project is just a matter of copying and pasting, as shown in the following steps. To get started, just do the following:

1. Open the project or MIDI file from which you want to copy data.

2. In the Track view, select the clip(s) that you want to copy. You can also select an entire track or a number of whole tracks to copy.

3. Select Edit > Copy to open the Copy dialog box (see Figure 6.16). Make sure the Events in Tracks option is activated and then click OK.

Figure 6.16
Using the Copy dialog box, you can copy data within a Project or from one Project into another Project

4. Open the project to which you want to paste the data.

5. In the Track view, select the track where you want to start pasting the data. If you copied more than one track, the first copied track will be pasted to the selected track and the other copied tracks will be pasted to consecutive tracks after the selected one.

6. Set the Now time to the point in the track you would like the data to be pasted.

7. Select Edit > Paste to open the Paste dialog box (see Figure 6.17). You don't have to change any of the parameters here (I'll go over them in more detail in Chapter 8). Click OK.

Figure 6.17
The Paste dialog box takes any previously copied data and places it where you specify

SONAR copies the data you selected from the first project or MIDI file and places a copy of the data into the second project within the tracks and at the Now time you specify. In addition to reusing your own material, you can share material with a friend this way.

Importing Audio Files

You learned about audio files in Chapter 3. SONAR allows you to import Wave, Apple AIFF, MPEG, Windows Media, and Next/Sun audio files. This is important because at some time you might record some audio using another program, and you might want to use that data within one of your SONAR projects. Doing so is really simple; just follow these steps:

1. Select the track to which you want to import the audio file.

2. Set the Now time to the point in the track that the file should be placed.

3. Select File > Import Audio to open the Import Audio dialog box.

4. Choose the audio file you want to import.

5. If you want to listen to the file before you import it, click the Play button.

6. If the audio file is a stereo audio file, you can have either the left and right channels merged into one track or split between two different tracks (starting with the one you selected). To have the file split, activate the Stereo Split option.

7. Click Open.

SONAR then imports the file and inserts it into the track(s) you selected at the Now time you specified.

NOTE

If the sampling rate of the audio file that you are importing is different from your project's sampling rate, SONAR will make a copy of the original file and convert the sampling rate of the copied audio file to match the sampling rate of the project.

Synchronization

One other aspect related to recording that you should know about is *synchronization*. This subject is fairly complicated and a bit beyond the scope of this book, but you might need to utilize synchronization in two somewhat popular situations. So, I'll cover a few of the basics and explain how to use synchronization in those two particular situations.

Basics

All music is based on time. Without time, there is no music. To record and play music data, SONAR needs a timing reference. It uses this reference to determine the exact measure, beat, and tick at which an event should be stored during recording or at which it should be played. When you work with SONAR alone, it uses one of two different clock sources as its reference: either the clock built into your computer (internal) or the clock built into your sound card (audio). By default, SONAR uses the internal clock as its timing reference. Because the internal clock cannot be used if you have audio data in your project, SONAR automatically changes the clock to audio when a track's source is set to an audio input or when an audio file is inserted into the project. So, the built-in clock on your sound card provides the timing for all the data that you record into a project, and it allows SONAR to keep all the tracks synchronized during playback. This is internal synchronization.

Sometimes, though, you might need to synchronize SONAR externally with another piece of equipment. For example, if you have a drum machine (a special type of MIDI instrument that plays only drum sounds) containing some special songs that you programmed into it, you might like to have the data in your current SONAR project play along with the data contained in the drum machine. You would have to synchronize SONAR to the drum machine. In this situation, the drum machine would be known as the *master* device, and SONAR would be the *slave* device. The master would send messages to the slave, telling it when to start and stop playback and telling it what tempo to use so that they can stay in sync with one another. To accomplish this, you need to use what is called MIDI Sync.

MIDI Sync

MIDI Sync is a special set of MIDI messages that allow you to synchronize MIDI devices to one another. These messages include Start (telling a slave device to start playback at the beginning of the song), Stop (telling a slave device to stop playback), Continue (telling a slave device to continue playback from the current location in the song—the Now time in SONAR), Song Position Pointer or SPP (telling a slave device to jump to a specific time position in the song—the Now time in SONAR), and Clock (a steady pulse of ticks sent to the slave device telling it the speed of the current tempo of the song).

To synchronize SONAR with an external MIDI device using MIDI Sync, follow these steps:

1. Configure your drum machine (or other MIDI device you want to use as the master) to transmit MIDI Sync messages. You'll have to refer to the user's guide for your device on how to do so.

2. In SONAR, open the project that you want to synchronize. Then select
    Options > Project to open the Project Options dialog box and click the
    Clock tab (see Figure 6.18).

Figure 6.18
Using the Project
Options dialog box,
you can configure
SONAR for
synchronization

3. In the Source section, click the MIDI Sync option and click OK.

4. Follow the steps outlined earlier for recording or playing MIDI tracks, but
    when you activate recording or playback, SONAR won't respond right
    away. Instead, it will display a message that says "Waiting for MIDI Sync."

5. After you see this message, start playback on your master device. It will
    then send a Start message to SONAR, and both the device and SONAR
    will play through the song in sync with one another. In the case of the
    drum machine, you will hear it play its sounds in time with the music
    being played by SONAR.

6. To stop playback, don't use the commands in SONAR; instead, stop
    playback from the master device. It will send SONAR a Stop message, and
    SONAR will stop at the same time automatically.

While working with SONAR via MIDI Sync, just remember to start, stop, and navigate
through the project using the master device instead of SONAR. Otherwise, all the other
steps for recording and playback are the same.

CHAPTER 6

NOTE

You cannot record or play audio tracks in SONAR while using MIDI Sync. If you
have some previously recorded MIDI data stored in a drum machine (or other
MIDI device) that you want to use in your SONAR project, first use MIDI Sync to
transfer that data into SONAR. Then use the drum machine (or other MIDI
device) as a playback device.

SMPTE/MIDI Time Code

You might need to use synchronization when you're composing music to video. Here,
though, the synchronization method is different because a VCR is not a MIDI device, so
MIDI Sync won't work. Instead, you have to use SMPTE/MIDI Time Code. You learned a
little about SMPTE in Chapter 5, so you know that it is a timing reference that counts
hours, minutes, seconds, and frames (as in video frames). But you didn't really learn how
it works.

NOTE

In addition to video, SMPTE/MIDI Time Code is often used to synchronize a
sequencer to an external multitrack tape recorder or DAT (digital audio tape)
deck. The procedure for doing so (explained below) is the same.

SMPTE is a complex audio signal that is recorded onto a tape track (in the case of video,
it's recorded onto one of the stereo audio tracks) using a time code generator. This signal
represents the absolute amount of time over the length of the tape in hours, minutes,
seconds, and frames. A sequencer (such as SONAR) reading the code can be synchronized
to any exact moment along the length of the entire tape recording. In this case, the VCR
would be the master, and SONAR would be the slave. When you play the tape in the VCR,
SONAR will play the current project in sync to the exact hour, minute, second, and frame.

Reading the time code from tape requires a SMPTE converter, which translates the SMPTE
code into MTC (MIDI Time Code). The MIDI Time Code is read by the MIDI Interface and
sent to the sequencer (SONAR). MIDI Time Code is the equivalent of SMPTE, except that
it exists as special MIDI messages rather than an audio signal. As SONAR receives MTC,
it calculates the exact measure, beat, and tick that corresponds to the exact time reading.
This means you can start playback anywhere along the tape, and SONAR will begin
playing or recording MIDI or audio data at precisely the right point in the current project
in perfect sync.

As an example, say you need to compose some music to video. This video could be your own or a video from a client. To synchronize SONAR to the video, you need to follow these steps:

1. If the video is your own, you need to add SMPTE time code to it using a SMPTE generator. This process is called *striping*. I won't go into the details of doing that here. You'll need to purchase a SMPTE generator and read the instructions in the included manual on how to stripe SMPTE to tape. If the video is from a client, he or she will probably stripe the tape before sending it to you.

TIP
You also need a SMPTE converter to read the time code from the tape. If you have a professional MIDI Interface attached to your computer, it may provide SMPTE generating and converting capabilities. Check the user's manual to be sure. You might be able to save yourself some money. I use a Music Quest 8Port/SE MIDI Interface from Opcode (they are no longer in business, but check **www.midiman.com** for other options), and it includes multiple MIDI ports as well as SMPTE capabilities.

2. In SONAR, open the project you want to synchronize. Then select Options > Project to open the Project Options dialog box and click the Clock tab.

3. In the SMPTE/MTC Format section, you need to select a frame rate for the time code. If you're composing music to your own video, just use the default selection, 30 Frame Non-Drop. If you're composing music for a client, he or she should let you know what frame rate you need to use.

NOTE
Different types of video material use different tape speeds for recording. The frame rate corresponds to how many frames per second are used to record the video to tape. For film, 24 frames per second is used. For video, several different rates are used depending on whether the video is recorded in color or black-and-white and so on. For more information about frame rates, you should consult the user's guide for your SMPTE generating/reading device.

4. You might also need to enter a SMPTE/MTC Offset in hours, minutes, seconds, and frames. Whether you need to enter an Offset depends on whether the video material starts at the very beginning of the time code stripe, which is a value of 00:00:00:00.

NOTE

When you stripe a tape with SMPTE, the time code usually starts with a value of 00 hours, 00 minutes, 00 seconds, and 00 frames. However, the actual video material on the tape may start a bit later, say at 00 hours, 01 minutes, 20 seconds, 00 frames. If that's the case (and your client should let you know this fact), you need to enter an Offset of 00:01:20:00 into SONAR so that SONAR will begin playing the project at that time rather than at the initial time code value.

5. After you finish entering the settings, click OK.

6. Now you can follow the steps outlined earlier for recording or playing MIDI tracks, but when you activate recording or playback, SONAR won't respond right away. Instead, it will display a message saying "Waiting for 30 Frame" (or whatever frame rate you selected).

7. After you see this message, start playback on your master device (in this case, start the tape playing in the VCR). It will then send SMPTE code to SONAR, and both the device and SONAR will play through the song in sync with one another. In the case of the VCR, you will see it play the video in time with the music that is being played by SONAR.

8. To stop playback, don't use the commands in SONAR; instead, stop playback from the master device.

TIP

If you would rather control playback from the master device (the VCR) entirely without having to first start it in SONAR, select Transport > Loop And Auto Shuttle to display the Loop/Auto Shuttle dialog box. Then activate the Loop Continuously option and click OK.

A little confused? Well, as I said, synchronization is a complicated subject. You'll find a little more information in the SONAR User's Guide and the Help files, but it isn't any easier to understand than the information I've provided here. Your best bet is to experiment as much as possible with synchronization and get a good beginner's book on audio recording. Knowing how to utilize synchronization is worthwhile if a situation that requires it ever arises.

7

Editing Basics

After you've finished recording all your tracks, it's time to do some editing. Actually, if you're like me, you might end up doing some editing during the recording process. This is especially true for MIDI tracks, because it's so easy to fix the pitch or timing of a note quickly if you happen to make a mistake or two. You'll do most of your editing after the fact, though, and SONAR provides a number of different tools to get the job done. I briefly described these features in Chapter 2, but, in this chapter, I'll go into more detail about the following:

▶ Dealing with tracks and clips in the Track view

▶ Editing MIDI note and controller messages in the Piano Roll view

▶ Creating and editing drum tracks in the Piano Roll view

▶ Editing audio data in the Track view

▶ Editing individual events in the Event List view

▶ Changing the tempo via the Tempo view

CAUTION

Before you do any kind of editing to your recently recorded material, I suggest you make a backup of your project file. This way, if you totally mess things up during the editing process, you'll still have your raw recorded tracks to fall back on. Take a look at Appendix B, "Backing Up Your Project Files," for more information.

Arranging with the Track View

The first part of the editing process has to do with arranging the material in your project. Of course, you can do any kind of editing at any time you like. You don't have to follow exactly what I say, but it's just logical to start with arranging. Basically, this step involves rearranging the tracks and clips in your project so that they provide a better representation of the song you're trying to create. For example, after listening to the project a few times, you might find that the guitar part in the second verse sounds better in the first verse, or you might want the vocal to come in a little earlier during the chorus. You can accomplish these (and many other) feats by manipulating your tracks and clips.

Dealing with Tracks

You already learned how to work with the Track view in terms of setting up track properties, navigating within SONAR, and recording new tracks. However, I haven't talked about actually manipulating the tracks themselves and the data within them. Manipulating includes selecting, sorting, inserting, and otherwise changing your original data.

Scrolling

As you already know, the Track view consists of two areas: The Track pane (on the left) shows the track properties and the Clips pane (on the right) shows the track data. The Clips pane contains scroll bars (see Figure 7.1). These scroll bars work the same as scroll bars in any standard Windows application. You either click the arrows to move the display, or you click and drag the scroll bars to move the display.

Figure 7.1
Using the scroll bars, you can access additional information that doesn't fit on the screen

Horizontal scroll bar

arrows   Vertical scroll bar

The horizontal scroll bar allows you to display all the data within all the tracks. As you scroll to the right, the measure numbers on the Time Ruler increase. Scrolling doesn't change the Now time, though (as you learned in Chapter 5). The vertical scroll bar affects both the track and clips pane areas. As you move the bar up or down, the different Tracks within the Project are displayed, starting from 1 (at the top of the list).

In addition to the Track view, scroll bars are available in all the other views. In the Piano Roll view, you can scroll horizontally to display the data in a track similar to the clips in the Track view. You also can scroll vertically to display different MIDI note ranges. The

Event List view is the oddball, because it only lets you scroll vertically to display all the events within a track as one long list. I'll describe the different views later in this chapter.

Zooming

The Track view (as well as other views, except the Event List view) also provides zooming functions. Using these functions, you can magnify the data in a track in case you want to do some really precise editing. If you take a look at the bottom-right corner of the Track view (see Figure 7.2), you'll notice two sets of buttons (one along the bottom and one along the side) that have little pictures of magnifying glasses on them.

Figure 7.2
The zoom features reside in the bottom-right corner of the view

Using the buttons along the bottom, you can magnify the track data horizontally. So, by clicking on the Zoom In button (the button with the magnifying glass with a + sign shown on it), the clips grow bigger in size horizontally and give you a more detailed look at the data they contain. Clicking on the Zoom Out button, of course, does the opposite. And the same buttons along the side of the Track view perform the same functions, except that they affect the display vertically. You'll also notice that as you zoom in vertically, the track parameters will be shown beneath each track in the Track pane. In addition, you'll notice a little control in between each set of zoom buttons. These controls show you the current level of magnification being used.

TIP
Click and hold the mouse on either zoom control, and up pops a zoom meter. You can use the meter to quickly set the zoom level by dragging your mouse (see Figure 7.3).

Figure 7.3
You can also change the zoom level via the zoom meters

In addition to the Zoom In and Zoom Out buttons on the right side of the view, you'll find another button with an empty magnifying glass shown on it. This button activates the Zoom tool. The Zoom tool can also be activated by clicking the Zoom tool button in the Track View toolbar (see Figure 7.4) or by pressing Z on your computer keyboard.

Figure 7.4
Activate the Zoom tool using either of the Zoom tool buttons

Zoom tool

You can use this tool to select a range of data and just zoom in on that selection. To use it, simply do the following:

1. Click one of the Zoom tool buttons.
2. Move your mouse pointer within the Clips pane, and it turns into a magnifying glass.
3. Click and drag anywhere within the area to select some data (see Figure 7.5).

Figure 7.5
You just click and drag to make a selection with the Zoom tool

4. Release the mouse button. SONAR then zooms in on the selection (both horizontally and vertically, depending on how you drag the mouse), and your mouse pointer returns to normal.

You have to click the Zoom tool button every time you want to use it.

Selecting

To manipulate your tracks in a project for editing, you have to be able to select them. In Chapter 6, I mentioned how to select a single track: You simply click the track number of the track you want to select. But sometimes you might want to have more than one track selected at one time. You also might need a quick way to select all the tracks in your project. Or after going through the trouble of selecting a number of tracks, you might want to deselect one or two while keeping the others selected. You accomplish these tasks as follows:

► To select more than one track, hold down the Ctrl key on your computer keyboard as you click the Track numbers.

► To select all tracks in a project, select Edit > Select > All or press Ctrl+A on your computer keyboard.

► To deselect all tracks in a project, select Edit > Select > None or press Ctrl+Shift+A on your computer keyboard.

► To deselect a track while keeping others selected, just hold down the Ctrl key on your computer keyboard as you click the track number.

By the way, all these procedures also work in the other views. The only difference is the items being selected. Just remember that to select a single item, you simply click it. To select more than one item, you hold down the Ctrl key on your computer keyboard as you click. To select all or none of the items, you choose Edit > Select. Some special selection features are also available, but I'll talk about them later in this chapter and in Chapter 8.

Sorting

You can change the order in which the tracks appear in a couple of different ways. Being able to sort the tracks can be useful if you want to keep related tracks together in the track list. For instance, you might want to keep all the percussion tracks or all the vocal tracks together. It's easier to work on your song when the tracks are grouped together in this way—at least, it is for me.

Click and Drag

The easiest way to move a track within a list is simply to drag it to a new location. Just move your mouse pointer over the little icon next to the name parameter of the track you want to move (see Figure 7.6) and then click and drag it up or down anywhere within the list. When you release your mouse button, the track moves to the new location and takes on a new track number.

Figure 7.6
Click and drag a track icon to move the track within the Track List

Track Sort

You also can use the Track Sort function to sort tracks in the list based on the track properties. You use this function as follows:

1. Select Track > Sort to open the Sort Tracks dialog box (see Figure 7.7).

Figure 7.7
Using the Sort Tracks dialog box, you can rearrange the tracks in the Track view

2. In the Sort By section, select the track property by which you want to sort the tracks.
3. In the Order section, select whether you want the tracks to be sorted in ascending or descending order.
4. Click OK.

SONAR then sorts the tracks according to the settings you specified. And remember, the track numbers for the tracks are changed as well, because the tracks have been moved to new locations within the list. Each track maintains its parameter settings and data, though.

Inserting

If you ever need to insert a new track in between two existing tracks within the list, you can do the following:

1. Right-click the track number of the track above which you want to insert a new track.
2. From the pop-up menu, select Insert Audio Track or Insert MIDI Track, depending on the type of track you need.

SONAR moves the current track down one location in the list and inserts a new track at the location you clicked on. For example, if you right-click Track 2 and select Insert MIDI Track, SONAR moves Track 2 (and all the tracks below it) down by one and inserts a new MIDI Track at number 2 in the list.

Cloning

If you ever need to make a copy of a track, you can do the following:

1. Select the track you want to copy.

2. Select Track > Clone to open the Clone dialog box (see Figure 7.8).

Figure 7.8
You can make a copy of a track by using the Clone dialog box

3. You can choose to copy the events within the track, the track properties, the effects (Fx) assigned to the track (I'll talk more about effects in Chapter 11), or all of the above. Simply activate the appropriate options. There is also an option for preserving linked clips (I'll talk more about linked clips later in this chapter).

4. You can also choose how many copies of the track you want to make by entering a number for the Repetitions parameter.

5. To designate the number of the first copied track, enter a number for the Starting Track parameter. Your first copied track will use this number and all other copies will be consecutively numbered after this one.

6. Click OK.

SONAR makes a copy (or copies) of the track you selected according to the parameter settings you specified. If you want to move the track(s) to a new location in the list, you can do so as explained earlier.

Erasing

Getting rid of tracks that you no longer need is very easy. Simply select the track, and select Track > Delete. But SONAR also provides another erasing function that's a little more flexible. Instead of erasing the track entirely, it allows you to delete all the data in the track while keeping the track properties intact. To do so, just select the Track, and then choose Track > Wipe. Nothing could be easier.

Hiding

If you open the View Options menu (which I'll explain later) and click the Track Manager selection (see Figure 7.9), you can access the Track Manager. Using the Track Manager, you can hide tracks in the Track view. To hide tracks, do the following:

Figure 7.9
Choose the Track Manager selection in the View Options menu to open the Track Manager

1. Choose the Track Manager selection in the View Options menu to open the Track Manager (see Figure 7.10). You will see a list of all the tracks in the Track view. You will also see some other items (aux bus, mains, etc.). Don't worry about those for now. I'll talk more about them in Chapter 12.

Figure 7.10
Use the Track Manager to hide tracks in the Track view

TIP

You can also open the Track Manager by pressing the M key on your computer keyboard while you are using the Track view.

2. To hide an individual track, click to remove the check mark next to that track in the list. Then click OK.

3. To hide a group of tracks (such as all the audio tracks or all the MIDI tracks), click the appropriate button—Toggle Audio, Toggle MIDI—to select the appropriate group. Then press the spacebar on your computer keyboard to remove the check marks. Finally, click OK.

Of course, you can also make tracks appear again by doing the opposite of the preceding procedures. These changes to the Track view are in appearance only. They don't affect what you hear during playback. For example, if you hide an audio track that outputs data during playback, you still hear that data even if you hide the track. Hiding tracks can come in handy when you want to work only on a certain group of tracks at a time and you don't want to be distracted or overwhelmed by the number of controls being displayed.

TIP

You can quickly hide a single track by right-clicking on its track number and choosing Hide Track from the pop-up menu. To make the track visible again, however, you need to use the Track Manager. You can also quickly hide all selected tracks by pressing Shift+H on your computer keyboard, and all tracks can be shown by pressing A on your computer keyboard.

The View Options Menu

In addition to all of the features I've already described, SONAR provides some predefined options for zooming and the appearance of tracks. These options are available from the View Options menu, which can be accessed by clicking the small downward arrow button located to the right of the Zoom tool button in the Track view toolbar (see Figure 7.11).

Figure 7.11
Use the View Options
menu for additional
zooming and track
appearance options

Each of the selections in the View Options menu has a different function. They work as
follows:

▶ **Show and Fit Selection**—Choosing this option will make it so that the data
in the selected tracks is made to fit within the current dimensions of the
Track view, and only the selected tracks are shown. All other tracks are
hidden. This also works if you simply select some data within a track or
track(s), which I'll explain in the Dealing with Clips section of this chapter.

▶ **Fit Tracks to Window**—Choosing this option will make it so that the
vertical zoom is set to make all the tracks fill the current dimensions of
the Track view vertically.

▶ **Fit Project to Window**—Choosing this option will make it so that both the
vertical and horizontal zoom functions are set to make all the tracks fill
the current dimensions of the Track view both vertically and horizontally.

▶ **Show Only Selected Tracks**—Choosing this option will keep all currently
selected tracks visible and will hide any unselected tracks.

▶ **Hide Selected Tracks**—The opposite of the Show Only Selected Tracks
option, choosing this option will hide all currently selected tracks and
keep all unselected tracks visible.

▶ **Show All Tracks**—Choosing this option will make all tracks in the project
visible.

▶ **Track Manager**—As I mentioned earlier, choosing this option will give
you access to the Track Manager dialog box.

▶ **Undo View Change**—Choosing this option will undo the last view change
you made to the Track view.

▶ **Redo View Change**—Choosing this option will redo the last view change
you undid using the Undo View Change option.

Dealing with Clips

Unless you insert, copy, or erase tracks in your project, you're not actually doing any kind of data manipulation. If you move a track in the track list or sort the tracks, that doesn't change the data within them. To make changes to the data within your project, you have to manipulate the clips within the tracks.

Clip Properties

For organizational purposes, SONAR allows you to change the way clips are displayed. To change the properties, you can right-click a clip and select Clip Properties from the pop-up menu to open the Clip Properties dialog box (see Figure 7.12). Here, you can assign a name to the clip (which doesn't have to be the same name as the track in which the clip resides) and the color of the clip.

Figure 7.12
To change the name or color of a clip, you use the Clip Properties dialog box

The name and the color of a clip don't affect the data within your project, but you can also change the start time of the clip in this dialog box. This is the position within the project at which the clip begins. If you enter a new start time for the clip, the clip is moved within the track to the new time and, during playback, SONAR will play the clip at the new time as well. This move does change the data within your project.

View Options

You can also change whether the names you assign to clips will be displayed and whether clips will be displayed with a graphical representation of the data they contain. In other words, if a clip contains audio data, it shows a drawing of what the sound wave for the audio data might look like. For MIDI data, the clip shows a mini piano roll display.

To change these options, just right-click anywhere within the Clips pane and select View Options from the pop-up menu to display the Track View Options dialog box (see Figure 7.13). Activate the appropriate options (Display Clip Names and Display Clip Contents) and click OK.

Figure 7.13
Using the Track View Options dialog box, you can show or hide clip names and contents

Using the Track View Options dialog box, you also can specify whether left-clicking or right-clicking will change the Now time (the Left Click Sets Now or Right Click Sets Now options), whether to display vertical rule lines for the Time Ruler (Display Vertical Rules option), and which views open automatically when you double-click a MIDI or audio clip. Another option allows you to choose whether or not to display the Audio Scale, which I'll talk about later in this chapter.

Selecting

You select clips the same way you select tracks. To select a single clip, click it. To select more than one clip, hold down the Ctrl key on your computer keyboard while clicking on the clips you want to select. You know the rest.

There is one additional selection method that doesn't apply to tracks, and that method is selecting only a portion of a clip. This procedure is known as working with partial clips. This capability is useful when you want to split a single clip into smaller ones or combine one clip with another to make a larger clip. I'll describe this topic in more detail later in this chapter.

To select only part of a clip, hold down the Alt key on your computer keyboard and drag your mouse pointer across the clip to select a part of it. You can also drag across several clips (or even over several tracks) to make a partial selection of multiple clips.

NOTE
When you're making selections or moving data, the start and end times of your selections or data are affected by the Snap to Grid. You learned how to use the Snap to Grid feature in Chapter 5.

Splitting and Combining

Using partial selections, you can combine and split clips into new, smaller or larger ones. Combining clips is very easy. Just select the clips you want to combine and choose Edit > Bounce to Clip(s). SONAR then creates one new clip from the old, selected ones.

Bounce To Track(s)

The Bounce to Clip(s) function, however, works only on clips that are on the same track. If you want to combine clips from different tracks, you have to use the Bounce to Track(s) function as follows:

NOTE
The Bounce to Track(s) function also has a limitation: It works only with audio tracks.

1. Select the clips you want to combine.
2. Choose Edit > Bounce to Track(s) to open the Bounce to Track(s) dialog box (see Figure 7.14).

Figure 7.14
Use the Bounce to Track(s) function to combine clips from multiple tracks

Bounce to Track(s) - [Selected 2:1:0 - 4:1:0]

Destination: <6> New Track

Format: Mix to Single Track Stereo Event(s)

Source Bus(es):
A (C-Media PCI)

☐ Each Source to Separate Submix

Mix Enables
☑ Track Mute/Solo
☑ Track Automation
☑ Clip Automation
☑ Aux Automation
☑ FX Automation
☑ Master Automation
☑ Track FX
☑ Aux Returns
☑ Master FX

OK   Cancel   Help

CHAPTER 7

3. Since you are combining clips from multiple tracks into one clip, the new clip has to reside on a single track. In the Destination drop-down list, choose the track on which you want your new combined clip to reside.

4. The Bounce to Track(s) function lets you determine the format of your new clip. In the Format drop-down list, choose the format you would like to use. Choose Mix to Single Track Stereo Event(s) to create a single stereo track from your combined clips. Choose Mix to Separate Left And Right Tracks to create two new tracks, each holding the left and right stereo channels of your new audio data respectively. Choose Mix Stereo Content to Mono to create a single mono track from your combined clips.

5. In the Source Bus(es) section, choose the buses that you would like SONAR to use when combining your clips.

6. In the Mix Enables section, activate the automation and effects options you would like to have included in the new clip from the clips being combined. You should usually keep all these options activated. I'll talk more about effects and automation in chapters 11 and 12.

7. Click OK.

SONAR combines all your clips into one new clip and puts it in the track you specified.

The Split Function

SONAR enables you to split clips using its Split function. It works like this:

1. Select the Clip(s) that you want to split.

2. Choose Edit > Split to open the Split Clips dialog box (see Figure 7.15).

Figure 7.15
Using the Split Clips dialog box, you can split clips into new, smaller clips in a variety of ways

3. Choose the Split option you want to use. The Split At Time option lets you split a clip at a certain measure, beat, or tick. The Split Repeatedly option lets you split a clip into a bunch of smaller clips instead of just two new smaller ones. Just enter at what measure you want the first split to occur and at how many measures you want each consecutive split to occur after that. For example, if you have a clip that begins at measure 2 and ends at measure 7, and you want to create three two-bar clips out of it, enter 2 for the starting measure and 2 for the split interval. The Split At Each Marker option lets you split clips according to the markers you set up in the Track view. You learned about markers in Chapter 5. Finally, the Split When Silent For At Least option lets you split clips at any place where silence occurs within them. You can set the interval of silence that SONAR has to look for by entering a number of measures.

4. If you are splitting MIDI clips, you have the option of having them split non-destructively, which means that any data (such as note durations) that extends beyond the split point isn't deleted, just the appearance of the clip(s) is changed. To do this, activate the Use Nondestructive Cropping When Splitting MIDI Clips option. More than likely you will usually want to have this option activated.

5. Click OK.

The Split Tool

In addition to the Split function, you can split clips graphically with your mouse using the Split tool. You access this tool via the Split tool button on the Track view toolbar (see Figure 7.16).

Figure 7.16
Access the Split tool using the Split tool button on the Track view toolbar

By using the Split tool, you can split long audio and MIDI clips into smaller ones by clicking and dragging with your mouse. To use the Split tool, simply do the following:

1. Click the Split tool button in the Track view toolbar.

2. Move your mouse pointer within the Clips pane, and it turns into a pointer with a pair of scissors attached to it.

3. Click and drag anywhere within the Clips pane to select some data (see Figure 7.17). You can make a selection over multiple clips and multiple tracks simultaneously if you'd like.

Figure 7.17

You just click and drag to make a selection with the Split tool

4. Release the mouse button. SONAR then splits all the selected clips according to the boundaries of the selection.

5. When you are done using the Split tool, be sure to activate the Select tool (press T on your computer keyboard) so you don't accidentally split some clips by mistake when you're just trying to make a selection.

Moving and Copying

You can also change the arrangement of your data by moving and copying clips to new locations, either within the same tracks or into other tracks. One way to move a clip is to use the Clip Properties dialog box and enter a new start time for the clip. You can also move a clip by simply clicking and dragging it to a new location with your mouse. As long as the track you're dragging the clip into doesn't contain any other existing clips, you have nothing to worry about. SONAR simply moves the clip to its new location.

If the track contains existing data, though, SONAR asks how you want the data to be handled by displaying the Drag and Drop Options dialog box (see Figure 7.18). You then have to choose one of three options: Blend Old and New, Replace Old with New, or Slide Over Old to Make Room.

NOTE

If you have the Ask This Every Time option in the Drag and Drop Options dialog box activated, then SONAR will always open the box whenever you drag data, even if there is no existing data in the track to which you're dragging. If you don't want this to happen, deactivate the Ask This Every Time option.

Figure 7.18
If you move a clip within a track that contains existing material, SONAR displays the Drag and Drop Options dialog box

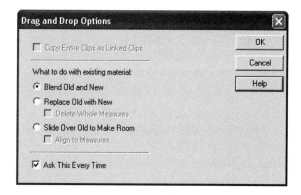

If you choose the Blend Old and New option, the clip you're moving simply overlaps any existing clips. This means that the clips remain separate, but they overlap so that, during playback, the data in the overlapping sections plays simultaneously. If you choose the Replace Old with New option, the overlapping portion of the clip you are moving replaces (which means erases and takes the place of) the portion of the clip being overlapped. If you choose the Slide Over Old to Make Room option, the start times of any existing clips are simply changed to make room for the new clip. So, during playback, the new clip plays at the time it was placed at, and the existing clips play a little later, depending on how much their start times had to be changed.

If you would rather copy a clip instead of just moving it, you can use SONAR's Copy, Cut, and Paste functions. Actually, using the Cut function is the same as moving a clip. If you use the Copy function, though, you can keep the original clip in its place and put a copy of it in the new location. This procedure works as follows:

1. Select the clip(s) you want to copy.
2. Select Edit > Copy to open the Copy dialog box (see Figure 7.19).

Figure 7.19
To copy clips, you use the Copy dialog box

3. Choose the type(s) of data you want to copy. Usually, you should choose the Events in Tracks option.

4. Click OK.

5. Click the track number of the track into which you want to copy the clip(s).

6. Set the Now time to the point within the track at which you want to place the clip(s).

7. Select Edit > Paste to open the Paste dialog box. Then click the Advanced button to open the advanced Paste dialog box (see Figure 7.20).

Figure 7.20
The advanced Paste dialog box provides many different options for copying data in SONAR

8. Choose the options you want to use. Most of these options are self-explanatory. Setting the Starting at Time option is the same as setting the Now time in Step 6. Setting the Starting At Track option is the same as setting the Track in Step 5. The Repetitions option simply lets you create more than one copy of the clip if you want. I've already talked about the What to do with existing material options. The only new ones are the Paste as New Clips and Paste into Existing Clips options. The Paste as New Clips option creates a new clip and then follows the overlapping rules that you choose with the What to do with existing material options. The Paste into Existing Clips option, however, merges the clip that you are copying with any existing clips that it overlaps. You end up with material from both clips merged into one.

9. Click OK.

If some of these options sound a little confusing, just experiment with them a bit. Make an extra backup of your project, and then use it to go wild with the copying and pasting functions. Try every possible combination, and soon you'll get the hang of using them.

TIP

You can also quickly copy a clip by holding down the CTRL key on your computer keyboard and clicking and dragging the clip to a new location. A copy of the clip is made and placed at the new location. In addition, when moving or copying clips to other tracks, you can constrain the start position of the clip(s) by holding down the Shift key while dragging the clip(s).

CHAPTER 7

Linked Clips

You may have noticed a few other options in the Paste dialog boxes—namely, the Linked Repetitions and Link to Original Clips options. These options deal with a special feature in SONAR called linked clips. Using this feature, you can link copies of a clip to each other so that any changes you make to one clip will affect the others that are linked to it. This way, you can easily create repeating patterns and then make changes to the patterns later.

For example, you might have a cool drum pattern in a clip that takes up one measure and you want to repeat that pattern through the first eight measures of your song. You can simply copy the clip and then paste it (setting the Repetitions to 7 and activating the Linked Repetitions and Link to Original Clips options). SONAR then copies your clip and pastes seven identical, linked copies of it. If you make any changes to one of the clips, these changes affect them all. For instance, you can change the snare drum from sounding on beat 2 to sounding on beat 3 in one of the Clips, and the change happens in all of them. Linked clips is a very fun, cool, and time-saving feature.

NOTE

There are a few things that will not affect sibling linked clips: clip envelopes, slip editing, splitting, and Groove clip enable/disable.

If you ever want to unlink linked clips, just follow these steps:

1. Select the Clips you want to unlink. You don't have to unlink all linked clips in a group. For example, if you have four linked clips, you can select two of them to unlink, and the two that you leave unselected remain linked.

2. Right-click one of the selected clips and select Unlink from the pop-up menu to open the Unlink Clips dialog box.

3. Choose an unlink option. The New Linked Group option unlinks the selected clips from the other clips but keeps them linked to each other. The Independent, Not Linked At All option totally unlinks the clips from any others.

4. Click OK.

Linked clips are shown with dotted outlines in the Clips pane of the Track view. When you unlink them, they appear as normal clips again.

Erasing

Deleting any clips that you no longer need is an easy process; just follow these steps:

1. Select the clips you want to delete.

2. Select Edit > Delete to open the Delete dialog box (see Figure 7.21).

Figure 7.21
In the Delete dialog box, you can determine the type of data you want to erase

3. Make sure the Events in Tracks option is activated.

4. If you want to have SONAR remove the space that's created when you delete the clip(s), activate the Delete Hole option. SONAR moves any other existing clips in the track backward (toward the beginning of the project) by the amount of time opened when you delete the clip(s). Just give it a try, and you'll see what I mean.

5. If you activate the Shift by Whole Measures option as well, the existing clips are only moved back to the nearest whole measure.

6. Click OK.

Inserting

Instead of manipulating existing data, you may sometimes need to introduce silent parts into your project. You can do so by using SONAR's Insert > Time/Measures feature. This feature allows you to insert blank space in the form of measures, ticks, seconds, or frames. You also can insert the space either into the whole project or into selected tracks. It works like this:

1. Select Edit > Select > None to clear any currently selected data in the project.

2. If you want to insert space into the whole project, skip to Step 3. Otherwise, select the track(s) into which you want to insert space.

3. Set the Now time to the point in the track(s) or project at which you want the space inserted.

4. Select Insert > Time/Measures to open the Insert Time/Measures dialog box (see Figure 7.22).

Figure 7.22
In the Insert Time/Measures dialog box, you can insert blank space into selected tracks or the entire project

5. The At Time parameter reflects the current Now time. Type a new time here, or make adjustments if you'd like.

6. For the insert parameter, type the number of units of blank space you want to have inserted.

7. Select the type of unit you want to have inserted. You can choose to insert measures, ticks, seconds, or frames.

8. In the Slide section, choose the types of data that will be affected by the insert process. The types of data you select will be moved to make room for the new blank space. Of course, you'll almost always want to have the Events in Tracks option activated. When you're inserting space into selected tracks, the Events in Tracks option is usually the only one you want to have activated. When you're inserting space into the entire project, on the other hand, you'll more than likely want to have all the options activated.

9. Click OK.

SONAR then inserts the number of measures, ticks, seconds, or frames you typed into the Insert parameter at the Now time you specified. It also moves the types of data you selected by sliding the data forward in time (toward the end of the project). So, for instance, if you inserted a measure of blank space into the entire project at measure 2, then all the data in all the tracks starting at measure 2 is shifted forward by one measure. Whatever data was in measure 2 is now in measure 3, and any data that was in measure 3 is in measure 4, and so on.

Slip Editing

Up until now, all of the editing functions I've described in this chapter work by making permanent changes to the MIDI and audio data in your clips and tracks. This is called *destructive processing*, because it "destroys" the original data by modifying (or overwriting) it according to any editing that you apply.

NOTE

As you know, you can remove any destructive processing done to your data by using SONAR's Undo function. You can also load a saved copy of your project containing the original data. But neither of these restoration methods is as convenient as using nondestructive processing.

In contrast to destructive processing, SONAR also includes some editing functions (called *slip editing* functions) that provide *nondestructive* processing. The slip editing functions are nondestructive because they don't apply any permanent changes to your data. Instead, they are applied only during playback, letting you hear the results while leaving your original data intact.

The slip editing functions can be used to crop the beginning or end of a clip, shift the contents of a clip, or shift-crop the beginning or end of a clip.

Cropping a Clip

To crop the beginning or end of a clip, do the following:

1. If you want to crop the beginning of a clip, position your mouse over the left end of the clip until the cursor turns into a square (see Figure 7.23).

Figure 7.23
Position your mouse over the left end of the clip to crop the beginning

2. Click and drag your mouse toward the right so that the clip changes length, as shown in Figure 7.24.

Figure 7.24
Click and drag to the right to shorten the Clip from the beginning

3. If you want to crop the end of a clip, follow steps 1 and 2, but adjust the right end of the clip rather than the left end, so that it looks like what is shown in Figure 7.25.

Figure 7.25
Click and drag the right end of the clip to crop the end

When you crop a clip, the data that is cropped is not deleted. Instead, the data is masked so that you will not hear it during playback. So, if you crop the first two beats in a one-measure clip, those first two beats will not sound during playback. And if you crop the last two beats in a one-measure clip, those last two beats will not sound during playback.

NOTE

When you crop a clip, the length of the clip is altered. The space where the cropped data used to be will be filled with silence during playback. So, you may need to make some adjustments to the position of your clips within your tracks.

TIP

If you ever want to apply your cropping changes to a clip permanently, choose Edit > Apply Trimming.

Shifting a Clip

Instead of cropping a clip (and thus changing its length) you can also shift the data inside a clip without changing the length of the clip. To shift a clip, do the following:

1. Press and hold the Alt+Shift keys on your computer keyboard.

2. Position your mouse over the middle of the clip until the cursor turns into a square (see Figure 7.26).

Figure 7.26
To shift a Clip, position your mouse in the middle of the Clip

3. Click and drag to the left to shift the data in the clip toward the beginning of the clip.

4. Click and drag to the right to shift the data in the clip toward the end of the clip.

When you shift a Clip, the data in the beginning or end of the clip is cropped, but the length of the clip is not altered, as shown in Figure 7.27.

Figure 7.27
Shifting a clip still crops the data but doesn't alter the length of the clip

Shift-Cropping a Clip

Shift-cropping is a combination of the aforementioned functions. When you shift-crop a clip, the data in the clip is shifted and the length of the clip is altered. To shift-crop a clip, do the following:

1. Press and hold the Alt+Shift keys on your computer keyboard.

2. Position your mouse over the left or right end of the clip (depending on whether you want to shift-crop the beginning or end of the clip) until the cursor turns into a square.

3. Click and drag to the left or right to alter the length of the clip and shift the data inside the clip at the same time.

The slip editing functions can be a very powerful alternative to cutting and pasting. Since the data from the clips isn't deleted, you can edit the clips at any time to specify what portions of their data will sound during playback. So, for example, if you have a clip that contains a vocal phrase and the first word in the phrase isn't quite right, you can crop it. But, later on, if you decide that the word actually sounded good, just uncrop it and, like magic, your data is restored.

TIP

SONAR provides some additional non-destructive editing functions called *envelopes*. I'll talk more about envelopes in Chapter 12.

Audio Editing

Although SONAR provides separate views for precise editing of MIDI data, it doesn't provide a dedicated view for editing audio data. Instead, the Track view doubles as an audio editor. To edit audio in the Track view, you simply use all of the functions described previously in this chapter to edit any audio clips in your tracks. There are some other, more sophisticated functions available for editing audio data that I'll describe in Chapter 8.

There are, however, a few things you should keep in mind while editing audio in the Track view.

Audio Waveforms

When examining audio clips, you'll notice that they display the audio waveforms corresponding to the audio data inside them.

NOTE

An *audio waveform* is a graphical representation of sound. Let me try to explain using the cup and string analogy. Remember when you were a kid, and you set up your own intercom system between your bedroom and your tree house using nothing but a couple of paper cups and a long piece of string? You poked a hole in the bottom of each cup and then tied one end of the string to one cup and the other end of the string to the other cup. Your friend would be in the tree house with one of the cups, and you would be in your bedroom with the other. As you talked into your cup, your friend could hear you by putting his cup to his ear, and vice versa. Why did it work?

Well, when you talked into the cup, the sound of your voice vibrated the bottom of the cup, making it act like a microphone. This movement, in turn, vibrated the string up and down, and the string carried the vibrations to the other cup. This movement made the bottom of that cup vibrate so that it acted like a speaker, thus letting your friend hear what you said. If it were possible for you to freeze the string while it was in motion and then zoom in on it so you could see the vibrations, it would look similar to the audio waveforms shown in Figure 7.28.

Continued

As you can see, a waveform shows up and down movements just like a vibrating string. A line, called the *zero axis,* runs horizontally through the center of the waveform. The zero axis represents the point in a waveform at which there are no vibrations or there is no sound, so the value of the audio data at the zero axis is the number zero (also known as *zero amplitude*). When a waveform moves above or below the zero axis, vibrations occur, and thus there is sound. The amplitude value of a waveform in these places depends on how high above or how low below the zero axis the waveform is at a certain point in time (shown on the Time Ruler).

Figure 7.28
An audio waveform is similar to a vibrating string if you could freeze and zoom in on it to observe the vibrations

Snap to Zero Crossing

Another thing to keep in mind is that you need to make sure to edit your audio data at zero crossings in the waveform to avoid noisy pops or clicks. You can do so by activating the Snap to Audio Zero Crossings feature, which you access via the Snap to Grid dialog box. Just open the Snap to Grid dialog box by clicking on the Snap To Grid Options button in the Track view toolbar (see Figure 7.29) or press Shift+N on your computer keyboard. Then put a check mark next to the Snap to Audio Zero Crossings option.

Figure 7.29
Use the Snap To Grid Options button to access the Snap to Grid dialog box

The Snap to Audio Zero Crossings feature (when activated) makes sure that, when you make a selection or perform an edit, your selections or edits fall on zero crossings in the audio waveform.

NOTE
Remember the description of the zero axis? Well, any point in an audio waveform that lands on the zero axis is called a *zero crossing.* It's called that because, as the waveform moves up and down, it crosses over the zero axis.

Why is it important that your selections and edits line up with zero crossings? Because a zero crossing is a point in the audio waveform at which no sound is being made, it provides a perfect spot at which to edit the waveform—for example, when you're cutting and pasting pieces of audio. If you edit an audio waveform at a point where it's either above or below the zero axis, you might introduce glitches, which can come in the form of audible pops and clicks. You get these glitches because you cut at a moment when sound is being produced. You also get them because, when you're pasting pieces of audio together, you cannot guarantee that the ends of each waveform will line up perfectly (except, of course, if they both are at zero crossings).

Audio Scaling

Lastly, SONAR provides some special zooming features when you are working with audio tracks. These are the *audio scaling* features, and they allow you to zoom in on the audio waveforms shown inside the clips within your audio tracks. Audio scaling allows you to measure the amplitude of your audio data and it comes in handy for doing very precise audio editing.

When working with audio tracks, you'll notice some numbers displayed along the left side of the Clips pane in the Track view (see Figure 7.30). This is the audio scale, and it displays a measurement of the amplitude of the audio data in your audio tracks.

Figure 7.30
Use the audio scale to measure the amplitude of your audio

The measurement can be shown in decibels, as a percentage, or as a zoom factor. To change the measurement display, right-click anywhere in the audio scale area and choose an option (see Figure 7.31).

Figure 7.31
Change the audio scale
measurement display
by right-clicking

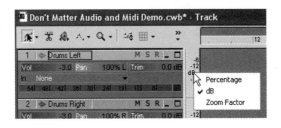

To change the audio scale factor for a single audio track, just left-click and hold your mouse on the audio scale of the track. Then drag your mouse up or down to change the audio scale factor. You'll notice that the audio waveform display for the track changes as you move your mouse. This allows you to zoom in and out of the audio waveform, but it doesn't affect the Track view zooming that I talked about earlier in the chapter.

You can also change the audio scaling factor for all audio tracks at once using the Zoom Out Vertical, Zoom In Vertical, and Vertical Zoom Control functions I talked about earlier in the chapter. To use them for audio scaling, just hold down the Ctrl key on your computer keyboard while you manipulate the functions with your mouse.

Using the Piano Roll View

By manipulating the tracks and clips in your project, you can change the overall structure, but to fix single-note mistakes and make smaller changes, you need to do some precision editing. You do so by selecting individual or multiple tracks or clips in the Track view and then using the view menu to open the data within one of the other available views. For editing MIDI data, that would be the Piano Roll view. (You also can edit MIDI data as standard music notation in the Staff view, which I'll talk about in Chapter 13.)

Using the Piano Roll view (see Figure 7.32), you can add, edit, and delete MIDI note and controller data within your MIDI tracks. Looking somewhat like a player piano roll, the Piano Roll view represents notes as colored shapes on a grid display with the pitches of the notes designated by an on-screen music keyboard.

Figure 7.32
The Piano Roll view
resembles that of the
old player piano rolls
used in the late 1800s
and early 1900s

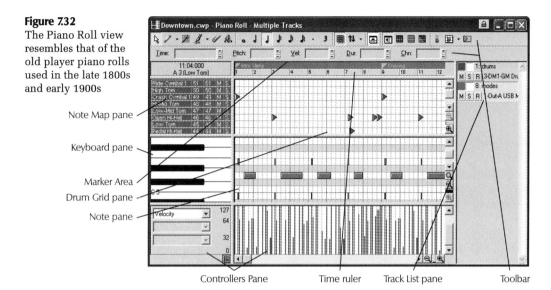

Note Map pane

Keyboard pane

Marker Area
Drum Grid pane

Note pane

Controllers Pane   Time ruler   Track List pane   Toolbar

CHAPTER 7

More precisely, the Piano Roll view consists of seven major sections: the toolbar (containing all the view's related controls), the Drum Grid pane (showing the drum notes in the currently displayed track), the Note Map pane (displaying the drum instruments represented by the note shown in the Drum Grid pane), the Note pane (showing the melodic notes in the currently displayed track), the Keyboard pane (displaying the pitch values of the notes shown in the Note pane), the Controllers pane (showing the MIDI controller data in the currently displayed track), and the Track List pane (showing a list of all the tracks currently being displayed—the Piano Roll view can display the data from more than one track at one time).

You'll also notice that the Piano Roll view has scroll bars and zoom tools just like the Track View. These tools work the same way as they do in the Track view. In addition, a Snap to Grid function is represented by the Grid button in the toolbar (see Figure 7.33). Other similarities are the marker area and the Time Ruler, which are located just above the Drum Grid pane. Basically, you can use the Piano Roll view to edit and view the data within the MIDI tracks of your project in more detail.

Figure 7.33
Use the Grid button
to access the Piano Roll
view's Snap to
Grid function

You can open the view in three different ways:

▶ In the Track view, select the track(s) you want to edit and then choose View > Piano Roll.

▶ In the Track view, right-click a track or clip and choose View > Piano Roll from the pop-up menu.

▶ In the Track view, double-click a MIDI clip in the clips pane.

Whichever method you choose, SONAR then opens the Piano Roll view and displays the data from the track(s) you selected.

Working with Multiple Tracks

If you select more than one track to be displayed at one time, the Piano Roll view shows the data from each track using a unique color. For example, the notes and controllers from one track may be shown as yellow, and the data from another track may be shown as blue.

NOTE
The one exception to the use of track colors is that tracks with numbers ending in the same digit (that is, 1, 11, 21, and so on) must all share the same color. There's no way around this. You can change the color used by each number group, however, by using the Colors dialog box, which you access by selecting Options > Colors. You learned how to customize SONAR's colors in Chapter 3.

Each track is also listed in the Track pane with a set of individual controls (see Figure 7.34).

Figure 7.34
The data from multiple
tracks is shown with
different colors, and
each track is listed in
the Track pane

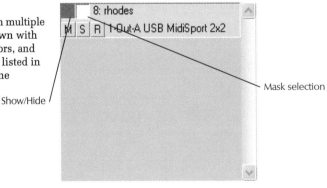

Show/Hide

Mask selection

CHAPTER 7

The Track Pane

When you open the Piano Roll view, the names and numbers of the tracks you selected are listed in the Track pane. For convenience, the associated Mute, Solo, and Record buttons for each track are also provided. Plus, you'll notice two other controls available for each track in the list:

▶ **Mask Selection**—The white button shown next to each track in the Track pane is the Mask Selection button. This button determines whether the notes for its associated track can be edited. When the button is white, the notes appear in color in the Drum Grid and Note panes, and they can be edited. When the button is gray, the notes appear gray in the Drum Grid and Note panes, and they cannot be edited. Clicking on the Mask Selection button toggles it on and off.

▶ **Show/Hide Track**—The button shown to the left of the Mask Selection button is the Show/Hide Track button. This button determines whether the notes for its associated track will be displayed in the Drum Grid and Note panes. When the button is in color (which is the same color as the notes for that Track), the notes are shown in the Drum Grid and Note panes. When the button is white, the notes are not shown in the Drum Grid and Note panes. Clicking on the Show/Hide Track button toggles it on and off.

The Track Tools

In addition to the Track pane controls, six other track-related controls are located in the toolbar (see Figure 7.35):

Figure 7.35
Use the Track controls via the Piano Roll toolbar to manipulate your displayed tracks

Pick Tracks   Show/Hide   All Tracks   Invert Tracks
Controller pane
Show/Hide   No Tracks
Track pane

▶ **Invert Tracks**—Clicking on this button toggles the Show/Hide Track buttons for each of the tracks in the Track pane. This means that if one track has its Show/Hide Track button on and another track has its button off, clicking on the Invert Tracks button turns off the first track's Show/Hide button and turns on the second track's Show/Hide button. It toggles the current state of each Show/Hide Track button.

▶ **No Tracks**—Clicking on this button turns off the Show/Hide Track buttons for each track in the Track List pane. No matter what state each Show/Hide Track button is in (either on or off), the No Track button turns them all off.

▶ **All Tracks**—This button is the exact opposite of the No Tracks button. Clicking on the All Tracks button turns on the Show/Hide Track buttons for each track in the Track List pane.

▶ **Show/Hide Track Pane**—Clicking on this button simply toggles between having the Track pane open or closed.

▶ **Show/Hide Controller Pane**—Clicking on this button simply toggles between having the Controller pane open or closed. I'll talk more about the Controller pane later in this chapter.

▶ **Pick Tracks**—While you have the Piano Roll view open, you might want to add or remove some of the tracks in the Track pane. Instead of having to close the Piano Roll view, select other tracks in the Track view, and then open the Piano Roll view again, you can use the Pick Tracks feature.

Clicking on the Pick Tracks button opens the Pick Tracks dialog box. This box displays a list of all the tracks in your project. You can select one or more tracks from the list. (Hold down the Ctrl key on your computer keyboard to select multiple tracks.) After you click the OK button, the tracks that you selected are listed in the Track pane.

TIP

If you have two or more tracks that contain the same exact notes, those notes overlap one another in the Drum Grid and Note panes. What determines which track's notes are on top is the order of the tracks in the Track pane. For example, if Track 4 is listed above Track 2 in the Track pane, the data from Track 4 overlaps the data from Track 2 in the Note pane. If you want to change this order (meaning you want the data from Track 2 to overlap the data from Track 4), you can click and drag the Track listing in the Track pane to a new position in the list.

Dealing with Notes

When you open a melodic MIDI track in the Piano Roll view, the notes in that track are displayed in the Note pane. Each note is represented by a colored rectangle. The horizontal location of a note designates its Start time when you line up the left side of the rectangle with the numbers in the Time Ruler, and the vertical location of a note designates its pitch when you line up the whole rectangle with the keys in the Keyboard pane. The length of the rectangle designates the duration of the note (for instance, quarter note, eighth note, and so on).

You can add new notes to a track or edit the existing ones using the tools represented by the first six buttons in the toolbar, from left to right on the left side of the Piano Roll view (see Figure 7.36).

Figure 7.36
Add and edit notes using the tools represented by the first six toolbar buttons

Select \ Draw line \ Erase

Draw   Pattern Brush   Scrub

Selecting

Using the Select tool, you can select notes for further manipulation, such as deleting, copying, moving, and so on. Essentially, you select notes the same way you select clips in the Track view. To select a single note, click it. To select more than one note, hold down the Ctrl key on your computer keyboard while clicking on the notes you want to select or click and drag your mouse over the notes you'd like to select. You know the rest.

One additional selection method involves the Keyboard pane. To select all the notes of a certain pitch, you can click one of the keys in the Keyboard pane. You can also drag your mouse pointer across several keys to select the notes of a number of different pitches.

Editing

After you've made a selection, you can copy, cut, paste, move, and delete the notes the same way you do with clips in the Track view. You can also edit notes individually by using the Draw tool. Using this tool, you can add (which I'll describe shortly) and edit the notes in the Note pane.

To change the Start time of a note, simply drag the left edge of its rectangle left or right. This action moves it to a different horizontal location along the Time Ruler.

To change the pitch of a note, simply drag the middle of its rectangle up or down. This action moves it to a different vertical location along the Keyboard pane.

To change the duration of a note, simply drag the right edge of its rectangle left or right. This action changes the length of the rectangle and thus the duration of the note.

Of course, sometimes you might want to make more precise changes to a note. There are two ways to do this. The first way is to use the Select tool to select the note and then use the Time, Pitch, Vel (Velocity), Dur (Duration), and Chn (MIDI Channel) parameters in the toolbar to change those characteristics of the note.

You can also use the Note Properties dialog box. Just right-click a note to open the Note Properties dialog box (see Figure 7.37).

Figure 7.37
In the Note Properties dialog box, you can make precise changes to a note in the Piano Roll view

Note Properties

Time:	5:03:000
Pitch:	D 5
Velocity:	111
Duration:	2:464
Channel:	6
Fret:	0
String:	0

OK
Cancel
Help

CHAPTER 7

In the Note Properties dialog box, you can make precise changes to the Start time, pitch, velocity, duration, and MIDI channel of an individual note by typing numerical values. If you're wondering about the fret and string parameters, I'll describe them in Chapter 13.

Drawing (or Adding)

In addition to editing, the Draw tool allows you to add notes to a track by literally drawing them in. To do so, just follow these steps:

1.   Select the Draw tool by clicking on its toolbar button.

2.   Select a duration for the new note(s). If you look a little further over in the toolbar, you'll notice a number of buttons with note values shown on them (see Figure 7.38). Clicking on these buttons determines the duration for your new note(s). For example, if you click the Quarter Note button, the duration is set to a quarter note. You'll also see two additional buttons: one representing a dotted note and another representing a triplet note. So, if you want your notes to be dotted or triplets, click one of those buttons as well.

Figure 7.38
Use the duration toolbar buttons to choose a duration for you new note

3.   Click anywhere within the Note pane at the point at which you want to place the new note(s). Remember, the horizontal position of the note determines its Start time, and the vertical position of the note determines its pitch.

TIP

When drawing notes, first click on an existing note to apply the same note properties (velocity, duration, and channel) to new notes you want to create.

Erasing

Even though you can select and delete notes (as I described earlier), the Piano Roll view includes an Erase tool for added convenience. To use it, just select the Erase tool and then click any note(s) in the Note pane that you want to delete. You can also click and drag the Erase tool over a number of notes to erase them all at once.

TIP

You can also use the Draw tool to erase notes if you activate the Auto-Erase feature. Just click the downward arrow located to the right of the Draw tool button in the toolbar and choose the Auto-Erase option from the menu. Now when you click an existing note, it will be erased. But if you click anywhere there isn't an existing note, a new note will be "drawn." In addition, Auto-Erase can be temporarily enabled/disabled by holding down the Alt key on your computer keyboard.

Scrubbing

When you're editing the data in a track, the procedure usually involves making your edits and then playing back the project to hear how the changes sound. However, playing back very small sections can be a bit difficult, especially when you're working with a fast tempo. To remedy this situation, SONAR provides a Scrub tool.

Using the Scrub tool, you can drag your mouse pointer over the data in the Piano Roll view and hear what it sounds like. To use it, simply select the Scrub tool by clicking on its button in the toolbar. Then click and drag your mouse pointer over the data in the Drum Grid and/or Note panes. Dragging left to right plays the data forward (what would normally happen during playback), and dragging right to left enables you to hear the data played in reverse. This capability can be useful for testing very short (one or two measure) sections.

TIP

Instead of using the Scrub tool, you might want to try a more useful technique for hearing what your changes sound like. Did you know that you can edit the data in your project as it's being played back? Of course, it's a bit difficult to edit anything while SONAR is scrolling the display as the project plays. I like to work on a small section of a project at a time. I set up a section of the project to loop over and over, and as SONAR is playing the data, I make any changes I think might be needed. Because the data is being played back while I edit, I can instantly hear what the changes sound like. This procedure is much easier than having to keep going back and forth, making changes and manually starting and stopping playback. You learned about looping in Chapter 6. By the way, you can use any of the views to edit your data while SONAR is playing a project. This tip is not just for the Piano Roll view.

NOTE

I'm sure you noticed that I didn't talk about the Draw Line tool or the Pattern Brush tool. I'll be covering those later on in this chapter.

Dealing with Drum Tracks

Because drum tracks are a bit different from regular MIDI tracks, SONAR provides some special features for dealing with drum tracks. What do I mean by different? Well, notes in a drum track usually represent a number of different percussion instruments grouped all in the same track. Each note pitch in a drum track represents a different instrument. It used to be that if you wanted to work easily with each specific instrument, you would have to split a drum track into many different tracks—one track for each note pitch. This would allow you to mute and solo different instruments, as well as do other things that couldn't be done when all the drum notes where grouped together on the same track.

With SONAR's new drum specific features, you no longer have to go through the trouble of creating separate tracks for each drum instrument, and you also have the flexibility of specifying different MIDI channels and MIDI ports for each instrument (among other things) using *drum maps*.

Drum Maps

A drum map allows you to define your drum instruments for SONAR, thus "telling" SONAR how each note pitch in a drum track should be handled. Each note pitch defined in a drum map can have its own instrument name, MIDI channel, MIDI port, velocity offset, and velocity scale. I know this sounds a little confusing, but hang in there with me for a moment.

Assigning Drum Maps

The easiest way to explain drum maps is to show you how to assign a drum map to a MIDI track and explain the results. So, let's use an example to help clarify things a bit:

1. Choose File > Open, and select the demo project file included with SONAR named Downtown.cwp. Then click Open to load the project.

2. Close the Auto-Send Sysx, File Info, Big Time, and Staff view windows. You won't need them.

3. Select track 1 (drums) by clicking on its number, and then choose View > Piano Roll to open the track in the Piano Roll view. This is what a drum track looks like without a drum map assigned to it. You can see the notes in the track, but you don't know what percussion instruments they represent. And you can't easily work with each individual instrument because there is no way to mute or solo a specific group of note pitches. In addition, all the notes in the track have to share the same MIDI port and channel as specified by the parameters in track 1. To get beyond these limitations, we need to assign a drum map to track 1.

4. Close the Piano Roll view, and in the Track view expand track 1 (drums) so that you have access to its Out parameter. Then click the Out parameter to display the Out menu (see Figure 7.39).

Figure 7.39
Use a track's Out parameter to assign a drum map to the track

5. Highlight the New Drum Map option, and then choose GM Drums (Complete Kit) from the extended menu. This assigns the GM Drums (Complete Kit) drum map to track 1. SONAR ships with a number of predefined drum maps, as you can see from the list (plus hundreds more on the SONAR 2 CD).

6. Select track 1 by clicking on its number, and then choose View > Piano Roll to open the track in the Piano Roll view again. Also, choose Edit > Select > None to get rid of the selection.

This time the track data looks a bit different, right? Instead of the Note pane, the Drum Grid pane is shown, and instead of rectangles there are triangles representing the notes, even though these are the same notes as they were before.

More importantly is what is shown in the Note Map pane. Each row in the Note Map pane represents a different percussion instrument. By lining up the notes in the Drum Grid pane with the rows in the Note Map pane, you can see what instrument the notes represent. And even though all these note pitches (instruments) reside on the same MIDI track, each instrument can be muted or soloed individually using the M and S buttons next to each instrument name in the Note Map pane. This makes working with drum tracks so much easier.

Creating Drum Maps

Of course, there may be times when the predefined drum maps included with SONAR might not provide what you need. In that case, you'll need to create a drum map of your own. To do that, you need to use the Drum Map Manager (see Figure 7.40), which can be accessed by choosing Options > Drum Map Manager.

Figure 7.40
Use the Drum Map
Manager to create
and manage your
drum maps

The Drum Map Manager is divided into three sections. The first section (Drum Maps Used in Current Project) lists all the drum maps being used in the current project. It also allows you to delete existing drum maps or create new ones. The second section (Map Settings) shows all the parameter settings for the selected drum map. It also allows you to define each instrument in the drum map by specifying note pitches, instrument names, MIDI channels, MIDI out ports, velocity offsets, and velocity scales. And the third section lists all the MIDI output port and channel pairs that are used by the selected drum map. It also allows you to specify a MIDI bank and patch for each port/channel combination.

To create a drum map of your own, follow these steps:

1. With a project already open in SONAR, choose Options > Drum Map Manager to open the Drum Map Manager window.

2. Click the New button in the first section (Drum Maps Used in Current Project) of the window to create a blank drum map. Don't worry about naming or saving it yet. We'll do that later.

3. Click the New button in the second section (Map Settings) of the window to create a new instrument mapping complete with default parameter settings, as shown in Figure 7.41.

Figure 7.41
New instrument
mappings initially
contain default
parameter settings

4. Double-click the In Note parameter for the new instrument mapping and enter a number (from 0 to 127) to specify the source pitch for this instrument. I'll explain what I mean by source pitch in a moment.

NOTE

Note pitches in MIDI are represented by a range of numbers (0 to 127). These numbers represent the note pitches C0 (pitch/octave) to C8, with the number 60 (C4) being middle C. Unfortunately, you have to enter numbers for note values in the Drum Map Manager. There is no way to directly enter the pitch/octave of a note. However, after you enter a number, the pitch/octave of the note is displayed.

5. Double-click the Out Note parameter for the new instrument mapping and enter a number (from 0 to 127) to specify the destination pitch for this instrument.

NOTE

A drum map is sort of like a MIDI data processor. After you assign a drum map to a MIDI track, SONAR passes all the data in that MIDI track through the drum map for processing during playback. As SONAR reads each note from the MIDI track, it compares the pitch of the note to all of the source pitches (In Note parameters) in the drum map. If it finds a match, it converts the incoming note to the destination pitch (Out Note parameter) of the matching source pitch. For example, if you set up an instrument mapping in your drum map with an In Note pitch of C4 and an Out Note pitch of D5, any incoming notes that have a pitch of C4 would be converted to a pitch of D5.

Why is this useful? Well, more often than not the In Note and Out Note parameters for an instrument mapping will be the same. But there may be times when you have a MIDI drum track that was recorded using a MIDI percussion synth other than what you have in your studio. This means that the drum sounds in your MIDI percussion device will be different and are probably triggered with different pitches. Using a drum map, you can map the pitches from the MIDI track to the different pitches used by your MIDI percussion device. This saves you the work of having to rewrite all the note pitches in the MIDI track.

6. Double-click the Name parameter for the new instrument mapping and enter a name for the instrument. For example, if you are creating your own General MIDI drum map and you had entered 56 for both the In Note and Out Note parameters, that would mean you were creating an instrument mapping for a cowbell sound because the number 56 represents a cowbell in General MIDI. So, for the name you would enter something like Cowbell.

7. Double-click the Chn (channel) parameter and enter a MIDI channel for the instrument. This should be the same MIDI channel that is being used by your MIDI percussion synth to play this particular instrument sound.

8. Double-click the Out Port parameter and choose a MIDI output port for the instrument. This should be the same MIDI output port that is being used by your MIDI percussion synth to play this particular instrument sound.

9. If you find that this instrument sound in your MIDI track is too loud or soft, you can add an offset to the MIDI velocity of the notes for that instrument sound. Just double-click the Vel+ parameter and enter a number from −127 to +127. This number is then either subtracted or added to the MIDI velocity value of each incoming note for this instrument sound.

10. You can also adjust the loudness of an instrument sound using the V Scale parameter. Instead of having to designate a set value to be added to or subtracted from the MIDI velocity values of the incoming notes, you can apply a velocity scale. Just double-click the V Scale parameter, and enter a value from 10% to 200%. A value of 100% means there is no change. A value below 100% means the velocity values will be decreased. A value above 100% means the velocity values will be increased.

11. Repeat steps 3 through 10 to create as many instrument mappings in the drum map as you need. If you ever make a mistake, you can use the Undo button to remove your last change. And to delete an instrument mapping, just click the Delete button.

12. In the third section (Ports and Channels) of the window, you can set the bank and patch parameters for each MIDI port/channel combination used in the drum map. Basically, this is where you designate the drum set sounds that should be used by each MIDI percussion synth connected to your computer system. Your MIDI percussion synths should allow you to choose from a number of different drum sets.

13. To save your drum map, type a name in the Presets parameter, and click the Save button (located just to the right of the Presets parameter showing the picture of a computer disk).

When you go to assign a drum map to a MIDI track, you'll see your new drum map listed there along with all the others.

Composing Drum Tracks

Once you've assigned a drum map to a MIDI track, you can start composing the percussion parts for your project. By opening the track in the Piano Roll view, you can use the Note Map pane and Drum Grid pane to add, edit, and delete drum notes. Most of the procedures that I described earlier in the Dealing with Notes section of this chapter (for selecting, editing, drawing (adding), and erasing notes) can be applied here. But there are a few differences of which you need to be aware. Instead of just describing these differences, I'd like to show you by walking you through the procedure that I use to compose my own drum patterns. Here is how it goes:

1. Choose File > New and select the Normal template to create a new project. Assuming you haven't changed the Normal template, you'll be presented with four blank tracks. Select the first three tracks and choose Track > Delete, leaving you with one MIDI track as your new drum track.

2. Assign a drum map to the MIDI track. For this example, let's use the GM Drums (Complete Kit) drum map. You'll need to use a synth that has a General MIDI compatible mode. Most modern synths have this capability.

3. If you need to set a bank and patch for your synth, choose Options > Drum Map Manager. In the third section (Ports and Channels) of the window, set a bank and patch for single port/channel listing there. Close the Drum Map Manager.

TIP

You can also use a DXi synth to play the sounds for your drum track. I'll talk more about DXi's in chapter 10, but for now, follow these directions to set one up:

1. Choose Insert > DXi Synth > EDIROL VSC.

2. In the Insert DXi Synth Options dialog box, deactivate the MIDI Source Track option. Then click OK.

3. The VSC DXi window will open. Close it.

4. Choose Options > Drum Map Manager to open the Drum Map Manager.

5. While holding down the Ctrl and Shift keys on your computer keyboard, double-click one of the Out Port parameters in the Map Settings list and choose EDIROL VSC 1 from the menu.

6. Close the Drum Map Manager.

Now the EDIROL VSC DXi will play any notes you add to your MIDI drum track. If you need to change the sound card output for the DXi, expand track 2 in the Track view and change its Out parameter.

4. I like to create my drum tracks by composing small sections at a time, and I also like to hear my music as I'm composing it. SONAR allows me to do this using it playback looping features. Let's say I want to create a one-measure drum pattern starting at the very beginning of the project and going to the beginning of measure 2. To set up a playback loop for this example, just choose Transport > Loop and Auto Shuttle. Set the Loop Start parameter to 1:01:000 and the Loop End parameter to 2:01:000. Then activate the Stop At The End Time and Loop Continuously options. Then click OK.

5. To continue with our drum composing exercise, choose View > Piano Roll to open the MIDI drum track in the Piano Roll view. You'll be presented with the Note Map pane filled with all the instruments available in the drum map you assigned to track 1, and a blank Drum Grid pane. Scroll the window vertically downward until you can see the last instrument (Acoustic Bass Drum) in the Note Map pane. You might also want to increase the horizontal zoom of the window a bit so that the first measure of the track fills the window.

6. The best way to start composing a drum pattern is to lay down a solid beat foundation—that means creating a kick drum part. You'll see in the list that we've got two kick drum sounds available to us: Bass Drum 1 and Acoustic Bass Drum. To audition an instrument, just click its name in the list. Personally, I like the Acoustic Bass Drum, so let's use that for this exercise. For the kick drum part of the pattern, let's lay down a basic four quarter note beat. To do that, activate the Draw tool, and choose the quarter note duration using the Quarter Note button in the toolbar. Then place a note at each of the four beats in the first measure of the track as shown in Figure 7.42.

Figure 7.42
Start a drum pattern
with a solid kick drum
beat foundation

TIP

If have a hard time placing the notes exactly on the beats, activate the Snap To Grid function by clicking the Snap To Grid button (see Figure 7.43). Then right-click the Snap To Grid button to set the function to a musical time interval that you want to use (in this case a quarter note).

Figure 7.43
Use Snap To Grid to
help you place the
notes in your drum
pattern

You can also have SONAR display a visual grid over the Drum Grid pane to help you in placing notes by clicking on the Show/Hide Grid button (see Figure 7.44) or pressing I on your computer keyboard. I also like to click the downward arrow button to the right of the Show/Hide Grid button and choose the Follow Snap Settings option. This makes the visual grid use the same resolution settings as the Snap To Grid function. So if you change the Snap To Grid resolution, the visual changes along with it.

Figure 7.44
Use the Show/Hide
Grid button to display
a visual grid to help
with note placement
as well

7. Choose Transport > Play (or press the Spacebar on your computer keyboard) to start playback and listen to the drum pattern so far. It sounds good, but now we need to add an accompanying instrument to emphasize the beat, like a snare drum part. We've got two snare drum instruments available in the list: Electric Snare and Acoustic Snare. I think I'm going to go with the Acoustic Snare sound for this example, so play a quarter note at beats 2 and 4 in the pattern for the Acoustic Snare instrument, as shown in Figure 7.45. You should now hear both the kick and snare instruments playing.

Figure 7.45
Add some acoustic snare to the drum pattern

TIP

Remember that if you make any mistakes, you can use the same editing techniques I talked about earlier in the chapter to fix things. If you need to delete a note, you can use the Erase tool or the Auto-Erase feature of the Draw tool. If you place a note on the wrong beat, just use the Select tool to click and drag the note right or left along the grid. Or if you place a note in the wrong instrument row, just use the Select tool to click and drag the note up or down to the correct instrument row.

Also, if the Drag and Drop Options dialog box keeps popping up and you don't want it to, just deactivate the Ask This Every Time option in the box.

8. Now let's spice up the pattern a bit with a closed hi-hat rhythm. Instead of quarter notes, however, let's use sixteenth notes. Change the Snap To Grid to a sixteenth note resolution, then place notes at every sixteenth note line on the grid using the Closed Hi-Hat instrument as shown in Figure 7.46.

Figure 7.46
Add a rhythmic closed
hit-hat part to the
drum pattern

9. The closed hit-hat part is missing something. Usually a part like this will emphasize each beat in a pattern by playing each sixteenth note that falls on a beat a little louder than the rest. To make this happen, we need to adjust the velocity of these four notes using the Show Velocity Tails feature. To activate the feature, click the Show Velocity Tails button (see Figure 7.47) or press Y on your computer keyboard.

Figure 7.47
Use the Show Velocity
Tails feature to adjust
note velocities

10. You'll notice some vertical lines attached to each of the notes in the pattern. These lines represent the MIDI velocity for each note. To adjust the velocity of a note, using the Draw tool, hover your mouse over the lines of a note until your mouse turns into a pointer with some vertical lines attached to it. Then click and drag your mouse up to increase the note's velocity or down to decrease the note's velocity. For our example, increase the velocity of the four closed hit-hat notes that reside right on each beat of the pattern to 127 (see Figure 7.48).

TIP

You can also adjust the velocity of multiple notes simultaneously by first selecting the notes and then holding down the Shift key on your computer keyboard while you adjust the velocity of one of the selected notes.

Figure 7.48
Increase the velocity of the four closed hit-hat notes that sit right on each beat

NOTE

Instead of using the Show Velocity Tails feature to change the velocity of each note graphically, you can make changes more precisely by selecting notes with the Select tool and then entering a new value in the Vel parameter of the toolbar.

11.   Our new drum pattern sounds pretty good, no? I know it's basic, but I mainly want to show you how to use all the tools at your disposal. To go on to create more patterns, just repeat steps 4 through 10. In step 4, just change the loop points to cover the next measure in the track, or several measures if you want to create longer drum patterns.

TIP

If you ever want to audition the entire drum track, you'll need to disable looping playback and then enable it again to continue working on your current drum pattern. A quick way to do this is to set up a key binding for the Loop On/Off function.

Also, remember that, as you're listening to your drum patterns, you can mute and solo individual instruments by using the M and S buttons next to each instrument in the Note Map pane. And for quick access to the drum map parameter settings for an individual instrument, just double-click the instrument.

The Pattern Brush

If you're not inclined to composing your own drum parts, then you'll really enjoy SONAR's Pattern Brush tool. Also found in the Piano Roll view (see Figure 7.49), the Pattern Brush tool allows you to create drum parts by "painting" in whole drum patterns that have already been composed for you.

Figure 7.49
Access the Pattern Brush tool in the Piano Roll view

Composing with the Pattern Brush

To compose drum parts using the Pattern Brush tool, follow these steps:

1. Set up a MIDI drum track as I explained in the Composing Drum Tracks section of this chapter.

2. Click the downward arrow to the right of the Pattern Brush button in the Piano Roll view toolbar. The first four options in the menu allow you to adjust how the Pattern Brush will work. The Velocity option allows you to specify an exact MIDI velocity to which all your notes will be set. The Note Duration option makes it so that all your notes use the duration specified in the Piano Roll view toolbar. Personally, I don't use those settings very much since you can achieve the same thing using the Draw tool, as I described earlier in the chapter. The Use Pattern Velocities and Use Pattern Polyphony options tell SONAR to use the MIDI velocities and rhythms from the predefined patterns, which can be chosen from the remaining menu selections. So basically, you'll almost always want to have the Use Pattern Velocities and Use Pattern Polyphony options activated. Activate them now for this example.

3. The lower part of the Pattern Brush menu allows you to choose predefined drum patterns that you can use to compose your drum tracks. In this example, for our first pattern, let's choose Kick+Snare Patterns (D-F) > Funky 1.

4. Choose the Pattern Brush tool by clicking on the Pattern Brush button in the toolbar. Then click and drag your mouse from left to right over the first measure in your drum track. It doesn't matter at what vertical location you drag. The drum notes are automatically placed with the correct instruments at the correct rhythmic locations (see Figure 7.50). Is that cool, or what?

Figure 7.50
Just click and drag the
Pattern Brush to
automatically create a
drum part

5. Let's add another instrument to our drum part by choosing a different
    Pattern Brush pattern. This time try the Dumbec, Egg Shaker, Finger Bongos,
    and Guiro Patterns > Egg Shaker 1 pattern. Click and drag the Pattern Brush.
    You'll notice that this adds a Maracas instrument to the drum part.

6. Let's add one more final touch. Choose Conga Patterns > Congas 1 for the
    Pattern Brush pattern, and "paint" the instrument into the drum part (see
    Figure 7.51).

Figure 7.51
Add a conga
instrument to the
drum part

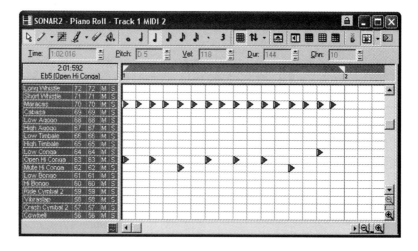

7. The drum part sounds pretty good, but it could use a few adjustments. The Open Hi Conga and Mute Hi Conga instruments are a bit low in volume. Double-click each instrument and set their Vel+ parameters to 36 and 45, respectively. You see, this is where the Vel+ and V Scale settings can come in handy.

8. The Mute Hi Conga instrument still can't really be heard because it sounds at the same time as the snare drum. To fix this, activate the Select tool and then drag both notes for that instrument to the left by one sixteenth note (see Figure 7.52). Just because you are using predefined patterns doesn't mean you can't make changes to them. Many times you'll find that you come up with something even better.

Figure 7.52
Fix the Mute Hi Conga with some small adjustments

You can keep going to add more instruments to the drum part or add more drum parts (measures) to the drum track. The process is really intuitive. Don't be afraid to experiment. If something doesn't sound good, just change it. Choose Edit > Undo and try a different pattern. Or make small adjustments like I showed you earlier. I guarantee you'll have a lot of fun with the Pattern Brush while creating your own drum tracks.

Creating Pattern Brush Patterns

After you've created some of your own drum patterns, you may want to save them for future use in other projects. You can do this by converting them into patterns that can be used with the Pattern Brush. Follow these steps to do so:

1. After you've finished creating a drum pattern as I've described in the previous sections, close the Piano Roll view and switch to the Track view.

2. You'll notice a clip in the Clips pane of the Track view that represents the drum pattern you just created (see Figure 7.53). Click the clip to select it and then choose Edit > Copy. Make sure the Events in Tracks option is activated in the Copy dialog box, and then click OK.

Figure 7.53
A clip in the Track view represents your newly created drum pattern

3. Choose File > New. Then select the Pattern Brush Template and click OK. Also, close the File Info window. In the Track view of this new project, you'll see a single MIDI track with a bunch of markers placed in it. Each marker is there to represent a different pattern. You can put as many patterns in a Pattern Brush file as you'd like, but the last marker in the file always has to be an END marker.

4. Set the Now time to the beginning of the project.

5. Choose Edit > Paste, leave the Paste dialog box settings as they are, and click OK. Your drum pattern is pasted in the place of the first pattern in the project.

6. You can add more patterns if you like, but for now just delete the rest of the pattern markers, and move the END marker to the beginning of measure 2 (2:01:000) as shown in Figure 7.54. You can also change the name of the first pattern marker to something that describes the pattern. This name will later be displayed in the Pattern Brush menu.

Figure 7.54
Paste your drum patterns in a new file with markers

7. Choose File > Save As. Set the Save As Type parameter to MIDI Format 0. Type in a name for the file. Also be sure to save the file in the same folder location as is specified in the Patterns parameter of the Global Options > Folders dialog box. Initially, SONAR has this location set to the C:\Program Files\Cakewalk\SONAR 2\Pattern Brush Patterns folder. Click Save.

After you restart SONAR, your new Pattern Brush patterns will be displayed in the Pattern Brush menu for you to use in future projects.

Dealing with Controllers

When you open a MIDI track in the Piano Roll view, in addition to the notes in the Drum Grid and Note panes, SONAR displays the MIDI controller data for that track in the Controllers pane (see Figure 7.55). Because there are many different types of MIDI controller messages, to help you avoid confusion, the Piano Roll view displays only one type at a time.

TIP

If you need to see multiple controllers simultaneously (in the same track), use track envelopes in the Track view. I'll talk more about envelopes in chapter 12.

You can tell the type of MIDI controller that's being displayed by looking at the Control Type drop-down lists located to the left of the Controllers pane. The first list shows the type of controller being displayed. The second list shows the number of the controller being displayed. And the third list shows the MIDI channel being used for that controller. You can change the values for any of these lists by simply clicking on them and selecting a new value from the list that pops-up. Initially, MIDI Note Velocity is shown when you open the Piano Roll view.

Figure 7.55
MIDI Controller data for a track is displayed in the Controller pane when you open the Piano Roll view

Each controller is represented by a colored line that runs from the bottom of the Controller pane toward the top. The height of the line designates the value of the controller according to the ruler on the left side of the Controller pane. This ruler gives you a reference to go by for determining the value of a controller; it usually runs from 0 to 127, starting at the bottom of the Controller pane and going all the way to the top. The values can be different according to the type of controller being edited. The horizontal location of a controller designates its Start time according to the Time Ruler at the top of the Piano Roll view.

NOTE

In one instance, the controllers in the Controller pane and the ruler values appear differently. If you select the pitch wheel event type for editing, you'll notice that, instead of originating at the bottom of the Controller pane, the controllers start at the center and extend either up or down (see Figure 7.56). They do so because values for the pitch wheel range from –8192 to 0 to +8191, which you can see in the ruler values. Other than that, pitch wheel events are handled exactly the same as any other types.

Figure 7.56
The pitch wheel is the one exception to how controllers are displayed in the Controller pane

Editing

You edit controllers exactly the same way as you do notes in terms of selecting, copying, cutting, deleting, pasting, and so on. Unfortunately, no precision editing is available such as is available with the Note Properties dialog box, although you can edit the numerical values of controllers via the Event List view (which you'll learn about later in the chapter). One other exception is that you can't move controllers by simply dragging them like you can with notes. You have to cut and paste them instead.

Erasing and Scrubbing

The Eraser and Scrub tools work with controllers exactly the same as they do with notes.

Drawing

You add controllers pretty much in the same way you add notes, but with a couple of exceptions. When you're using the Draw tool, in addition to clicking in the pane to add a single controller, you can also click and drag within the pane to add a whole series of controllers at once.

In addition, you can use another tool, called the Draw Line tool (its button is located right next to the Draw tool button in the toolbar), to create a smooth series of controllers starting at one value and smoothly increasing or decreasing to another value. Without this tool, it's a bit difficult to achieve the same effect by drawing freely with the Draw tool.

TIP

When using the Draw tool, you can hold down the Shift key on your computer keyboard to make the Draw tool behave like the Draw Line tool.

To use the Draw Line tool, you just click anywhere within the Controller pane at the controller value you want to begin with and then drag either to the left or right within the pane to draw a line that ends at a different time and a different value. When you release the mouse button, SONAR adds a smooth series of controller values from the first point to the second point in the pane.

Inserting

SONAR provides one other way to add a smooth series of controller values to your tracks: the Insert Series of Controllers function. I find using the Draw Line tool in the Piano Roll view much more intuitive, but if you need to add controllers over a very long span of time, the Insert Series of Controllers function can be useful. You use it as follows:

1. Select the track to which you want to add the controller values. You can do so either in the Piano Roll view or the Track view.

2. Select Insert > Series of Controllers to open the Insert Series of Controllers dialog box (see Figure 7.57).

Figure 7.57
Using the Insert Series
of Controllers dialog
box, you can add a
series of controllers
that change smoothly
from one value to
another

3. In the Insert section, choose the type of controller you want to add, the number of the controller (if appropriate), and the MIDI channel you want the controller to use.

4. In the Value Range section, type numbers for the Begin and End parameters. These numbers determine the values of the controller over the range of the series. For example, if you're using a volume controller type, you can have an instrument get louder over time by typing in a small value for Begin and a larger value for End. If you want the instrument to get softer over time, you type a larger value for Begin and a smaller value for End.

5. In the Time Range section, type the measure, beat, and tick values for the location in the project where you want the series of controllers to be inserted.

TIP

You can also set the Time Range parameters before you open the Insert Series of Controllers dialog box by dragging your mouse pointer over the Time Ruler in either the Piano Roll view or the Track view. This action sets up a selection within the project that is automatically used to set the From and Thru values of the Time Range parameters.

Bank/Patch Change

The one type of data that the Piano Roll view doesn't allow you to manipulate is the bank/patch change. This type of event is useful when you want the sound of your MIDI instrument to change automatically during playback of your Project. SONAR provides an Insert Bank/Patch Change function that you can use in case you need it.

Utilizing the Insert Bank/Patch Change function is very simple. You just do the following:

1. Click the name of the track in the Track pane into which you want to insert the bank/patch change.

2. Set the Now time to the measure, beat, and tick at which you want the bank/patch change to occur.

3. Select Insert > Bank/Patch Change to open the Bank/Patch Change dialog box.

4. Choose a Bank Select Method, Bank, and Patch from the appropriate drop-down lists.

5. Click OK.

SONAR then inserts a bank/patch change event in the track at the Now time you specified. By the way, you can insert (and also edit) bank/patch change events by using the Event List view; I'll describe that task later in this chapter.

Using the Event List View

For the most precise data editing (meaning individual events and their properties), you have to use the Event List view (see Figure 7.58). Using this view, you can add, edit, and delete any kind of event in any track within the entire project. The Event List view doesn't resemble any of the other views; instead of providing a graphical representation of your data, it provides a numerical representation, which you can edit and view. The Event List view displays events as one long list of columns and rows (similar to that of a spreadsheet). Each row holds the data for a single event, and the event's different properties are separated by columns.

Figure 7.58
You can use the Event
List view to edit Events
numerically using a
spreadsheet-like format

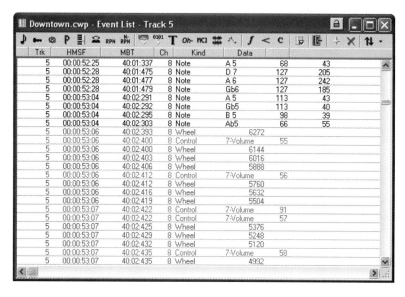

You can use the first column in the list to select events (which I'll describe later). The second column (titled Trk) shows the track number in which an event is stored. The third column (titled HMSF) shows the start time of an event as hours, minutes, seconds, and frames. The fourth column (titled MBT) also shows the start time of an event, but as measures, beats, and ticks. If an event is a MIDI event, the fifth column (titled Ch) shows the MIDI channel to which that event is assigned. The sixth column (titled Kind) shows the type of data an event holds (for example, a MIDI note event). The seventh column (titled Data) actually spans across the seventh, eighth, and ninth columns (the last three), and these columns hold the data values associated with each event. For instance, for a MIDI note event, the seventh column would hold the pitch, the eighth column would hold the velocity, and the ninth column would hold the duration for the note.

Because the Event List view doesn't have any graphical data to contend with, it doesn't provide any Snap to Grid, Zoom, Time Ruler, or Marker features. It does allow you to scroll the list up and down and left and right so that you can access all the events shown. It also provides a toolbar full of buttons (which I'll describe later). One button that you'll recognize, though, is the Pick Tracks button. Just as with the other views, the Event List view allows you to display the data from multiple tracks at once.

Opening the View

You open the Event List view via the Track view. You simply select one or more tracks and then either select View > Event List or right-click one of the selected tracks and choose View > Event List from the pop-up menu. You can also press Alt+4 on your computer keyboard. That's all there is to it.

Filtering Events

Many different types of events are available in SONAR, and sometimes having to wade through them all in the Event List view can get a bit confusing, especially when you're displaying the data from multiple tracks. To help you deal with the problem, the Event List view allows you to filter out each of the event types from being displayed. This filtering does not affect the data at all; it just helps to unclutter the list display if that's what you need.

The first eighteen buttons in the toolbar represent different event types. Initially, all these buttons are set so that all event types are shown in the list when you open the Event List view. By clicking on a button, you can filter out its associated event type from the list. You can click as many of the buttons as you like to filter out multiple types of events. Clicking on a button again turns off its associated event type filter so that the events can be shown in the list again. To see the type of event each button is associated with, just hover your mouse pointer over a button until the pop-up text appears showing the name of the event type.

The Event Manager

If you find it easier to deal with the event types by name rather than by using the buttons, you can use the Event Manager. Just click the Event Manager button on the toolbar (the one with the check mark shown on it) to open the Event Manager dialog box (see Figure 7.59).

Figure 7.59
You can use the Event Manager dialog box to filter Event types by name

Initially, all the event types are activated so that they will be displayed in the list. To filter out a certain type, just click it to remove its check mark. You can also use the All/None buttons to quickly activate or deactivate groups of event types. Click the Close button when you're done.

TIP

You can also filter out event types by simply right-clicking anywhere within the Event List and then selecting an event type from the pop-up list.

Editing Events

If you've ever used a spreadsheet application, you'll be right at home with editing events in the Event List view. To navigate through the list, you use the arrow keys on your computer keyboard. These keys move a small, rectangular cursor through the list. This cursor represents the Now time. As you move the cursor up and down through the list, the Now time changes to reflect the time of the event upon which the cursor is positioned. You can also move the cursor (which I'll call the Now time cursor from now on) left and right to access the different event parameters.

Changing

To change an event parameter, just position the Now time cursor over the parameter, type a new value, and then press the Enter key on your computer keyboard to accept the new value.

TIP

You can also change an event parameter by double-clicking on it and then clicking on the little plus or minus buttons that appear to increase or decrease the value, respectively.

You can change the start time in the HMSF or MBT columns, the MIDI channel, the type of event, and most or all of the values in the data columns, depending on the type of event you're editing. The only thing you can't change is the track number of an event.

Changing the type of an event via the parameter in the Kind column is a bit different from changing the values of the other parameters. Instead of typing a new value, you must either press the Enter key on your computer keyboard or double-click the parameter. This action opens the Kind of Event dialog box (see Figure 7.60). The Kind of Event dialog box displays a list of all the event types available. Select the type of event you want to use and then click OK.

Figure 7.60
You use the Kind of
Event dialog box to
change the type of
an event

Kind of Event

MIDI
- ⊙ Note
- ○ Key Aftertouch
- ○ Controller
- ○ Patch Change
- ○ Channel Aftertouch
- ○ Pitch Wheel
- ○ RPN
- ○ NRPN

Special
- ○ Sysx Bank
- ○ Sysx Data
- ○ Text
- ○ Lyric
- ○ MCI Command
- ○ Audio
- ○ Shape

Notation
- ○ Expression
- ○ Hairpin
- ○ Chord

OK
Cancel
Help

Selecting

If you ever need to copy, cut, or paste events in the Event List view, you have to select them first. To select a single event, just click in the first column of the row representing the event. You can also select more than one event by dragging your mouse pointer within the first column of the list. If you want to remove a selection, click or drag a second time.

Inserting

You can also add new events to the list by using the Insert function. It works as follows:

1. Position the Now time cursor at the point in the list at which you want to insert a new event.

TIP
Setting the position of the Now time cursor in the Event List view isn't very intuitive. Because the list gives you such a specific close-up look at your data, it's sometimes hard to tell where in your project the Now time cursor is pointing. You might find it easier using one of the other views (such as the Track view or the Piano Roll view) to position the Now time cursor. That way, you get a graphical representation of your project and a better feel for the placement of the cursor. Then you can simply switch to the Event view, and the cursor will be positioned exactly at (or at least very close to) the point where you want to insert the new event.

2. Either press the Insert key on your computer keyboard or click the Insert Event button in the toolbar (the one with the bright yellow star shown on it). SONAR creates a new event in the list using the same parameter values as the event upon which the Now time was positioned.

3. Edit the event parameters.

TIP

When you're changing the type of event using the Kind parameter, the values in the Data columns change according to the type of event you choose. For a list of all the types of events available, along with all their associated parameters, look in the SONAR help file under Editing MIDI Events And Controllers > The Event List View > Event List Buttons And Overview.

Special Events

Two types of Events in SONAR can be accessed only via the Event List view. You can't manipulate them in any of the other views. The first one, called a text event, allows you to add notes to the data in your project. I'm not talking about musical notes, I'm talking about text notes—you know, like those little sticky notes you have plastered all over your studio. Text events can act as little reminders to yourself in case you need to keep track of some kind of special information in certain parts of your project. I've never had a lot of use for text events, but it's nice to know they're available if I need them.

The other type of special event is called the MCIcmd event, or the Windows Media Control Interface (MCI) command event. You can use the MCIcmd event to control the multimedia-related hardware and software in your computer system. For example, by setting the type of an event to MCIcmd and setting the event's Data parameter to PLAY CDAUDIO, you can make the audio CD inside your CD-ROM drive start to play. You can also use MCIcmd events to play audio files, video files, and more. But the problem is that none of these files can be synchronized to the music in your project, so you can't really use these events for too many things. In addition, the subject of MCI commands can be complex and are well beyond the scope of this chapter. If you want to find more information, take a look at the following area on the Microsoft Web site: **http://msdn.microsoft.com;** do a search for the term MCI.

Deleting

Erasing events from the list is as easy as it gets. Just move the Now time cursor to the row of the event you want to remove and then click the Delete Event button in the toolbar (the one with the big red X shown on it). You can also press the Delete key on your computer keyboard.

If you want to delete more than one event at once, select the events you want to remove and then select Edit > Delete to open the Delete dialog box. The parameters in this dialog box work the same way as described in the Track view section of this chapter.

Playing

If you want to quickly preview the event you're currently editing, you can have SONAR play back that single event by holding down the Shift key on your computer keyboard and then pressing the spacebar. If you continue holding the Shift key, each press of the spacebar scrolls down through the list and plays each event. This capability is especially useful for testing MIDI note events.

TIP

You can print a hard copy reference of the Event List if you have a printer connected to your computer system. While the Event List view is open, just select File > Print to print a copy of the list. You can also preview the list before printing it by choosing File > Print Preview.

Using the Tempo View

You learned how to set the initial tempo for a project by using the Tempo toolbar in Chapter 4. But, in addition to the initial project tempo, you can also have the tempo change automatically during playback. To allow you to specify tempo changes within a project, SONAR provides the Tempo view (see Figure 7.61). The Tempo view has some similarities to the Piano Roll view in that it displays a graphical representation of the data you need to manipulate—in this case, tempo. The Tempo view shows the tempo as a line graph with the horizontal axis denoting time (via the Time Ruler) and the vertical axis denoting tempo value.

Figure 7.61
The Tempo View displays the tempo in a project as a line graph

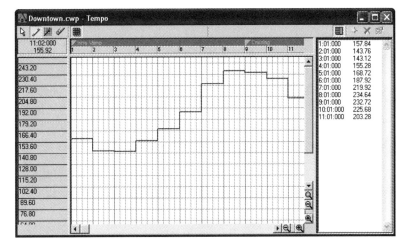

More precisely, the Tempo view consists of three major sections: the toolbar (located at the top of the view, containing all the view's related controls), the Tempo pane (located in the main part of the view, displaying all the tempo changes in the project as a line graph), and the Tempo List pane (located at the right of the view, showing a list of all the tempo changes within the project). Because tempo affects the whole project, no track selection tools are available here.

Because the Tempo view shows tempo changes graphically, it has scroll bars and zoom tools just like in the Piano Roll view. And, of course, these tools work the same here. In addition, this view provides a Snap to Grid function, which is represented by the Grid button in the toolbar. The Tempo view also contains a marker area and a Time Ruler located just above the Tempo pane. Along the left of the Tempo pane are the tempo measurements, which are used to show the value of the tempo changes displayed in the line graph.

Opening the View

To open the Tempo view, simply select View > Tempo or press Alt+9 on your computer keyboard. You don't need to select a track or clip or anything else. For a new project (or a project that doesn't contain any tempo changes), the Tempo view displays a straight horizontal line located vertically on the graph at the tempo measurement value that corresponds to the current tempo setting for the Project. So, for instance, if your project has a main tempo of 100, then the line is shown at a tempo measurement of 100 on the graph. In addition to the horizontal line, a single entry in the Tempo Change pane shows the measure, beat, and tick at which the tempo event occurs, along with the tempo value itself. In this example, it is 1:01:000 for the measure, beat, and tick, and 100 for the tempo value.

Editing

Just as you can edit controller messages graphically in the Piano Roll view, you can use the Tempo view to edit tempo changes. Also, just as in the Piano Roll View, the Tempo view provides Select, Draw, Draw Line, and Erase tools. All these tools work the same way they do in the Piano Roll View. You can use the Select tool to select individual and groups of tempo changes by clicking and dragging. Using the Draw tool, you can literally draw in tempo changes on the line graph in the Tempo pane. The Draw Line tool enables you to create smooth tempo changes from one value to another by clicking and dragging. And using the Erase tool, you can erase single and multiple tempo changes by clicking and dragging. As you draw and erase within the Tempo pane, the line graph changes its shape accordingly to display how the tempo will change over time as the project plays. An increase in the tempo (*accelerando*, in musical terms) is shown as an incline in the line graph, and a decrease in tempo (*diminuendo*, in musical terms) is shown as a decline in the line graph.

The Tempo Change Pane

As I mentioned earlier, tempo changes are also listed numerically in the Tempo List pane. Luckily, you can edit them here, too. I find it easier and more accurate to add and edit tempo changes via the Tempo Change pane rather than drawing them in.

Inserting

To add a new tempo change to the list, do the following:

1. Set the Now time to the measure, beat, and tick at which you want the tempo change to occur.

2. Click the Insert Tempo button in the toolbar (the one with the bright yellow star shown on it) to open the Tempo dialog box (see Figure 7.62).

Figure 7.62
In the Tempo dialog box, you can add and edit tempo events

3. Enter a value for the tempo parameter. You can also tap out a tempo by clicking on the Click Here To Tap Tempo button. When you click repeatedly on the button, SONAR measures the time between each click and calculates the tempo at which you're clicking. It then enters the value into the tempo parameter automatically.

TIP

Instead of using your mouse to click the Click Here To Tap Tempo button, you might find it easier (and more accurate) to use the spacebar on your computer keyboard. Click the button with your mouse once just to highlight it and then use your spacebar to tap out a tempo value.

4. Make sure the Insert A New Tempo option is activated.

5. You shouldn't have to enter a value for the Starting at Time parameter because you set the Now time earlier. However, you can change it here if you'd like.

6. Click OK.

SONAR adds the new tempo change and displays it in the Tempo Change pane as well as on the graph in the Tempo pane.

Deleting and Editing

You can also edit or remove a tempo change from the list by using the appropriate toolbar buttons. First, select the tempo change you want to edit or delete by clicking on it in the list. If you want to delete the tempo change, click the Delete Tempo button in the toolbar (the one with the big red X shown on it). If you want to edit the tempo change, click the Tempo Properties button in the toolbar (the very last button at the right end of the toolbar). This action opens the Tempo dialog box. Make any changes necessary, as per the same settings I described for inserting a new tempo change.

Using the Tempo Commands

In addition to the Tempo view (and the Tempo toolbar), SONAR provides two other tempo-related functions. The Insert Tempo Change function works the same as adding a new tempo change in the Tempo Change pane in the Tempo view. However, this function can be used from within any of the other views. To access it, just select Insert > Tempo Change to open the Tempo dialog box (which you learned about earlier).

SONAR also provides a function that allows you to insert a series of tempos so that you can have the tempo change smoothly from one value to another over time. Using it is similar to using the Draw Line tool in the Tempo view, but here you specify your values numerically. You use this function as follows:

1. Select Insert > Series of Tempos to open the Insert Series of Tempos dialog box (see Figure 7.63).

Figure 7.63
You can change the tempo smoothly from one value to another by using the Insert Series of Tempos dialog box

2. In the Tempo Range section, enter a beginning and an ending value for the range of tempos to be inserted.

3. In the Time Range section, enter a beginning and an ending value for the range of time in your project in which you want the tempo changes to occur.

TIP

If you make a selection by dragging your mouse pointer in the Time Ruler of the Track view, for instance, before you select Insert > Series of Tempos, the Time Range values in the Insert Series of Tempos dialog box are set according to your selection. This shortcut makes it easier to see where in your Project the tempo changes will be inserted.

4. For the Step parameter, enter a beat and tick value for how often you want a tempo change to be inserted within the Time Range you specified. For example, if you enter a value of 1.00, then the Insert Series of Tempos function will insert a new tempo change at every beat within the Time Range you specified.

5. Click OK.

SONAR then inserts a smooth series of tempo changes starting and ending with the Tempo Range values you specified within the time range you specified. Any existing tempo changes are overwritten.

8

Exploring the Editing Tools

In Chapter 7, you learned about some of the essential editing features found in SONAR, including all the views (and the tools they provide), as well as how to manipulate your data via copy, cut, paste, move, delete, and so on. Although these features provide a lot of power, you might be asking yourself, "Is that all there is?" Not likely! In addition to its fundamental tools, SONAR provides a full arsenal of sophisticated editing features. Some can be used to process audio data, some to process MIDI data, and some to process both kinds of data. One aspect they all have in common, however, is that they can be accessed within more than one view (similar to the copy, cut, and paste functions). Of course, as you learned previously, for MIDI data, you'll be using the Track, Piano Roll, Staff, and Event views, and for audio data, you'll be using the Track view.

This chapter covers the following:

▶ Advanced data selection
▶ Changing the loudness of audio clips
▶ Equalization
▶ Quantization
▶ Transposition
▶ Various advanced timing features

Advanced Data Selection

As you learned in the preceding chapter, you can select the data in your project within each of the views by using some basic clicking and dragging techniques. SONAR also provides some more sophisticated data selection features that enable you to use time as well as individual event properties for more precise editing.

By Time

If you ever need to select a range of data within a project that is based on time rather than data that is neatly tucked away into individual clips, you can select Edit > Select > By Time to do so. For example, say you need to copy the data in Track 8 that falls between the range of 4:2:010 (measure, beat, tick) and 13:3:050. But what if that data is stored in multiple clips within that range, and the clips don't neatly start and end at the beginning and ending times that you specified? That's the kind of situation for which this feature is useful. It works like this:

1.   Choose Edit > Select > By Time to open the Select by Time dialog box (see Figure 8.1).

Figure 8.1
You can use the Select by Time dialog box to define a time range within your project in which data will be selected for editing

2.   Type the beginning (From) and ending (Thru) measure, beat, and tick values to define the range of time you want to select. Then click OK. You use this dialog box to select a range of time within your project, but it doesn't select any actual data. For that, you need to select the track(s) you want to edit.

3.   In the Track view, select the track(s) containing the data you want to edit.

SONAR selects the data within the clips within the tracks within the time range you specified so that you can edit it by using copy, cut, and the other features that you'll learn about in this chapter.

TIP
You can also make time selections within any of the views by simply clicking and dragging on the Time Ruler or by ALT dragging within a clip (you learned about this approach in Chapter 7); however, by choosing Edit > Select > By Time, you can make more precise selections because you can enter the exact numerical values for the measures, beats, and ticks that define the range.

By Filter

For really precise editing tasks, you can choose Edit > Select > By Filter. Using this approach, you can refine a selection that you've already made with any of the other methods discussed previously. For instance, if you select some clips or tracks in the Track view, you can then choose Edit > Select > By Filter to zero in on (so to speak) your selection even further to the individual events within those clips and tracks based on their event properties.

Say you have a MIDI track in which you want to change all the notes with a pitch of C4 to C5. You can easily select only those notes by choosing Edit > Select > By Filter and then change their pitch by using the Transpose feature (which you'll learn about later). All the C4 pitches are then changed to C5, but none of the other notes in the track are affected. This feature works as follows:

1. Select the clip(s), track(s), or set of events you want to use as your initial selection. You can select clips and tracks in the Track view or a group of events in the Piano Roll view, Event view, or Staff view.

2. Choose Edit > Select > By Filter to open the Event Filter - Select Some dialog box (see Figure 8.2).

Figure 8.2
You can use the Event Filter - Select Some dialog box to set the criteria for the type of data you want to have selected

3. Does this dialog box look familiar? The Event Filter - Select Some dialog box is the same as the Event Filter - Search dialog box, which you learned about in Chapter 5. The same information about how to use all the options applies here, so go ahead and set the options as you'd like.

TIP
As with the Event Filter - Search dialog box, the Event Filter - Select Some dialog box enables you to save presets for instant access to your favorite settings. By the way, presets are also available in many of the features that you'll learn about later in this chapter. I described how to use them in Chapter 5.

4. Click OK.

SONAR searches through the data in your initial selection, finds the events that fall under the filter parameters you specified, and then selects those events while leaving any other events alone. If you want to refine your selection even further, just choose Edit > Select > By Filter again on the previous selection results.

Some Selection Applications

Of course, just describing the selection features that you have at your disposal doesn't always convey the types of things you can accomplish with them. The following section provides a small sample of what you can do with the advanced data selection features in SONAR.

Specific Deletions

I've heard from many people asking about how to go about deleting specific notes or data within a MIDI track, while at the same time leaving other data in the track alone. Here's an example of how that is done:

1. Select the clip(s), track(s), or set of events you want to use as your initial selection. You can select clips and tracks in the Track view or a group of events in the Piano Roll view, Event view, or Staff view.

2. Choose Edit > Select > By Filter to open the Event Filter - Select Some dialog box.

3. Click the None button to deactivate all the available options.

4. Activate the options for the type of data that you want to delete. For example, if you want to delete all notes with the value of C5 within a track, activate the Note option. Then set the Key Min and Key Max parameters to C5. Leave all the other parameters as they are.

5. Click OK. This selects all the notes with a value of C5 within your initial selection.

6. Choose Edit > Delete to open the Delete dialog box. You learned about this function in chapter 7.

7. Set the appropriate options. For this example, just make sure the Events In Tracks option is activate so that the selected notes will be deleted.

8. Click OK.

SONAR deletes all the selected data from your initial selection. In this case, all the notes with a value of C5 have been deleted. You can use this procedure for any other kinds of specific data deletions as well. And you can also use it to manipulate selected data in other ways. For example, instead of deleting all the C5 notes, maybe you wanted to transpose them? In that case, instead of using the Delete function, you would use the Transpose function by choosing Process > Transpose in Step 6 above. I'll talk more about the Transpose function later on in this chapter.

Advanced Audio Editing

By using the cut, copy, paste, and slip editing tools in the Track view, you can manipulate the data in your audio tracks in a variety of ways. SONAR also provides a number of advanced features you can use to adjust the volume, apply equalization, and even reverse the data within audio clips. You access all these features by choosing Process > Audio.

Adjusting Audio Volume

If you ever need to adjust the volume of an audio clip, you can use a number of different SONAR features to increase or decrease the volume of your data.

3 dB Louder

Using the 3 dB Louder feature, you can increase the volume of audio data by 3 dB each time you apply it. So, if you want to increase the volume of your data by 6 dB, you can apply the 3 dB Louder feature to it twice. To use it, simply select the audio data you want to change and choose Process > Audio > 3 dB Louder. SONAR processes the data and you can see the results via the higher amplitude value(s) in the audio waveform(s).

CAUTION
Remember the description about setting your input level during the recording process in Chapter 6? I mentioned that you have to be careful not to set the level too high because it could overload the input and cause your audio to be distorted. Well, when you're raising the volume of audio data, you also have to watch out not to raise it too high. Setting it too high can cause clipping. Clipping occurs when SONAR attempts to raise the amplitude of audio data higher than 100 percent. The top and bottom of the waveform become clipped, and when you play the audio it sounds distorted. So, be careful when using the 3 dB Louder feature. Be sure to keep an eye on the amplitude levels of your audio waveforms, and also be sure to listen to your audio data right after you increase its volume to see if it sounds okay. If you hear distortion, then use Undo to remove the volume change.

3 dB Quieter

The 3 dB Quieter feature works in the same way as the 3 dB Louder feature except that it decreases the volume of audio data by 3 dB.

CAUTION

You also have to be careful when using the 3 dB Quieter feature—not because you might introduce distortion into the audio, but because every time you use it, it degrades the audio slightly. For instance, if you use the 3 dB Quieter feature to lower the volume of audio data and then use the 3 dB Louder feature to raise the volume, the quality of the audio will not be the same as it was originally. This difference is due to the limitations of processing digital audio signals, a subject that is a bit complex to explain here. More than likely, though, you won't be able to hear the difference in quality, because it really is only a slight degradation, so you don't need to worry about it too much.

Normalize

Like the 3 dB Louder feature, the Normalize feature also raises the volume of audio, but in a different way. Instead of just simply raising the volume, Normalize first scans the audio waveform to find its highest amplitude level. It subtracts that amplitude level from the maximum level, which is 100 percent. Normalize then takes that value and uses it to increase the volume of the audio data. So, when all is said and done, the highest amplitude in the waveform is 100 percent, and all the other amplitude values are increased.

In other words, if an audio waveform has its highest amplitude value at 80 percent, Normalize subtracts that value from 100 percent to get 20 percent. It then increases the volume of the audio data by 20 percent so that the highest amplitude value is 100 percent, and all the other amplitude values are 20 percent higher. Basically, you can use Normalize to raise the volume of audio data to the highest it can be without causing any clipping.

To use Normalize, simply select the audio data, and choose Process > Audio > Normalize.

CAUTION

You knew this caution was coming, didn't you? When you use the Normalize feature, just like the 3 dB Louder and 3 dB Quieter features, you have to be careful. If you raise the volume of audio data to its maximum, you can easily introduce clipping to the signal if you process it later with some of the other editing or effects features in SONAR. Usually, you should use the Normalize feature only after you know you're not going to do any more processing on that particular audio data. Then again, you probably shouldn't even use the Normalize feature at all (see the tip at the end of the "Crossfade" section).

Fade

If you want to get a little more creative with your volume changes, you can build much more complex volume changes by using the Fade/Envelope feature as follows:

NOTE

A *fade-in* is a gradual and smooth increase from a low volume (loudness) to a higher volume. This increase in volume is also called a *crescendo* in musical terms. A *fade-out* is the exact opposite—a gradual and smooth decrease from a higher volume to a lower volume. In musical terms, this decrease in volume is called a *decrescendo*.

1. Select the audio data to which you want to apply the fade. Then choose Process > Audio > Fade/Envelope to open the Fade/Envelope dialog box (see Figure 8.3). The dialog box displays a graph. The left side of the graph displays amplitude values, 0 to 100 percent from bottom to top. Inside the graph is a line, which represents the fade that will be applied to your selected audio data. If you look at the line from left to right, the left end of the line represents the beginning of your audio data selection and the right end of the line represents the end of your audio data selection. When you first open the dialog box, the line runs from the bottom left to the top right of the graph. If you leave it this way, a straight linear fade-in is applied to your audio data, because, as you look at the graph, the left end of the line is set at 0 percent, and the right end of the line is set at 100 percent. So, the volume of the audio data would begin at 0 percent and fade all the way up to 100 percent. See how it works?

Figure 8.3
You can use the Fade/Envelope dialog box to apply fades to your audio data

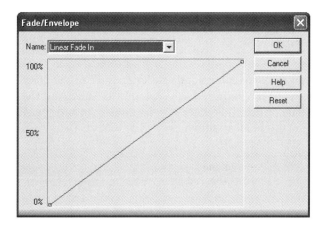

CHAPTER 8

2. You can change the shape of the fade line in one of two ways. You can simply select one of the six available presets from the drop-down list at the top of the dialog box. Alternatively, you can change the fade line graphically by clicking and dragging the small squares at the ends of the line. These squares are called Nodes.

3. If you want to create some really complex fades, you can add more Nodes by clicking anywhere on the fade line. The more Nodes you add, the more flexibility you have in changing the shape of the line (see Figure 8.4).

Figure 8.4
You can create some really complex fades by adding more Nodes

4. After you've finished setting up the graph the way you want it, click OK.

SONAR changes the volume of your audio data selection according to the fade you defined in the Fade/Envelope dialog box.

In addition to the Fade/Envelope feature (which allows you to apply destructive fades to your data), SONAR allows you to apply non-destructive fades. To apply a fade non-destructively, do the following:

1. If you want to create a fade-in for an audio clip, position your mouse in the upper-left corner of the clip until the shape of the mouse changes to a triangle. Then click and drag the mouse toward the right end of the clip to define the fade, as shown in Figure 8.5.

Figure 8.5
Apply a non-destructive fade-in to a clip by clicking in the upper-left corner of the clip and dragging toward the right

2. If you want to create a fade-out for an audio clip, position your mouse in the upper-right corner of the clip until the shape of the mouse changes to a triangle. Then click and drag the mouse toward the left end of the clip to define the fade, as shown in Figure 8.6.

Figure 8.6
Apply a non-destructive fade-out to a clip by clicking in the upper-right corner of the clip and dragging toward the left

CHAPTER 8

3. You can also define the shape of a fade if you would rather not use the straight linear process. SONAR provides three choices: Linear, Slow Curve, and Fast Curve. To change the type of fade, position your mouse on the fade line at the top of the clip so the shape of the mouse changes to a triangle. Then right-click and choose a fade type from the pop-up menu (see Figure 8.7).

Figure 8.7
Change the fade type by right-clicking at the top of the fade line

TIP

If you use a particular type of fade most often, you can set the default fade types. Just click the small downward arrow next to the Enable/Disable Automatic Crossfades button to reveal a menu, which will let you choose the default types for fade-in, fade-out, and crossfades (see Figure 8.8). I'll talk about crossfades in the next section of this chapter.

Figure 8.8
Set the default fade type using the Enable/Disable Automatic Crossfades menu

TIP

The non-destructive fade feature doesn't allow you to define complex fades by adding nodes as with the Fade/Envelope feature, but you can apply non-destructive complex fades or volume changes to a clip (or an entire track) using envelopes. I'll talk more about envelopes in Chapter 12.

Crossfade

A *crossfade* is a special kind of fade that can be applied only to overlapping audio clips. This kind of fade can come in handy when you want to make a smooth transition from one style of music to another or from one instrument to another. It is especially useful when you're composing to video; you can change smoothly from one type of background music to another as the scene changes. Of course, it has many other types of creative uses as well.

When you apply a crossfade to two overlapping audio clips, it works like this: During playback, as the Now time reaches the point at which the two audio clips overlap, the first audio clip fades out and the second audio clip fades in at the same time. You can apply a crossfade as follows:

1. Select the two overlapping audio clips to which you want to apply the crossfade.

TIP
The two audio clips you select don't have to reside on the same track; they only have to overlap in time.

2. Choose Process > Audio > Crossfade to open the Crossfade dialog box (see Figure 8.9).

Figure 8.9
You can apply a crossfade to two overlapping audio Clips by using the Crossfade dialog box

CHAPTER 8

3. Notice that the Crossfade dialog box looks almost exactly the same as the Fade/Envelope dialog box. It works almost exactly the same, too. You can choose from three preset fades, and you can manipulate the fade line with your mouse by adding, clicking, and dragging nodes. The only difference here is that an additional line appears on the graph. The gray line represents the second selected audio clip and can't be manipulated directly. As you make changes to the purple line, the gray line mimics it. This feature ensures that the volumes of both audio clips are synchronized and provides a perfectly smooth crossfade. So, go ahead and make your changes as discussed earlier.

4. Click OK.

SONAR applies the crossfade to the parts of the two audio clips that are overlapping. When you play back the audio, you hear the data from the first clip gradually fade out at the same time the data from the second audio clip gradually fades in.

In addition to the Crossfade feature (which allows you to apply destructive crossfades to your data), SONAR allows you to apply non-destructive crossfades. To apply a crossfade non-destructively, do the following:

1. Activate the Enable/Disable Automatic Crossfades button located in the Track view toolbar, which I mentioned earlier. You can also just hit the X key on your computer keyboard for a much quicker method.

2. Click and drag one audio clip so that it overlaps another audio clip. Both clips must reside on the same track.

3. In the Drag and Drop Options dialog box, choose the Blend Old and New option.

4. Click OK. SONAR overlaps the clips and automatically applies a perfect crossfade to the overlapping sections, as shown in Figure 8.10.

Figure 8.10
SONAR automatically applies a crossfade to the overlapping sections of the clips

5. As with fades, you can also define the shape of a crossfade if you would rather not use the straight linear process. SONAR provides nine different choices. To change the type of crossfade, position your mouse in the crossfade area. Then right-click and choose a crossfade type from the pop-up menu (see Figure 8.11).

Figure 8.11
Change the crossfade type by right-clicking in the crossfade area

TIP

If you use a particular type of crossfade most often, you can set the default crossfade type. Just click the small downward arrow next to the Enable/Disable Automatic Crossfades button in the Track view toolbar to reveal a menu, which will let you choose the default crossfade type. As I mentioned earlier, this is also how you define the default fade-in and fade-out types.

CHAPTER 8

Equalization (EQ)

You have a radio in your car, right? Maybe even a cassette or CD player, too? If so, then you've probably used equalization without even knowing it. Adjusting the bass and treble controls on your car radio is a form of equalization. Equalization (EQ) enables you to adjust the tonal characteristics of an audio signal by increasing (boosting) or decreasing (cutting) the amplitude of different frequencies in the audio spectrum.

NOTE

When a musical object (such as a string) vibrates, it emits a sound. The speed at which the object vibrates is called the *frequency*, which is measured in vibrations (or cycles) per second. This measurement is also called *Hertz* (Hz). If an object vibrates 60 times per second, the frequency would be 60 Hz. The tricky point to remember here, though, is that most objects vibrate at a number of different frequencies at the same time. The combination of all these different vibrations makes up the distinct sound (or *timbre*) of a vibrating object. That's why a bell sounds like a bell, a horn sounds like a horn, and so on with all other types of sounds.

Of course, we humans can't perceive some very slow and some very fast vibrations. Technically, the range of human hearing resides between the frequencies of 20 Hz and 20 kHz (1 kHz is equal to 1,000 Hz). This range is known as the *audio spectrum*.

Equalization enables you to manipulate the frequencies of the audio spectrum, and because sounds contain many of these frequencies, you can change their tonal characteristics (or timbre).

In other words, using EQ, you can bump up the bass, add more presence, reduce rumble, and sometimes eliminate noise in your audio material. Not only that, but you can also use EQ as an effect. You know how, in some of the modern dance tunes, the vocals sound like they're coming out of a telephone receiver or an old radio? That's an effect done with EQ.

SONAR provides two different types of EQ features: Graphic EQ and Parametric EQ. (Actually, seven different EQ features are available, but I'll describe the other five in Chapter 11.) Both have their strengths and weaknesses.

Graphic EQ

You might already be familiar with graphic equalizers, because they are sometimes included on boom boxes and home stereo systems. SONAR's Graphic EQ feature simulates a hardware-based graphic equalizer. It even looks similar (see Figure 8.12).

Figure 8.12
The Graphic EQ feature resembles that of a real graphic equalizer

The Graphic EQ feature provides ten different frequencies (called *bands*) you can adjust. Each band can either be boosted or cut by 12 dB. You simply drag the appropriate slider up (boost) or down (cut) to increase or decrease the amplitude of that frequency. But herein lies the weakness of Graphic EQ. Although it's very easy to use, you are limited by the frequencies you can manipulate. You can't change any of the frequencies below, above, or in between the ones provided. Still, Graphic EQ is very useful if you want to make quick equalization changes, and the frequencies provided are the most common ones. It works like this:

1. Select the audio data you want to change.
2. Choose Process > Audio > Graphic EQ to open the Graphic EQ dialog box.
3. Adjust the sliders for the frequencies that you want to cut or boost.

CAUTION

Be careful when you're boosting frequencies, because doing so also increases the overall volume of the audio data. If you raise the volume too high, you could introduce clipping into the data.

4. Click the Audition button to hear the first few seconds of the processed audio before you go ahead and accept the settings. That way, you can decide whether you like the way it sounds. By listening to a few seconds of the audio, you can test whether any clipping occurs. When you're done listening, click Stop. By the way, SONAR includes the Audition button in many of its other features, too, and it always works in exactly the same way.

TIP

If clipping does occur, but you really want to boost some of the frequencies in your audio data, click Cancel to exit the Graphic EQ dialog box without making any changes. Now, lower the volume of the audio data by using the 3 dB Quieter feature. Then go back and try to apply the EQ again. By lowering the volume of the audio first, you can make enough room to allow more frequency boosting.

5. If you want to be able to use the same EQ settings again later without having to keep making the same slider adjustments, save them as a preset. You learned about presets in Chapter 5.
6. Click OK.

SONAR processes the selected audio data, and, when you play it back, it should sound the same way it did when you listened to it using the Audition feature.

TIP

By default, the Audition feature plays only the first few seconds of the selected data. You can adjust the Audition time by selecting Options > Global to open the Global Options dialog box. Under the General tab, set the Audition Commands For option to the number of seconds you want to use for the Audition feature. I usually like to keep this set anywhere between 5 and 10 seconds.

Parametric EQ

Parametric equalization, on the other hand, is much more powerful and flexible, but it's also a lot more complex and difficult to understand. With the Parametric EQ feature, you're not limited to specific frequencies. You can specify an exact frequency to adjust, and you can cut or boost by much larger amounts. You can also process a range of frequencies at the same time, such as cutting all frequencies above 10 kHz by 20 dB (which would reduce all the frequencies between 10 kHz and 20 kHz but leave the frequencies between 20 Hz and 10 kHz alone). I can explain the Parametric EQ feature a little better by showing you how it works:

1. Select the audio data you want to change.

2. Choose Process > Audio > Parametric EQ to open the Parametric EQ dialog box (see Figure 8.13).

Figure 8.13
The Parametric EQ feature provides a lot more power, but it's also more difficult to use

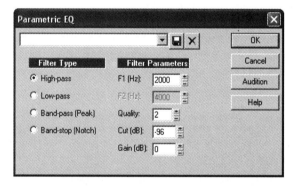

3. Choose one of the options in the Filter Type section: High-Pass, Low-Pass, Band-Pass (Peak), or Band-Stop (Notch). Then set the appropriate parameters in the Filter Parameters section. You can use the F1 and F2 parameters to set the frequencies you want to adjust. They work differently depending on the type of filter you choose (I'll talk more about this in a minute). The Cut parameter enables you to reduce the volume of the frequencies. To change this setting, just enter a negative number (such as –20) to cut by that number of decibels. The Gain parameter allows you to boost the volume

of the frequencies. To change this setting, just enter a positive number (such as +20) to boost by that number of decibels. You can set the Quality parameter to determine how precise the Parameter EQ feature will be when processing your audio.

If you really want to zero in on a frequency or range of frequencies, use a higher value for the Quality parameter (200 being the highest). This setting gives you a sharper (for lack of a better term) sound. A low value (such as 2) allows the Parametric EQ feature to slightly process the other frequencies not defined specifically or outside the range, which gives you a smoother sound. It's a bit difficult to describe. Experiment with it a little, and you'll be able to hear the difference.

If you select the High-Pass filter type, all the frequencies below the frequency that you set in the F1 parameter will be cut, and all the frequencies above it will be boosted, depending on how you set the Cut and Gain parameters. If you select the Low-Pass filter type, all the frequencies above the frequency that you set in the F1 parameter will be cut, and all the frequencies below it will be boosted, depending on how you set the Cut and Gain parameters.

If you select either the Band-Pass (Peak) or Band-Stop (Notch) filter types, you have to set up a range of frequencies using both the F1 and F2 parameters. Use the F1 parameter to mark the beginning of the range and the F2 parameter to mark the end of the range. For the Band-Pass (Peak) filter type, any frequencies outside the range are cut, and frequencies within the range are boosted, depending on how you set the Cut and Gain parameters. For the Band-Stop (Notch) filter type, any frequencies outside the range are boosted and frequencies within the range are cut, depending on how you set the Cut and Gain parameters.

4. Click the Audition button to hear the first few seconds of the processed audio before you go ahead and accept the settings. That way, you can decide whether you like the way it sounds. By listening to a few seconds of the audio, you can test whether any clipping occurs. When you're done listening, click Stop.

5. If you want to be able to use the same EQ settings again later without having to keep making the same parameter adjustments, save them as a preset.

6. Click OK.

SONAR processes the selected audio data, and, when you play it back, it should sound the same way it did when you listened to it using the Audition feature.

CHAPTER 8

Applications

Right about now, you might be saying to yourself, "Okay, EQ sounds pretty cool, but what can I do with it?" Well, you can use EQ in many different ways to process your audio. To begin with, you might want to try some of the presets that come included with SONAR. Not very many are provided for the Graphic EQ and Parametric EQ features, but you can find enough to give you a taste of what EQ can do. After that, you might want to try experimenting with some of the settings described in the following sections.

Fullness

To make your audio sound a little fuller, try boosting the range of frequencies between 100 and 300 Hz by 6 dB. To do so, use the Parametric EQ feature with the Band-Pass (Peak) filter type and set the filter parameters to the following: F1 = 100, F2 = 300, Quality = 2, Cut = 0, and Gain = 6.

Punch

To add a little more punch to your audio, try boosting the range of frequencies between 800 Hz and 2 kHz by 6 dB. To do so, use the Parametric EQ feature with the Band-Pass (Peak) filter type and set the filter parameters to the following: F1 = 800, F2 = 2000, Quality = 2, Cut = 0, and Gain = 6.

Noise Reduction

EQ can also be used as a simple means of reducing noise in your audio. This is especially true for high frequency hiss. Use the Parametric EQ feature with the Low-Pass filter type and set the filter parameters to the following: F1 = 18000, Quality = 2, Cut = –96, and Gain = 0.

To get rid of buzzing or humming noises with EQ, use the Parametric EQ feature with the Band-Stop (Notch) filter type and set the filter parameters to the following: F1 = 60, F2 = 60, Quality = 100, Cut = –96, and Gain = 0.

Specific Sounds

EQ is handy for molding specific types of sounds, such as stringed instruments like guitar and bass. For example, to give a bit of a different sound to an acoustic or electric guitar, try using the Graphic EQ feature with the following settings: 32 Hz = –12, 64 Hz = 0, 130 Hz = +4, 260 Hz = +7, 500 Hz = +6, 1 k = +3, 2 k = 0, 4 k = +4, 8.3 k = +7, and 16.5 k = 0.

For a bass guitar, trying using the Graphic EQ feature with the following settings: 32 Hz = –12, 64 Hz = 0, 130 Hz = +6, 260 Hz = +7, 500 Hz = +5, 1 k = +1, 2 k = 0, 4 k =0, 8.3 k = +6, and 16.5 k = +12.

And So On

I could go on and on with equalization applications, but that would fill a whole book on its own. Don't be afraid to experiment. The more you practice using the EQ features, the more skilled you will become at applying them. Keep one point in mind, though: With just the right amount of spices, a meal tastes great. Too many spices, and the taste starts taking a turn for the worse. The same goes for applying EQ to your audio. Too much EQ will make your projects sound amateurish.

Getting Rid of Silence

When you record an audio track in SONAR, even though there may be pauses in your performance (such as between musical phrases), your sound card still picks up a signal from your microphone or instrument, and that data is recorded. Although you might think that the data is just recorded silence, in actuality, it contains a very minute amount of noise that may come from your sound card itself or the microphone or instrument connected there. More often than not, you can't really hear this noise, because it's masked by the other music data in your project. And even during quiet passages, if you have only one or two audio tracks playing, the noise is probably still inaudible. With a large number of audio tracks, however, the noise can add up.

In addition, during playback, SONAR still processes those silent passages even though they don't contain any actual music. These passages take up valuable computer processing power and disk space. To remedy this problem, SONAR provides the Remove Silence feature. This feature automatically detects sections of silence in audio clips according to a loudness threshold that you set. Then, by first splitting long audio clips into shorter ones, it removes the resulting clips containing only silence. Thus, SONAR doesn't process that extra data during playback, and it doesn't save it to disk when you save your project.

To detect silent passages in audio, the Remove Silence feature uses a digital noise gate. Depending on the parameter settings you specify, this noise gate opens up when the Remove Silence feature comes upon a section in your audio that has an amplitude level greater than the one you set. It identifies this part of the audio as acceptable sound and lets it pass through. When the level of audio dips below a certain amplitude level that you set, the noise gate identifies that part of the audio as silence, and it closes to stop it from passing through. At that point, the Remove Silence feature splits the audio clip with one new clip containing just the music and another new clip containing just the noise. This process happens over and over until the whole initial audio clip is finished being scanned.

You use this feature as follows:

1. Select the audio data that you want to scan for silence.

2. Choose Process > Audio > Remove Silence to open the Remove Silence dialog box (see Figure 8.14).

Figure 8.14
You can use the
Remove Silence feature
to clean up your audio
tracks and make them
more manageable

3. Type a value for the Open Level parameter. This parameter determines how loud the audio data has to be to make the noise gate open, thus identifying the data as acceptable sound.

4. Type a value for the Close Level parameter. This parameter determines how soft the data has to be to make the noise gate close, thus identifying the data as silence.

5. Type a value for the Attack Time parameter. This parameter determines how quickly (in milliseconds) the noise gate will open to the amplitude set in the Open Level parameter. If the beginning of your audio data starts off soft (such as with a fade in), and its amplitude is below the Open Level setting, it could get cut off by the noise gate. For example, the beginnings of the words in a vocal part might be cut. To prevent this problem, you can set the Attack Time parameter so that the noise gate takes this kind of situation into consideration.

6. Type a value for the Hold Time parameter. This parameter determines how long the noise gate will remain open even when the amplitude level of the audio dips below the Close Level. This parameter is useful when the level of your audio goes up and down very quickly, which could make the noise gate react when it's not supposed to (such as during quick percussion parts). By setting a Hold Time, you can make sure that musical passages containing quick sounds don't get cut by mistake.

7. Type a value for the Release Time parameter. This parameter is the same as the Attack Time parameter but in reverse. It determines how quickly the noise gate will close after the amplitude of the audio reaches the Close Level. This feature is useful if your audio data gradually gets softer at the end, such as with a fade out.

8. Type a value for the Look Ahead parameter. This parameter determines how long (in milliseconds) the amplitude of the audio must stay above the Open Level before the noise gate will open. Basically, this setting lets you fine-tune how the noise gate determines whether the audio being scanned is acceptable sound or silence.

9. If you want SONAR to delete the audio clips that contain only silence, activate the Split Clips option. Otherwise, the silent portions of the audio won't be deleted; they will just be reduced to vacant space, but your clips will remain as they are.

10. You can save your settings as a preset, and you can use the Audition feature to hear the results of your settings if you'd like.

11. Click OK.

SONAR scans the selected audio clip and then splits it up into pieces (and also removes the clips containing only silence) according to the settings that you specified.

TIP

Unless the musical passages and silent passages of your audio are separated pretty neatly, it can be difficult to get the right settings for the Release Time feature to perform accurately. You might find it easier and more precise if you simply split the audio clips by hand using the Split function. The process is a bit more time-consuming, though.

Audio to MIDI Conversion

In chapter 1, you learned about the differences between MIDI and audio data. MIDI data represents recorded performance instructions, and audio data represents actual sound. Because audio data is actual sound, SONAR doesn't really know what's being recorded in an audio Track except that it's a bunch of numbers that represent sound. It can't tell whether the sound is notes being played on an instrument, or a voice singing lyrics, or even if it's the sound of birds chirping on a sunny summer afternoon.

With recent advances in digital audio processing technology, however, under certain circumstances, audio data can be scanned for rhythmic values. This means that a program can scan audio data and determine the rhythm of the instruments being played. It can then convert that data into MIDI notes. SONAR provides a feature that gives you this capability.

CHAPTER 8

Extract Timing

With the Extract Timing feature, SONAR can scan audio data for quick percussive changes in volume and by that be able to determine the rhythm of the music. It can then convert those rhythmic values into MIDI notes and velocity messages. The Extract Timing feature works best with single-note melodies and percussion performances.

You might want to use this feature in a number of different situations. One of the most obvious is in converting melodies (such as a melody played on a piano) into MIDI notes. The Extract Timing feature would pick up only the rhythm of the notes, but you could easily add the pitches by hand. To take this example one step further, you can create a new MIDI melody by scanning a percussion Track. The new melody would then play in sync with the rhythm Track, emphasizing the same notes, beats, and so on. Using this feature is a great way to sync a bass line to a percussion part. Another situation may arise in which you already have a bunch of MIDI Tracks recorded, and you have some existing percussion audio sample beats that you want to use in your Project. With the Extract Timing feature, you can convert the audio rhythm pulses into tempo changes for your song so that the MIDI Tracks play at the same tempo as the audio samples. You can also use the Extract Timing feature to create your own templates for the Groove Quantize feature (which you'll learn about later in this chapter). Here's how Extract Timing works:

1. Select the audio data that you want to scan for rhythmic values.

2. Choose Process > Audio > Extract Timing to open the Extract Timing dialog box (see Figure 8.15).

Figure 8.15
You can detect the rhythm of audio recordings by using the Extract Timing feature and then apply that rhythm to your MIDI data

3. In the Pulse Analysis section, set the Trigger Level parameter. This parameter (set in decibels) tells SONAR how loud the audio data being scanned has to be in order to be considered a rhythmic value. For example, if you have a snare drum track, and each snare drum hit has a volume of –50 dB, you have to set the Trigger Level to at least –50 dB for the snare drum to be picked up. If you have audio data with many varied volume levels, you'll have to experiment with the Trigger Level to be sure all the rhythmic values are picked up.

4. Set the Minimum Length parameter. This parameter (set in milliseconds) tells SONAR how much time should be allowed between rhythmic values. If you set the Minimum Length parameter too low, many extraneous values (that aren't really rhythmic values) may be picked up. If you set it too high, not all the legitimate rhythmic values will be picked up. As you do with the Trigger Level parameter, you'll have to experiment with Minimum Length parameter to find the right setting for the audio material being scanned.

5. Activate or deactivate the Find A Steady Rhythm option. This option tells SONAR to look for a steady rhythm within the audio material being scanned. For example, if you have a snare drum Track that has even hits on each beat but also has some syncopated hits in between the beats, activating the Find A Steady Rhythm option will weed out the syncopated hits and just pick up the rhythm values that are steady.

6. Set the appropriate parameters in the Timing Synthesis section. The options and values set here depend on what you want to do with the Extract Timing feature. If you want to match the tempo of some existing MIDI Tracks to the tempo of some existing audio material, activate the Insert Tempo Changes option. Then set the Expected Pulse Duration parameter to the length of rhythmic values in your audio material. For example, if you are scanning some percussion material that has a snare drum being played as steady quarter notes, you can set the Expected Pulse Duration parameter to Quarter. If you want to convert the rhythmic values from your audio material into MIDI notes so that you can use the data in some of the situations described earlier, you can activate the Convert Each Pulse To MIDI Note option. Then enter the pitch at which you want all the MIDI notes to be set. And if you want the Velocity values of the MIDI notes to match the volume levels of the rhythmic values being scanned, under Note Velocities, activate the Vary With Pulse Level option. Otherwise, you can set all the MIDI notes to the same Velocity by activating the Set All To Same Value option and then entering a value for the Velocity you would like to use.

CHAPTER 8

7. Click the Audition button. In this case, the button works a bit differently from any of the other editing and effects features in SONAR. Instead of hearing anything, you'll see some red marks placed over the audio material that you selected in the Track view (see Figure 8.16). These marks represent the rhythmic values that will be picked up by the Extract Timing feature. You need to see if they match up to the rhythmic values in the audio material. If they do, you can move on to the next step; otherwise, you might need to adjust some of the parameters a little more to make everything line up correctly.

Figure 8.16
Before leaving the Extract Timing dialog box, you should use the Audition feature to make sure the correct rhythmic values from the audio material are being picked up

8. Click OK.

Depending on the parameter settings you chose, SONAR scans the selected audio data and attempts to detect the rhythmic values of the material. If you activated the Insert Tempo Changes option, SONAR inserts tempo changes into your Project so that the MIDI Tracks will play along at the same tempo as the audio material. If you activated the Convert Each Pulse To MIDI Note option, SONAR temporarily stores the MIDI note data into the Clipboard. From here, you can paste the data into a Clip or Track using the Track or Piano Roll Views, and use it to create a new melody or bass line that plays along with the audio material.

Extract Timing Example

The Extract Timing feature is a bit complicated, and it may be difficult to understand why you might need it. So, let's take a look at a sample application:

1. Open the sample project called Don't Matter Audio and MIDI Demo.cwb that is included with SONAR.
2. Close the File Info window and the Staff view. You won't need them.
3. Select the first clip in Track 5 (Guitar).
4. Choose Process > Audio > Extract Timing to open the Extract Timing dialog box.
5. Set the Trigger Level parameter to –17 dB.
6. Set the Minimum Length parameter to 50 milliseconds.

7. Because the audio material that you're scanning has an irregular rhythm, make sure the Find A Steady Rhythm option is deactivated.

8. Activate the Convert Each Pulse To MIDI Note option, and set the note value to G#4.

9. Under Note Velocities, activate the Vary With Pulse Level option.

10. Click OK. SONAR scans the audio material, converts the rhythmic values to MIDI note and velocity data, and stores the data in the Clipboard.

11. Choose Edit > Paste to open the Paste dialog box.

12. Set the Starting at Time parameter to 2:01:000 (measures, beats, ticks).

13. Set the Repetitions parameter to 3.

14. Set the Starting at Track parameter to New.

15. Click OK.

SONAR creates a new Track (Track 10) containing three Clips, each containing the rhythmic data that was scanned from the first Clip of the guitar Track. Before you play the project back to hear how it sounds, be sure to set the Output and Channel for Track 10. Set it so that the Track uses your General MIDI-compatible MIDI instrument and uses MIDI channel 10 (the standard channel for drums). When you play the project, you'll hear a cowbell sound playing along in time with the rest of the Tracks. In particular, it should have close to the same rhythm as the audio material in the guitar Track. Some of the MIDI notes may be slightly off, but you can fix their timing in the Piano Roll View. In any case, this example illustrates just one of the many applications for which you can use the Extract Timing feature.

Play It Backward

Assuming you're old enough to remember vinyl recordings, did you ever take a record and play it backward to see whether your favorite band had left some satanic messages in their songs or perhaps a recipe for their favorite lentil soup? Well, guess what? You can do the same thing with your audio data. SONAR lets you flip the data in an audio clip so that it plays in reverse.

This feature doesn't have much practical use, but combined with some other processing, it can render some cool effects. To use it, simply select the audio clip you want to change and choose Process > Audio > Reverse. Now the data in that clip will play backward.

TIP

If you want to reverse the data in an entire track, make sure to combine all the audio clips in the track into one big audio clip first. If you don't, the data in each separate clip will be reversed, which is not the same as reversing the entire track. Try it, and you'll hear what I mean.

CHAPTER 8

TIP

With the combination of the audio editing features discussed so far in this chapter and the audio effects features described in Chapter 11, there's no doubt that SONAR packs a lot of audio data editing power. But there may be times when you still want to use your favorite dedicated audio editing application such as Sonic Foundry's Sound Forge (**www.sonicfoundry.com**), Syntrillium's Cool Edit (**www.syntrillium.com**), or Steinberg's WaveLab (**www.steinberg.net**). The people at Cakewalk included a little-known feature that enables you to access your favorite audio editing applications from within SONAR. I've tested the previously mentioned products, but there might be others that can use the feature as well.

To use your audio editing software from within SONAR, simply select the audio data that you want to edit. Then select the Tools menu. At the bottom of the menu, you should see your software listed there. Choose the program that you want to run. Your audio editing software then opens with the audio data you selected, ready to be processed. Make any changes you want and then close the audio editing software. Before closing, the program first asks whether you want to save the changes you made. Click Yes. The program closes, and you return to SONAR. SONAR then tells you that the audio data has changed and asks whether you would like to reload it. Click Yes. That's all there is to it. And now you have easy access to all the power of your audio editing software as well as SONAR. Isn't that cool?

If your audio editing software doesn't show up in the Tool menu automatically, you can add it to the menu manually by manipulating the Windows Registry. For more information on how to do this, check out my article (Adjusting the Cakewalk Tools menu) in issue 2 of the DigiFreq newsletter. You can download the issue for free at: **http://www.digifreq.com/digifreq/issues.asp**

The Edit Menu

Up until now, I've talked about editing features that pertain strictly to audio data. The remainder of SONAR's editing features are more diverse in their use, meaning some can be used with MIDI data, some with audio data, and some with both. The one aspect they all have in common is that they are accessed via the Process menu. Because of their diversity, I'll go through each feature one by one, explaining what it does, along with how and why you would want to use it. Of course, I'll also let you know what kinds of data each feature works with.

Deglitch

Occasionally, you might find that, while you're playing your MIDI instrument, some unintended notes get recorded along with the legitimate musical material. This is especially true for people who play a MIDI guitar. The strings on a MIDI guitar can easily trigger notes when they're not supposed to. To help with this problem, SONAR provides the

Deglitch feature. Using this feature, you can filter out any notes from your MIDI data that don't fall within the right pitch, velocity, and duration range for the music you're recording. It works like this:

1. Select the MIDI data from which you want to filter any unwanted notes.

2. Choose Process > Deglitch to open the Deglitch dialog box (see Figure 8.17).

Figure 8.17
Using the Deglitch feature, you can filter out any unintended notes from your MIDI data by specifying acceptable pitch, velocity, and duration ranges

3. If you want to filter out notes by pitch, activate the Pitch option. Then, for the Notes Higher Than parameter, type the maximum note value allowed in your material. For example, if the highest note in your MIDI data should be C5, then you should set the Notes Higher Than parameter to C5. If the Deglitch feature finds any notes within the data that have a pitch higher than C5, it will delete them.

4. If you want to filter out notes by velocity, activate the Velocity option. Then, for the Notes Softer Than parameter, type the minimum velocity value allowed in your material. For example, if the lowest velocity in your MIDI data should be 15, then you should set the Notes Softer Than parameter to 15. If the Deglitch feature finds any notes within the data that have a velocity lower than 15, it will delete them.

5. If you want to filter out notes by duration, activate the Duration option. Then, for the Notes Shorter Than parameter, type the minimum duration value allowed in your material. Also, be sure to specify whether the duration should be measured in ticks or milliseconds by choosing either the Ticks option or Milliseconds option via the Format parameter. As an example, if the lowest duration in your MIDI data should be 20 ticks, then you should set the Notes Shorter Than parameter to 20 and the Format parameter to Ticks. If the Deglitch feature finds any notes within the data that have a duration lower than 20 ticks, it will delete them.

6. Click OK.

SONAR scans the selected MIDI data and removes any notes that fall within the criteria you set. By the way, you can scan for pitch, velocity, and duration all at once by having all the options activated if you'd like.

Slide

Remember back in Chapter 7, when I described how to move clips in the Track view by dragging and dropping them or by using the Clip Properties dialog box to change their Start times? Well, the Slide feature performs the same function. You can use it to move clips backward or forward within a track. So why does SONAR provide the same functionality more than once? Because the Slide feature has a few differences. Instead of just working with clips, you can use it with any kind of selected data from a group of MIDI notes to single events. And instead of having to specify an exact Start time (as in the Clips Properties dialog box), you can move data by any number of measures, ticks, seconds, or frames. In addition, the Slide feature doesn't give you the option of blending with, replacing, or sliding over existing events in a track. It simply moves the selected data so that it overlaps with any existing data. You use it as follows:

1. Using the appropriate view, select the MIDI data or audio clips that you want to move.

2. Choose Process > Slide to open the Slide dialog box (see Figure 8.18).

Figure 8.18
You can use the Slide feature to move any kind of data, not just Clips

3. If you want to move events, be sure the Events In Tracks option under the Slide parameter is activated. If you would also like to move any markers that happen to fall within the same time range as the selected data, activate the Markers option.

4. For the By parameter, type the number of units by which you want to move the selected data. If you want to move the data backward in time, enter a negative number. If you want to move the data forward in time, enter a positive number.

5. Choose the type of unit by which you want to move the selected data by activating the appropriate option. You can select Measures, Ticks, Seconds, or Frames.

6. Click OK.

SONAR moves the selected data backward or forward in time by the amount you specified and the unit type that you chose.

Quantize

Even though you may be a great musician, you're bound to occasionally make mistakes when playing your instrument, especially when it comes to timing. No one I know can play in perfect time during every performance, and having to listen to a metronome while you play can sometimes be distracting. Instead of playing notes at the exact same time as the metronome sounds, you'll more than likely play some of them either a little ahead or a little behind the beat. You may even hold some notes a little longer than you're supposed to. Usually, if these timing errors are slight enough, they'll make your performance sound more "human" than anything else. But if the mistakes are large enough to stand out, they can make your performance sound sloppy. At this point, the Quantize feature can come in handy. It can help you correct some of the timing mistakes you make.

To understand how to use the Quantize feature, you first have to know how it works. The Quantize feature scans the MIDI events in your selected data one by one, and it changes the Start time of each event so that it is equal to the nearest rhythmic value you specify. You specify this rhythmic value by using the Resolution parameter. So, if you want all the events in your data to be moved to the nearest sixteenth note, you can set the Resolution parameter to Sixteenth. The Quantize feature uses this value to set up an imaginary (for lack of a better word) time grid over your data. In this case, the grid is divided into sixteenth notes.

During the scanning process, the Quantize feature moves an imaginary pointer along the grid one division at a time. Centered around the pointer is an imaginary window, of which you can set the size using the Window parameter. As the Quantize feature moves its pointer and window along the grid, it looks to see whether any of your Events are in the vicinity. Any events that fall within the window have their Start times changed so that they line up with the current position of the pointer. Any events that fall outside the window are left alone. This procedure continues until the Quantize feature comes to the end of the data you selected. Actually, there's a little more to the procedure than that, but I'll explain the rest as I describe how to use the feature:

1. Select the data that you want to quantize. It can be anything from all the data in your project, to a single track or clip, or a selected group of events.

2. Select Process > Quantize to open the Quantize dialog box (see Figure 8.19).

Figure 8.19
The Quantize dialog box provides a number of parameters you can set to determine exactly how you want your data to be corrected

3. In the Resolution section, set the Resolution parameter. This parameter determines what rhythmic value will be used to set up the imaginary grid and what will be the nearest rhythmic value to which the events in your data will be aligned. It's best to set this parameter to the smallest note value found in your data. For instance, your data may contain quarter notes, eighth notes, and sixteenth notes. Because the smallest note value in your data is the sixteenth, you would set the Resolution parameter to Sixteenth.

4. In the Change section, activate the appropriate options for the types of events and the event properties you want to have quantized. You'll almost always want to have the Start Times option activated. Along with the Start Times of events, you can also quantize the durations of MIDI note events by activating the Note Durations option. You'll almost always want to have this option activated as well. If you don't, the ends of some notes may overlap the beginnings of others, which may not sound very good. You might not want to quantize the Start Times of Events but just the durations only if you want to create a staccato (separated notes) feel to your music. The Only Notes, Lyrics, and Audio option, when activated, makes it so only MIDI note, lyric, and audio events are quantized, leaving any other events (such as MIDI controller events) alone. You'll usually want to keep this option activated, too; otherwise, the Quantize feature will move controller events to the nearest grid point, which can actually screw up their timing.

TIP

Even though the Quantize feature can change the Start times of audio Clips, don't be confused into thinking that it can correct the timing of your audio data. It can't. Remember, audio data is different from MIDI data. The Quantize feature can move an entire audio clip to the nearest rhythmic value. However, if you record a sloppy performance as audio data, you cannot correct it except by doing the recording over again.

Continued

You can use one trick, however, to quantize a monophonic (one note at a time) melody or percussion part that was recorded as an audio clip. If you split the clip into smaller clips, each containing one note of the melody, then each note will have its own Start time, and you can use the Quantize feature to change the timing of each note.

5. In the Options section, set the Strength parameter. Quantizing your data so that all the events are aligned in perfect time with the grid can make your performance sound mechanical (like it is being played by a machine). So, instead of having the Quantize feature move an event to the exact current pointer position on the grid during the scanning process, you can have it move the event only slightly toward the pointer, thus taking the sloppiness out of the performance but keeping the "human" feel. You can do so by setting a percentage for the Strength parameter. A value of 100 percent means that all events will be moved to the exact grid point. A value of 50 percent means that the events will be moved only halfway toward the grid point. You'll have to experiment with this parameter to find the best-sounding setting.

6. Set the Window parameter. This parameter tells SONAR how close to the current grid point an event has to be in order to be quantized. If the event falls inside the window, it is quantized. If it falls outside the window, it isn't. You set the Window parameter by using a percentage. A value of 100 percent means the window extends halfway before and halfway after the current pointer position on the grid. So, basically all events get moved; if they don't fall inside the window at the current pointer position, they will fall inside at the next position. A value of 50 percent means the window extends only one-quarter of the way before and after the current pointer position, meaning only half of the events in your selection will be processed.

7. Set the Offset parameter. This parameter is an extra setting thrown in to make the Quantize feature even more flexible (and complicated) than it already is. When the Quantize feature sets up its imaginary grid over your selected data, the grid is perfectly aligned to the measures and beats in your project. So, if your data selection started at the beginning of your project, the grid would be set up starting at 1:01:000 (measure, beat, tick). If you enter a value for the Offset parameter (in ticks), the grid is offset by the number of ticks that you enter. For example, if you enter an Offset of +3, the grid would be set up starting at 1:01:003 instead of 1:01:000. This means that if the current event being scanned was initially supposed to be moved to 1:01:000, it would be moved to 1:01:003 instead. Basically, you can use this parameter to offset the selected data from the other data in your project, in case you want to create some slight timing variations, and so on. It works similarly to the Time Offset parameter in the Track view, which you learned about in Chapter 4.

CHAPTER 8

8. Set the Swing parameter, which is yet another parameter that makes the Quantize feature more flexible (and more difficult to understand). You might use it to work on a song that has a "swing" feel to it, similar to that of a waltz, where the first in a pair of notes is played longer than the second. It's difficult to explain, but essentially the Swing parameter distorts the grid by making the space between the grid points uneven. If you leave the parameter set at 50 percent, it doesn't have any effect. If you set it to something like 66 percent, the space between the first two points in the grid becomes twice as much as the space between the second and third points. This pattern of long space, short space gets repeated throughout the length of the grid, and your data is aligned according to the uneven grid points. You'll need to experiment with this parameter a bit to hear the effect it has on your data.

9. Click the Audition button to hear how the quantized data will sound. Go back and make any parameter changes you think might be necessary.

10. If you want to use the same settings again later, save them as a preset.

11. Click OK.

SONAR quantizes the selected data, and when you play it back, it should sound the same way it did when you listened to it using the Audition feature.

TIP
SONAR provides additional quantizing features with the Quantize MIDI Effect. See chapter 11 for more information.

Groove Quantize

Not only can quantizing be used to correct the timing of your performances, but you can also use it to add a bit of creative flair. The Groove Quantize feature works in almost the same way as the Quantize feature, but it's slightly more sophisticated. Instead of using a fixed grid (meaning you can set the grid to use only straight rhythmic values such as sixteenth notes), it uses a grid with rhythmic values that are based on an existing rhythmic pattern called a groove pattern. This groove pattern can contain any kind of musical rhythm, even one taken from an existing piece of music.

Basically, the Groove Quantize feature works by imposing the timing, duration, and velocity values of one set of Events onto another set. For example, suppose you record a melody that comes out sounding a bit too mechanical, but your friend slams out this really kickin' MIDI bass line that has the exact "feel" you want. You can copy the bass clip data and use it as a groove pattern to groove quantize the melody clip data. By doing so, you impose the timing, duration, and velocity values (depending on your parameter settings) from the bass line on to the melody. Thus, the melody will have the same rhythm as the bass line but keep its original pitches.

The preceding example is just one of the many uses for the Groove Quantize feature. Just like the Quantize feature, the Groove Quantize feature provides Strength parameters to give you control over how much influence a groove pattern has over the data you're quantizing. You can define via percentages how much the timing, duration, and velocity values of the events will be affected, so you can use this feature for all kinds of editing tasks. You can correct off-tempo tracks, add complex beat accents to each measure of a tune, synchronize rhythm and solo tracks, align tracks with bad timing to one with good timing, and steal the "feeling" from tracks, as I explained in the preceding example.

As a matter of fact, groove quantizing has become so popular that companies now sell groove pattern files so that you can steal the "feeling" from tracks that have been recorded by professional keyboard, drum, and guitar players. It's almost like having Steve Vai play on your latest tune! Just look in any copy of *Electronic Musician* or *Keyboard* magazine, and you'll see advertisements for these types of products. Of course, you need to know how to use the Groove Quantize feature before you can make use of these groove pattern files, so let me tell you how:

1. If you want to grab the timing, duration, and velocity values from existing data, first select and copy that data so that it is placed into the Clipboard. Otherwise, you can use one of the groove patterns that comes included with SONAR (which I'll show you how to choose later).

2. Select the data that you want to groove quantize.

3. Choose Process > Groove Quantize to open the Groove Quantize dialog box (see Figure 8.20).

Figure 8.20
The Groove Quantize
dialog box provides a
number of parameters
you can set to deter-
mine exactly how you
want your data to be
groove quantized

4. Set the Groove File parameter. If you're grabbing the values from existing
    data, as explained previously, then select Clipboard from the drop-down list
    and skip to Step 6. Otherwise, choose an existing groove file. SONAR ships
    with only one groove file (Cakewalk DNA Grooves.grv), so unless you've
    created your own groove files, choose the Cakewalk DNA Grooves.grv file. If
    you have other groove files available, you can load them by clicking on the
    small button to the right of the Groove File parameter to bring up the Open
    Groove File dialog box. Just select a file and then click Open.

5. Set the Groove Pattern parameter. Each groove file can contain any number
    of groove patterns. The groove file that comes with SONAR contains twelve
    different groove patterns. Choose the groove pattern you want to use.

6. The rest of the parameters for the Groove Quantize feature are the same as
    for the Quantize feature. You need to set the Resolution parameter; the
    Only Notes, Lyrics, And Audio; and the Window parameters. The Window
    Sensitivity parameter is the same as the Window parameter for the Quantize
    feature, but one additional Window parameter is available here. You can
    choose the If Outside Window parameter to have Groove Quantize change
    events even if they fall outside the window. If you select Do Not Change,
    then events outside the window are left alone (just as with the Quantize
    feature). If you select Quantize to Resolution, any events outside the window
    are moved to the nearest grid point as specified by the Resolution parameter.
    If you select Move to Nearest, then the Window Sensitivity parameter is

ignored, and all events outside the window are moved to the nearest grid point as defined by the groove pattern. If you select Scale Time, SONAR looks at the events located right before and after the current event being scanned (as long as they are within the window), and it sets their relative timing so that they're the same. The Scale Time parameter is very difficult to explain, so you should try it out to hear what kind of effect it has on your music.

7. You also need to set the Strength parameters. They work the same as with the Quantize feature, but instead of just having one parameter for affecting the timing of events, three Strength parameters are provided to give you control over how the Groove Quantize feature will affect the time, duration, and velocity of each event. If you want the events to have the exact same timing, duration, and velocity of their counterparts in the groove pattern, then set all these parameters to 100 percent. Otherwise, you can make it so the events take on only some of the "feel" of the events in the groove pattern by adjusting the percentages of these parameters.

8. Click the Audition button to hear how the quantized data will sound. Go back and make any parameter changes you think might be necessary.

9. If you want to use the same settings again later, save them as a preset.

10. Click OK.

SONAR quantizes the selected data so that (depending on your parameter settings) the timing, duration, and velocity of the events sound exactly or somewhat like those in the groove pattern you used. By the way, if the groove pattern is shorter than the material you are quantizing, the Groove Quantize feature will loop through the groove pattern as many times as necessary to get to the end of your selected data. For example, if you use a groove pattern that is only one measure long, but your selected data is three measures, then the timing, duration, and velocity values of the groove pattern will be repeated over each of those three measures.

Saving Groove Patterns

If you create your own groove pattern by grabbing the timing, duration, and velocity values from existing data, you can save it for later use as follows:

1. After you've gone through steps 1 through 4 in the preceding example on how to use the Groove Quantize feature, and you've set the Groove File parameter to Clipboard, click the Define button at the bottom of the Groove Quantize dialog box to open the Define Groove dialog box (see Figure 8.21).

CHAPTER 8

Figure 8.21
Using the Define
Groove dialog box, you
can save your own
groove patterns and
groove files

2. In the Groove Library File section, select an existing groove file via the File parameter. You can also type a new name to create your own new groove file.

NOTE

SONAR supports two types of groove files. One type is the DNA groove files, which contain only timing data but are compatible with other sequencing software. The groove files being sold by other companies are usually in this file format. SONAR also has its own proprietary groove file format that stores timing, duration, and velocity data. Unless you really need to share your groove files with others who don't own SONAR, I suggest you save your files in the SONAR format, because it provides more flexibility. To do so, be sure to activate the Cakewalk Groove File Format option in the Define Groove dialog box.

3. If you want to replace an existing groove pattern in the current groove file, just select one from the list via the Pattern parameter. If you want to save your groove pattern under a new name, type the name via the Pattern parameter.

TIP

You can also delete existing groove patterns in the current groove file. Just select the groove pattern you want to delete via the Pattern parameter and click the Delete button. SONAR then asks you to confirm the deletion process.

4. Click OK. If you're replacing an existing groove pattern, SONAR will ask you to confirm the replacement process.

SONAR saves your new groove pattern inside the groove file that you selected (or created) under the name that you specified.

TIP

For examples of some cool applications for the Groove Quantize feature, look at the SONAR Help in the Editing MIDI Events and Controllers > Changing the Time of a Recording > Quantizing section.

Interpolate

Throughout the text of this book, I've mentioned the name SONAR quite a few times. What if I want to change all those instances of the phrase to SONAR 2.0 instead? Luckily, I'm using a word processing program on my computer, so all I would have to do is use the search and replace feature to have the program automatically make the changes for me. I mention this point because the Interpolate feature is similar to the search and replace feature you find in most word processing programs. The difference is that the Interpolate feature works with event properties, and in addition to simply searching and replacing, it can scale whole ranges of event properties from one set of values to another set of values. This means that you can easily transpose notes, change key signatures, convert one type of controller message into another type of controller message, and so on. It works like this:

1. Select the data that you want to change.

2. Choose Process > Interpolate to open the Event Filter - Search dialog box. You learned about this dialog box and its parameters in Chapter 5.

3. Set all the available parameters so that SONAR can select the exact Events that you want to process.

4. Click OK to open the Event Filter - Replace dialog box (see Figure 8.22). This dialog box is also almost the same as the Event Filter - Search dialog box. It has the same settings, except some of the settings are not available, because here you need to enter only the values to which you want to change the original selected data. So, enter the replacement values in the appropriate parameters.

Figure 8.22
In the Event Filter -
Replace dialog box,
you can enter the
replacement values
only for the data you're
trying to change

5. Click OK.

SONAR selects all the events in your initial selection according to the parameters you set
the in Event Filter - Search dialog box. It then changes the values of those events according
to the parameters you set in the Event Filter - Replace dialog box.

Interpolation Applications

You didn't think I was going to leave you high and dry trying to figure out such a complicated feature, did you? Actually, when you get the hang of it, using the Interpolate feature
isn't too difficult, especially if you're just trying to make straight replacements of data.
Anyway, the following sections describe some of the changes you can accomplish with
this feature.

Straight Replacement

If all you want to do is replace one value with another, setting up the parameters in both
dialog boxes is fairly easy. Say you want to change all the notes having a pitch of C#2
with notes having a pitch of D#7. To do so, set up the Event Filter - Search dialog box so
that only the Note option is activated in the Include section. Then type C#2 for both the
Key Min and Key Max parameters and click OK. In the Event Filter - Replace dialog box,
type D#7 for the Key Min and Key Max parameters and click OK. All the C#2 notes are then
changed to D#7 notes. Pretty easy, no? And you can use this approach with any of the data.
Earlier, I mentioned changing one type of controller message to another. Just use the
Control option along with the Number Min and Number Max parameters as you did with
the Note option and the Key Min and Key Max parameters.

TIP

You can also use wildcards when designating an octave number for the pitch of a note. In regards to the above example, say you want to change all the C# notes to D notes, not just the ones in octave 2 to octave 7. Instead of using C#2, you can use C#?, and instead of using D#7, you can use D#?. The ? is the wildcard, which stands for any octave.

Scaling Values

When you're working with ranges of values, you can use the Interpolate feature to scale them from one range to another. This capability is useful in limiting certain values to keep them within a set of boundaries. For example, some of the note velocities in one of your MIDI tracks may be a bit high, and you want to quiet them down a bit. Usually, quieting them would mean having to use the Piano Roll view to change them all one by one. With the Interpolate feature, you can compress their range down in a couple of easy steps. To do so, set up the Event Filter - Search dialog box so that only the Note option is activated in the Include section. Then type 0 for the Velocity Min and 127 for the Velocity Max and click OK. In the Event Filter - Replace dialog box, type 0 for the Velocity Min and 100 for the Velocity Max and click OK. All the note velocities are then scaled down from a range of 0 to 127 to a range of 0 to 100. See how it works? You can use this approach with any of the other value ranges, too.

Inverting Values

You also can invert any of the value ranges by reversing the Min and Max parameters. For example, what if you want to make all the loud volume controller messages soft and the soft volume controller messages loud? To do so, set up the Event Filter - Search dialog box so that only the Control option is activated in the Include section. Then type 7 (the number for volume controller messages) for both the Number Min and Number Max parameters. Also, type 0 for Value Min and 127 for Value Max and click OK. In the Event Filter - Replace dialog box, type 7 for both the Number Min and Number Max parameters. Also, type 127 for Value Min and 0 for Value Max and click OK. All the loud sections of your selected data then become soft and vice versa. Again, you can use this technique for any of the other value ranges.

As a matter of fact, you can change a whole bunch of different parameters at once (even mix straight replacement, scaling, and inverting) by activating the appropriate parameters in the Event Filter - Search dialog box. For instance, you could easily set up all three of the preceding examples so that you would have to use the Interpolate feature only one time to process the same data. This feature is very powerful. You should experiment with it as much as possible because, in the long run, it can save you a lot of editing time.

TIP

You also can find some other Interpolate application ideas in the SONAR Help file under the Editing MIDI Events and Controllers > Searching for Events > Event Filters section.

Length

The Length feature is one of the very simple but also very useful features provided in SONAR. Using it, you can change the size of a clip or group of selected data by specifying a percentage. It works like this:

1. Select the data that you want to change.

2. Choose Process > Length to open the Length dialog box (see Figure 8.23).

Figure 8.23

You can change the size of Clips or selected groups of Events by using the Length feature

3. Activate the Start Times, Durations, and/or Stretch Audio options. Activating the Start Times option makes the Length feature change the Start Times of the selected events so that the entire selection will change in size. Activating the Durations option makes the Length feature change the durations of the selected events. If you activate the Durations option without the Start Times option, the Length feature will change only the size of the durations of the selected events. This feature can be useful if you want to create a staccato effect for your notes. And if you want the length of your audio data to be changed, you can activate the Stretch Audio option.

4. Enter a value for the By Percent parameter. A value of 100 percent doesn't make any changes at all. A value of 50 percent changes the selection to half of its original length. And a value of 200 percent changes the selection to twice its original length.

5. Click OK.

SONAR changes the size of the clip(s) or entire selection of events according to your parameter specifications.

TIP
For a more intuitive way to change the length of your data (meaning you can enter a length using an actual time value instead of a percentage), use the Fit to Time feature, which you'll learn about later in this chapter.

Retrograde

The Retrograde feature works similarly to the Reverse feature that you learned about earlier in this chapter. Instead of reversing the data in audio clips, however, the Retrograde feature reverses MIDI data. This means you can have your MIDI data play backward if you apply this feature. Just select the data you want to reverse and then select Process > Retrograde. SONAR reverses the order of the selected events. In other words, if you were looking at the data via the Event view, the data is changed so that essentially the list is flipped upside down. That's about it.

Transpose

Transposition is a common occurrence when you're composing music, and SONAR's Transpose feature enables you to transpose quickly and easily. It works like this:

1. Select the data that you want to transpose.

2. Choose Process > Transpose to open the Transpose dialog box (see Figure 8.24).

Figure 8.24
By entering a number of steps, you can transpose the pitches of note Events up or down using the Transpose feature

3. You can use the Transpose feature to transpose the pitches of your note events either chromatically so that they can be changed by half steps or diatonically so that they remain in the current key signature of your project. If you want to transpose chromatically, leave the Diatonic Math option deactivated. If you want to transpose diatonically, activate the Diatonic Math option.

4. If you have selected any audio data, you can opt to have its pitch changed as well. To do so, activate the Transpose Audio option.

5. Enter a value for the Amount parameter. A positive value transposes up, and a negative value transposes down. If you are transposing chromatically, this value corresponds to half steps. If you are transposing diatonically, the Transpose feature changes the pitches of your notes according to the major scale of the current key signature. So, for example, if you enter a value of +1 and the key signature is D major, a D becomes an E, an E becomes an F#, and so on.

6. Click OK.

SONAR transposes the pitches of the notes (or audio) in the selected data according to your parameter settings.

TIP

SONAR includes an even more powerful transpose feature, but instead of being used as an editing function, it is used as an effect. I'll talk more about the transpose effect in chapter 11.

Scale Velocity

You learned about scaling the velocity values of events earlier in the description of the Interpolate feature. Using the Scale Velocity feature, you can do the same thing, but this feature has one extra option that enables you to scale the velocities by a percentage rather than enter exact values or a range of values. It works like this:

1. Select the data that you want to change.

2. Choose Process > Scale Velocity to open the Scale Velocity dialog box (see Figure 8.25).

Figure 8.25
You can scale the velocities of note Events by percentages if you use the Scale Velocity feature

3. If you want to scale the velocities by percentages, activate the Percentages option. Otherwise, the values that you enter will be exact velocity values.

4. Enter values for the Begin and End parameters. For example, you can use the Scale Velocity feature to create crescendos and decrescendos. To create a crescendo, enter a small value (such as 0 or 50 percent) for the Begin parameter and a larger value (such as 127 or 150 percent) for the End parameter. Do the opposite for a decrescendo.

5. Click OK.

SONAR scales the velocity values of the note events within the selected data according to your parameter settings.

TIP

You can create crescendos and decrescendos with more precise control by drawing them with the Draw Line tool in the Controller pane of the Piano Roll view. You learned how to use this tool in Chapter 7.

Fit to Time

As I mentioned earlier, the Fit to Time feature works similarly to the Length feature: Using it, you can change the size of clips and selected groups of data. But instead of having to use a percentage, you can specify an actual time (according to the Time Ruler) at which the data will end. For example, if you have a clip that begins at 1:01:000 and ends at 4:02:000, the Start time of the clip remains the same, but you can change the End time of the clip so that it stops playing at the exact moment you specify. This feature is great when you need to compose music to a precise length such as for a radio commercial or a video. It works like this:

1. Select the data that you want to change.

2. Choose Process > Fit to Time to open the Fit to Time dialog box (see Figure 8.26).

Figure 8.26
You can specify the
exact length of clips or
selected groups of
events by using the Fit
to Time feature

3. The Original Time Span section shows the beginning and end times for the selected data. In the Adjust to End at New Time section, enter a new end time for the selected data. You can enter either hours, minutes, seconds, and frames or measures, beats, and ticks. To change the format, click the Format button.

4. In the Modify by Changing section, activate either the Tempo Map option or the Event Times option. If you want the actual data to be changed (meaning the Start times of every event in the selection will be adjusted to accommodate the new end time), activate the Event Times option. If you would rather leave the data as it is and just have SONAR insert tempo changes into the project to accommodate the new end time, activate the Tempo Map option. The key difference here is that using the Tempo Map option affects the entire project, and all the data in all the tracks during the selected time will play at a different rate. If you want the data in only one track to be affected, you must use the Event Times option.

5. If you want to change the length of audio clips, you have to activate the Stretch Audio option.

6. Click OK.

SONAR either changes the length of the selected data or inserts tempo changes into the project (depending on your parameter settings) to accommodate the new end time that you specify.

Fit Improvisation

Having to play along with a metronome while recording in SONAR can be a nuisance sometimes. Depending on the type of music you are performing, using the metronome might not be conducive to your mood during the performance, which means you may end up with a less than acceptable recording. Some people just can't stand using a metronome. The problem is, if you don't use the metronome while recording in SONAR, your data will not line up correctly to the measure, beat, and tick values along the Time Ruler. Therefore, editing your music can be a lot more difficult.

If you are one of those people who hates metronomes, then you're in luck. SONAR allows you to record your MIDI tracks without using the metronome but still line up your data correctly after the fact by using the Fit Improvisation feature. This feature works by adding tempo changes to your Project according to an additional reference track that you must record. This reference track gives SONAR an idea of the tempo at which you were playing when you were recording your MIDI track without the metronome. The following is a more detailed version of how this feature works:

1. Record a MIDI track without using the metronome. For the most accurate results, try to play using as steady a tempo as possible.

2. Choose Options > Global to open the Global Options dialog box. Click the MIDI tab. Be sure only the Notes option in the Record section is activated. This filters out any extraneous events when you're recording your reference track so that they don't mess up the timing. The more accurate your reference track, the better. After you're done recording it, you can go back to the Global Options dialog box and change the options back to the way they were.

3. Record a reference MIDI track. To do so, simply tap out the tempo of your initial MIDI recording by hitting a key on your MIDI instrument for every beat. So, if you recorded a track in 4/4 time, you would have to hit the key four times for every measure of music you recorded. Also, be sure that the first note in your reference track has a Start time of 1:01:000 so that it starts at the very beginning of the project. You can adjust it manually by using the Event view or Piano Roll view if you have to.

4. Select the reference track.

TIP

If you record your reference track in several takes, resulting in multiple clips rather than one long clip for a single take, combine the multiple clips into one using the Bounce To Clips function before choosing the Fit Improvisation command.

5. Choose Process > Fit Improvisation.

SONAR scans your reference track, analyzing where the beats fall, and adds tempo changes to your project so that the data in your recorded track lines up with the measure, beat, and tick values on the Time Ruler. Now you can edit your data just as you would any other data that was recorded along with the metronome.

9

Composing with Loops

In addition to creating music by recording and editing your MIDI and audio performances, SONAR allows you to compose music with *sample loops*. Sample loops are short (though not always) audio recordings that you can piece together to create whole musical performances. Using them is a great way to add some acoustic audio tracks to your project without having to actually do any recording or having to know how to play an instrument. For example, you can buy a CD full of sample loops that contain nothing but acoustic drum beats. Not only can you buy drum loops, but you can also get real guitar solos, vocal chorus recordings, orchestral recordings, and more. You can create a whole project just by using sample loops, and SONAR even provides you with the tools to create your own loops. In this chapter, I'll tell you about all the loop-based features that SONAR provides, including the following:

▶ Groove clips
▶ Creating and saving Groove clips
▶ The Loop Construction view
▶ Working with Groove clips
▶ The Loop Explorer view
▶ Project pitch and pitch markers

Groove Clips

In SONAR, sample loops are known as Groove clips. If you're familiar with Sonic Foundry's ACID software, you won't have any trouble with Groove clips, since they are Cakewalk's equivalent to Sonic Foundry's loops for ACID. Like loops for ACID, Groove clips automatically take care of the sometimes tedious chore of matching the playback tempo and pitch of each loop you use in a song. This is because Groove clips are sample loops with extra information stored within them that lets SONAR know their basic tempo, pitch, and playback properties. SONAR can then accurately shift the tempo and pitch of the Groove clips so that they match the tempo and pitch of the current project. Why is this important? Because not all sample loops are recorded at the same tempo and pitch, and in order to use them in the same song, they have to "groove" with one another, so to speak. Before loops for ACID or Groove clips came along, a musician would have to match the tempo and pitch of multiple loops manually, and, let me tell you, it's not a fun task. Of course, not all sample loops contain the extra information I mentioned earlier. Plain sample loops need to be converted into Groove clips before you can use them within a SONAR project. But don't worry—it's not nearly as difficult as you might think.

Creating Groove Clips

As a matter of fact, any audio clip in SONAR can easily be converted into a Groove clip with a few clicks of your mouse. To convert a regular audio clip into a Groove clip, do the following:

1. Right-click an audio clip in the Clips pane of the Track view and choose Clip Properties from the pop-up menu to open the Clip Properties dialog box.

2. Click the Groove-Clips tab to display the Groove Clips parameters (see Figure 9.1).

Figure 9.1
Use the Clip Properties dialog box to convert an audio clip into a Groove clip

3. Activate the Enable Looping option. That's basically all you need to do, but there are some extra parameters that you need to deal with if you want some extra control over how SONAR will handle your new Groove clip.

TIP
Instead of opening the Clip Properties dialog box to enable looping for an audio clip, you can just right-click the clip and choose Groove-Clip Looping from the pop-up menu. You can also just select the clip (or multiple clips) and press Ctrl+L on your computer keyboard. These methods are quicker, but they don't give you access to the extra parameters.

4. When you activate the Enable Looping option for a clip, SONAR automatically activates the Stretch To Project Tempo parameter and makes a guess as to how many rhythmic beats are in the clip and the original tempo of the clip. If the beats are inaccurate, you can change the number of beats for the clip by entering a new number in the Beats In Clip parameter. These parameters must be accurate for SONAR to be able to change the playback tempo of the clip to follow the tempo of your project.

5. In addition to changing the tempo of the clip, SONAR can also change the pitch of the clip to follow the pitch of the project. This ensures that Groove clips stay in tune with one another within the same project. If you want SONAR to control the pitch of the clip, activate the Follow Project Pitch option.

TIP

Not all Groove clips should follow the pitch of the project. Why? Well, if you have a Groove clip that contains percussive data like a drum instrument performance, you don't want the pitch of that clip to change, because it will just make the drum performance sound strange. For these types of Groove clips, only the Stretch To Project Tempo option should be activated. The Follow Project Pitch option should be activated only for clips containing pitch-related performances such as guitar, bass, woodwinds, horns, strings, vocals, and the like.

6. When you activate the Follow Project Pitch option, you have to tell SONAR the original pitch of the material in the clip. SONAR doesn't automatically determine the pitch for you. To tell SONAR the original pitch of the clip, choose a pitch from the Reference Note drop-down list. For example, if the notes played in the clip are based on a C chord, choose C in the Reference Note drop-down list. How do you know the original pitch of the clip? You'll have to figure it out by listening to it.

7. If you want to transpose the pitch of the clip so that it plays differently from the project pitch, you can enter a value (measured in semitones) for the Pitch parameter. This parameter can come in handy if you are composing with orchestral instrument loops that need to be played in a different key.

8. If the pitch of the clip is slightly out of tune, you can adjust it by entering a value (measured in Cents) for the Fine Pitch parameter.

9. Click OK.

SONAR will now treat your original audio clip as a Groove clip. If the tempo or pitch of the project changes (I'll talk more about this later), the Groove clip will be stretched and transposed accordingly. In addition, you'll notice that in the Track view, a regular audio clip is shown as a rectangle, but when a clip is converted into a Groove clip, it is shown as a rectangle with rounded corners (see Figure 9.2).

CHAPTER 9

Figure 9.2
A Groove clip is
indicated as a rectangle
with rounded corners

The Loop Construction View

Of course, there may be times when SONAR doesn't seem to stretch your Groove clips
accurately. If this occurs, you'll hear slight anomalies in the audio when you change the
tempo of your project. To correct this, you can try using the Loop Construction view to
convert your audio clip. To utilize the Loop Construction view, do the following:

1. Right-click the audio clip in the Clips pane of the Track view, and choose
   View > Loop Construction (or double click the clip) to open the Loop
   Construction view (see Figure 9.3).

Figure 9.3
Instead of the Clip
Properties dialog
box, use the Loop
Construction view to
convert your clips

2. Along the top of the view, you'll see a toolbar containing all of the same parameters found in the Clip Properties dialog box. From left to right are the Save Loop To WAV File function (more about this later); Enable Looping option; the Beats In Clip parameter; the Enable Stretching option (which is the same as the Stretch To Project Tempo option); the Orig. BPM parameter (which is the same as the Original Tempo parameter); the Follow Project Pitch option; the Root Note parameter (same as the Reference Note parameter); and the Pitch parameters (same as the Pitch and Fine Pitch parameters. You can set these parameters as explained in the previous section.

3. The last three toolbar parameters are Stop Preview, Preview Loop, and Preview Bus. The Preview Loop and Stop Preview parameters let you listen to the loop currently displayed in the Loop Construction view. The Preview Bus parameter lets you choose which virtual main will be used to play the loop. I'll talk more about virtual mains in Chapter 12.

4. You'll also notice a second toolbar as well as the audio waveform of the loop currently displayed in the Loop Construction view. I'll talk more about the second toolbar in a minute. For now, notice that when you activate the Enable Looping option, SONAR automatically adjusts two of the parameters in the second toolbar and adds vertical lines to the audio waveform (see Figure 9.4). These lines are slicing markers. Slicing markers designate a specific place in a loop where the timing data needs to be preserved when the timing of the loop is being stretched in order to fit the project tempo. The slicing markers make it so that a loop can be stretched without having its pitch change at the same time.

Figure 9.4
SONAR uses slicing markers to maintain the audio quality of a loop when it is stretched

NOTE
Normally when you stretch (change the length of) audio data, the pitch is changed as well. Make the data shorter, and the pitch is raised. Make the data longer, and the pitch is lowered. By slicing the data into smaller pieces, the data can be stretched very accurately, preserving its original quality without changing its pitch. This slicing happens in real-time during playback, and it's non-destructive (meaning the original data is not changed).

5. To control the way that SONAR automatically adds slicing markers to your loop, you need to adjust the Basic Slicing and the Trans Detect (short for Transient Detection) sliders, which are located in the second toolbar. The Basic Slicing slider works by placing slicing markers at specific rhythmic locations in the loop according to the Beats In Clip parameter (mentioned earlier). For example, if you set the Basic Slicing slider to Eighth Notes, slicing markers will be placed at every eighth note location in your loop. If your loop contains four beats, it will have seven slicing markers. You would think there should be eight slicing markers—since there are two eighth notes to every beat and two multiplied by four is eight—but the beginning of a loop never needs a slicing marker, so there is one fewer than expected. When adjusting the Basic Slicing slider, it's usually best to go with a note value equal to the smallest rhythmic value in your audio data performance. For example, if your loop contains sixteenth notes, try setting the Basic Slicing slider to 16th Notes. You can also try a setting that is one value lower, which in this case would be eighth notes. Just be aware that too few or too many slicing markers will introduce unwanted artifacts into the audio when your loops are being stretched.

6. When adjusting the Trans Detect slider, slicing markers are placed at the beginning of detected transients in the audio data of the loop. Transients are large spikes (big changes in volume) in the audio waveform. Because of this, the Trans Detect slider works best when working with percussive material. A setting of about 90 percent usually works well. And you'll usually want to use a combination of the Basic Slicing and Trans Detect sliders to get the optimum number of slicing markers set up in your loop.

7. If the Basic Slicing and Trans Detect sliders don't provide enough Slicing Markers or provide the wrong placement, you can use the Select, Erase Marker, and Default All Markers tools to create, erase, and adjust the slicing markers manually. The first three buttons in the second toolbar correspond to the Select, Erase Marker, and Default All Markers tools, respectively. Use the Select tool to move existing slicing markers by clicking and dragging the marker triangles in the marker area above the audio wave-form display (see Figure 9.5). You can also use the Select tool to create your own slicing markers by simply double-clicking in the marker area. Manually made or changed markers are shown with a blue triangle.

Figure 9.5
Use the Select tool to create or move slicing markers

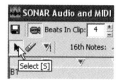

8. To erase a slicing marker, just choose the Erase Marker tool and click the triangle of the slicing marker that you want to erase.

9. If you moved any of the automatically created slicing markers and you want to put them back to their original positions, just click the Default All Markers button. If you created any slicing markers manually, those markers will remain untouched.

10. Once you are finished adjusting all the parameters for your new Groove clip, close the Loop Construction view.

You can usually rely on the automatic settings that SONAR provides, but just in case, it's good to know that you have total control over how your Groove clips are handled.

Saving Groove Clips

When you create Groove clips within a SONAR project, those clips are saved along with the project, but what if you want to use your Groove clips in another project? Or maybe you'd like to share the clips with your friends? This is where the Save Loop To WAV File function (mentioned earlier) comes in handy. The Save Loop To WAV File function lets you save your Groove clips to disk as a special WAV file. Unlike most ordinary WAV files (that just contain audio data), the Groove clip WAV files contain all the special looping information that I talked about earlier. Here's how it works:

1. With your Groove clip still open in the Loop Construction view, click the Save Loop To WAV File button to open the Save As dialog box.

2. Use the Save In drop-down list to navigate to the location on your disk drive to which you want to save the file.

3. Type in a name for the file in the File Name parameter.

4. Click Save.

Your Groove clip is saved to disk as a WAV file that contains the audio data for the clip plus all the looping information that you set, such as the Beats In Clip, Root Note, Pitch, and slicing markers. The next time the clip is opened, this information will automatically be loaded as well.

CHAPTER 9

Working with Groove Clips

Once you've created your Groove clips, you can use them to compose music in a current project or to create an entirely new project altogether. Composing with Groove clips involves a combination of dragging and dropping to add clips to a project and slip editing to make the clips conform to music you are trying to create.

TIP

You can also export multiple Groove clips at once by using the File > Save As function. In the Save As dialog box, activate the Copy All Audio With Project and Create One File Per Clip options. Any Groove clips in your project will then be saved as ACID-compatible WAV files.

The Loop Explorer View

If you have some Groove clips stored on disk in the WAV file format, you can use the Loop Explorer view to add them to your project. The Loop Explorer view lets you examine and preview your stored Groove clips as well as add them to your project via dragging and dropping with your mouse. To use the Loop Explorer view, do the following:

1. Choose View > Loop Explorer to open the Loop Explorer view (see Figure 9.6). The Loop Explorer view is very similar to the Windows Explorer.

Figure 9.6
Use the Loop Explorer view to add existing Groove clips to your project

2. In the Folders pane, navigate to the folder on your disk drive that contains your Groove clip files. Then select the folder. Its contents are then displayed in the File pane.

3. Your Groove clip files can be displayed as large or small icons, a list of file names, or a detailed list of file names. Just use the Views drop-down list to choose your option (see Figure 9.7).

Figure 9.7
Use the Views drop-down list to choose the Groove clip file display option

4. To preview a Groove clip, select its file in the File pane and then click the Play button in the Loop Explorer view toolbar. To stop playback, click the Stop button. If you would like a file to start playing automatically as soon as you select it, activate the Auto-Preview option (see Figure 9.8). As in the Loop Construction view, you can choose which virtual main to use for the loop playback. I'll talk more about virtual mains in Chapter 12.

Figure 9.8
Use the Play, Stop, and Auto-Preview options to preview a Groove clip file

5. To add a Groove clip to a project, just drag and drop the clip from the Loop Explorer view into the clips pane of the Track view. If you drag the clip onto an existing track, the clip will be added to that track. If you drag the clip onto a blank area of the Clips pane, a new track containing the clip will be created for you. Also, depending on the horizontal position to which you drag and drop, the clip will be added to the track at the closest measure position in the track. For example, if you drag and drop the clip anywhere inside of measure two within the track, the clip will be added to the track with its beginning at the beginning of measure two.

6. You can keep the Loop Explorer view open for as long as you need to continue dragging and dropping Groove clips into your project.

After you've added your Groove clips, you can slip edit them to make them conform to the music you are trying to create. I talked about slip editing back in Chapter 7, but, later in this chapter, I'll give you an example of how to use the technique with Groove clips.

TIP
You can also add Groove clips to a project by using the Import Audio feature. I talked about this feature back in Chapter 6.

CHAPTER 9

Project Pitch

Controlling the pitch of the Groove clips in your project is extremely easy. The first thing you need to do is set the default pitch for the entire project. This is called the project pitch. To set the project pitch, do the following:

1. Make sure the Markers toolbar is visible by choosing View > Toolbars. Then activate the Markers option and click Close.

2. In the Markers toolbar, use the Default Groove-Clip Pitch drop-down list to set the initial pitch for your project (see Figure 9.9). For example, if you want the music in your project to start using a C chord, choose C in the Default Groove-Clip Pitch drop-down list.

Figure 9.9
Use the Default Groove-Clip Pitch drop-down list to set the initial pitch of your project

Pitch Markers

Once you've set the initial pitch for your project, all the Groove clips will automatically be transposed to play using that pitch until you change it. To change the project pitch at specified points within your project, you need to use pitch markers. I talked about markers back in Chapter 5, and while pitch markers work almost the same as regular markers, they do have a slight difference.

Create Pitch Markers

Creating pitch markers is essentially the same as creating regular markers. You simply set the Now time to the measure, beat, and tick at which you want to place the marker in the project, activate the Marker dialog box, and type in a name. But you also have to designate a pitch setting for that marker, which tells SONAR to change the project pitch at that point in the project. To create a pitch marker, just do the following:

1. Set the Now time to the measure, beat, and tick or the SMPTE time at which you want to place the marker in the object.

2. Select Insert > Marker to open the Marker dialog box (see Figure 9.10). You can also open the Marker dialog box in one of these ways: by pressing F11 on your computer keyboard; holding the Ctrl key on your computer keyboard and clicking just above the Time Ruler (the Marker section) in the Track,

Staff, or Piano Roll views; right-clicking in a Time Ruler; clicking on the Insert Marker button in the Markers toolbar; or clicking on the Insert Marker button in the Markers view.

Figure 9.10
Using the Marker dialog box, you can create a pitch marker

3. Type a name for the marker.
4. If you want the marker to be assigned to a measure/beat/tick value, you don't need to do anything more.
5. If you want the marker to be assigned to a SMPTE time, activate the Lock To SMPTE (Real World) Time option.

NOTE

If you use the Lock To SMPTE (Real World) Time value, your marker is assigned an exact hour/minute/second and frame value. It retains that value no matter what. So, even if you change the tempo of the project, the marker keeps the same time value, although its measure/beat/tick location may change because of the tempo. This feature is especially handy when you're putting music and sound to video and you need to have cues that always happen at an exact moment within the project.

By leaving a marker assigned to a measure/beat/tick value, however, you can be sure that it will always occur at that measure, beat, and tick even if you change the tempo of the project.

6. Assign a pitch to the marker using the Groove-Clip Pitch drop-down list.
7. Click OK.

When you're finished, your pitch marker (and its pitch) is added to the marker section (just above the Time Ruler) in the Track, Staff, and Piano Roll views.

TIP

Usually, you add markers to a project while no real-time activity is going on, but you can also add markers while a project is playing. Simply press the F11 key on your computer keyboard, and SONAR creates a marker at the current Now time. The new marker is automatically assigned a temporary name, which you can later change. You also need to add a pitch to each marker after you stop playback, because SONAR will not automatically assign pitches to markers.

Name Change

To change the name of a pitch marker, follow these steps:

1. Right-click the marker in the Marker section of the Time Ruler in one of the views to open the Marker dialog box. Alternatively, select View > Markers to open the Markers view, and double-click the marker in the list to open the Marker dialog box.

2. Type a new name for the marker.

3. Click OK.

Time Change

Follow these steps to change the time value of a pitch marker numerically:

1. Right-click the marker in the Marker section of the Time Ruler in one of the views to open the Marker dialog box. Alternatively, select View > Markers to open the Markers view and double-click the marker in the list to open the Marker dialog box.

2. Type a new measure/beat/tick value for the marker. If you want to use an SMPTE value, activate the Lock To SMPTE (Real World) Time option and then type a new hour/minute/second/frame value for the marker.

3. Click OK.

You can also change the time value of a pitch marker graphically by simply dragging the marker within the marker section of the Time Ruler in one of the views with your mouse. Drag the marker to the left to decrease its time value or drag it to the right to increase its time value. Simple, no?

Make a Copy

To make a copy of a pitch marker, follow these steps:

1. Hold down the Ctrl key on your computer keyboard.

2. Click and drag a pitch marker in the Marker section of the Time Ruler in one of the Views to a new time location.

3. Release the Ctrl key and mouse button. SONAR displays the Marker dialog box.

4. Enter a name for the marker. You can also change the time by typing a new value if you'd like. The time value is initially set to the time corresponding to the location on the Time Ruler to which you dragged the marker.

5. Click OK.

Delete a Pitch Marker

You can delete a marker in one of two ways—either directly in the Track, Staff, or Piano Roll views or via the Marker view. Here's the exact procedure:

1. If you want to use the Track, Staff, or Piano Roll views, click and hold the left mouse button on the marker that you want to delete.

2. If you want to use the Markers view, select View > Markers to open the Markers view. Then select the marker that you want to delete from the list.

3. Press the Delete key on your computer keyboard.

A Groove Clip Exercise

Now that I've talked about how to create Groove clips and how to use them in a project, let's put that knowledge to practical use by working through a detailed exercise so that you can actually see Groove clips in action. Are you ready? Let's go:

1. Start SONAR. A blank new project should open automatically. If not, then choose File > New and choose the Normal template from the New Project File dialog box to create one.

2. If there are any tracks in the project, delete them. You should now have a totally blank Track view.

3. Set the Default Project Pitch to C and set the tempo for the project to 114 bpm. Also activate the Snap to Grid feature and, in the Snap to Grid dialog box, choose the Musical Time: Measure options and Move To mode.

4. Choose File > Open and open the demo project that comes with SONAR called SONAR Audio and MIDI Demo2.cwb.

5. If the File Info window appears, close it. Then choose Window > Tile In Rows to adjust the view layout so you can see the Track views from both projects.

6. Drag-and-drop the first clip in Track 1 from the demo project into your new project. If the Drag and Drop Options dialog box appears, click OK. SONAR will automatically create a new track for the clip. Make sure the clip is positioned at the very beginning of the track (see Figure 9.11). Zoom in a bit so that you can see the data in the clip.

Figure 9.11
Drag-and-drop the clip
to the beginning of the
new track

7. Drag-and-drop the clip in Track 1 at measure 6 from the demo project into Track 1 of your new project. Position the start of this clip at measure 2 and slip edit the clip so that its end extends to the beginning of measure 12 (see Figure 9.12). If the Drag and Drop Options dialog box appears, choose the Slide Over Old To Make Room option and activate Align To Measures. Then click OK.

Figure 9.12
Slip edit the clip in
Track 1 to extend its
end to measure 12

8. Drag-and-drop the clip in Track 1 at measure 13 from the demo project into Track 1 of your new project. Position the start of this clip at measure 12. If the Drag and Drop Options dialog box appears, choose the Slide Over Old To Make Room option and activate Align To Measures. Then click OK.

9. Drag-and-drop the clip (named Kick and Crash) in Track 1 at measure 37 from the demo project into Track 1 of your new project. Position the start of this clip at measure 13. If the Drag and Drop Options dialog box appears, choose the Slide Over Old To Make Room option and activate Align To Measures. Then click OK. Track 1 in your new project now contains all the drum parts (see Figure 9.13). Play the project to hear what it sounds like so far.

Figure 9.13
Track 1 contains all the drum parts for the project

10. Close the SONAR Audio and MIDI Demo2 project. Then pop your SONAR CD into your CD-ROM drive and open the Loop Explorer. Navigate to the Audio Loops\Smart Loops\Electric Guitars\Mid Tempo loops folder.

11. Drag-and-drop the Shorty 1 C maj.wav file from the Loop Explorer into your new project. Drop the clip somewhere underneath Track 1 in the new project so that SONAR will create a new track (Track 2, Shorty 1). Position the start of the clip at measure 2. Widen the track so that you can see the data in the clip.

12. Slip edit the clip in Track 2 so that its end goes to the beginning of measure 13. Play the song. Sounds kind of dull, huh? Okay, let's add some pitch markers.

13. Place pitch markers at the beginning of measures 2, 6, 8, 10, 11, and 12. Give these markers the following pitches respectively: C, F, C, G, F, C. Your project should now look like what is shown in Figure 9.14.

Figure 9.14
Place some pitch markers to make the project more interesting

14. Play the project. Sounds better, right? The guitar doesn't sound quite right when it's transposed to G in measure 10, though, does it? SONAR seems to be transposing down instead of up. Normally, there's no way around this by just using pitch markers. Instead, we need to create a Groove-Clip that is independent of the project pitch. Slip edit the clip in Track 2 so that its end goes to the beginning of measure 10 rather than 13. Drag another copy of the Shorty 1 C maj.wav file from the Loop Explorer into Track 2, and position the start of the clip at measure 10. Now right-click the clip and choose Clip Properties > Groove-Clips. Deactivate the Follow Project Pitch option and enter a value of 7 for the Pitch parameter. This will transpose the clip up 7 semitones to G, and it won't be affected by the project pitch. Click OK.

15. Drag another copy of the Shorty 1 C maj.wav file from the Loop Explorer into Track 2, and position the start of the clip at measure 11. Then slip edit the clip so that its end goes to the beginning of measure 13. Ah, now that sounds better.

16. Let's add a bass track by navigating to the Audio Loops\Smart Loops\Bass Guitars\Mid Tempo Loops folder in the Loop Explorer. Now drag the Straight Slap 2 D.wav file into your new project. Drop the clip somewhere underneath Track 2 so that SONAR will create a new track (Track 3, Straight Slap). Position the start of the clip at measure 2. Widen the track so that you can see the data in the clip.

17. Slip edit the clip in Track 3 so that its end goes to the beginning of measure 13. Play the song. Cool! Now it's starting to sound like a real song. There's still one thing missing, though.

18. Close the Loop Explorer. Then open another sample project that comes with SONAR called Don't Matter Audio and MIDI Demo.cwb. Close the File Info window, as well as the Staff view. Also, choose Window > Tile In Rows to reposition the Track views.

19. Drag-and-drop the first clip in Track 6 (Horns Left) from the demo project into your new project. Drop the clip somewhere underneath Track 3 in the new project so that SONAR will create a new track (Track 4, Horns Left). Position the start of the clip at measure 3. Widen the track so that you can see the data in the clip. Also, make sure that the panning for the track is set to 100 percent left.

20. Right-click the new clip in Track 4 and choose Clip Properties to open the Clip Properties dialog box. Click the Groove-Clips tab. Activate the Enable Looping option. Activate the Follow Project Pitch option. Choose D in the Reference Note drop-down list. Click OK.

21. Select the Horns Left clip and choose View > Loop Construction to open the clip in the Loop Construction view. Adjust the Trans Detect slider to a value of 90 percent. Then adjust the Basic Slicing slider to a value of 16th Notes. Close the Loop Construction view.

22. Copy the Horns Left clip (using the Edit > Copy feature) and then paste (using the Edit > Paste feature) copies of the clip at the following measures: 6, 8, and 10. Now slip edit the clip in measure 10 so that its end extends to measure 12. The Horns Left track should look like what is shown in Figure 9.15.

Figure 9.15
Copy and paste the clips in the Horns Left track

23. Drag-and-drop the first clip in Track 7 (Horns Right) from the demo project into your new project. Drop the clip somewhere underneath Track 4 in the new project so that SONAR will create a new track (Track 5, Horns Right). Position the start of the clip at measure 3. Widen the track so that you can see the data in the clip. Also, make sure that the panning for the track is set to 100 percent right.

24. Right-click the new clip in Track 5 and choose Clip Properties to open the Clip Properties dialog box. Click the Groove-Clips tab. Activate the Enable Looping option. Activate the Follow Project Pitch option. Choose D in the Reference Note drop-down list. Click OK.

25. Select the Horns Right Clip and choose View > Loop Construction to open the clip in the Loop Construction view. Adjust the Trans Detect slider to a value of 90 percent. Then adjust the Basic Slicing slider to a value of 16th Notes. Close the Loop Construction view.

26. Copy the Horns Right clip (using the Edit > Copy feature) and then paste (using the Edit > Paste feature) copies of the clip at the following measures: 6, 8, and 10. Now slip edit the clip in measure 10 so that its end extends to measure 12.

27. The final version of your new project should look like what is shown in Figure 9.16.

CHAPTER 9

Figure 9.16
The final version of our example project should look like this

28.   Play the project. Sounds cool, no?

Now you have a good working knowledge of how to use Groove clips. You can add to this exercise by creating more tracks and inserting more clips. Don't forget that you can also change the mix by adjusting the volume and pan parameters for each track. Plus, since these are audio tracks, you can apply real-time effects as well. For more information on effects, read Chapter 11.

TIP

Change the tempo of the example project to 120 bpm. Play the project. Isn't that great? SONAR automatically adjusts the Groove clips so that they will play at the correct speed whenever you change the tempo of the project.

10

Software Synthesis

In Chapter 1, I talked about the differences between MIDI and digital audio. MIDI is simply performance data. MIDI data alone does not produce any sound. In order to have sound produced from your MIDI data, you need a MIDI instrument. Usually, a MIDI instrument comes in the form of a MIDI synthesizer keyboard or module. These are hardware-based synthesizers. Today, however, personal computers have become so powerful that it is now possible to simulate a MIDI synthesizer via a computer software program. This process is known as software synthesis, and basically it has the power to turn your computer into a full-fledged MIDI synthesizer module. SONAR has built-in software synthesis features. In this chapter, I'll tell you all about the software synthesis features that SONAR provides, including the following:

► DX Instruments

► Setting up and playing DX Instruments

► The Virtual Sound Canvas

► The DreamStation

► The Cyclone

► The DR-008

► The ReValver

► SoundFonts and LiveSynth Pro

► ReWire Instruments

DX instruments (DXi's for short) are a new technology developed by Cakewalk based on Microsoft's DirectX technology. DXi's come in the form of plug-ins that can simulate any kind of hardware-based synthesizer module. As a matter of fact, many DXi's have interfaces that look like on-screen versions of a hardware-based synth, with all kinds of knobs and switches that can be tweaked with your mouse. Because DXi's are plug-ins, they can be used interchangeably within SONAR just like effects plug-ins (see Chapter 11 for more information about effects).

NOTE
In basic terms, a *plug-in* is a small computer program that, by itself, does nothing but, when used with a larger application, provides added functionality to the larger program. You, therefore, can use plug-ins to easily add new features to a program. In SONAR's case, plug-ins provide you with additional ways to produce music through the use of DXi's.

What's more, DXi's are based on standard computer code known as DirectX. SONAR enables you to use any audio plug-ins that are DirectX-compatible. DirectX is a special computer code built into Windows that controls all its multimedia functions, such as playing audio and video. This means that, in addition to the DXi's that come included with SONAR, many more will be available for purchase from other third-party vendors.

Using DX Instruments

Using a DXi to generate music is just like using a hardware-based synth, except that, because a DXi is software-based, it is run on your computer as an application from within SONAR. You control the settings of a DXi by tweaking on-screen parameters. You can generate sound with a DXi either in real-time, as you perform on your MIDI keyboard, or by using data from a pre-existing MIDI track. To use a DXi in your SONAR project, do the following:

1. Create a new project or open a pre-existing project.

2. Right-click in the Track pane of the Track view and choose Insert Audio Track to create a new audio track. Then widen the track to display its parameters.

3. Set the In parameter to None, and set the Out parameter to one of your sound card outputs.

4. Right-click in the Fx parameter of the audio track and choose DXi Synth > (name of the DXi you want to use) to set up a DXi for that track (see Figure 10.1). If you ever want to remove a DXi, just right-click its name in the Fx parameter and choose Delete from the pop-up menu.

Figure 10.1
To use a DXi, add it to
the Fx parameter of an
audio track

NOTE

Even though DXi's are software-based, they still need to use a sound card output
(which is hardware) in order to generate sound. Adding a DXi to an audio track
allows the DXi to use the output of the track to generate sound. You can also add
DXi's to the aux bus and main Fx bins. For more information about aux buses
and mains, read Chapter 12.

5. After you add a DXi to the Fx parameter of the audio track, the window for
    that DXi appears showing the Property Page (or control interface) of the
    DXi (see Figure 10.2). Using those controls, you can set up the DXi's para-
    meters, such as the sounds it will produce, and so on. After you've finished
    setting the DXi's parameters, you can close the window to get it out of the
    way. If you need to access the DXi's controls again, just double-click the
    name of the DXi in the Fx parameter of the audio track.

Figure 10.2
When added to the Fx
parameter, a window
appears showing all the
controls available for
the DXi that you chose

6. If you opened a pre-existing project that already contains MIDI tracks, you can skip this step. Otherwise, right-click in the Track pane of the Track view and choose Insert MIDI Track to create a new MIDI track. Then widen the track to display its parameters.

7. Set the In parameter to the MIDI channel being used to receive data from your MIDI keyboard. Then click the Out parameter to display a list of available outputs. In addition to your MIDI interface outputs, the list will also show any DXi's that you have previously set up (see Figure 10.3). Choose the DXi that you want to use.

Figure 10.3
After you set up a DXi, it will be displayed in the Out parameter list of your MIDI track

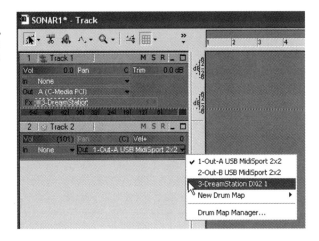

8. Set the Ch (channel), Bnk (bank), and Pch (patch) parameters for the MIDI track. The settings you choose for these parameters depend on the DXi that you are using. For the Ch parameter, choose the same channel to which the DXi is set. The Bnk and Pch parameters automatically display different settings depending on the DXi. The parameters will show what sound presets the DXi has available. Choose the bank and patch that correspond to the sound that you want to use.

9. Either start performing some music on your MIDI keyboard or start playback of the project. Whichever action you choose, you should hear sound coming from the DXi.

NOTE

When you use a DXi in real-time by performing on your MIDI keyboard, you might hear a delay between the time you press a key on your keyboard and the time it takes for the DXi to produce sound. This is caused by sound card latency. In order to prevent this delay, you need to use WDM drivers for your sound card, and you also need to adjust the Latency slider to its lowest possible setting. I talked about WDM drivers and latency in chapters 2 and 3.

Those are the basic steps you need to take in order to use DXi's in your projects.

The Insert DXi Synth Function

There is actually an easier way to add a DXi to a project, but I wanted to be sure you knew everything that was needed to add one manually. And it allowed me to explain the process in more detail as well. More often than not, however, you'll probably use the Insert DXi Synth function. This function allows you to automatically add a DXi to a project along with the accompanying audio and MIDI tracks needed for the DXi. Here is how the Insert DXi Synth function works:

1. Create a new project or open a pre-existing project.

2. Choose Insert > DXi Synth > (name of the DXi you want to use) to open the Insert DXi Synth Options dialog box (see Figure 10.4).

Figure 10.4
Use the Insert DXi
Synth function as a
quick way to add a
DXi to a project

3. In the Create These Tracks section, activate the MIDI Source Track option if you want a MIDI track for your DXi to be automatically created.

4. In the Create These Tracks section, activate either the First Synth Output (Audio) option or the All Synth Outputs (Audio) option if you want the audio track(s) for your DXi to be automatically created.

NOTE
Some DXi's provide multiple audio outputs, similar to some hardware-based synthesizers. This gives you more control over how the sounds of the DXi are processed and routed. For example, if a DXi can produce 16 different instrument sounds at the same time and has 4 outputs (like the Virtual Sound Canvas DXi, which I will talk about later), you can group those 16 instruments into 4 different sections and send them to their own outputs. This means you could send all drum sounds to one output, all guitar sounds to another output, etc. You could then apply different effects to each out (or group of sounds). Each output of a DXi requires its own audio track. So, if you choose the All Synth Outputs option in the Insert DXi Synth Options dialog box, and the DXi provides 4 outputs, then 4 separate audio tracks will be created.

5. In the Open These Windows section, activate the Synth Property Page option if you want the DXi's Property Page (or control interface) to be opened after the DXi is added to the project.

6. In the Open These Windows section, activate the Synth Rack View option if you want the Synth Rack View (which I will talk about shortly) to be opened after the DXi is added to the project.

7. Click OK. The DXi you chose is added to the project along with the MIDI track and audio track(s) depending on the options you activated in the Insert DXi Synth Options dialog box.

8. If you chose to have a MIDI track automatically created for you, you still need to set the track parameters. Set the Ch (channel), Bnk (bank), and Pch (patch) parameters for the MIDI track as I described in the previous section of this chapter.

9. Either start performing some music on your MIDI keyboard or start playback of the project. Whichever action you choose, you should hear sound coming from the DXi.

Don't worry if the instructions in the last two sections seem a bit generic. I'll provide some more specific examples on how to use the DXi's that come included with SONAR a little later. Before we get to that, let me tell you about the Synth Rack view.

The Synth Rack View

When you add a DXi to a project, the DXi is listed as an entry in SONAR's Synth Rack view (see Figure 10.5).

Figure 10.5
All DXi's in a project are listed in the Synth Rack view

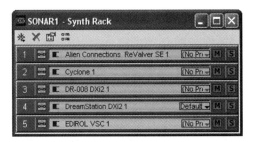

The Synth Rack view allows you to manage all the DXi's in a project by letting you add, remove, and change DXi's, as well as manipulate their properties.

Adding a DXi

To add a DXi to a project using the Synth Rack view, just click the Insert DXi Instruments And Rewire Devices button (see Figure 10.6). Then choose a DXi from the pop-up menu. This will open the Insert DXi Synth Options dialog box. From here you can follow the same steps as shown in the Insert DXi Synth Function section of this chapter.

Figure 10.6
Use the Insert DXi
instruments and
Rewire devices
button to add a
DXi to a project via
the Synth Rack

Removing a DXi

To remove a DXi from a project using the Synth Rack view, select the DXi you want to remove by clicking on its number in the Rack. Then click the Delete button (see Figure 10.7).

Figure 10.7
Use the Delete button
to remove a DXi from
a project via the
Synth Rack

NOTE

If there are any MIDI or audio tracks associated with the deleted DXi, they will not be removed from the project. You have to delete those tracks manually if you no longer want them in the project.

DXi Properties

To access the Property Page (or control interface) of a DXi via the Synth Rack view, select the DXi by clicking on its number. Then click the Properties button (see Figure 10.8).

Figure 10.8
Use the Properties
button to access a DXi's
Property Page via the
Synth Rack

TIP

You can also just double-click the number of a DXi in the Synth Rack to open the DXi's Property Page.

Synth Rack Parameters

When a DXi is listed in the Synth Rack, the DXi is shown using a graphical representation that has a number of control parameters that can be used to manipulate certain aspects of the DXi. These include turning a DXi on/off, showing its patch point, showing its name, displaying its current preset, and muting and/or soloing the DXi (see Figure 10.9).

Figure 10.9
Use the Synth Rack control parameters to manipulate a selected DXi

DXi Number
Audio On/Off
Patch Point

Solo
Mute
DXi Preset
DXi Name

DXi Audio Connection

Just like a hardware-based synth, a DXi can be turned on or off. To do so, just click the Audio On/Off parameter of the DXi in the Synth Rack. Internally, this changes the DXi's connection to SONAR's audio engine. When the DXi is on, it is connected to the audio engine, which means it produces sound and it also takes up some of your computer's processing power. When the DXi is off, it is not connected to the audio engine, which means it does not produce sound and it doesn't use any of your computer's processing power. Using the Audio On/Off parameter is an easy way to disable/enable a DXi without having to keep adding or removing it (and its associated tracks) to/from a project.

NOTE

You may sometimes notice that the Audio On/Off button doesn't work. This is because DXi's are "connected" to a project in two different ways. When you add a DXi manually to a project by inserting it into the Fx bin of an audio track, the DXi is treated like an effect and can't be disconnected from the SONAR audio engine without being completely removed from the project. When you add a DXi via the Insert DXi Synth function, the DXi is inserted into the In (input) of the audio track, which means it can be disconnected from the SONAR audio engine without having to be removed from the project.

Continued

CHAPTER 10

Why two connection methods? Well, because while most DXi's are software synthesizers, there are some that must be used as effects (like the Alien Connections ReValver SE included with SONAR, which I'll talk about later). The DXi's that provide effects processing must be treated like effects, otherwise they won't work. You'll need to refer to the documentation of your DXi to determine if it is a software synth or an effect.

DXi Patch Point

You can tell how a DXi is "connected" to a project by hovering your mouse over the Patch Point parameter of the DXi in the Synth Rack. One symbol designates that the DXi is connected to the In (input) of an audio track (see Figure 10.10).

Figure 10.10
This DXi is connected to the In (input) of an audio track

Another symbol designates that the DXi is connected to the Fx bin of an audio track (see Figure 10.11).

Figure 10.11
This DXi is connected to the Fx bin of an audio track

DXi Presets

You can change the current synth preset (sound) of a DXi in the Synth Rack by clicking on the DXi's Preset parameter. This displays a pop-up menu allowing you to choose the preset you want to use. Unfortunately, this only works with SONAR presets, meaning the presets listed in the Presets drop-down list of the Property Page of a DXi. Some DXi's have their own method of storing presets and some DXi's multitimbral (they can produce more than one different sound at the same time). For these DXi's, you'll need to access their Property Pages to change their presets.

DXi Mute and Solo

You can also mute and solo DXi's in the Synth Rack by clicking on their Mute and Solo DXi buttons. This is just like muting and soloing tracks in the Track view. And just like muting a track, when you mute a DXi, it no longer produces any sound but it is still processed by your computer. Muting a DXi doesn't disconnect it from the SONAR audio engine. If you want to mute and disconnect a DXi, use the Audio On/Off parameter instead.

The Virtual Sound Canvas

SONAR ships with a number of DXi's, one of which is the Virtual Sound Canvas DXi (or VSC DXi for short). The VSC DXi simulates the Roland Sound Canvas, which is a hardware-based MIDI playback module. The VSC DXi is multitimbral (meaning it can play more than one different sound at a time—up to sixteen), has a polyphony of 128 voices (meaning it can play up to 128 notes at a time), and comes with 902 built-in sounds as well as 26 different drum sets. The sounds in the VSC DXi can't be changed, and you can't create your own sounds, but the selection is quite varied, so I don't think you'll run out any time soon.

VSC DXi Basics

If you examine the main interface for the VSC DXi (see Figure 10.12), you'll notice that it provides sixteen parts, one part for each of the sixteen available MIDI channels. Part 1 corresponds to MIDI channel 1, Part 2 to MIDI channel 2, and so on. Each part provides a number of adjustable parameters. These parameters include the instrument, volume, pan-pot, expression, reverb, chorus, and delay.

Figure 10.12
You can adjust the VSC DXi parameter settings using its main interface

Selecting Instruments

"Instruments" refers to the sounds or programs or patches that the VSC DXi provides. To assign an instrument to a part, just click the Instrument drop-down list that corresponds to the part and choose an instrument from the pop-up menus (see Figure 10.13).

Figure 10.13
Choose an instrument for a part using the instrument drop-down list

Preview the Instrument

To test the instrument and hear what it sounds like, click the Prev (preview) button for the part (see Figure 10.14).

Figure 10.14
To test the sound of the instrument, click the part's Prev button

Additional Instruments

The VSC DXi provides two different categories of instruments. One category is a set of GM (General MIDI)-compatible instruments. The other category is a set of GS (Roland GS format)-compatible instruments. The Roland GS format is similar to GM in that it provides a standardized set of rules for MIDI synths, but they usually pertain only to Roland MIDI devices. The GS format provides an expanded set of rules to include many more instruments as well as additional features not covered by GM. To switch between the GM and GS modes for the VSC DXi, click the Setup button at the bottom of the VSC DXi window to open the Setup dialog box (see Figure 10.15). Then under the Performance tab, choose the GM2 or GS option for the Generator Mode parameter and click OK.

Figure 10.15
Choose between two sets of instruments using the Generator Mode parameter

Adjusting Volume, Panpot, and Expression

To adjust the volume, panpot, and expression parameters for each part, do the following:

1. In the Fader Function section, choose the parameter you would like to adjust. To adjust volume, click the Volume button. To adjust panpot (panning), click the Panpot button. To adjust expression (velocity depth), click the Expression button.

2. When you click a parameter button, it will light up with a green color (see Figure 10.16). This indicates that all the sliders in the Fader sections for each part now correspond to the parameter that you selected. For example, if you chose the Volume parameter, each slider would control the volume of its corresponding part.

Figure 10.16
Activating a parameter makes it light up with a green color

3. Click and drag the sliders in the Fader sections for each part to adjust the selected parameter (see Figure 10.17).

Figure 10.17
Click and drag the
Fader sliders to adjust
the chosen parameter
for each part

Applying Effects

In addition, the VSC DXi provides effects that can be applied to each part individually. This gives you a lot more flexibility than if you were to apply SONAR's effects because, with the VSC DXi effects, each part can have a different amount of effects applied. With SONAR's effects you would have to apply them to all the parts in the same amount because you would be assigning the effects to the audio track to which the VSC DXi is assigned. For more information about effects, read Chapter 11.

Assigning effects to parts works in exactly the same way as adjusting the volume, panpot, and expression parameters. Just click the appropriate effect parameter button in the Fader Function section, and then adjust the Fader sliders for each part. The Fader sliders determine how much of the effect is applied to the each part. For example, you could have a large amount of reverb on one part and a small amount of reverb on another part.

The only difference is that each effect provides a number of variations. Each part cannot have its own effect variation. All parts use the same effect variation. To change the variation of an effect, just click the Macro arrow next to the effect and choose a variation from the pop-up menu (see Figure 10.18).

Figure 10.18
Choose effect
variations using the
Macro arrows

TIP

Some of the VSC DXi parameters can be set by simply setting the corresponding MIDI track parameters. For instance, by changing the Vol, Pan, Bnk, Pch, Chr, and Rev parameters of the MIDI track driving one of the VSC DXi Parts, you can control the volume, panpot, instrument, chorus effect, and reverb effect parameters for that part. When you save your project, those parameters are stored along with it. But there is an advantage to adjusting parameters within the VSC DXi itself. You can save all the VSC DXi parameters as a preset using the Preset drop-down list and Preset Save and Delete buttons located at the top of the window. By saving a number of parameter configurations as presets, you can quickly switch between configurations to test out different instrumentation for the project you are working on.

Multiple Outputs

In the previous section of this chapter (Applying Effects), I mentioned that, when applying SONAR's effects to the VSC DXi, you would have to apply the same effect to all the Parts because they share the same audio track. This isn't entirely true. The VSC DXi provides four separate audio outputs to which any of the 16 available Parts can be assigned. Each VSC DXi output gets its own audio track, so you could essentially separate the 16 Parts into four different groups, each of which can use its own set of SONAR effects. This can come in handy if you want to apply one type of effect to your drum instruments, another type of effect to your guitar instruments, and so on.

Earlier, I talked about how to set up a DXi to use multiple outputs in a project, but you still need to set up the internal parameters of the DXi, and this procedure is different for each DXi. To designate which Parts are assigned to the four available outputs in the VSC DXi, do the following:

1. In the VSC DXi, click the Setup button to open the VSC Settings dialog box. Then click the Output Assign tab (see Figure 10.19).

Figure 10.19
Use the VSC Settings dialog box to assign Parts to different outputs

2. In the displayed grid, you'll see the Part numbers shown along the top and the Output numbers shown along the left. To assign a Part to a specific output, just line up your mouse with Part number along the top and the Output along the left. Then click at that grid point to make the assignment.
3. If you want to reset all Part assignments to Output 1, click the Change All Parts To Output 1 button.

4. You can also turn off multiple outputs using the Don't Use Multiple Outputs option. This keeps your grid assignments intact if you want to temporarily send all Parts to Output 1.

5. Click OK.

VSC DXi Exercise

Now that I've covered all the boring parameter basics for the VSC DXi, what do you say we kick it up a notch? How about working through an exercise so that you can hear what the VSC DXi is really capable of?

To give you an idea of the amount of power that the VSC DXi provides, try this:

1. Choose File > Open and select the sample project that comes included with SONAR called "Latin.cwp." Click Open.

2. Click Cancel in the Auto-Send Sysx dialog box.

3. Close the File Info window, the Staff view, and the Big Time view. Then delete Track 1. You won't need them.

4. Choose Insert > DXi Synth > EDIROL VSC.

5. In the Insert DXi Synth Options dialog box, activate the All Synth Outputs and Synth Property Page options. Make sure all the other options are deactivated and then click OK.

6. In the Track view, change the names of Tracks 11, 12, 13, and 14 to Drums, Bass, Piano, and Brass respectively.

7. Select Tracks 1 through 10. Then choose Track > Property > Outputs, and choose EDIROL VSC in the MIDI Outputs drop-down list. Click OK.

TIP
If you ever need to change the parameters for more than one track at a time, just select the tracks that you want to adjust, then use the Track > Property menu to change the properties for all of those tracks simultaneously.

8. Press the spacebar on your computer keyboard to start playback of the project. Notice that in the VSC DXi window, all the MIDI tracks are being played by only four different parts—2, 3, 4, and 10. This works out perfectly since the VSC DXi provides up to four separate audio outputs. We've already set up our audio tracks, but now we need to assign the VSC DXi parts to the different outputs.

9. In the VSC DXi window, click the Setup button to open the VSC Settings dialog box. Then click the Output Assign tab. In the grid, assign Part 2 to Output 2 (Bass audio track), Part 3 to Output 3 (Piano audio track), Part 4 to Output 4 (Brass audio track), and Part 10 to Output 1 (Drums audio track) as shown in Figure 10.20. Then click OK.

Figure 10.20
Assign Parts 2, 3, 4, and 10 to Outputs 2, 3, 4, and 1 respectively

10.   Expand the four audio tracks in the Track view so you can see their play-back meters. Then play the project again. You should notice that the drum, bass, piano, and brass instruments are now playing through tracks 11, 12, 13, and 14 respectively (see Figure 10.21). This allows us to apply different SONAR audio effects to each separate group of instruments.

Figure 10.21
Each group of instruments is now assigned to its own audio track

11.   I'll talk more about effects in chapter 11, but, in the meantime, let's add some effects to each group of instruments. Right-click the Fx parameter of track 11 (Drums) and choose Audio Effects > Cakewalk > FxReverb. In the Cakewalk FxReverb window, choose the Drum Room—Small, Warm preset. Then close the window. Now do the same for track 13 (Piano).

12.   Right-click the Fx parameter for track 14 (Brass) and choose Audio Effects > Cakewalk > FxChorus. In Cakewalk FxChorus window, choose the Big Stereo Spread preset. Then close the window.

13.   Play the project one last time. Then just sit back and listen.

Can you believe all of that sound is coming from one little software synthesizer? Of course, you can always try out different effects. Don't be afraid to experiment. For the full scoop on effects, read chapter 11.

TIP

One more thing about the VSC DXi is that even though some of the sounds aren't the greatest, this DXi works wonderfully as a scratch-pad synth—meaning you can use it to work out your musical ideas and then use some more professional equipment for the final production. In addition, if you have a songwriting partner (or team) and everyone is using SONAR, then everyone has access to the VSC DXi. This means that you can use the VSC DXi to work out your song ideas and you can be sure that the project will sound exactly the same no matter if it is played on your computer or someone else's.

The DreamStation

Another of the DXi's included with SONAR is the DreamStation. The DreamStation DXi simulates an analog modular synth (see Figure 10.22).

Figure 10.22
The DreamStation DXi puts the power of analog synthesis in your hands

The DreamStation DXi provides three oscillator modules, an amplifier module, filter module, lfo (low frequency oscillator) module, envelope module, vibrato and portamento features, and controls pertaining to synth output, such as volume and panning. By adjusting the controls provided by each of the modules, you can create your own unique synthesizer sounds just like you would with a hardware-based analog synth.

Unfortunately, covering the topics of analog synthesis, as well as how to create your own sounds with the DreamStation Dxi, would easily fill an entirely separate book. Instead, I'll show you how to load and save pre-existing sounds (called instruments) in the DreamStation DXi, and I'll provide an example of how you can use the DreamStation DXi in your SONAR projects.

NOTE

Although I won't be going into the subjects of analog synthesis or how to create your own sounds with the DreamStation DXi, you can find some good introductory synthesis information on the following Web sites: **http://tilt.largo.fl.us/faq/ synthfaq.html** and **http://nmc.uoregon.edu/emi/emp_win/main.html**. And for more specific information about the DreamStation DXi (as well as some free downloadable instruments), check out this site: **http://www.audio-simulation.de/**

TIP

There is one way you can create your own sounds with the DreamStation DXi automatically, and without having to know anything about analog synthesis. Just hold down the Shift key on your computer keyboard and then click the CLR button at the top of the DreamStation DXi window. This makes the DreamStation DXi randomly set all of its parameters, thus automatically creating a new sound. Many of the sounds may not be useable, but click enough times and you could come up with something very cool.

Loading and Saving Instruments

The DreamStation DXi sounds are called instruments. You can save and load instruments for your own use, and you can also share instruments with others. To load and save instruments for your own use, follow these procedures:

▶ To load an instrument, choose an instrument name from the Preset drop-down list at the top of the DreamStation DXi window. The DreamStation DXi comes with ninety-five pre-existing Instruments.

▶ To save an instrument, type a name for the instrument in the Preset parameter and then click the Save button (the one with the picture of a floppy disk shown on it). Your new instrument will show up in the Preset drop-down list.

▶ To delete an instrument from the Preset drop-down list, select the instrument from the list and then click the Delete button (the one with the large red X shown on it).

In addition to saving and loading instruments for your own use, you can save and load instruments as DSI files to share with other SONAR and DreamStation users. To use DSI files, follow these procedures:

▶ To load a DSI file, click the Load button at the top of the DreamStation DXi window. Choose your DSI file in the Open dialog box and then click Open.

▶ To save the current instrument as a DSI file, click the Save button. In the Save As dialog box, type in a name for the DSI file and then click Save.

A DreamStation DXi Exercise

Okay, now let's have some fun. To hear the DreamStation DXi in action, try the following exercise:

1. Choose File > Open and select the sample project file that comes included with SONAR called "Downtown.cwp." Click Open.

2. Click Cancel in the Auto-Send Sysx dialog box.

3. Close the File Info window, as well as Staff and Big Time views. You won't need them.

4. We'll use the VSC DXi to play our drum tracks. Choose Insert > DXi Synth > EDIROL VSC. In the Insert DXi Synth Options dialog box, activate the First Synth Output option and make sure the other options are deactivated.

5. Select tracks 1, 2, and 3. Then choose Track > Property > Outputs and select EDIROL VSC in the MIDI Outputs drop-down menu of the Track Outputs dialog box. Click OK.

6. Choose Insert > DXi Synth > DreamStation DXi2. In the Insert DXi Synth Options dialog box, activate the First Synth Output and Synth Property Page options. Click OK.

7. In the DreamStation DXi window, choose Bass: 01-Soft Bass in the Preset drop-down list. Then close the window.

8. In the Track view, assign the Out of track 4 to DreamStation DXi2 1. Also adjust the Vol of track 4 to 75.

NOTE

One drawback to the DreamStation DXi is that it's "single" timbral rather than multi-timbral. This means that it can play only one kind of sound at a time. In addition, the DreamStation DXi only provides one audio output. It doesn't have multiple outputs like the VSC DXi. Luckily, the DreamStation DXi doesn't take up much computer processing power, so you can set up multiple instances, each playing a unique sound.

9. Set up another instance of the DreamStation DXi using the steps we covered earlier. In the DreamStation DXi window, choose Organ: 02-Jazz in the Preset drop-down list and then close the window. Then set the Out of track 5 to DreamStation DXi2 2 and the Vol to 50.

10. Set up another instance of the DreamStation DXi. In the DXi window, choose Synth: 09-Brass in the Preset list and then close the window. Then set the Out parameters of tracks 6 and 7 to DreamStation DXi2 3 and the Vol parameters to 40.

11. Set up another instance of the DreamStation DXi. In the DXi window, choose Synth: 21-Analogic 2 in the Preset list and then close the window. Then set the Out of track 8 to DreamStation DXi2 4 and the Vol to 50.

12. Set up one last instance of the DreamStation DXi. In the DXi window, choose Synth: 16-Rhodes in the Preset list and then close the window. Then set the Out of track 9 to DreamStation DXi2 5 and the Vol to 80.

13. Play the project.

That's a cool sound, isn't it? Of course, you can also liven things up even more by applying some effects. The nice thing about using multiple instances of the DreamStation DXi is that each instance can have different effects applied to it.

The Cyclone

The Cyclone DXi is the equivalent of a very powerful MIDI sample playback device. Like the VSC DXi, the Cyclone is multitimbral (meaning it can play more than one different sound at a time—up to sixteen), but instead of having built-in sounds, the Cyclone allows you to load in your own sounds in the form of audio sample loops in the WAV file format. The music-making possibilities of this DXi are astonishing to say the least.

Cyclone Basics

If you examine the main interface for the Cyclone (see Figure 10.23), you'll notice that it provides sixteen parts (called Pad Groups), one Pad Group for each of the sixteen available MIDI channels. Pad Group 1 for MIDI channel 1, Pad Group 2 for MIDI channel 2, and so on (although you can assign any MIDI channel to any Pad Group if you'd like).

Figure 10.23
You can adjust the
Cyclone parameters
using its main interface

Each Pad Group provides a number of adjustable parameters. These parameters include
the sample file, volume, pan, sync, loop, mute, and solo (see Figure 10.24).

Figure 10.24
Each Pad Group
provides some
adjustable parameters

Loading Sample Files

To load a sample file into a Pad Group, click the Load button. Then select a WAV file in
the Open dialog box and click Open. If you later want to remove a file from a Pad Group,
right-click the Pad Group and choose Clear Pad from the pop-up menu.

Loop Bin Loading

When you load a sample file into a Pad Group, the sample file is also listed in the Loop Bin (see Figure 10.25).

Figure 10.25
Sample files loaded
into Pad Groups are
also listed in the
Loop Bin

The Loop Bin lists all the sample files in the current Cyclone Sound Bank. You can load sample files into the Loop Bin separately and then apply them to Pad Groups later on if you'd like. Just click the Loop Bin Load button, choose a sample file in the Open dialog box, and click Open. To apply a sample file from the Loop Bin to a Pad Group, just drag and drop the file from the Loop Bin onto the Pad Group.

TIP

You can also use the Loop Explorer view to apply sample files to Pad Groups. Just drag and drop files from the Loop Explorer onto the appropriate Pad Groups. I talked about the Loop Explorer view in chapter 9.

If you want to delete a file from the Loop Bin, select the file and click the Trash button.

CAUTION

If you delete a file from the Loop Bin that is being used by any of the Pad Groups, that file is also deleted from those Pad Groups.

Previewing Sample Files

To preview a sample file listed in the Loop Bin, just select the file and then click the Preview button in the Cyclone toolbar (see Figure 10.26).

Figure 10.26
Preview sample files
using the Preview
button in the
Cyclone toolbar

To stop the sample file preview, click the Stop button. You can also preview a sample file that's already loaded into a Pad Group by clicking on the number of the Pad Group. Click the number of the Pad Group a second time to stop playback.

Adjusting Pad Group Parameters

To adjust the volume, pan, mute, solo, sync, and loop parameters for each Pad Group, do the following:

> ▶ Volume and Pan—Click and hold your mouse on the onscreen knob, then drag your mouse up or down to raise or lower the value. If you'd like to reset the parameter to its default value, just double-click it.

> ▶ Mute and Solo—To mute or solo a Pad Group, just click the Mute or Solo buttons.

> ▶ Sync—Activating the Sync parameter will synchronize the playback tempo of the sample file loaded into the Pad Group with the playback tempo of the current SONAR project.

> ▶ Loop—Activating the Loop parameter will loop the playback of the sample file loaded into the Pad Group so that the file keeps repeating over and over again.

The Pad Inspector

Each Pad Group also provides a number of other adjustable parameters, which are accessed via the Pad Inspector (see Figure 10.27). To see the Pad Inspector parameter values for a Pad Group, just click the number of Pad Group.

Figure 10.27
Use the Pad Inspector to adjust additional Pad Group parameters

Output

Like the VSC DXi, the Cyclone provides multiple audio outputs (up to 17—16 individual outputs and one mix output). Each Pad Group can be assigned to its own separate output using the Output parameter. If you choose the Mix Only option, the sound from the Pad Group will only be sent to the mix output, which contains a mix of all the sound coming from all the Pad Groups in Cyclone.

MIDI In

As I mentioned earlier, Cyclone can play up to 16 different sounds at once, each one assigned to its own MIDI channel. Use the MIDI In parameter to assign a MIDI input channel to a Pad Group. Then any MIDI data coming into that channel will be used to trigger playback of that Pad Group. If you choose the MIDI Omni option, then the Pad Group will receive MIDI data from all 16 MIDI channels.

Root

The Root parameter determines the original pitch of the sample file loaded into a Pad Group. If you load an ACID-compatible WAV file or a SONAR Groove Clip WAV file into a Pad Group, the Root parameter will be set for you automatically. If you load a regular WAV file into a Pad Group, you will have to determine the pitch of the file yourself and set the Root parameter manually.

Velocity and Key Map

When a Pad Group receives MIDI note messages via its assigned MIDI channel, those MIDI note messages trigger the playback of the sample file loaded into the Pad Group. You can limit the range of notes and their velocities that can be used to trigger the Pad Group by setting the Velocity and Key Map parameters as follows:

> ▶ Velocity Low—Set this to the lowest note velocity value you would like used to trigger the Pad Group.

> ▶ Velocity High—Set this to the highest note velocity value you would like used to trigger the Pad Group.

> ▶ Key Map Unity—Set this to the note value that will be used to play the sample file in the Pad Group at its Root pitch. Most of the time, you'll probably set this parameter to the same pitch value as the Root parameter.

> ▶ Key Map Low—Set this to the lowest note value you would like used to trigger the Pad Group.

> ▶ Key Map High—Set this to the highest note value you would like used to trigger the Pad Group.

Pitch Markers

I talked about pitch markers back in chapter 9. They are used to change the pitch of groove clips in a project. You can also use them to change the pitch of Pad Groups throughout a project. If your project uses pitch markers, and you would like your Pad Group(s) to change pitch along with the markers, activate the Pitch Markers option for the Pad Group(s) in the Pad Inspector.

The Loop View

When you select a sample file listed in the Loop Bin, its audio waveform is displayed in the Loop view section of the Cyclone main interface (see Figure 10.28).

Figure 10.28
The Loop view
displays sample file
audio waveforms

If the selected sample file is an ACID-compatible loop or a SONAR Groove Clip, then the Loop view will also display any slices contained in the file, which are designated by vertical dotted lines shown on the audio waveform.

NOTE

In chapter 9 I talked about Groove Clips and the Loop Construction view. When you open a Groove Clip in the Loop Construction view, you'll notice that SONAR breaks the clip down into small sections. These sections are called slices. Slices are based on the beat values and audio waveform spikes (transients) in a clip. Slices allow SONAR to accurately change the tempo and pitch of a Groove Clip. In Cyclone, however, you can use slices to break sample files apart and create new sample files by combining the slices from several different files. This is where the Pad Editor comes into play.

The Pad Editor

When you load a sample file into a Pad Group, a track for that Pad Group is created in the Pad Editor (see Figure 10.29). This track contains green colored blocks with each separate block representing a different slice in the sample file. At the end of the track is a white *track handle* that marks the point in the track at which the track will loop back to the beginning.

Figure 10.29
Examine and manipulate Pad Group sample file slices with the Pad Editor

Using the Pad Editor, you can select, change and edit slices to create entire compositions out of nothing but sample file slices if you'd like.

Selecting

To select a slice, just click its associated green block. If you'd like to select more than one slice, hold down the Shift key on your computer keyboard as you click the blocks. Also, to select all the slices in a track, double-click the track number.

The Slice Inspector

You can edit the parameters of a slice using the Slice Inspector. Each slice has adjustable pitch, gain (volume), and panning. Just select the slice you'd like to change and then click and drag your mouse over the parameter knobs. You can also change the settings by double-clicking on the numerical values and typing in new values.

Changing Slices

You can also change slices in a track by deleting them, moving them, or swapping them with slices from a different sample file. To delete a slice, just select it and press the Delete key on your computer keyboard.

You can move slices by clicking and dragging them with your mouse. To move a slice within the same track, click and drag the slice left or right. To move a slice to a different track, click and drag the slice up or down.

To swap a slice with another slice from a different file, first select a sample file in the Loop Bin so that its audio waveform is shown in the Loop view. Then click and drag a slice from the Loop view into the Pad Editor (see Figure 10.30).

Figure 10.30
Click and drag slices from the Loop view to the Pad Editor to swap slices

Cyclone DXi Exercise

With the boring basics out of the way, let's have some fun and give the Cyclone a whirl. To hear what the Cyclone can do, try the following exercise:

1. Choose File > New and select the Normal template in the New Project File dialog box to create a new project. If any preconfigured tracks appear in the Track view, delete them.

2. Choose Insert > DXi Synth > Cyclone to add an instance of the Cyclone to the project. In the Insert DXi Synth Options dialog box, activate the First Synth Output and Synth Property Page options while leaving the other options deactivated.

3. Put your SONAR CD into your CD-ROM drive.

4. Choose View > Loop Explorer to open the Loop Explorer view.

5. Load the following file into Pad Group 1: D:\Audio Loops\Smart Loops\Dry Studio Kit (sample loops)\Funky 2.wav.

6. Load the following file into Pad Group 2: D:\Audio Loops\Smart Loops\Bass Guitars (sample loops)\Mid Tempo loops\Eigth G.wav.

7. Load the following file into Pad Group 3: D:\Audio Loops\Smart Loops\Electric Guitars (sample loops)\Mid Tempo loops\Funk Junk 13 G.wav.

8. Load the following file into Pad Group 4: D:\Audio Loops\Smart Loops\Percussion Kit (sample loops)\Claves 1.wav.

9. Click the numbers of Pad Groups 1 through 4 to start them playing. Sounds pretty good, huh? But also a little boring. I think we need to spice up this groove a bit.

10. Load the following file into the Loop Bin: D:\Audio Loops\Smart Loops\Dry Studio Kit (sample loops)\DSK (with Power Snare)\Funky 2.wav. The file will be selected and shown in the Loop view.

11. Drag and drop the 5th slice in the Loop view onto the 5th slice in the Pad 1 track of the Pad Editor (see Figure 10.31).

Figure 10.31
Drag and drop slices from the Loop view to the Pad Editor to replace slices (sounds) in a track

12. Drag and drop the 13th slice in the Loop view onto the 13th slice in the
     Pad 1 track. Then click the Pad Group 1 number to hear it play. Click it
     again to stop playback.

TIP

You may have noticed when listening to Pad Group 1 that the new snare drum
sound gets cut off. This can happen when you replace slices in a sample file
because not all slices are exactly the same length. To remedy this, you can
choose to have cut slices play through as if they weren't being cut off by having
Cyclone allow the tail ends of the slices play. To do this, select the Pad Group
(by clicking on its number) in which the slice resides. Then activate the Tail
option for that Pad Group, which is located at the bottom of the Pad Inspector.

13. Okay, the drums in Pad Group 1 sound pretty good, but the bass in Pad
     Group 2 is extremely boring. Load the following file into the Loop Bin:
     D:\Audio Loops\Smart Loops\ Bass Guitars (sample loops)\Mid Tempo
     loops\Marmalade 4 G.wav.

14. Drag and drop the first three slices from the Loop view onto the last three
     slices in the Pad 2 track of the Pad Editor. You'll notice that the track han-
     dle for that track has been moved out of position. You need to drag the
     track handle to the left so that it lines up with the other track handles (see
     Figure 10.32). This will make sure all the tracks loop at the same time.
     Play both Pad Groups 1 and 2 to hear what the groove sounds like so far.

Figure 10.32
Move the Pad 2
track handle in
the Pad Editor

15. I think we'll leave the guitar in Pad Group 3 alone, but the percussion in
     Pad Group 4 needs some tweaking. Load the following file into the Loop
     Bin: D:\Audio Loops\Smart Loops\ Percussion Kit (sample loops)\Bongos
     Roll 1 (2 beats).wav.

16. Drag and drop the last four slices from the Loop view onto the last four
     slices in the Pad 4 track of the Pad Editor. Adjust the track handle so that
     it lines up with the other track handles.

17. Click the numbers of Pad Groups 1 through 4 to hear the entire groove. Cool, no?

18. To save your current Cyclone setup as a file for later editing, click the Export Sound Bank button in the Cyclone toolbar (see Figure 10.33).

Figure 10.33
Use the Export Sound Bank function to save your current Cyclone set up as a Cyclone file

That was just a small taste of what can be accomplished with the Cyclone. This is one very powerful tool. In addition to creating entire compositions out of audio slices, it can also be used for sample playback via MIDI tracks in a project, live sample triggering via a MIDI keyboard, and you can even use it to create entirely new sample files. I'm sure you'll get a lot of creative use out of the Cyclone DXi.

TIP

For more information and tutorials concerning the Cyclone DXi, be sure to read through pages 85 to 89 and pages 583 to 594 of the SONAR User's Guide.

I'll also be providing additional Cyclone coverage in future issues of my DigiFreq music technology newsletter. You can sign up for a free subscription at: **http://www.digifreq.com/digifreq/**

The DR-008 (SONAR XL)

If you purchased the XL version of SONAR, you also received a copy of the DR-008 DXi. Like the Cyclone DXi, the DR-008 DXi is a sample playback synth, but rather than focusing on sample loops and slices, the DR-008 provides advanced sample playback and synthesis of drum and percussion instruments. You can think of it as a very high tech drum machine, and so much more (see Figure 10.34).

Figure 10.34
The DR-008 DXi is a
very advanced sample
playback and drum
instrument synthesizer

The DR-008 provides 96 different pads, each of which can be loaded with any AIFF or WAV sample file for playback. These pads represent single sample or synth playback modules which can be triggered via MIDI note messages from your MIDI tracks in SONAR. With 96 pads at your disposal, this means you can have an extremely large percussion ensemble at your disposal all playing from a single DXi.

The DR-008 is very complex. As a matter of fact, it's the most complex DXi included with SONAR. Covering how to use the DR-008 in detail could probably fill an entire book alone. So, instead, I'll show you how to load and save settings, and I'll provide an example of how you can use the DR-008 in your SONAR projects.

NOTE

Although I won't be going into detail on how to use the DR-008, you can find a lot of good information in the manual that comes included with the DXi. You should be able to find the manual on your hard drive in the following location: C:\Program Files\Cakewalk\Shared DXi\Fxpansion\DR-008\DR-008_Manual.pdf. In addition, you can find even more information about the DR-008 on the Fxpansion web site: **http://www.fxpansion.com**.

Kits, Presets, and Sample Files

You can work with sounds in the DR-008 DXi in a number of different ways. Sounds come in the form of kits, presets, and sample files. To get sound out of the DR-008, you must have at least one pad loaded with a preset or sample file. But you can also group different pad settings together as a kit. A sample file is just a basic sound file loaded into a pad without any parameter settings. A preset can be a sample file or synth module loaded into a pad along with accompanying parameter settings. And a kit is a file containing all the sample files and settings for every pad in the DR-008.

Loading a Kit

To load a kit into the DR-008 DXi, do the following:

1.   Click the Load button in the toolbar at the top of the DR-008 DXi window (see Figure 10.35).

Figure 10.35
To load a kit, click
the Load button in
the toolbar

2.   Choose Load Settings from the pop-up menu.
3.   Select a kit file in the Load Bank dialog box. Kit files have a DR8 extension. For example, ManytoneAcousticMulti.dr8 would be a kit file.

NOTE
The DR-008 DXi includes a selection of kits, which are located in the following folder on your hard drive: C:\Program Files\Cakewalk\Shared DXi\Fxpansion\DR-008\KITS.

4.   Click Open to load the kit.

The DR-008 DXi loads the kit file that you selected and highlights the pads loaded with sounds that make up that kit. From here you can either play the kit with its default pad presets; load additional pad presets from separate files; or adjust the pad settings of the current kit and save your own pad presets.

Loading and Saving Presets

To load additional pad presets for the current kit, do the following:

1.   Double-click an empty pad.
2.   From here you can either load a preset or a raw sample file into the pad. Select a preset or file from the Select a DR-008 File dialog box. Preset files have a DRS extension and sample files have either a WAV or AIF extension.

NOTE
The DR-008 DXi includes a selection of presets and sample files, which are located in the following folders on your hard drive: C:\Program Files\Cakewalk\Shared DXi\Fxpansion\DR-008\PRESETS and C:\Program Files\Cakewalk\Shared DXi\Fxpansion\DR-008\Samples.

3. Click Open to load the preset or sample file. The DR-008 DXi loads the preset or sample file into the pad and highlights the pad indicating it is ready to be used.

If you've adjusted the settings of a pad and you would like to save a new preset, do the following:

1. Right-click the pad and choose Save from the pop-up menu.

2. In File Name parameter of the Save Settings As dialog box, type in a name for the new preset and give it a DRS extension.

3. Click Save to save the new preset.

You can also save groups of presets into a kit.

Saving a Kit

If you would like to save all the current pad presets as a kit, do the following:

1. Click the Save button in the toolbar at the top of the DR-008 DXi window (see Figure 10.36).

Figure 10.36
To save a kit, click the Save button in the toolbar

2. Choose Save Samples And Settings In Bank from the pop-up menu.

3. In the File Name parameter of the Save Settings As dialog box, type in a name for the new kit and give it a DR8 extension.

4. Click Save to save the new kit.

A DR-008 DXi Exercise

To hear the DR-008 in action, try the following exercise:

1. Choose File > Open and select the sample project that comes included with SONAR called "Latin.cwp." Click Open.

2. Click Cancel in the Auto-Send Sysx dialog box.

3. Close the File Info window, the Staff view, and the Big Time view. Then delete tracks 1, 2, 3, 4. You won't need them.

4. Choose Insert > DXi Synth > DR-008 DXi2.

5. In the Insert DXi Synth Options dialog box, activate the First Synth Output and Synth Property Page options while leaving the other options deactivated. Then click OK.

6. In the Track view, select tracks 1 through 7. Then choose Track > Property > Outputs, and choose DR-008 DXi2 1 in the MIDI Outputs drop-down list. Click OK.

7. In the DR-008 DXi window, click the Load button and choose Load Settings from the pop-up menu.

8. In the Load Bank dialog box, select the JSquare's DanceFloor Kit.dr8 file and click Open.

9. In the Track view, right-click the Fx parameter of track 8 and choose Audio Effects > Cakewalk > FxReverb from the pop-up menu.

10. In the Cakewalk FxReverb dialog box, choose the preset called Drum Room—Small, Warm.

11. Play the project.

This is just a basic example of what can be done with the DR-008. Be sure to read through the manual, and experiment with all the different kits, presets, and sample files included with the DXi.

The ReValver

Unlike all the other DXi's included with SONAR, the ReValver DXi is actually an audio effect. You use it to apply amplifier simulation effects to your audio tracks.

NOTE

For more information about amplifier simulation effects and audio effects in general, read chapter 11.

The best way to describe the ReValver DXi is to actually show it to you in action. To use the ReValver in a project, do the following:

1. Choose File > Open and select the sample project file that comes included with SONAR called "Don't Matter Audio and Midi Demo.cwb." Click Open.

2. Close the File Info window and the Staff view. Then delete all the tracks in the projects except for the Guitar track. You won't need the others for this demonstration.

3. Right-click the Fx parameter of the Guitar track and choose DXi Synth > Alien Connections ReValver SE to apply the ReValver DXi to the track.

NOTE

As I mentioned earlier in the chapter, the ReValver DXi must be added to a project via the Fx bin of an audio track rather than through the Insert DXi Synth Options dialog box. Since the ReValver DXi is an audio effect rather than a regular DXi, it will not work if you apply it using the dialog box.

CHAPTER 10

4. In the ReValver DXi window, you'll see a virtual rack mount bay containing virtual rack mount modules used to virtually emulate preamplifiers, power amplifiers, speakers, and effects (see Figure 10.37). The first module in the rack is permanent and controls the ReValver DXi. In the first module, adjust the In and Out parameters to control the input and output levels of the ReValver.

Figure 10.37
The main ReValver interface looks like a virtual rack mount bay

5. Click Bypass to temporarily turn ReValver processing off and on. This allows you to compare the audio signal with the ReValver applied and without it applied.

6. Click Clear to delete the current configuration of modules in the rack.

7. Click Save to save the current configuration of modules in the rack as a ReValver preset file.

8. Click Load to open a ReValver preset file.

NOTE
The ReValver DXi includes a selection of preset files, which are located in the following folder on your hard drive: C:\Program Files\Cakewalk\Shared DXi\ReValver SE\presets\.

9. By clicking on a module, you can move, remove, replace, bypass, reset, as well as load and save individual presets for a module by choosing the appropriate option from the pop-up menu.

10. To add a new module to the rack, click in an empty rack space and choose Insert Module Here from the pop-up menu to open the Choose Module dialog box (see Figure 10.38).

Figure 10.38
Use the Choose Module dialog box to insert a new module into the rack mount space

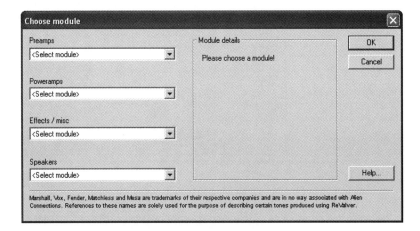

11. To add a preamplifier module, choose one from the Preamps list. To add a power amplifier, choose one from the Poweramps list. To add an effect, choose one from the Effects / misc list. To choose a speaker simulator, choose one from the Speakers list. Then click OK.

12. If you play the project, you should hear the Guitar track being processed by the ReValver. The audio signal is processed starting with the first module in the rack and ending with the last module in the rack. This means that the order in which the modules appear in the rack makes a difference as to how the audio is processed and how it sounds.

13. You can also adjust the individual parameters of some of the modules to affect processing. Each module is different.

Those are the basic steps required for using the ReValver DXi. For more in-depth information about how ReValver works and how to adjust the parameters of each individual module, you should read the ReValver manual by clicking the Help button in the first ReValver module.

ReWire

In addition to DX Instruments, there are software-based synthesizers that run as separate applications. This means that, normally, they can not be connected in any way to a sequencing application like SONAR. If, however, the software synth application supports a technology called ReWire, the synth can be used within SONAR, almost exactly like a DX Instrument.

ReWire is a virtual connection technology that allows two different music applications to connect to one another and share audio data, synchronize their internal clocks, and share transport control. For example, one of the most popular software synthesizers on the market that supports ReWire is called Reason. Reason provides built-in synthesis and sequencing features. When using ReWired with SONAR, you can stream audio from Reason to SONAR just like you would with a DX Instrument. In addition, the sequencer aspects in both Reason and SONAR would be completely synchronized, meaning that the Now Time in SONAR would correspond to the exact same sequencer time in Reason. And both applications would share common transport functions, meaning that using the Play, Stop, Rewind, etc. functions in one application would trigger that same function in the other application and vice versa. The ReWire technology is very powerful and allows you to use SONAR with any other ReWire compatible application on the market.

TIP

For more information about Reason, visit: **http://www.propellerheads.se/ products/reason/frame.html**

As far as using the ReWire functions in SONAR, to be honest, there really isn't much more I can say that isn't already covered in the SONAR User's Guide. Instead of just rehashing the same information, I would recommend that you read through pages 365 to 369 of the

Guide. If you have questions, don't be afraid to post them in the discussion area of my DigiFreq music technology web site: **http://www.digifreq.com/digifreq/**.

TIP

For more information about the ReWire technology in general, be sure to visit: **http://www.propellerheads.se/products/rewire/frame.html**

SoundFonts

Last and somewhat least (I'll explain in a moment), SONAR includes the LiveSynth Pro DXi. This DXi allows you to use SoundFonts even if you don't have a SoundFont-compatible sound card. Unfortunately, the version of LiveSynth Pro DXi included with SONAR is only a trial version. You get full use of the DXi for 30 days, but after that you are limited to using SoundFonts that are 1 MB or less in size. Most good SoundFonts are larger than that.

TIP

For a review of the full shipping version of the LiveSynth Pro DXi product, go to: **http://www.digifreq.com/digifreq/reviewdetails.asp?ProdReviewID=8**

NOTE

Most modern MIDI instruments and sound cards use sample-playback to produce sounds. Sample-playback can produce some very realistic sounds. The reason for this realism lies in the fact that a sample-playback device plays samples, which are actually audio recordings of real-life instruments and sounds. When the sample-playback device receives a MIDI Note On message, instead of creating a sound electronically from scratch, it plays a digital sample, which can be anything from the sound of a piano note to the sound of a coyote howling.

A SoundFont is a special type of digital sample format, which works only with a SoundFont-compatible sound card. The SoundFont format was developed by Creative Labs, the makers of the ever-popular Sound Blaster line of sound cards. Most recent Sound Blaster-model sound cards are SoundFont compatible. For more information about Sound Blaster sound cards, check out **http://www. soundblaster.com/**. For more information about SoundFonts (as well as free SoundFont downloads), check out the following Web sites:

▶   **http://www.soundblaster.com/resources/read.asp?ArticleID=12**

▶   **http://www.soundfonts.com/**

▶   **http://www.hammersound.com/**

Using the LiveSynth Pro DXi

To use the LiveSynth Pro DXi to play SoundFonts, do the following:

1. Create a new project or open a pre-existing project.

2. Choose Insert > DXi Synth > LiveSynth Pro SE.

3. In the Insert DXi Synth Options dialog box, activate the First Synth Output and Synth Property Page options.

4. Click OK. The LiveSynth Pro window opens (see Figure 10.39).

CHAPTER 10

Figure 10.39
Use the LiveSynth Pro DXi to play SoundFonts with any sound card

5. In the LiveSynth Pro window, click the Browse button and choose the SoundFont file you want to use. Click Open. The name of the SoundFont file appears in the Filename parameter.

NOTE

SONAR includes a selection of SoundFont files, which are located in the following folder on your hard drive: C:\Program Files\Cakewalk\SONAR 2\Sample Content\Soundfonts\.

6. Choose an unused bank number and type it into the Bank parameter.

7. Click the Load button. LiveSynth Pro then loads your selected SoundFont into your selected bank. The Bank and SoundFont are listed in the Currently Loaded SoundFont Bank(s) list.

8. Repeat steps 5 through 7 to load additional SoundFonts. If you want to remove a SoundFont from the list, select the SoundFont and click the Unload button.

9. When you're finished loading SoundFonts, close the LiveSynth Pro window.

10. If you opened a pre-existing project that already contains MIDI tracks, you can skip this step. Otherwise, right-click in the Track pane of the Track view and choose Insert MIDI Track to create a new MIDI track. Then widen the track to display its parameters.

11. Set the In parameter to the MIDI channel which is being used to receive data from your MIDI keyboard and set the Out parameter to LiveSynth Pro.

12. Set the Ch (channel) parameter to the same MIDI channel as your MIDI keyboard. Set the Bnk (bank) parameter to the same bank containing the SoundFont you want to use for this MIDI track. Set the patch parameter to one of the patches available in the SoundFont. You'll see a list of available patches.

13. Repeat steps 10 through 12 to set up any additional new or pre-existing MIDI tracks.

After you record some data into your MIDI tracks or if the tracks already contained data, when you play the project, your MIDI tracks will drive the LiveSynth Pro, which will in turn play the appropriate sounds from the SoundFonts you have loaded.

Using SoundFonts with a Compatible Sound Card

If you have a SoundFont-compatible sound card (like the Sound Blaster Live), you can play SoundFonts with your sound card instead of the LiveSynth Pro DXi. The procedure for using a sound card to play SoundFonts is as follows:

1. Create a new project or open a pre-existing project.

2. Choose Options > SoundFonts to open the SoundFont Banks dialog box.

3. Select an emtpy bank, and click the Attach button to open the SoundFont File dialog box.

4. Choose the SoundFont file you want to load and click Open. The Sound-Font you chose is loaded into the bank you selected.

5. Repeat steps 3 and 4 to load any additional SoundFonts.

6. To remove a SoundFont from your project, just select it in the list and click Detach.

7. Click Close when you're finished loading SoundFonts.

8. If you opened a pre-existing project that already contains MIDI tracks, you can skip this step. Otherwise, right-click in the Track pane of the Track view and choose Insert MIDI Track to create a new MIDI track. Then widen the track to display its parameters.

9. Set the In parameter to the MIDI channel which is being used to receive data from your MIDI keyboard and set the Out parameter to SoundFont Device.

10. Set the Ch (channel) parameter to the same MIDI channel as your MIDI keyboard. Set the Bnk (bank) parameter to the same bank containing the SoundFont you want to use for this MIDI track. Set the patch parameter to one of the patches available in the SoundFont. You'll see a list of available patches.

11. Repeat steps 8 through 10 to set up any additional new or pre-existing MIDI tracks.

After you record some data into your MIDI tracks or if the tracks already contained data, when you play the project, your MIDI tracks will drive your SoundFont-compatible sound card, which will in turn play the appropriate sounds from the SoundFonts you have loaded.

TIP

If you want to share your project with someone, and the project uses Sound-Fonts, be sure to send copies of the SoundFonts along with the project file. Of course, if you purchased the SoundFonts and they are copyrighted, the other person will have to purchase them as well. Sending copies of copyrighted SoundFonts to friends is a no-no. Thanks for respecting the rights of all the hard working musicians out there.

CHAPTER 10

11

Effects: The Really Cool Stuff

Just as adding spices to a recipe makes it taste better, adding effects to your music data makes it sound better. Effects can make the difference between a dull, lifeless recording, and a recording that really rocks. For example, you can apply echoes and background ambience to give the illusion that your song was recorded in a certain environment, such as a concert hall. You can also use effects to make your vocals sound rich and full. And the list goes on. SONAR provides a number of different effects features that you can use to spice up both your MIDI and audio tracks. Although applying these effects to your data isn't overly complicated, understanding what they do and how to use them can sometimes be confusing. So, this chapter covers the following topics:

▶ Plug-ins

▶ Offline and real-time processing

▶ Audio effects: Chorus, Equalization, Reverb, Delay, Flanging, Pitch Shifting, and Time/Pitch stretching

▶ MIDI effects: Quantization, Delay, Filtering, Arpeggio, Chord analyzing, Transposition, and Velocity

▶ The Session Drummer

Offline or Real-Time?

SONAR's effects features are very similar to its editing features (which you learned about in Chapter 8), but they do have a couple of differences. One difference is that, although the Effects features come included with SONAR, they are not actually a part of the main application. Instead, they come in the form of plug-ins.

NOTE

In basic terms, a plug-in is a small computer program that, by itself, does nothing, but when it is used together with a larger application, it provides added functionality to the larger program. You therefore can use plug-ins to easily add new features to a program. In SONAR's case, plug-ins provide you with additional ways to process your MIDI and audio data. As a matter of fact, Cakewalk offers additional plug-in products for sale (Audio FX 3) so that you can add even more power to your copy of SONAR.

What's more, Cakewalk isn't the only vendor that can sell plug-ins for SONAR. You can use plug-ins from a number of different third-party vendors, because many plug-ins are programmed using standard computer code. SONAR enables you to use any audio plug-ins that are DirectX-compatible. DirectX is special computer code built into Windows that controls all its multimedia functions, such as playing audio and video. So, if you are looking for new audio plug-ins to add to SONAR, just make sure they are DirectX-compatible (it will say so on the package), and you can be sure they will work.

Unfortunately, no standard computer code is available for MIDI plug-ins yet. However, Cakewalk has been kind enough to share its code with other vendors, so you can purchase additional MIDI plug-ins, too. Actually, SONAR includes a few MIDI plug-ins from other vendors, but I'll talk more about them later.

TIP

For a great source of DirectX plug-ins that you can download and use for free, check out **http://www.directxfiles.com/**

TIP

Although SONAR only supports plug-ins that are DirectX-compatible, you can also use VST-compatible plug-ins with SONAR by utilizing a VST wrapper. VST is a special plug-in format that was developed by Steinberg (**www.steinberg.net**). A VST wrapper is a program that allows a DirectX host application (like SONAR) to run VST plug-ins. The wrapper sort of acts like a translator and lets a DirectX host "understand" how to communicate with VST plug-ins.

There are several VST wrappers available. The three most common wrappers in use are VST Adapter from Fxpansion (**www.fxpansion.com**), DirectiXer from ToneWise (**www.tonewise.com**), and VST DX Wrapper from SpinAudio (**www.spinaudio.com**).

Because the Effects features are plug-ins, not only do they add functionality to SONAR, but they also add more flexibility. Unlike the editing features, the Effects features can be used to process your data in two different ways: offline and real-time.

Offline Processing

You already know what offline processing is, because you've performed it while using SONAR's editing features. With offline processing, the MIDI and audio data in your clips and tracks are permanently changed. Therefore, offline processing is also called *destructive processing* because it "destroys" the original data by modifying (or overwriting) it according to any processing that you apply.

NOTE
As you know, you can remove any offline processing done to your data by using SONAR's Undo feature. You can also load a saved copy of your project containing the original data. But neither of these restoration methods is as convenient as using real-time processing, which I'll explain shortly.

The basic procedure for using effects in offline mode is essentially the same as when using any of SONAR's editing features. You just follow these steps:

1. Select the data that you want to change.

2. Choose the MIDI or audio effect feature that you want to use by choosing either Process > Audio Effects or Process > MIDI Effects.

3. Make the appropriate parameter adjustments in the dialog box that appears.

4. Click the Audition button to test the current parameter settings. Make further adjustments if necessary.

5. If you're using an audio effect, click the Mixing tab (see Figure 11.1). These parameters determine how your data will be processed. If you select the Process In-Place, Mono Result option, SONAR takes your originally selected data, processes it with the chosen effect, and then replaces it with the processed data. This means your original data is overwritten. If your original data was in stereo, it is converted into *mono* (or *monophonic*, meaning only one channel, whereas stereo has two channels, left and right). If you select the Process In-Place, Stereo Result option, SONAR takes your originally selected data, processes it with the chosen effect, and then replaces it with the processed data. Again, this means your original data is overwritten. Also, if your original data was in mono, it is converted into stereo. If you select the Create A Send Submix option, SONAR takes your selected data, mixes it all together into a stereo signal, processes it with the chosen effect, and then places it into a new stereo track, which you designate by setting the Return Track parameter. In addition, if you activate the Keep Original Data option, your original data is left untouched. If you deactivate the Keep Original Data option, your original data is deleted.

Figure 11.1
The Mixing
parameters are
available only when
you're using an audio
effect in offline mode

6. Click OK to close the dialog box.

SONAR processes the data by applying the effect according to the parameter settings you specified. It's very simple. Don't worry; I'll go over each individual effect and its corresponding parameters later in the chapter.

Real-Time Processing

On the other hand, real-time processing doesn't change the actual data in your clips and tracks. Instead, the Effects features are applied only during playback, letting you hear the results while leaving your original data intact. Therefore, real-time processing is also called *nondestructive,* because it doesn't apply any permanent changes to your data. By simply turning off the Effects features, you can listen to your data as it was originally recorded.

The basic procedure for using effects in real-time mode isn't any more difficult than using them in offline mode, although it is a little different, as you can see here:

1. In the Track view, right-click in the Fx field of the track to which you want to add an effect. A pop-up menu appears.

NOTE
You can also apply effects in real-time by using the Console view, but I'll talk about that approach in Chapter 12.

2. Choose the effect you want to use from the pop-up menu. Depending on whether the track is for MIDI or audio, the list of effects is different. The effect you choose is added to the list in the Fx field.

3. The corresponding window for the effect is opened automatically. You can also open an effect window by double-clicking the effect in the Fx field.

NOTE

In real-time mode, the parameters of an effect are displayed in a window instead of a dialog box. You therefore can access any of the other features in SONAR while still having access to the effect parameters. You also can use more than one effect at the same time, which I'll talk about in a moment.

4. Make the appropriate parameter adjustments.

5. Start playback of the project. You immediately hear the results of the effect being applied to the data in the track. While the project plays, you can make further parameter adjustments if necessary.

TIP

If you want to make a quick comparison between how the original data sounds and how it sounds with the effect applied, some of the effects provide a Bypass button. This button (located within the effect window) is available only when you're applying effects to audio tracks.

When you activate the button, it bypasses (or turns off) the effect so that you can hear how the original data sounds. When you deactivate the button, you can hear how the data sounds with the effect being applied. You can also bypass an effect by clicking on the green box next to the name of the effect in Fx field.

NOTE

Notice that no Audition button is shown in the effect window. It isn't needed, because in real-time mode you can hear the results as the project plays. Also, notice that no Mixing tab is shown. In real-time mode, all mixing is handled via the Console view, which I'll talk about in Chapter 12. In addition, effects used in real-time mode don't provide a Cancel button. Instead, they provide a Reset And Cancel button, which still applies the effect to the track but with the default parameter settings. Any parameter settings that you changed are removed.

6. If you want to add another effect to the same track (or add some effects to different tracks), go back to Step 1. You either can leave the effects windows open, or you can close them. It doesn't matter. You can also let the project continue to play as you add new effects. As soon as you add an effect to the Fx field, you hear the results according to the current parameter settings.

7. If you want to remove an effect, right-click the effect you want to remove and select Delete from the pop-up menu.

TIP

If you apply more than one Effect to a track, the order in which the effects appear in the Fx field determines the order they are applied to the data in the track. For example, if you have the Chorus and Reverb effects added to the Fx field (in that order) of an audio track, SONAR first applies the Chorus effect to the data. It then takes the result of that application and applies the Reverb effect to it. This means that the order in which you apply effects to a track matters. If you apply effects in a different order, you get different results. This makes for some interesting experimentation. To change the order of the effects listed in the Effects bin, simply drag and drop the name of an effect left or right within the list.

You can simply go on using SONAR with the real-time effects in place. Remember that you will be aware of the results only during playback. The original data looks the same even if you examine it in the various views. Also, doing any editing to your original data doesn't change how the effects are applied to it. For example, if you have a track set up with some effects applied and you transpose the pitch of one of the clips within that track, during playback SONAR still applies the effects to the track in the same way. When the Now time reaches the point in the track containing the transposed clip, you simply hear the effect applied to the transposed data. This is one of the features that make real-time effects so flexible.

TIP

You can also apply real-time effects during recording. For example, this allows you to add some reverberation (which I'll explain later) to a vocal part to make it sound more appealing to the performer while his or her part is being recorded. This helps a performer get "in the groove" more, so to speak. In order to apply real-time effects during recording, you have to activate Input Monitoring, which I talked about in Chapter 6.

Advantages and Disadvantages

You might be asking yourself, "Why don't I just use real-time processing all the time, because it's so much more flexible?" Well, applying effects in real-time is very flexible, but in a couple of instances, you need to apply them offline. The first has to do with your computer's processing power. Most of SONAR's effects need to perform complex mathematical calculations to achieve their results. Applying effects in real-time means that not only does your computer have to deal with these calculations, but it also has to deal with SONAR playing back your MIDI and audio data. All these things going on at once can put a lot of strain on your computer's CPU. So, if you use too many effects in real-time at once, your computer might not be able to keep up. You may hear skips in playback or

SONAR might stop playing altogether. If this ever happens, you need to apply some of the effects offline and keep only a few of them going in real-time. You lose a bit of flexibility in terms of being able to make changes to your data, but there's no limit to the number of effects you can apply to your data offline.

TIP

One thing that you can do to make applying effects offline a little more flexible is to select the Create A Send Submix option and to activate the Keep Original Data option under the Mixing tab when you're applying an effect. Also be sure to set the Wet parameter to 100%. This way, you can keep your original data intact and place only the output from the effect in another track. Although this approach doesn't allow you to change how the effect is applied, you can adjust how much of the effect you want to hear by adjusting the volumes of the two tracks. If you want to hear more of the original data, raise the volume on the original data track and lower the volume on the track that contains the processed data—and vice versa if you want to hear more of the processed data.

Applying effects offline also comes in handy when you want to process some specifically selected data. For example, if you want to process a short segment of data within a track or within a clip, you have to do it offline. In real-time, you can apply effects only to whole tracks.

TIP

Actually, you can apply real-time effects to specific parts of a track by using automation, but it's a bit more complicated that just applying an effect offline. I'll explain automation in chapter 12.

Audio Effects

SONAR provides more than thirty different audio effects. If you choose either Process > Audio Effects or Process > Audio Effects > Cakewalk, you'll notice that some of these effects cover the same type of processing. Why would Cakewalk include multiple effects that accomplish the same tasks?

Well, some of the effects are designed to work with mono audio signals, and others are designed to work with stereo audio. They include parameters for both the left and right stereo channels. In addition, some of the effects process audio with a lower level of quality, and they include fewer parameter settings. So why include them? Because they provide one advantage: They don't take up as much computer processing power. This means you can apply more of the lower-quality effects to your tracks in real-time, especially if you have a slow computer system.

You also may have noticed that some of the effects mimic some of SONAR's editing features (as is the case with EQ). They mimic these effects so that you can process your data with these features in real-time. SONAR's editing features can't be used in real-time because they aren't plug-ins. The Effects features, however, come with their own sets of parameters, so I'll go over them here for you step by step.

NOTE

Because I've already covered how to apply effects offline and in real-time, I'm just going to include the basic offline steps (along with parameter descriptions) in each of the following explanations. For detailed step-by-step procedures for applying Effects offline and in real-time, refer to the previous sections in this chapter.

Equalization

I talked about the how, what, and why of equalization back in Chapter 8. In addition to the two EQ editing features, SONAR provides four EQ effects (actually, there are five if you have SONAR XL) for you to use. These are similar to the Parametric EQ editing feature.

2-Band EQ

As a matter of fact, the 2-Band EQ effect has the same exact parameters available as the Parametric EQ editing feature, but instead of one set of parameters, it has two. With these two parameters, you can apply two different types of equalization to your data at once. You use it as follows:

1. Select the audio data that you want to process.

2. Choose Process > Audio Effects > Cakewalk > 2-Band EQ to open the 2-Band EQ dialog box (see Figure 11.2).

Figure 11.2
You can use the 2-Band EQ effect to apply two different types of equalization to your data at once

3. Under the Settings tab, activate one or both of the Active options to turn on each type of EQ.

4. Set the F1, F2, Gain, and Cut parameters. I explained these parameters in the Equalization section of Chapter 8.

NOTE

You've probably noticed that one parameter setting is missing: the Q (or Quality) parameter. It isn't here because the 2-Band EQ effect has a permanent Q parameter setting of 2. This is one of the factors that keeps this effect from taking up too much computer processing power. If you need more flexibility, use the Parametric EQ or FxEq effects, which are explained later.

5. Click the Audition button to test the current parameter settings. Make further adjustments if necessary.
6. Set the appropriate options under the Mixing tab.
7. If you want to use the current settings at a later time, save them as a preset.
8. Click OK.

SONAR processes the data by applying the effect according to the parameter settings you specified.

ParamEq

The ParamEq effect provides only one band of EQ and only three parameter settings, but it also takes up the least CPU processing power, although this doesn't really make much difference since it can't be used in real-time. Here is how it works:

1. Select the audio data that you want to process.
2. Choose Process > Audio Effects > ParamEq to open the ParamEq dialog box (see Figure 11.3).

Figure 11.3
The ParamEq Effect provides a single band of parametric EQ

3. Set the Center parameter. This sets the center frequency (80 Hz to 16 kHz) for the EQ, around which the frequencies will be boosted or cut.

CHAPTER 11

4. Set the Bandwidth parameter. This parameter is the same as the Q parameter mentioned earlier. It affects how many other frequencies around the center frequency will be affected. A low value means fewer frequencies around the center frequency will be affected. A high value means more frequencies around the center frequency will be affected.

5. Set the Gain parameter. This parameter determines whether the frequencies will be cut (use a negative value) or boosted (use a positive value), and by how much (–15 dB to +15 dB).

6. Click the Audition button to test the current parameter settings. Make further adjustments if necessary.

7. Set the appropriate options under the Mixing tab.

8. If you want to use the current settings at a later time, save them as a preset.

9. Click OK.

SONAR processes the data by applying the effect according to the parameter settings you specified.

Parametric EQ

Even though the Parametric EQ effect also provides parametric equalization, its parameters are a bit different from those previously mentioned. You use it like this:

1. Select the audio data that you want to process.

2. Select Process > Audio Effects > Cakewalk > Parametric EQ to open the Parametric EQ dialog box (see Figure 11.4).

Figure 11.4
The Parametric EQ effect also provides parametric equalization but with slightly different parameter settings

3. In the Band section under the Transfer function tab, select the number of the EQ band you want to modify. Like the 2-Band EQ effect, the Parametric EQ effect enables you to set up more than one equalization type at once. In this case, you can have up to four different equalization types set up to process your data at the same time. This way, you can do some very complex equalization processing.

4. You'll notice a couple of familiar parameters in the Band Data section: Gain and Q. They work just as they do in all the other EQ features. You can set the Gain from −24 to +24 dB, and you can set the Q from 0.1 to 30. The Center Freq (short for frequency) parameter works a bit differently depending on what type of equalization you choose in the Band Type section. Essentially, it determines the frequency below which other frequencies will be cut or boosted, above which other frequencies will be cut or boosted, or exactly where boosting or cutting will occur. You can set the Center Freq from 16 to 22050 Hz. Choose the settings for these parameters that you want to use.

5. In the Band Type section, choose the type of equalization you want to use. If you choose the Low Shelf option, any frequencies below the Center Freq are either boosted or cut depending on how you set the Gain parameter. If you choose the High Shelf option, any frequencies above the Center Freq are either boosted or cut depending on how you set the Gain parameter. If you choose the Peak option, the exact frequency designated by the Center Freq parameter is the frequency that is boosted or cut depending on how you set the Gain parameter.

TIP

You've probably noticed that in addition to the parameter settings, the Parametric EQ dialog box contains a graph display. This graph shows all the current equalization settings for all four types (bands). Along the left, it shows the amplitudes (gain), and, along the bottom, it shows the frequencies. The shape of the line drawn on the graph shows you what frequencies in the audio spectrum are either boosted or cut, but that's not all. Four colored points on the graph represent each EQ band. Red is for band 1, blue for band 2, green for band 3, and purple for band 4. By clicking and dragging on these points, you can graphically change the Gain and Center Freq settings for each of the EQ types (bands), essentially "drawing" the EQ settings. You still have to manually set the Band Type and Q settings, though.

6. If you want to set up more than one equalization type, go through steps 3 through 5 again.

7. Click the Audition button to test the current parameter settings. Make further adjustments if necessary.

8. Set the appropriate options under the Mixing tab.

CHAPTER 11

9. If you want to use the current settings at a later time, save them as a preset.

10. Click OK.

SONAR processes the data by applying the effect according to the parameter settings you specified.

FxEq

Like Parametric EQ, the FxEq effect provides multiple EQ bands (with many of the same parameters) for you to adjust, but instead of four, you now have eight bands at your disposal, plus hi-shelf and lo-shelf filters. The FxEq effect is the most powerful of all the EQ effects provided (unless you have SONAR XL, which I'll talk about shortly), but it also takes up the most CPU processing power. Here is how it works:

1. Select the audio data that you want to process.

2. Choose Process > Audio Effects > Cakewalk > FxEq to open the FxEq dialog box (see Figure 11.5).

Figure 11.5
The FxEq Effect provides eight bands of parametric EQ plus single hi-shelf and lo-shelf filters

3. In the Bands section, click the number of the EQ band you want to modify to select it. To turn a band on or off, click the green button located just above the band number.

4. When you select a band, you'll notice that the Voice section displays the name of the selected band as well as the Gain setting for that band. To adjust the Gain, just drag the appropriate slider for the selected band up or down.

TIP

You can adjust the amplitude range for all the EQ bands by setting the dB Scale control, which is located just above the Monitor section. Setting the dB Scale control limits the Gain range for each of EQ bands. For example, setting the dB Scale to 15 dB means that the Gain for each EQ band can only be adjusted from –15 dB to +15 dB.

5. Selecting a band also displays the Center Frequency and Bandwidth (Q) for that band in the sections of the same names. The Center Frequency and Bandwidth parameters work the same as they do for the Parametric EQ effect, which I explained earlier.

6. If you want to set up more than one EQ band, go through steps 3 through 5 again.

7. You can also set up a hi-shelf and/or a lo-shelf filter using the controls in the Shelf section. These parameters work just like the High Shelf and Low Shelf band types in the Parametric EQ effect, which I explained earlier.

8. To adjust the final output volume of the FxEq effect, use the Trim control.

9. You can also determine if the FxEq effect will process the left, right, or both channels of a stereo signal by using the controls in the Monitor section.

10. Click the Audition button to test the current parameter settings. Make further adjustments if necessary.

11. Set the appropriate options under the Mixing tab.

12. If you want to use the current settings at a later time, save them as a preset.

13. Click OK.

SONAR processes the data by applying the effect according to the parameter settings you specified.

Equalizer (Sonar XL)

If you purchased the XL version of SONAR, you'll have one additional EQ effect at your disposal. This is the Equalizer effect from Sonic Timeworks. It's probably one of the best EQ effects you'll ever use because of its high quality output, flexibility, and low CPU usage. Like the FxEq, the Equalizer provides multiple EQ bands for you to adjust, but in this case it's six bands, plus high cut and low cut filters. Here is how it works:

1. Select the audio data that you want to process.

2. Choose Process > Audio Effects > Timeworks > Equalizer (Sonar XL) to open the Equalizer dialog box (see Figure 11.6).

CHAPTER 11

Figure 11.6
The Equalizer Effect
provides six bands of
parametric EQ plus
high cut and low
cut filters

3. In the mid-section of the dialog box, there are six EQ bands. Bands don't need to be selected in order for their parameters to be adjusted, but you can turn a band on or off by clicking on its Bypass button located at the bottom of the band's parameter controls. You can also turn the entire Equalizer effect on or off by clicking the Bypass button in the Global section of the dialog box.

4. To adjust the gain for a band, just drag its Gain slider up or down.

TIP

To make precise parameter adjustments, hold down the CTRL key on your computer keyboard as you drag a slider up or down with your mouse. To specify an exact value, click the number value shown for the parameter and then type in a new value using your computer keyboard.

5. There are also center frequency (Freq) and bandwidth (Q) parameters available for each band. These parameters work the same as they do for the Parametric EQ effect, which I talked about earlier.

TIP

Normally the frequency parameter of a band can range from 20 to 20,480 Hz. If you want to limit the frequency range of a band, click the L button located at the top of the band's parameter controls. This will limit the frequency range to 20 to 600 Hz. This can be useful when you want to use a band only for low frequency adjustments. To set the frequency range back to normal, click the ALL button located to the right of the L button.

6. To reset a band to its last known parameter values, click the Reset button located at the bottom of the band's parameter controls. You can also reset the parameters for all the bands by clicking the Reset button in the Global section of the dialog box.

7. If you want to set up more than one EQ band, go through steps 3 through 6 again.

8. You can also set up high and/or low shelf filters using the special buttons located at the bottom of the band parameter controls (right above the Reset buttons) for the first and sixth bands. Clicking these special buttons will convert the first band into a low shelf filter and the sixth band into a high shelf filter. These filters work just like the High Shelf and Low Shelf band types in the Parametric EQ effect, which I talked about earlier.

9. In addition to the high and low shelf filters, you can apply Low Cut and High Cut filters, which are the two extra sets of parameter controls you see at the extreme left and right sides of the dialog box, respectively. You can adjust the frequency and resonance of these filters. The Resonance parameter allows you to boost or cut the specified frequency, although anything below the low frequency will be cut and anything above the high frequency will be cut.

NOTE

The difference between the high/low shelf filters and the high/low cut filters are that the shelf filters allow you to either boost or cut frequencies above or below their designated center frequency. With the cut filters, frequencies are always cut.

TIP

You've probably noticed that in addition to the parameter settings, the Equalizer dialog box provides two different modes of operation: Standard and Graphic. If you click the Graphic Mode button located in the upper right corner of the dialog box, the Equalizer presents a graph display. This graph shows all the current equalization settings. The vertical part of the graph represents amplitude (gain), and along the bottom of the graph, you'll see the frequency measurements. The shape of the line drawn on the graph shows you what frequencies in the audio spectrum are either boosted or cut, but that's not all. Two gray balls represent the low and high cut filters, and six colored balls on the graph represent each EQ band. Dark blue, medium blue, light blue, yellow, light orange, and dark orange represent the six EQ bands, respectively. By clicking and dragging on these balls, you can graphically change the Gain and Frequency settings for each band, essentially "drawing" the EQ settings. You still have to manually adjust the Q settings and use Standard mode for all else.

In addition, Graphic mode provides a spectrum analysis graph. You can use spectrum analysis to analyze the frequency content in your audio and determine which frequencies need to be boosted or cut. To analyze the signal coming into the Equalizer effect, click the In button in the Spectrum section of the dialog box. To analyze the signal going out of the Equalizer effect, click the Out button. The animated spectrum graph shows the amplitudes of different frequencies within the signal as it is being played. It can tell you if there is too much bass or too much treble, and you can make the appropriate adjustments to make the audio sound better.

10.   To adjust the final output volume of the Equalizer effect, use the Outgain control in the Standard mode.

TIP

The Equalizer effect provides both Clean and Vintage processing. Clean processing gives you a more modern, clean, and crisp sound found in most EQ effects today. Vintage processing gives you a warmer, smoother type of sound found in early EQ effects. You'll have to listen to each processing type to determine which one is right for your audio material. To choose a processing type, click the Clean/Vintage buttons in the Global section of the dialog box.

11.   Click the Audition button to test the current parameter settings. Make further adjustments if necessary.

12.   Set the appropriate options under the Mixing tab.

13.   If you want to use the current settings at a later time, save them as a preset.

TIP

You can save Equalizer presets using the standard method for all SONAR effects, or you can use a special method by right-clicking anywhere within the dialog box. This will bring up a menu that will allow you to load and save presets to separate files that can then be shared with friends. Another advantage to saving presets this way is that if you use another program to access the Equalizer effect, your presets will be available from within that program too, and not just from within SONAR.

14.   Click OK.

SONAR processes the data by applying the effect according to the parameter settings you specified.

TIP

In addition to regular equalization tasks, the high quality of the Equalizer effect allows it to be used for mastering. Mastering is the procedure during which the final mixed down stereo audio for a song is processed with various effects (such as EQ, compression, and limiting) to give the song that final professional touch before it is burned to CD. There have been entire books written on the topic of mastering, but you can also find some good information on the Internet at these sites:

- **http://www.izotope.com/products/ozone/ozoneguide.html**
- **http://www.prorec.com/prorec/articles.nsf/files/**
  F717F79532C9067386256688001A7623
- **http://www.digido.com/cdmastering.html**

Also, be sure to sign up for my free DigiFreq music technology newsletter so you don't miss the mastering information I will be providing in future issues. To sign up, go to: **http://www.digifreq.com/digifreq/**

Delay

You know what an echo is, right? It's a repeating sound that mimics an initial sound. For example, if you yell the word *hello* in a large enclosed area (such as a concert hall or a canyon), you hear that word repeated (or echoed) back over and over until it fades away. This effect is exactly what delay allows you to do to your audio data. You can create echoes that vary in the number of repeats and time between each repeat. SONAR includes four delay effects.

Delay/Echo (Mono)

The Delay/Echo (Mono) effect is pretty straightforward in terms of operation. This effect is intended to be used with monophonic audio rather than stereo. It works like this:

1. Select the audio data that you want to process.

2. Select Process > Audio Effects > Cakewalk > Delay/Echo (Mono) to open the Delay/Echo (Mono) dialog box (see Figure 11.7).

Figure 11.7
Using the Delay/Echo (Mono) Effect, you can add echoes to your audio data

CHAPTER 11

3. Under the Settings tab, set the Delay Time parameter. This parameter determines how much time (in milliseconds) occurs between each echo. You can set the Delay Time from 0.02 to 5000 milliseconds (which is equal to 5 seconds).

TIP
Many professional musicians use delay to synchronize the echoes with the music. For instance, you can have the echoes play in time with each quarter note, eighth note, sixteenth note, and so on. All that's required for this cool trick is a little simple math.

Continued

Begin by figuring the Delay Time needed to synchronize the echoes to each quarter note. To do so, just divide 60,000 (the number of milliseconds in one second) by the current Tempo (measured in beats per minute) of your project. So, for a Tempo of 120 bpm, you get 500 milliseconds. If you set the Delay Time to 500, the resulting echoes sound at the same time as each quarter note.

To figure out the Delay Time for other note values, you just need to divide or multiply. Because an eighth note is half the value of a quarter note, you simply divide 500 by 2 to get 250 milliseconds. A sixteenth note is half the value of an eighth note, so 250 divided by 2 is 125. See how it works? If you want to find out larger note values, just multiply by 2. Because a half note is twice as long as a quarter note, you multiply 500 by 2 to get 1,000 milliseconds, and so on.

4. Set the Dry Mix and Wet Mix parameters. When you apply an Effect to your original data, you can determine how much of the effect and how much of the original data ends up in the final sound. This way, you can add a certain amount of effect without drowning out the entire original data. The Dry Mix parameter determines how much of the original data you will hear in the final signal, and the Wet Mix parameter determines how much of the effect you will hear in the final signal. You can set both of these parameters anywhere from 0 to 100 percent.

5. Set the Feedback Mix parameter. With some effects, you can take their resulting signals and send them back through to have the effect applied again multiple times. That's what the Feedback Mix parameter does. The resulting sound can be different depending on the effect. For delay effects, the Feedback Mix controls how many echoes occur. You can set it anywhere from 0 to 100 percent. The lower the value, the fewer the number of echoes. The higher the value, the more echoes. Unfortunately, there's no way to determine exactly how many echoes will occur according to the percentage. You'll have to experiment with this one.

6. Set the Mod Rate and Mod Depth parameters. These parameters are a bit difficult to describe. They enable you to add a "warble" type of effect to your audio data along with the echoes. The sound is also similar to that of the tremolo you hear on an electronic organ. To hear what I mean, check out the Fast Tremolo Delay preset. The mod rate determines the speed (in Hz or cycles per second) of the "warble," and the mod depth determines how much your audio data will be affected by it. This is just another one of those features that you have to experiment with to understand.

7. Click the Audition button to test the current parameter settings. Make further adjustments if necessary.

8. Set the appropriate options under the Mixing tab.

9. If you want to use the current settings at a later time, save them as a preset.

10. Click OK.

SONAR processes the data by applying the effect according to the parameter settings you specified.

Echo

The Echo effect is similar to the Delay/Echo (Mono) effect, except that it works with stereo audio and some of its parameters are slightly different. Here is how it works:

1. Select the audio data that you want to process.

2. Choose Process > Audio Effects > Echo to open the Echo dialog box (see Figure 11.8).

Figure 11.8
The Echo Effect is similar to the Delay/Echo (Mono) Effect, except that it works with stereo audio

3. If you would like the echoes from each stereo channel added to themselves, choose the Normal Pan option for the Delay parameter. If you would like the echoes from the left stereo channel to be heard in the right stereo channel and vice versa, choose the Swap Channels option for the Delay parameter.

4. I've explained the Wet Dry Mix parameter before, but in this case there is only one parameter rather than two. Setting the Wet Dry Mix parameter to 50 percent gives you an equal balance between the original audio signal and the effect audio signal. Setting the Wet Dry Mix to 0 percent means you'll hear only the original audio signal. Setting the Wet Dry Mix to 100 percent means you will hear only the effect audio signal.

5. Set the Feedback parameter. This parameter works just like the Feedback parameter in the Delay/Echo (Mono) Effect.

6. Set the Left Delay and Right Delay parameters. These parameters work just like the Delay Time parameter in the Delay/Echo (Mono) Effect, except that here you get a separate setting for each stereo channel.

7. Click the Audition button to test the current parameter settings. Make further adjustments if necessary.

8. Set the appropriate options under the Mixing tab.

9. If you want to use the current settings at a later time, save them as a preset.

10. Click OK.

SONAR processes the data by applying the effect according to the parameter settings you specified.

Delay

Very similar to Delay/Echo (Mono), the Delay effect has most of the same parameters. Because it works with stereo audio, however, there are two sets, plus a few extras. It works like this:

1. Select the audio data that you want to process.

2. Select Process > Audio Effects > Cakewalk > Delay to open the Delay dialog box (see Figure 11.9).

Figure 11.9
The Delay effect has a few additional parameters because it is designed to work with stereo audio

3. Set the Left Delay and Right Delay parameters. These parameters work the same way as the Delay Time parameter in the Delay/Echo (Mono) Effect. In this case, separate controls are available for the left and right stereo channels. A Link option is also available. Activating this option links the Left Delay and Right Delay parameters together so that, if you change the value of one, the other is set to the exact same value. Most of the time, you

should keep the Link option activated so that both stereo channels have the same amount of delay. However, setting different values for each channel can sometimes yield interesting results. Don't be afraid to experiment.

4. Set the Dry Mix and Wet Mix parameters. These parameters work the same way as the parameters of the same names in the Delay/Echo (Mono) effect. Separate controls are not available for each stereo channel in this case, but a Link option is available. Activating this option links the Dry Mix and Wet Mix parameters together, so if you increase the value of the Wet Mix, the value of the Dry Mix decreases and vice versa. This feature enables you to achieve a perfect balance between the original data and the effect.

5. Set the Left Feedback and Right Feedback parameters. These parameters work the same way as the Feedback Mix parameter in the Delay/Echo (Mono) effect. In this case, separate controls are available for the left and right stereo channels. A Cross Feedback parameter is also available. Using this parameter, you can take the resulting signal from the left channel and send it back through the right channel and the resulting signal from the right channel and send it back through the left channel. Essentially, this means that this parameter also provides control over the number of echoes that will occur and, at the same time, it helps to make the stereo field sound "fuller."

6. Set the LFO Depth and LFO Rate parameters. These parameters work the same way as the Mod Depth and Mod Rate parameters in the Delay/Echo (Mono) effect. In addition, two other options called Triangular and Sinusoidal are available. They determine the type of "warble" to be applied. The Triangular option creates a "coarse" or "sharp" sound, and the Sinusoidal option creates a "smooth" or "flowing" sound. You'll have to try them out to hear what I mean.

7. Click the Audition button to test the current parameter settings. Make further adjustments if necessary.

8. Set the appropriate options under the Mixing tab.

9. If you want to use the current settings at a later time, save them as a preset.

10. Click OK.

SONAR processes the data by applying the effect according to the parameter settings you specified.

FxDelay

The FxDelay effect allows you to create very complex echo effects by letting you set up multiple delays at once, such as setting up multiple Delay/Echo (Mono) effects at the same time to process your audio data. Here is how the FxDelay effect works:

1. Select the audio data that you would like to process.

2. Choose Process > Audio Effects > Cakewalk > FxDelay to open the FxDelay dialog box (see Figure 11.10).

Figure 11.10
The FxDelay effect lets
you create complex
echo effects

3. Set the Mix Level parameter. This parameter works just like the Wet Dry Mix parameter in the Echo effect.

4. Set the On options for each of the Voice parameters (1, 2, 3, and 4). The On options let you determine how many different delays you want to set up in your effect. You can have up to four different delays.

5. Each Voice (delay) comes with its own Gain, Delay, Pan, and Feedback parameters. This means that you can control the initial volume, echo time, panning in the stereo field, and feedback (number of echoes) of each Voice. To adjust the parameters for a voice, select the number of the voice via the Sel. options. Then, adjust the Gain, Delay, Feedback, and Pan parameters for that voice. You can do this for all four voices individually.

6. To adjust the Gain for all four voices simultaneously, use the Global parameter.

7. Set the Output Level parameter, which controls the overall volume level of the effect output.

8. Click the Audition button to test the current parameter settings. Make further adjustments if necessary.

9. Set the appropriate options under the Mixing tab.

10. If you want to use the current settings at a later time, save them as a preset.

11. Click OK.

SONAR processes the data by applying the effect according to the parameter settings you specified.

Chorus

Believe it or not, you'll find that SONAR's chorus effects (of which there are four) have many of the same parameters as its delay effects. Why? Because, technically, chorus is a form of delay. Chorus uses delay and detuning to achieve its results. You don't hear echoes when using chorus, though, because the delay is extremely short. Instead, chorus makes your audio data sound "fatter" or "fuller." The name *chorus* comes from the fact that people singing in a chorus produce a full sound because each person sings slightly out of tune and out of time—not enough to make the music sound bad, but actually better. You can use SONAR's chorus effects to achieve similar results with your audio data. The following sections describe how to use them.

Chorus (Mono)

The Chorus (Mono) effect is designed to work with monophonic audio rather than stereo. To apply the Chorus (Mono) effect, you do the following:

1. Select the audio data that you want to process.

2. Select Process > Audio Effects > Cakewalk > Chorus (Mono) to open the Chorus (Mono) dialog box (see Figure 11.11).

Figure 11.11
The Chorus (Mono) effect has the same exact parameters as the Delay/Echo (Mono) effect, although they provide different results

3. Under the Settings tab, set the Delay Time parameter. The only difference between this Delay Time parameter and the same parameter in the Delay/Echo (Mono) effect is that this one has a range of only 20 to 80 milliseconds. If you set this parameter high enough, you can actually get some quick repeating echoes out of it. For adding chorus to your audio, though, you should keep it set somewhere between 20 and 35.

4. Set the Dry Mix and Wet Mix parameters. I explained these parameters earlier.

5. Set the Feedback Mix parameter. Instead of setting the number of echoes to occur (as in the Delay/Echo (Mono) effect), this parameter determines the "thickness" of the chorus. The higher the value, the "thicker" the chorus.

6. Set the Mod Rate and Mod Depth parameters. Instead of adding a "warble" to your audio (as in the Delay/Echo (Mono) effect), these parameters determine how detuning is added to the chorus. The Mod Rate determines how quickly the detuning occurs, and the Mod Depth determines the amount of detuning. A high Mod Depth setting makes your audio sound really out of tune (which isn't usually desirable), but a lower setting produces a nice chorusing.

7. Click the Audition button to test the current parameter settings. Make further adjustments if necessary.

8. Set the appropriate options under the Mixing tab.

9. If you want to use the current settings at a later time, save them as a preset.

10. Click OK.

SONAR processes the data by applying the effect according to the parameter settings you specified.

Chorus

Very similar to Chorus (Mono), the Chorus effect has most of the same parameters. Because it works with stereo audio, however, there are a couple differences. It works like this:

1. Select the audio data that you want to process.

2. Choose Process > Audio Effects > Chorus to open the Chorus dialog box (see Figure 11.12).

Figure 11.12
The Chorus effect is similar to the Chorus (Mono) effect, except that it works with stereo audio

3. Set the Delay parameter. This parameter provides the same chorusing results as the Delay Time parameter in the Chorus (Mono) effect—but, of course, for stereo audio.

4. Set the Wet Dry Mix parameter. Set the value of the parameter low to hear more of the original audio data. Set the value of the parameter high to hear more of the effect audio data. Set the value of the parameter at 50 percent to hear an equal mix of the original and effect audio data.

5. Set the Feedback parameter. This parameter provides the same chorusing results as the Feedback Mix parameter in the Chorus (Mono) effect—but, of course, for stereo audio.

6. Set the Depth and Frequency parameters. They provide the same results as the Mod Depth and Mod Rate parameters in the Chorus (Mono) effect.

7. Set the Waveform parameter. The Sine and Triangle parameters determine the type of "warble" to be applied to the Chorus effect. The Triangle option creates a "coarse" or "sharp" sound, and the Sine option creates a "smooth" or "flowing" sound. You'll have to try them out to hear what I mean.

8. Set the LFO Phase parameter. This parameter allows you to change the sound of the "warble" (mentioned earlier) to give it a sort of "hollow" sound. You'll need to experiment to hear what I mean.

9. Click the Audition button to test the current parameter settings. Make further adjustments if necessary.

CHAPTER 11

10. Set the appropriate options under the Mixing tab.

11. If you want to use the current settings at a later time, save them as a preset.

12. Click OK.

SONAR processes the data by applying the effect according to the parameter settings you specified.

Chorus

Yes, there are actually two chorus effects with the same exact name, but they are accessed and operated differently. To apply this Chorus effect (which provides more features and better sounding output), you do the following:

1. Select the audio data that you want to process.

2. Select Process > Audio Effects > Cakewalk > Chorus to open the Chorus dialog box (see Figure 11.13).

Figure 11.13
The Chorus effect has the same exact parameters as the Delay effect, although they provide different results

3. Set the Left Delay and Right Delay parameters. They provide the same chorusing results as the Delay Time parameter in the Chorus (Mono) effect—but, of course, for the separate left and right stereo channels. You can also link these parameters together by activating the Link option.

4. Set the Dry Mix and Wet Mix parameters. I explained these parameters earlier.

5. Set the Left Feedback and Right Feedback parameters. They provide the same chorusing results as the Feedback Mix parameter in the Chorus (Mono) effect, but of course for the separate left and right stereo channels.

Also, just as the Cross Feedback parameter in the Delay effect enhances the delay, this Cross Feedback parameter enhances the chorus.

6. Set the LFO Depth and LFO Rate parameters. They provide the same results as the Mod Depth and Mod Rate parameters in the Chorus (Mono) effect. And I explained the Triangular and Sinusoidal parameters earlier in the "Delay" section.

7. Click the Audition button to test the current parameter settings. Make further adjustments if necessary.

8. Set the appropriate options under the Mixing tab.

9. If you want to use the current settings at a later time, save them as a preset.

10. Click OK.

SONAR processes the data by applying the effect according to the parameter settings you specified.

FxChorus

The FxChorus effect allows you to create very complex chorus effects by letting you set up multiple choruses at once, such as setting up multiple Chorus (Mono) effects at the same time to process your audio data. Here is how the FxChorus effect works:

1. Select the audio data that you would like to process.

2. Choose Process > Audio Effects > Cakewalk > FxChorus to open the FxChorus dialog box (see Figure 11.14).

Figure 11.14
The FxChorus Effect lets you create complex chorus effects

3. Set the Mix Level parameter. This parameter works just like the Wet Dry Mix parameter in the Echo effect.

4. Set the On options for each of the voice parameters (1, 2, 3, and 4). The On options let you determine how many different choruses you want to set up in your effect. You can have up to four different choruses.

5. Each voice (chorus) comes with its own Gain, Delay, Pan, Mod Depth, and Mod Freq parameters. This means that you can control the initial volume, chorus strength, panning in the stereo field, and depth and speed of the "warble" of each Voice. To adjust the parameters for a voice, select the number of the voice via the Sel. options. Then, adjust the Gain, Delay, Pan, Mod Depth, and Mod Freq parameters for that voice. You can do this for all four voices individually.

6. To adjust the Gain for all four voices simultaneously, use the Global parameter.

7. Set the Output Level parameter, which controls the overall volume level of the effect output.

8. Click the Audition button to test the current parameter settings. Make further adjustments if necessary.

9. Set the appropriate options under the Mixing tab.

10. If you want to use the current settings at a later time, save them as a preset.

11. Click OK.

SONAR processes the data by applying the effect according to the parameter settings you specified.

Flanging

Guess what? As with SONAR's chorus effects, you'll find that the program's flanger effects have many of the same parameters as its delay effects, too, because (yep, that's right) flanging is also a form of delay. Flanging produces a kind of "spacey" or "whooshy" type of sound. It does so by mixing a slightly delayed version of the original data with itself. As with chorus, you don't hear echoes because the delay occurs so quickly. It's difficult to describe what flanging sounds like, so you'll have to hear it for yourself. You can apply SONAR's flanging effects as described in the following sections.

Flanger (Mono)

The Flanger (Mono) effect is designed to work with monophonic audio, rather than stereo. To apply the Flanger (Mono) effect, you do the following:

1. Select the audio data that you want to process.

2. Select Process > Audio Effects > Cakewalk > Flanger (Mono) to open the Flanger (Mono) dialog box (see Figure 11.15).

Figure 11.15
The Flanger (Mono) effect has the same exact parameters as the Delay/Echo (Mono) effect, although they provide different results

3. Under the Settings tab, set the Delay Time parameter. The only difference between this Delay Time parameter and the same parameter in the Delay/Echo (Mono) effect is that this one has a range of only 1 to 20 milliseconds. If you set this parameter high enough, you can actually get some chorusing out of it. To add flanging to your audio, though, you should keep it set somewhere between 1 and 11.

4. Set the Dry Mix and Wet Mix parameters. I explained these parameters earlier.

5. Set the Feedback Mix parameter. Instead of setting the number of echoes to occur (as in the Delay/Echo (Mono) effect), this parameter determines the "thickness" of the flanging. The higher the value, the "thicker" the flanger.

6. Set the Mod Rate and Mod Depth parameters. Instead of adding a "warble" to your audio (as in the Delay/Echo (Mono) effect), these parameters determine the speed and amount of the flanging. The Mod Rate determines how quickly the flanging occurs, and the Mod Depth determines the amount of flanging. Check out some of the included presets to get an idea of what values to use for these parameters.

7. Click the Audition button to test the current parameter settings. Make further adjustments if necessary.

8. Set the appropriate options under the Mixing tab.

9. If you want to use the current settings at a later time, save them as a preset.

10. Click OK.

SONAR processes the data by applying the effect according to the parameter settings you specified.

CHAPTER 11

Flanger

Very similar to Flanger (Mono), the Flanger effect has most of the same parameters. Because it works with stereo audio, however, there are a couple differences. It works like this:

1. Select the audio data that you want to process.

2. Choose Process > Audio Effects > Flanger to open the Flanger dialog box (see Figure 11.16).

Figure 11.16
The Flanger effect is similar to the Flanger (Mono) Effect, except that it works with stereo audio

3. Set the Delay parameter. This parameter provides the same flanging results as the Delay Time parameter in the Flanger (Mono) effect—but, of course, for stereo audio.

4. Set the Wet Dry Mix parameter. Set the value of the parameter low to hear more of the original audio data. Set the value of the parameter high to hear more of the effect audio data. Set the value of the parameter at 50 percent to hear an equal mix of the original and effect audio data.

5. Set the Feedback parameter. This parameter provides the same flanging results as the Feedback Mix parameter in the Flanger (Mono) effect—but, of course, for stereo audio.

6. Set the Depth and Frequency parameters. They provide the same results as the Mod Depth and Mod Rate parameters in the Flanger (Mono) effect.

7. Set the Waveform parameter. The Sine and Triangle parameters determine the type of "warble" to be applied to the Chorus effect. The Triangle option

creates a "coarse" or "sharp" sound, and the Sine option creates a "smooth" or "flowing" sound. You'll have to try them out to hear what I mean.

8. Set the LFO Phase parameter. This parameter allows you to change the sound of the "warble" (mentioned earlier) to give it a sort of "hollow" sound. You'll need to experiment to hear what I mean.

9. Click the Audition button to test the current parameter settings. Make further adjustments if necessary.

10. Set the appropriate options under the Mixing tab.

11. If you want to use the current settings at a later time, save them as a preset.

12. Click OK.

SONAR processes the data by applying the effect according to the parameter settings you specified.

Flanger

Yes, there are actually two flanger effects with the same exact name, but they are accessed and operated differently. To apply this Flanger effect, you do the following:

1. Select the audio data that you want to process.

2. Select Process > Audio Effects > Cakewalk > Flanger to open the Flanger dialog box (see Figure 11.17).

Figure 11.17
The Flanger effect has the same exact parameters as the Delay effect, although they provide different results

3. Set the Left Delay and Right Delay parameters. They provide the same flanging results as the Delay Time parameter in the Flanger (Mono) effect, but for the separate left and right stereo channels. You can also link these parameters together by activating the Link option.

4. Set the Dry Mix and Wet Mix parameters. I explained these parameters earlier.

5. Set the Left Feedback and Right Feedback parameters. They provide the same flanging results as the Feedback Mix parameter in the Flanger (Mono) effect, but for the separate left and right stereo channels. Also, just as the Cross Feedback parameter in the Delay effect enhances the delay, this Cross Feedback parameter enhances the flanging.

6. Set the LFO Depth and LFO Rate parameters. They provide the same results as the Mod Depth and Mod Rate parameters in the Flanger (Mono) effect. I explained the Triangular and Sinusoidal parameters earlier in the "Delay" section.

7. Click the Audition button to test the current parameter settings. Make further adjustments if necessary.

8. Set the appropriate options under the Mixing tab.

9. If you want to use the current settings at a later time, save them as a preset.

10. Click OK.

SONAR processes the data by applying the effect according to the parameter settings you specified.

FxFlange

The FxFlange effect allows you to create complex flange effects by letting you set up multiple flanges at once, such as setting up multiple Flanger (Mono) effects at the same time to process your audio data. Here is how the FxFlange effect works:

1. Select the audio data that you would like to process.

2. Choose Process > Audio Effects > Cakewalk > FxFlange to open the FxFlange dialog box (see Figure 11.18).

Figure 11.18
The FxFlange effect
lets you create complex
flanging effects

3. Set the Mix parameter. This parameter works just like the Wet Dry Mix parameter in the Echo effect.

4. Set the On options for each of the voice parameters (1 and 2). The On options let you determine how many different flanges you want to set up in your effect. You can have up to two different flanges.

5. Each voice (flange) comes with its own Gain, Delay, Pan, Feedback, and Mod Freq parameters. This means that you can control the initial volume, flanging strength, panning in the stereo field, and depth and speed of the flanging of each voice. To adjust the parameters for a voice, select the number of the voice via the Sel. options. Then adjust the Gain, Delay, Pan, Feedback, and Mod Freq parameters for that voice. You can do this for both voices individually.

6. To adjust the Gain for both voices simultaneously, use the Global parameter.

7. Set the Level parameter, which controls the overall volume level of the effect output.

8. Click the Audition button to test the current parameter settings. Make further adjustments if necessary.

9. Set the appropriate options under the Mixing tab.

10. If you want to use the current settings at a later time, save them as a preset.

11. Click OK.

SONAR processes the data by applying the effect according to the parameter settings you specified.

CHAPTER 11

Reverberation

Reverb (short for reverberation) is also a form of delay, but it's special because, instead of distinct echoes, reverb adds a complex series of very small echoes that simulate artificial ambience. In other words, reverb produces a dense collection of echoes that are so close together that they create a wash of sound, making the original audio data sound like it's being played in another environment, such as a large concert hall. Using SONAR's reverb effects, you can make your music sound like it's being played in all kinds of different places, such as in an arena, a club, or even on a live stage. SONAR includes five reverb Effects.

Reverb (Mono)

The Reverb (Mono) effect is designed to work with monophonic audio, rather than stereo. To apply the Reverb (Mono) effect to your data, you do the following:

1. Select the audio data that you want to process.

2. Select Process > Audio Effects > Cakewalk > Reverb (Mono) to open the Reverb (Mono) dialog box (see Figure 11.19).

Figure 11.19
Using the Reverb
(Mono) effect, you can
add reverberation to
your audio data

3. Under the Settings tab, set the Decay Time parameter. When you're applying reverb to your data, you should imagine what type of environment you want to create. Doing so will help you in setting the effect parameters. Techni- cally, the Decay Time determines how long it takes for the reverberation to fade away, but you can think of it as controlling how big the artificial envi- ronment will be. The lower the Decay Time, the smaller the environment. The higher the Decay Time, the larger the environment. You can set the Decay Time from 0.20 to 5 seconds. So, if you want to make your music sound like it's playing in a small room, a good Decay Time might be about 0.25. If you want to make your music sound like it's being played on a live stage, a good Decay Time might be about 1.50. Be sure to check out some of the included presets for more sample parameter settings.

4. Set the Dry Mix and Wet Mix parameters. I explained these parameters earlier in the chapter. One point you should note, however, is that in the case of reverb, the Dry Mix and Wet Mix parameters also make a difference on how the effect sounds. If you set the Dry Mix high and the Wet Mix low, your audio data will sound like it's positioned closer to the "front" of the imaginary environment. If you set the Dry Mix low and the Wet Mix high, your audio data will sound like it's positioned farther away. For example, if you want to simulate what it sounds like to be seated in the very back row of a music concert, you can set the Dry Mix low and the Wet Mix high. You need to experiment to get the exact parameter settings.

5. In the Early Reflections section, choose one of the following options: None, Dense, or Sparse. When you make a sound in any enclosed environment, some very quick echoes always occur because of the reflective surfaces (such as walls) that you are standing next to. These echoes are known as *early reflections*. To make your reverb simulations sound more authentic, SONAR provides this parameter so that you can control the density of the early reflections. If you select None, no early reflections are added to the effect. The Sparse option makes the reflections sound more like distinct echoes, and the Dense option makes the reverb effect sound "thicker." Early reflections are more pronounced in larger spaces, so if you want to simulate a really large space, you'll probably want to use the Sparse option. If you want to simulate a moderately sized space, you'll probably want to use the Dense option. And if you want to simulate a small space (such as a room), you should use the None option.

6. In the Frequency Cutoff section, set the High Pass and Low Pass parameters. If you think these parameters look like equalization settings, you're right. Using these parameters also helps to create more authentic environment simulations because smaller, closed environments tend to stifle some frequencies of the audio spectrum, and larger environments usually sound brighter, meaning they promote more of the frequencies. The High Pass and Low Pass parameters work just like the EQ parameters I described earlier in the chapter. If you activate the High Pass parameter and set its frequency (in Hz), any frequencies above that frequency are allowed to pass and are included in the Effect, and any frequencies below that frequency are cut. If you activate the Low Pass parameter and set its frequency, any frequencies below that frequency are allowed to pass, and any frequencies above that frequency are cut. So, if you want to simulate a small room, you can leave the High Pass parameter deactivated, activate the Low Pass parameter, and set its frequency to around 8000 Hz. This setting would cut out any really high frequencies, making the room sound small and enclosed. For more examples on how to set these parameters, be sure to take a look at some of the included presets.

7.   Click the Audition button to test the current parameter settings. Make further adjustments if necessary.

8.   Set the appropriate options under the Mixing tab.

9.   If you want to use the current settings at a later time, save them as a preset.

10. Click OK.

SONAR processes the data by applying the effect according to the parameter settings you specified.

Reverb

To apply the Reverb effect to your data, you do the following:

1.   Select the audio data that you want to process.

2.   Select Process > Audio Effects > Cakewalk > Reverb to open the Reverb dialog box (see Figure 11.20).

Figure 11.20
The Reverb effect parameters are exactly the same as the Reverb (Mono) effect except that they control both the left and right channels of the signal if your audio is in stereo

3.   Under the Settings tab, set the Decay(s) parameter. It is exactly the same as the Decay Time parameter in the Reverb (Mono) effect except that it controls both the left and right channels of the signal if your audio is in stereo.

4.   Set the Dry Mix and Wet Mix parameters. They are exactly the same as the Dry Mix and Wet Mix parameters in the Reverb (Mono) effect except that they control both the left and right channels of the signal if your audio is in stereo. A Link option is also available, which I explained previously.

5.   Choose an early reflections option. The No Echo, Dense Echo, and Sparse Echo options are exactly the same as the None, Dense, and Sparse options in the Reverb (Mono) effect, respectively.

6. Activate and set the frequency cutoff parameters. The LP Filter and HP Filter parameters are exactly the same as the Low Pass and High Pass filters in the Reverb (Mono) effect, respectively.

7. Click the Audition button to test the current parameter settings. Make further adjustments if necessary.

8. Set the appropriate options under the Mixing tab.

9. If you want to use the current settings at a later time, save them as a preset.

10. Click OK.

SONAR processes the data by applying the effect according to the parameter settings you specified.

WavesReverb

The WavesReverb effect is a simplified reverb effect that provides only four adjustable parameters. Because of this, however, it also takes up the least CPU processing power, although this doesn't really matter since it can't be used in real-time. Here is how the WavesReverb effect works:

1. Select the audio data that you want to process.

2. Choose Process > Audio Effects > WavesReverb to open the WavesReverb dialog box (see Figure 11.21).

Figure 11.21
The WavesReverb effect provides reverb without taking up a lot of CPU processing power

3. Set the InGain parameter. This parameter determines how loud the audio signal coming into the effect will be. More often than not, you'll want to keep this set at 0.

4. Set the Reverb Mix parameter. This parameter determines the balance between the original audio signal and the effect audio signal. Set it to 0 to hear the full reverberation effect.

CHAPTER 11

5. Set the Reverb Time parameter. This parameter works just like the Decay Time parameter in the Reverb (Mono) Effect, except that it is limited to 3 seconds.

6. Set the HF Ratio. This parameter is similar to the Low Pass parameter in the Reverb (Mono) effect. Using a low value cuts out the high frequencies in the effect, and using a high value boosts the high frequencies in the effect.

7. Click the Audition button to test the current parameter settings. Make further adjustments if necessary.

8. Set the appropriate options under the Mixing tab.

9. If you want to use the current settings at a later time, save them as a preset.

10. Click OK.

SONAR processes the data by applying the effect according to the parameter settings you specified.

FxReverb

In contrast to the WavesReverb effect (as well as the other reverberation effects), the FxReverb effect provides the highest quality sound as well as the most adjustable parameters. Here is how it works:

1. Select the audio data that you want to process.

2. Choose Process > Audio Effects > Cakewalk > FxReverb to open the FxReverb dialog box (see Figure 11.22).

Figure 11.22
The FxReverb effect provides the best quality of all of SONAR's reverberation effects

3. Set the Room Size parameter. This parameter determines the size of the environment you are trying to simulate.

4. Set the Mix parameter. I explained this parameter earlier in the chapter. It is similar to the Wet Dry Mix parameter used in other effects. One point you should note, however, is that in the case of reverb, the Mix parameter

also makes a difference on how the effect sounds. If you set the Mix parameter low, your audio data will sound like it's positioned closer to the "front" of the imaginary environment. If you set the Mix parameter high, your audio data will sound like it's positioned farther away. For example, if you want to simulate what it sounds like to be seated in the very back row of a music concert, you can set the Mix parameter high. You need to experiment to get the exact parameter settings you desire.

5. Set the Decay Time parameter. When you're applying reverb to your data, you should imagine what type of environment you want to create. Doing so will help you set the parameters. Technically, the Decay Time determines how long it takes for the reverberation to fade away, but you can also think of it as controlling how big the artificial environment will be. It works in conjunction with the Room Size parameter. The lower the Decay Time, the smaller the environment, and vice versa. So, if you want to make your audio sound like it's playing in a small room, a good Decay Time might be about 0.5 seconds. If you want to make your audio sound like it's playing in a large area, a good Decay Time might be about 3 seconds.

6. Set the Pre Delay parameter. This parameter is similar to the Decay Time parameter, except that the Pre Delay determines the time between when your audio is first heard and when the reverb effect begins. This gives you even more control in determining your artificial environment. For small spaces, use a low setting (such as 1 millisecond). For large spaces, use a high setting (such as 70 milliseconds).

7. Set the High Frequency Rolloff and High Frequency Decay parameters. If you think these parameters look like equalization settings, you're right. Using these parameters also helps to create more authentic environment simulations because smaller, closed environments tend to stifle some frequencies of the audio spectrum, and larger environments usually sound brighter, meaning they promote more of the frequencies. When you set the High Frequency Rolloff parameter (in Hz), any frequencies below that frequency are allowed to pass and any frequencies above that frequency are cut. Setting the High Frequency Decay parameter determines how quickly the high frequencies above the High Frequency Rolloff are cut as the reverberation sounds. For examples on how to set these parameters, be sure to take a look at some of the included presets.

8. Set the Density parameter. This parameter determines the "thickness" of the reverberation. Experiment with it to hear what I mean.

9. Set the Motion Depth and Motion Rate parameters. In a real environment, reverberation is constantly changing as it sounds. It isn't static at all. The reverberant echoes actually move around the environment, which is what gives the environment a distinct sound. You can simulate this movement using the Motion Depth and Motion Rate parameters. The Motion Depth parameter determines how much movement there is and the Motion Rate

parameter determines the speed of that movement. For examples on how to set these parameters, be sure to take a look at some of the included presets.

10. Set the Level parameter, which controls the overall volume level of the effect output.

11. Click the Audition button to test the current parameter settings. Make further adjustments if necessary.

12. Set the appropriate options under the Mixing tab.

13. If you want to use the current settings at a later time, save them as a preset.

14. Click OK.

SONAR processes the data by applying the effect according to the parameter settings you specified.

Dynamics

SONAR includes a number of effects that allow you to apply dynamic processing to your audio data, including compression and limiting. What does that mean? Well, one way to explain it would be to talk about taming vocal recordings. Let's say you recorded this vocalist who can really belt out a tune but doesn't have very good microphone technique. When he sings, he just stays in one place in front of the mike. Professional singers know that during the quiet parts of the song, they need to sing up close to the mike, and during the loud parts, they need to back away so that an even amplitude level is recorded. If a singer doesn't do this, the amplitude of your recorded audio will be very uneven. That's where compression and limiting come in. Compression allows you to "squash" the audio signal so that the amplitude levels are more even. Limiting allows you to stop the amplitude of the audio signal from rising past a certain level to prevent clipping. This can happen if the performer sings too loudly. I'll talk about each of the available effects one at a time.

Compressor

The Compressor effect allows you to apply compression to your audio data. The effect works as follows:

1. Select the audio data that you want to process.

2. Choose Process > Audio Effects > Compressor to open the Compressor dialog box (see Figure 11.23).

Figure 11.23
Use the Compressor effect to apply compression to your audio data

3. Set the Threshold parameter. The Compressor effect uses a digital noise gate to identify the parts of your audio data that should be processed. The Threshold parameter determines at what amplitude level your audio data will start being compressed. When the amplitude of your audio data reaches the Threshold level, processing begins.

4. Set the Ratio parameter. This parameter determines how much processing is done to your audio data. A ratio of 1 means no processing is done. A ratio of 100 means that the audio is fully processed.

5. Set the Attack parameter. This parameter determines how quickly after the input level has reached the threshold that processing is applied. For example, if the input level reaches the threshold, it doesn't have to be compressed right away. A slow attack means the signal won't be compressed unless it lasts for a while. This is a good way to make sure fast, percussive parts are left alone, but long, drawn-out parts are compressed. The Predelay parameter works in conjunction with the Attack parameter by delaying the processing when the input signal is first detected.

6. Set the Release parameter. This parameter determines how quickly after the input level goes below the threshold that processing is stopped (or the digital noise gate is closed). If you set the Release parameter too low, your audio could be cut off. A longer Release allows processing to sound more natural. You'll have to experiment to get to the right setting.

7. Set the Gain parameter. This parameter allows you to adjust the overall amplitude of your audio after it is processed.

CHAPTER 11

8. Click the Audition button to test the current parameter settings. Make further adjustments if necessary.

9. Set the appropriate options under the Mixing tab.

10. If you want to use the current settings at a later time, save them as a preset.

11. Click OK.

SONAR processes the data by applying the effect according to the parameter settings you specified.

FX Compressor/Gate

The FX Compressor/Gate effect is similar to the Compressor effect, but it provides better quality processing and more features. Here is how it works:

1. Select the audio data that you want to process.

2. Choose Process > Audio Effects > Cakewalk > FX Compressor/Gate to open the FX Compressor/Gate dialog box (see Figure 11.24). The dialog displays a graph. The right side of the graph shows output amplitude and the bottom of the graph shows input amplitude. Inside the graph is a line representing the input amplitude and output amplitude as they relate to each other. Initially, the line is drawn diagonally, and you "read" it from left to right. This shows a 1:1 ratio between input and output amplitudes, meaning as the input level goes up 1 dB, the output level also goes up 1 dB.

Figure 11.24
The FX Compressor/Gate provides high quality compression with some extra features

3. Set the Compressor Thr (threshold) parameter. This parameter works the same way as the Threshold parameter in the Compressor effect.

4. Set the Compressor Ratio parameter. This parameter works the same way as the Ratio parameter in the Compressor Effect, except the values are numbered differently. A ratio of 1:1 means no processing is done. A ratio of 2:1 means that for every 2 dB increase in input amplitude, there is only a 1 dB increase in output amplitude. Thus, the amplitude is being compressed. If you set the Ratio parameter to its highest value (Inf:1), that causes limiting, so no matter how loud the input amplitude gets, it is limited to the level set by the Threshold parameter. I'll talk more about limiting later.

5. Set the Attack Time parameter. This parameter works the same way as the Attack parameter in the Compressor effect.

6. Set the Release Time parameter. This parameter works the same way as the Release parameter in the Compressor effect.

7. In addition to being able to compress audio data, the FX Compressor/Gate effect can cut out noises using a special noise gate (hence the name Compressor/Gate). By setting the Gate Thr (threshold) parameter, you can remove any unwanted noises that have an amplitude level that falls below the threshold. This is great for removing bad notes or string noise on guitar parts, for instance. Setting the Expander Ratio determines how soft the amplitudes below the Gate Thr will be made. For example, if you set the Expander Ratio to 100:1, then any sounds that fall below the Gate Thr will be cut out completely.

8. Set the Detection Algorithm parameter. This parameter establishes how the FX Compressor/Gate effect will determine the amplitude level of the incoming audio signal. Choosing the Average option tells the Effect to determine the average value of the input signal and use that to apply compression appropriately. Choosing the RMS (root mean square) option tells the Effect to determine the perceived loudness (as a listener would hear it over a period of time) of the input signal and use that to apply compression appropriately. The best method to use depends on the material being processed. You'll need to experiment to see which one works better.

9. Set the Stereo Interaction parameter. Choose the Maximum option to apply compression to both stereo channels equally. Choose the Side Chain option to apply compression only to the right channel of the stereo signal, while using the left channel signal to activate the threshold. This option can be used as a *ducking* effect, which can come in handy if you have music playing in the right channel and a voice-over playing in the left channel. As the voice comes in, the music is lowered so that listeners can hear the voice over the background music. For most applications, you'll want to use the Maximum option.

10. Activate the Soft Knee option to give a smoother transition as the input signal starts to be compressed.

CHAPTER 11

11.   Set the Output Gain parameter. This parameter allows you to adjust the overall amplitude of your audio after it is processed.

12.   Click the Audition button to test the current parameter settings. Make further adjustments if necessary.

13.   Set the appropriate options under the Mixing tab.

14.   If you want to use the current settings at a later time, save them as a preset.

15.   Click OK.

SONAR processes the data by applying the effect according to the parameter settings you specified.

FX Expander/Gate

Like the special noise gate option in the FX Compressor/Gate effect, the FX Expander/Gate effect allows you to cut out unwanted noises below a certain amplitude threshold. This effect takes less CPU processing power for those times when you don't need compression. Here is how it works:

1.   Select the audio data that you want to process.

2.   Choose Process > Audio Effects > Cakewalk > FX Expander/Gate to open the FX Expander/Gate dialog box (see Figure 11.25). The dialog box displays a graph. This graph is the same as the one in the FX Compressor/Gate effect.

Figure 11.25
Use the FX Expander/Gate effect to remove low volume noises from your audio data

3.   Set the Expander Thr (threshold) parameter. This parameter works the same as the Gate Thr parameter in the FX Compressor/Gate effect.

4. Set the Expander Ratio parameter. This parameter works the same as the Expander Ratio parameter in the FX Compressor/Gate effect.

5. Set the Attack Time parameter. This parameter works the same as the Attack Time parameter in the FX Compressor/Gate effect.

6. Set the Release Time parameter. This parameter works the same as the Release Time parameter in the FX Compressor/Gate effect.

7. Set the Detection Algorithm parameter. This parameter works the same as the Detection Algorithm parameter in the FX Compressor/Gate effect, except there is one additional option. Choosing the Peak option tells the effect to determine the peak value of the input signal and use that to apply processing appropriately.

8. Set the Stereo Interaction parameter. This parameter works the same as the Stereo Interaction parameter in the FX Compressor/Gate effect.

9. Activate the Soft Knee option to give a smoother transition as the input signal starts to be processed.

10. Set the Output Gain parameter. This parameter allows you to adjust the overall amplitude of your audio after it is processed.

11. Click the Audition button to test the current parameter settings. Make further adjustments if necessary.

12. Set the appropriate options under the Mixing tab.

13. If you want to use the current settings at a later time, save them as a preset.

14. Click OK.

SONAR processes the data by applying the effect according to the parameter settings you specified.

FX Limiter

The FX Limiter effect allows you to stop an audio signal from getting any louder than a specified amplitude level. This effect can be put to good use during recording to prevent your input signal from getting too high and causing distortion or clipping. Here is how the effect works:

1. Select the audio you want to process.

2. Choose Process > Audio Effects > Cakewalk > FX Limiter to open the FX Limiter dialog box (see Figure 11.26).

Figure 11.26
Use the FX Limiter
effect to prevent an
audio signal from
getting too loud

3. Set the Limiter Thr (threshold) parameter. This is the level that you don't want your audio signal level to go above. This means that the amplitude of the audio won't be able to get any higher than this value.

4. Set the Stereo Interaction parameter. I explained this parameter earlier.

5. Set the Output Gain parameter. This parameter allows you to adjust the overall amplitude of your audio after it is processed.

6. Click the Audition button to test the current parameter settings. Make further adjustments if necessary.

7. Set the appropriate options under the Mixing tab.

8. If you want to use the current settings at a later time, save them as a preset.

9. Click OK.

SONAR processes the data by applying the effect according to the parameter settings you specified.

FX Dynamics Processor

The FX Dynamics Processor effect (see Figure 11.27) combines all of the features of the previous dynamics effects into one. This means that this one effect can perform all of the functions of the FX Compressor/Gate, FX Expander/Gate, and FX Limiter effects. It also has the same parameter settings, which all work the same as in the previously described effects. Please review the previous sections in order to learn how to operate the parameters of this effect.

Figure 11.27
The FX Dynamics
Processor combines all
of the features of the
other dynamics Effects

CompressorX (Sonar XL)

If you purchased the XL version of SONAR, you'll have one additional dynamics effect at
your disposal. This is the CompressorX effect from Sonic Timeworks. It's probably one of
the best compression effects you'll ever use because of its high quality processing and
low CPU usage. Similar to the previously described dynamics effects, the CompressorX
provides compression and limiting. Here is how it works:

1. Select the audio data that you want to process.

2. Choose Process > Audio Effects > Timeworks > CompressorX (Sonar XL) to
    open the CompressorX dialog box (see Figure 11.28).

Figure 11.28
The CompressorX
Effect provides high-
quality compression
and limiting

3. To adjust the input signal level, just drag the In slider up or down.

CHAPTER 11

TIP

To make precise parameter adjustments, hold down the CTRL key on your computer keyboard as you drag a slider up or down with your mouse. To specify an exact value, click the number value shown for the parameter and then type in a new value using your computer keyboard.

4. Set the Threshold parameter. This parameter works the same way as the Threshold parameter in the Compressor effect.

5. Set the Ratio parameter. This parameter works the same way as the Ratio parameter in the Compressor effect.

6. Set the Attack parameter. This parameter works the same way as the Attack parameter in the Compressor effect.

7. Set the Release parameter. This parameter works the same way as the Release parameter in the Compressor effect, with one exception. Just to the right of the Release parameter is an Auto button. Activating this button tells the CompressorX effect to try and determine a release time for you automatically. This may or may not work depending on the material you are processing.

8. In addition to being able to compress audio data, the CompressorX effect can also apply limiting to your data. To turn limiting on or off, use the In button located below the Wall (short for brick wall limiting) parameter. Then adjust the Wall parameter as a limiting threshold. This works just like the Limiter Thr parameter in the FX Limiter effect.

9. Set the detection algorithm. You can do this by using the Peak and RMS buttons. These work the same as the detection algorithm parameters in the FX Expander/Gate effect.

10. Set the Knee parameter. Choosing Soft will give you a warmer quality to the compression. Choosing Hard will give you a harsher quality to the compression.

11. Set the Out parameter. This parameter allows you to adjust the overall amplitude of your audio after it is processed.

12. Click the Audition button to test the current parameter settings. Make further adjustments if necessary.

13. Set the appropriate options under the Mixing tab.

14. If you want to use the current settings at a later time, save them as a preset.

TIP

You can save CompressorX presets using the standard method for all SONAR effects, or you can use a special method by right-clicking anywhere within the dialog box. This will bring up a menu that will allow you to load and save presets to separate files that can then be shared with friends. Another advantage of saving presets this way is that if you use another program to access the CompressorX effect, your presets will be available from within that program too, and not just from within SONAR.

    14.   Click OK.

SONAR processes the data by applying the effect according to the parameter settings you specified.

TIP

In addition to regular compression/limiting tasks, the high quality of the CompressorX effect allows it to be used for mastering. Mastering is the procedure during which the final mixed down stereo audio for a song is processed with various effects (such as EQ, compression, and limiting) to give the song that final professional touch before it is burned to CD. There have been entire books written on the topic of mastering, but you can also find some good information on the Internet at these sites:

- **http://www.izotope.com/products/ozone/ozoneguide.html**
- **http://www.prorec.com/prorec/articles.nsf/files/**
  F717F79532C9067386256688001A7623
- **http://www.digido.com/cdmastering.html**

Also, be sure to sign up for my free DigiFreq music technology newsletter so you don't miss the mastering information I will be providing in future issues. To sign up, go to: **http://www.digifreq.com/digifreq/**

Distortion

Most of the time, bad-sounding audio isn't something that you want. Distortion is something you usually try to avoid when recording audio data. But sometimes distortion can be a good thing (as Martha Stewart would say). For example, if you want to dress up a guitar part for a rock song, adding a bit of distortion can make it sound really cool. Or maybe you want to add a bit of "grit" to a vocal part. Using the Distortion effect, you can achieve these sounds, and here's how:

    1.   Select the audio data that you want to process.

    2.   Choose Process > Audio Effects > Distortion to open the Distortion dialog box (see Figure 11.29).

Figure 11.29
Use the Distortion
effect to add distortion
to your audio data

3. Set the Edge parameter. This parameter determines by how much your audio data will be distorted. A low level means less distortion. A high level means more distortion.

4. Set the PostEQ Center Frequency and PostEQ Bandwidth parameters. These parameters allow you to apply equalization to the output signal of the Distortion effect. Using these parameters, you can achieve different sounding distortion effects. You'll need to experiment with them.

5. Set the PreLowpass Cutoff parameter. Any frequencies above the frequency you set for this parameter will be cut from the audio signal. You can use this to reduce the "harshness" that sometimes accompanies distorted audio so that you can achieve more of an effect rather than noise.

6. Set the Gain parameter. This controls the overall volume of the effect.

CAUTION

Don't set the Gain too high, because the distortion may damage your speakers (or ears, if you're using headphones). Start off with a nice low level when you are auditioning this Effect.

7. Click the Audition button to test the current parameter settings. Make further adjustments if necessary.

8. Set the appropriate options under the Mixing tab.

9. If you want to use the current settings at a later time, save them as a preset.

10. Click OK.

SONAR processes the data by applying the effect according to the parameter settings you specified.

Gargle

The Gargle effect provides something that is known as amplitude modulation. The effect modulates (or "vibrates") the amplitude (or volume) of your audio data. With this effect, you can achieve sounds such as the tremolo on an electronic organ. Here is how the Gargle effect works:

1. Select the audio data that you want to process.
2. Choose Process > Audio Effects > Gargle to open the Gargle dialog box (see Figure 11.30).

Figure 11.30
The Gargle effect lets you modulate the amplitude of your audio data

3. Set the Waveform parameter. Choose the Square option for a "harsh" sounding amplitude modulation. Choose the Triangle option for a "smooth" sounding amplitude modulation.
4. Set the Rate parameter. For a tremolo effect, use a low value, such as 7. For a very weird "ringing" effect, use a high value, such as 800.
5. Click the Audition button to test the current parameter settings. Make further adjustments if necessary.
6. Set the appropriate options under the Mixing tab.
7. If you want to use the current settings at a later time, save them as a preset.
8. Click OK.

SONAR processes the data by applying the effect according to the parameter settings you specified.

Changing Time and Pitch

In addition to the Length and Transpose editing features, SONAR provides the Pitch Shifter and Time/Pitch Stretch effects, which you also can use to change the length and pitch of your audio data. The effects, however, are more powerful and flexible. This is especially true of the Time/Pitch Stretch effect.

Pitch Shifter

The Pitch Shifter effect provides low quality, but it doesn't take up as much CPU processing power. In case you want to try out the Cakewalk FX Pitch Shifter, here's how it works:

1. Select the audio data that you want to process.

2. Select Process > Audio Effects > Cakewalk > Pitch Shifter to open the Pitch Shifter dialog box (see Figure 11.31).

Figure 11.31
The Pitch Shifter doesn't provide very good sound quality—for better quality, use the Time/Pitch Stretch effect

3. Under the Settings tab, set the Pitch Shift parameter. It is exactly the same as the Amount parameter in the Transpose editing function. You can use it to transpose the pitch of your audio data from −12 to +12 semitones (a whole octave down or up).

TIP

Normally, when you change the pitch of audio data, the length is altered, too. Raise the pitch and the data gets shorter, lower the pitch and the data gets longer. When this happens, though, the processed audio no longer plays in sync with the other data in your project. Luckily, you can use SONAR's pitch shifting effects to change pitch without changing the length of the audio data. The only problem to be wary of is that pitch shifting can produce unwanted artifacts if you use too large an interval. The famous Alvin & the Chipmunks were a product of this phenomenon. It's best to stay within an interval of a major third (four semitones) up or down if possible.

4. Set the Dry Mix and Wet Mix parameters. I explained these parameters earlier in the chapter, but in reference to pitch shifting, you should almost always keep the Dry Mix set to 0 percent and the Wet Mix set to 100 percent.

5. As far as the Feedback Mix, Delay Time, and Mod Depth parameters are concerned, they don't seem to have anything to do with the Cakewalk FX Pitch Shifter effect. Changing these parameters only introduces unwanted artifacts into the sound. My advice is to simply leave them set at their default values: Feedback Mix = 0, Delay Time = 0, and Mod Depth = 35.

6. Click the Audition button to test the current parameter settings. Make further adjustments if necessary.

7. Set the appropriate options under the Mixing tab.

8. If you want to use the current settings at a later time, save them as a preset.

9. Click OK.

SONAR processes the data by applying the effect according to the parameter settings you specified.

Time/Pitch Stretch

The Time/Pitch Stretch effect is much more advanced and flexible, and it provides better quality than the Pitch Shifter effect. That doesn't mean it's difficult to use. Some of the more advanced parameters can be a bit confusing, but I'll go over them one at a time. The effect works like this:

1. Select the audio data that you want to process.

2. Select Process > Audio Effects > Cakewalk > Time/Pitch Stretch to open the Time/Pitch Stretch dialog box (see Figure 11.32).

Figure 11.32
The Time/Pitch Stretch effect provides advanced time stretching and pitch shifting capabilities

3. Under the Settings tab, set the Source Material parameter. One of the reasons the Time/Pitch Stretch effect provides better quality than the Pitch Shifter effect is that it takes into account the type of audio data you are processing. You should select the appropriate value for the Source Material

parameter according to the type of data you want to process. For instance, if you are processing percussion data, you should set the Source Material parameter to Drums. If you can't find an appropriate setting in the supplied list, just set the Source Material parameter to Generic. This setting still usually provides good results.

4. Set the Time parameter. Using the Time parameter, you can change the length of your audio data as a percentage. If you want to make the data shorter, set the Time parameter to a percentage smaller than 100. For example, to make the data half of its original length, use a setting of 50 percent. If you want to make the data longer, set the Time parameter to a percentage larger than 100. For example, if you want to make data twice its original length, use a setting of 200 percent. To change the Time parameter, just type a value or use the horizontal slider.

TIP

I mentioned earlier that, when you're transposing audio, it's best to stay within a major third (four semitones) up or down if possible, because audio doesn't react very well to higher values. Well, the same concept applies when you're changing the length of audio data. You should try to stay within 10 percent longer or shorter if possible; otherwise, the results may not sound very good. This is another feature you have to experiment with.

5. Set the Pitch parameter. Using the Pitch parameter, you can transpose your audio data up or down one octave (in semitones). To change the Pitch parameter, just type a value or use the vertical slider.

TIP

Notice that a graph is shown in the Time/Pitch Stretch dialog box. Using this graph, you can change the Time and Pitch parameters by dragging the small blue square. Drag the square up or down to change the Pitch parameter. Drag the square left or right to change the Time parameter. Also, if you hold down the Shift key on your computer keyboard at the same time, the square automatically snaps to the exact grid points on the graph.

6. Under the Advanced tab, you'll see three parameters called Block Rate, Overlap Ratio, and Crossfade Ratio. These very advanced settings are used by the Time/Pitch Stretch effect to determine how your data will be processed. Luckily, you don't have to deal with them because they are automatically set to the appropriate values according to the setting you use for the Source Material parameter. So, basically, don't worry about them.

7. You'll also notice two other parameters under the Advanced tab: Accuracy and Algorithm. These parameters you do need to deal with. The Accuracy

parameter determines the quality of the effect processing. If you set the Accuracy parameter to High, you'll get better quality out of the Effect, but it will also take longer to process your data. The Algorithm parameter is strictly for use when you're processing audio data containing vocals. If you're processing any other kind of material, you should leave the Algorithm parameter set to Normal. In the case of vocal material, though, setting the Algorithm parameter to Formant Preserving tells the effect to preserve the original vocal characteristics when transposing the pitch up or down. Without the Algorithm parameter set to Formant Preserving, transposing your vocal material up can make it sound like Alvin & The Chipmunks, and transposing it down can make it sound like Fat Albert.

8. Click the Audition button to test the current parameter settings. Make further adjustments if necessary.

9. Set the appropriate options under the Mixing tab.

10. If you want to use the current settings at a later time, save them as a preset.

11. Click OK.

SONAR processes the data by applying the effect according to the parameter settings you specified.

Amplifier Simulation

For all you electric guitar players out there, SONAR provides the Amp Sim effect. Using this effect, you can simulate the sound of real-life guitar amplifiers, making your recorded guitar audio data sound like it's being played through different kinds of amps. To achieve this sound, the effect uses technology called *physical modeling*. In this technology, the characteristics of a real instrument or device are converted into a mathematical algorithm (called a *model*). The model can then be used to apply those same characteristics to your audio data to achieve more authentic sounding recordings. This explanation of the process is simplified, of course, but that's the gist of it. The Amp Sim effect works like this:

1. Select the audio data that you want to process.

TIP

Even though the Amp Sim effect was designed for guitar amplifiers, that doesn't mean you can't use it on other types of data. The distorted sounds the Effect produces also work well on vocals, especially if you're looking for that hard rock sound. Check out some of the music by Kid Rock to hear what I mean.

2. Select Process > Audio Effects > Cakewalk > Amp Sim to open the Amp Sim dialog box (see Figure 11.33).

Figure 11.33
Using the Amp Sim effect, you can simulate your music being played through different kinds of guitar amplifiers

3. Under the Settings tab in the Amp Model section, select the type of guitar amplifier you want to simulate. An additional parameter called Bright is also available in this section. It is similar to the Brightness switch found on many guitar amplifiers. It makes the effect sound brighter by boosting the high frequencies (everything above 500 Hz) of the audio spectrum.

4. In the Cabinet Enclosure section, select the type of cabinet you want to use for your virtual guitar amplifier. By setting this parameter, you can simulate different types of speaker enclosures. You have five options to choose from: No Speaker, 1×12, 2×12, 4×10, and 4×12. If you choose the No Speaker option, the effect sounds as though you plugged your guitar directly into the output of the amplifier and recorded the sound without using a microphone or the amplifier speakers. If you choose any of the other options, the effect sounds as though you played your guitar through an amplifier that has a certain number of speakers of a certain size and recorded the output by placing a microphone in front of the amp. For example, if you choose 4×12, the simulated amp would contain four speakers each at 12 inches in size. Also, when you select the other options, two other parameters become available: Open Back and Off-Axis. Activating the Open Back parameter makes the effect simulate a guitar amplifier that has a cabinet enclosure with an open (rather than a closed) back. Activating the Off-Axis parameter makes the effect sound as though you placed the virtual microphone (mentioned earlier) off to the side of the amplifier speaker rather than directly in front of it.

5. In the Tremolo section, set the Rate and Depth parameters. Setting these parameters allows you to add a "warble" type of sound to the effect. The

Rate parameter controls the speed of the tremolo, and the Depth parameter controls how much tremolo is added. There is also a bias control (like that found on most guitar amps) that lets you determine if the tremolo will add to the volume level of the effect or subtract from the volume level of the effect. In addition, by activating the Mono option, the tremolo will produce a mono output rather than stereo.

6. Set the Bass, Mid, and Treb parameters in the EQ section. These parameters act similarly to the parameters in SONAR's Graphic EQ editing feature (which I discussed in Chapter 8). Each parameter enables you to cut or boost a specific frequency by –10 or +10 dB. The Bass parameter is set to 60 Hz, the Mid parameter is set to 600 kHz, and the Treb parameter is set to 6000 kHz.

7. Set the Drive parameter. This parameter basically controls how much distortion is added to the audio data being processing.

8. Set the Presence parameter. This parameter acts like a high-pass EQ with a permanent frequency of 750 Hz. You can use it to boost some of the higher frequencies of the effect, giving it more "presence."

9. Set the Volume parameter. This parameter controls the overall volume of the effect. No Dry Mix or Wet Mix parameters are available for this effect, so you hear only the totally processed signal through this one.

10. Click the Audition button to test the current parameter settings. Make further adjustments if necessary.

11. Set the appropriate options under the Mixing tab.

12. If you want to use the current settings at a later time, save them as a preset.

13. Click OK.

SONAR processes the data by applying the effect according to the parameter settings you specified.

TIP

SONAR provides a "lite" version of the Amp Sim effect, called Amp Sim Lite. The lite version provides the exact same features, except there is no tremolo processing available. The Amp Sim Lite Effect can be useful if you want to apply amplifier simulation in real-time but not use as much CPU processing power as the Amp Sim effect. Access the Amp Sim Lite effect by choosing Process > Audio Effects > Cakewalk > Amp Sim Lite.

Analog Tape Simulation

Similar to the Amp Sim effect, the FX2 Tape Sim effect uses physical modeling to simulate a realistic audio situation. But instead of simulating the sound of a guitar amplifier, the FX2 Tape Sim effect simulates the sound of your audio data being played off an analog tape deck. Why would you want to simulate old recording technology, especially when you have the clean and crisp sound of digital recording? Well, analog tape recording provides a sort of "warm" sound that can't be produced with digital recording, and that sound can be used to create authentic jazz or blues recordings. And some musicians just prefer the warm sound of analog as opposed to the crisp sound of digital. The FX2 Tape Sim effect lets you achieve that warm sound, and here is how it works:

1. Select the audio data that you want to process.

2. Choose Process > Audio Effects > Cakewalk > FX2 Tape Sim to open the FX2 Tape Sim dialog box (see Figure 11.34).

Figure 11.34
Use the FX2 Tape Sim effect to simulate the warm sound of analog tape recordings

3. Choose the type of tape machine you would like to simulate by setting the Tape Speed and Eq Curve parameters. An additional parameter called LF Boost is available, which lets you add a small increase to the lower frequencies of the audio data, giving it an even "warmer" sound.

4. Set the Input Gain parameter. This parameter controls how loud the input signal into the effect will be. Usually, you'll just want to keep it set at 0 dB.

5. Set the Rec (short for Record) Level parameter. This parameter lets you control the level of the audio that would be recorded in an actual tape recording situation. Setting this parameter too high will cause distortion.

6. Set the Warmth parameter. This parameter controls that "warm" sound I talked about earlier.

7. Set the Hiss parameter. As in an actual tape recording situation, you usually get tape hiss. If you want to be totally authentic in your simulation, you can use this parameter to add hiss to your audio data. A setting of 0 will turn the Hiss parameter off.

8. Set the Output Gain parameter. This parameter controls the overall volume of the effect. No Dry Mix or Wet Mix parameters are available for this effect, so you hear only the totally processed signal through this one.

9. Click the Audition button to test the current parameter settings. Make further adjustments if necessary.

10. Set the appropriate options under the Mixing tab.

11. If you want to use the current settings at a later time, save them as a preset.

12. Click OK.

SONAR processes the data by applying the effect according to the parameter settings you specified.

An Effects Exercise

Before I begin talking about SONAR's MIDI effects, I thought it might be nice to work through a simple exercise on applying some of the audio effects to one of the sample projects that comes included with SONAR. This way, you get a chance to hear some of the effects in action. Just follow these steps:

1. Choose File > Open, choose the Don't Matter Audio and MIDI Demo.cwb file, and click Open to open that sample Project.

2. Close the File Info window and the Staff view. You don't need them right now.

3. In the Track view, select Tracks 1, 8, and 9. Then select Track > Delete to delete those tracks. They are MIDI tracks, and you don't need them for this exercise.

4. Add a little echo to the end of the horn tracks so that it trails off after the rest of the music stops playing. To do so, select the last clip in Track 5 (Horns Left) and the last clip in Track 6 (Horns Right). Then choose Process > Audio Effects > Cakewalk > Delay. Choose the preset called 120bpm Delay to automatically set the parameters for the effect. Under the Mixing tab, be sure the Process In-Place, Mono Result option is activated. Click OK.

TIP

If you want the delay effect on the horns to trail off at the end of the song, slip edit the ends of both of the clips that you just processed so that the ends of the clips extend to around the second beat in measure 9.

5. To make the horn tracks a little fuller, choose Edit > Select > None to get rid of the current data selection. Then select Tracks 5 and 6 entirely so that you can process all the data in the tracks. Choose Process > Audio Effects > Cakewalk > FxChorus. Choose the preset called Big Stereo Spread to automatically set the parameters for the effect. Under the Mixing tab, be sure the Process In-Place, Mono Result option is activated. Click OK.

6. The guitar track might sound nice with a bit of amp simulation applied to it, so select Track 4 (Guitar), and then choose Process > Audio Effects > Cakewalk > Amp Sim. Choose the preset called Solid State Clean to automatically set the parameters for the effect. Click OK.

7. The drum and bass tracks sound fine, but you can simulate the entire project being played in another environment by selecting all the tracks (1 through 6). Then choose Process > Audio Effects > Cakewalk > FxReverb. Choose the preset called Guitar – Small Blues Room. Under the Mixing tab, be sure the Process In-Place, Mono Result option is activated. Click OK.

8. Play the project to hear what it sounds like.

The result is quite a bit different from the original, isn't it? Personally, I think the horns may sound a bit too "big," but that can easily be changed. As a matter of fact, you can do anything you want. Don't be afraid to experiment to see what the different effects sound like. With judicious application of effects, you can make your music sound more professional. Just remember not to go overboard. And as with everything else in life, the more you practice, the better you become.

MIDI Effects

SONAR provides one set of eight MIDI effects, a couple of which (Chord Analyzer and Session Drummer) are not really effects—but I'll get into that later. It also provides a few third-party plug-ins from MusicLab, Inc. (**http://www.musiclab.com/**) and NTONYX Ltd. (**http://www.ntonyx.com/**). Some of them are "lite" versions. You can buy the full versions and other MIDI plug-ins from these vendors, too.

NOTE

To use the MusicLab and NTONYX MIDI plug-ins, you must install them separately. They are not automatically installed along with SONAR. To install the plug-ins, pop in your SONAR CD. In the SONAR Installation Welcome screen, choose Install. Then choose MusicLab MIDI FX and/or NTONYX MIDI FX to install the additional plug-ins.

Like the audio effects, some of the MIDI effects mimic some of SONAR's editing features. Again, they have this capability so that you can process your data with these features in real-time. You cannot use SONAR's editing features in real-time because they aren't plug-ins. In addition, the effects provide more power and flexibility, and they include additional parameters not found in the editing features, so I'll go over them here for you step by step.

NOTE

As I mentioned earlier, because I've already covered how to apply effects offline and in real-time, I'm just going to include the basic offline steps (along with parameter descriptions) in each of the following explanations. For detailed step-by-step procedures for applying effects offline and in real-time, refer to the previous sections in this chapter.

Automatic Arpeggios

In music, you can play the notes of a chord in a number of different ways. Most often, the notes are played all at once. You can also play them one at a time in sequence; this is called an arpeggio. SONAR's Arpeggiator effect automatically creates arpeggios for each note or chord in your selected MIDI data. Depending on how you set the parameters, however, you can achieve some very strange and interesting "melodies." This feature works as follows:

1. Select the MIDI data that you want to process.

2. Choose Process > MIDI Effects > Cakewalk FX > Arpeggiator to open the Arpeggiator dialog box (see Figure 11.35).

Figure 11.35
The Arpeggiator effect automatically converts your selected MIDI data into arpeggios

3. Set the Swing parameter. This parameter works the same way as the Swing parameter in the Quantize editing feature (which I talked about in Chapter 8). The only difference is that of 50 percent being the normal setting (meaning no "swing" is applied); in this case, 0 percent is the normal setting. And you can set this Swing parameter from −100 to +100 percent. More often than not, you'll want to keep it set to 0 percent.

CHAPTER 11

4. Set the Rate and Units parameters. These two parameters work together. The Rate parameter determines the amount of time between each note in the arpeggio. The Units parameter determines what units you want to use to set the Rate parameter. You can set the Rate parameter in notes, ticks, or milliseconds. By setting the Units parameter to Notes, you can easily synchronize the notes in the arpeggio to a certain note value so that you know they will play in sync with the rest of the music in your Project.

5. Set the Legato parameter. This parameter determines the duration of the notes in the arpeggio. If you set the Legato parameter to 1 percent (the lowest value), the notes in the arpeggio are played with a very short duration (as in a staccato fashion in which the note is played and let go very quickly). If you set the Legato parameter to 99 percent (the highest value), the notes in the arpeggio are played with a very long duration. To be exact, each note plays until the start of the next note in the arpeggio.

6. Set the Path parameter. This parameter determines the direction in which the notes in the arpeggio will be played. If you select Up, Up, the notes in the arpeggio consecutively go up in pitch. If you select Up, Down, the notes in the arpeggio first go up in pitch and then come back down. If you select Down, Down, the notes in the arpeggio consecutively go down in pitch. If you select Down, Up, the notes in the arpeggio first go down in pitch and then come back up.

7. Set the Play Thru option. If you activate the Play Thru option, your original data remains intact and plays along with the new arpeggio data. If you deactivate the Play Thru option, only the arpeggio data remains, and your original data is removed.

8. Set the Specify Output Range option, along with the Lowest Note and Span (Notes) parameters. If you activate the Specify output range option, additional notes are added so that the arpeggio will play smoothly over each octave in the range you specify. Otherwise, only your original is used to create the arpeggio. The Lowest note parameter determines the lowest note that will be included in the arpeggio. The Span (Notes) parameter determines the number of half-steps in the range (from 12 to 127).

9. Set the Use Chord Control option, along with the Lowest Note and Span (Notes) parameters. If you activate the Use chord control option, the Arpeggiator effect first analyzes the original data that falls in the range you specify, and it guesses at what chord is being played. If you use the effect in real-time mode, the name of the chord that is guessed is shown in the Chord Recognized field. The effect uses the recognized chord to create the notes for the arpeggio (meaning the notes in the arpeggio are based on the recognized chord).

10. Click the Audition button to test the current parameter settings. Make further adjustments if necessary.

11.   If you want to use the current settings at a later time, save them as a preset.

12.   Click OK.

SONAR processes the data by applying the effect according to the parameter settings you specified.

I know the parameter settings for the Arpeggiator effect can be a bit confusing. Sometimes it's difficult to tell what the results will be after you apply the effect. Basically, they'll be different depending on the data that you process. You'll have to experiment. By the way, this effect usually works best on slow, chord-based data. Of course, you can try it out on faster, different kinds of data. Like I said, be sure to experiment with it.

Chord Analysis

Earlier, I mentioned that a couple of the MIDI effects aren't really effects at all. The Chord Analyzer is one of them. This effect doesn't do anything to your data, meaning it doesn't make any changes. The Chord Analyzer simply looks at your data and guesses what kind of chord is being played.

Here's how the effect works:

NOTE
Although you can use the Chord Analyzer effect offline, it works best in real-time as your project is playing. Therefore, I'll go through the real-time procedure here instead of the offline procedure.

1.   In the Track view, right-click in the Fx field of the track to which you want to add an effect.

2.   Choose MIDI Effects > Cakewalk FX > Chord Analyzer to add the Chord Analyzer to the list.

3.   The Chord Analyzer window opens (see Figure 11.36).

Figure 11.36
The Chord Analyzer is best used in real-time

4. Set the Examine Every parameter. Using this parameter, you can control how often the Chord Analyzer effect analyzes your data. The lower the number, the more accurate it is at guessing the names of the chords being played. This feature also requires more processing power from your computer, but I've never had any problems keeping this parameter set at 1 (the lowest setting). So, unless you have trouble with playback, I recommend that you just leave this setting at its default value.

5. Start playback of the project. As the project plays, the effect analyzes your data and displays the name of the chord it thinks is being played, along with how the chord looks in music notation and on a piano keyboard.

This effect is useful as a learning tool, because it displays the chords being played on a piano keyboard and as music notation. Plus, it lists (in the Chord Recognized section) some possible alternatives you might want to try in place of the chord currently being used.

Echo Delay

Just as the delay effects enable you to add echoes to your audio data, the Echo Delay effect enables you to add echoes to your MIDI data. But because this effect works on MIDI data, some of the parameters are different, and some additional parameters are available as well. This feature works as follows:

1. Select the MIDI data that you want to process.

2. Choose Process > MIDI Effects > Cakewalk FX > Echo Delay to open the Echo Delay dialog box (see Figure 11.37).

Figure 11.37
You can use the Echo
Delay effect to add
echoes to your
MIDI data

3. Set the Delay and Delay Units parameters. These two parameters work together. The Delay parameter determines the amount of time between each echo. The Delay Units parameter determines what units you want to use to set the Delay parameter. You can set the Delay parameter in notes, ticks, and milliseconds. By setting the Delay Units parameter to Notes, you can easily synchronize the echoes to a certain note value so that you know they will play in sync with the rest of the music in your project.

TIP

You can also set the Delay parameter by clicking on the Tap button in the Echo Delay dialog box. Clicking on the button at a certain tempo sets the Delay parameter to that tempo.

4. Set the Decay parameter. This parameter determines whether the echoes get softer or louder (and by how much). If you set the Decay parameter to a value below 100 percent, the echoes get softer. If you set the Decay to a value above 100 percent, the echoes get louder.

5. Set the Echoes parameter. This parameter determines how many echoes you will have.

6. Set the Swing parameter. This parameter works the same way as the Swing parameter in the Quantize editing feature (which I talked about in Chapter 8). The only difference is that of 50 percent being the normal setting (meaning no "swing" is applied); 0 percent is the normal setting. And you can set this Swing parameter from –100 to +100 percent. More often than not, you'll want to keep it set to 0 percent.

7. Set the Transpose (Steps) parameter. If you'd like, you can have each echo transposed to a different pitch value. This way, you can create some interesting sounds. You can set the Transpose (Steps) parameter from –12 to +12 steps. You determine the types of steps by choosing either the Diatonic

(the pitches follow the diatonic musical scale) or the Chromatic (the pitches follow the chromatic musical scale) options.

8.   Click the Audition button to test the current parameter settings. Make further adjustments if necessary.

9.   If you want to use the current settings at a later time, save them as a preset.

10. Click OK.

SONAR processes the data by applying the effect according to the parameter settings you specified.

The Echo Delay effect is fairly easy to use, but just to give you a quick idea of what you can do with the effect, try the following example:

1.   Select File > Open, select the file called 2-Part Invention #13 in A minor.cwp, and click Open to open that sample project.

2.   Close all the windows except for the Track view.

3.   Play the project to see what the original data sounds like.

4.   Select Track 1.

5.   Choose Process > MIDI Effects > Cakewalk FX > Echo Delay.

6.   Choose the preset called 16th Note.

7.   Click OK.

8.   Play the Project again.

Hear that echo? You can achieve some pretty cool sounds by using this effect. As always, don't be afraid to experiment.

MIDI Event Filter

The MIDI Event Filter effect works almost exactly the same as the Select By Filter editing feature (which I talked about in Chapter 8). The only difference is that, instead of simply selecting the specified events, it deletes them. This feature gives you a quick way to remove specific kinds of MIDI data from your clips or Tracks. It works like this:

1.   Select the MIDI data that you want to process.

2.   Choose Process > MIDI Effects > Cakewalk FX > MIDI Event Filter to open the MIDI Event Filter dialog box (see Figure 11.38).

Figure 11.38
Using the MIDI
Event Filter effect, you
can easily remove
specific kinds of MIDI
data from your clips
and tracks

3. Set the appropriate parameters for the types of MIDI data that you want to remove. These settings are exactly the same as the settings for the Event Filter—Select Some dialog box (which I explained in Chapter 8).

4. Click the Audition button to test the current parameter settings. Make further adjustments if necessary.

5. If you want to use the current settings at a later time, save them as a preset.

6. Click OK.

SONAR processes the selected data and removes the types of MIDI data you specified via the effect parameter settings.

Quantize

The Quantize effect works almost exactly the same as the Quantize editing feature (which I talked about in Chapter 8). The only difference is that the effect provides a couple of additional parameters. It works like this:

1. Select the MIDI data that you want to process.

2. Choose Process > MIDI Effects > Cakewalk FX > Quantize to open the Quantize dialog box (see Figure 11.39).

Figure 11.39
The Quantize effect works almost exactly the same way as the Quantize editing feature

3. Set the Quantize parameter by activating/deactivating the Start Times and Note Durations options. These settings simply tell SONAR whether you want to quantize the start times and/or durations of each selected MIDI Event.

4. Set the Resolution parameter. This parameter works in exactly the same way as the Resolution parameter in the Quantize editing feature (which I talked about in Chapter 8).

5. Set the Tuplet option. Using this option, you can further define the Resolution parameter. For example, if you want to quantize your data according to an odd note value, activate the Tuplet option and set its related parameters to 5 and 4 (which would mean you want to quantize your data to the value of 5 notes occurring in the time of 4 notes).

6. Set the Strength, Swing, Window, and Offset parameters. These parameters work in exactly the same way as the Strength, Swing, Window, and Offset parameters in the Quantize editing feature (which I talked about in Chapter 8).

7. Set the Randomize By option. If you activate this option, a random time offset is applied to the timing of each quantized Event. You can use this option to achieve some very strange sounds. Do a little experimenting to hear what I mean.

8. Click the Audition button to test the current parameter settings. Make further adjustments if necessary.

9. If you want to use the current settings at a later time, save them as a preset.

10. Click OK.

SONAR processes the data by applying the effect according to the parameter settings you specified.

Transpose

Like the Transpose editing feature, the Transpose effect enables you to transpose your MIDI note data up or down by a number of half steps either chromatically or diatonically. However, the Transpose effect also provides some more advanced transposition methods. It works like this:

1. Select the MIDI data that you want to process.

2. Choose Process > MIDI Effects > Cakewalk FX > Transpose to open the Transpose dialog box (see Figure 11.40).

Figure 11.40
Using the Transpose effect, you can transpose your MIDI note data in a number of different ways

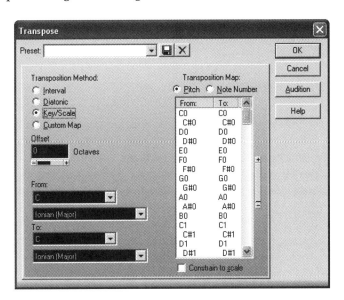

3. If you want to transpose your data by a simple musical interval, choose the Interval option for the Transposition Method parameter. Then enter the number of half steps –127 to +127) into the Offset parameter by which you want to transpose the data.

4. If you want to transpose your data diatonically so that the notes are changed according to degrees of a certain musical scale, choose the Diatonic option for the Transposition Method parameter. Then enter the number of scale degrees (–24 to +24) into the Offset parameter by which you want to transpose the data. Also, choose the musical scale you want to use by setting the Key parameter.

CHAPTER 11

TIP

If you want any of the notes in your data that don't fit within the chosen musical scale to be transposed so that they will fit, activate the Constrain To Scale option. This feature works well for pop music. For something like jazz, though, in which many different non-scale notes are used in the music, it's best to keep this option deactivated. This option works for both the Diatonic and Key/Scale Transposition Methods.

5. If you want to transpose your data from one musical key and scale to another, choose the Key/Scale option for the Transposition Method parameter. In the From and To parameters, choose the musical keys and scales by which you want to transpose your data. You can also transpose the data up or down by a number of octaves at the same time by setting the Offset parameter.

6. To specify exactly how each note in the musical scale will be transposed, choose the Custom Map option for the Transposition Method parameter. Using this option, you can define your own Transposition Map. This means that you can set what note each note in the musical scale will be transposed to. To change the transposition value of a note in the musical scale, select the note in the From column of the Transposition Map. Then click the plus or minus buttons to transpose that note up or down. This option is pretty tedious, but it gives you precise control over every musical note.

TIP

You can view notes in the Transposition Map either by note name or by MIDI note number. Simply select the appropriate option (Pitch or Note Number) located above the Transposition Map in the Transpose dialog box.

7. Click the Audition button to test the current parameter settings. Make further adjustments if necessary.

8. If you want to use the current settings at a later time, save them as a preset.

9. Click OK.

SONAR processes the data by applying the effect according to the parameter settings you specified.

Velocity

I'm tempted to compare the Velocity effect to the Scale Velocity editing feature (which I talked about in Chapter 8), but the effect not only enables you to scale MIDI velocity data, it also enables you to change it in many more advanced ways. As a matter of fact, you'll probably stop using the Scale Velocity editing feature when you get the hang of the Velocity effect, because you can use this effect as an editing tool as well. It works like this:

1. Select the MIDI data that you want to process.

2. Choose Process > MIDI Effects > Cakewalk FX > Velocity to open the Velocity dialog box (see Figure 11.41).

Figure 11.41
Using the Velocity
effect, you can change
your MIDI velocity
data in many more
ways than you can
using the Scale
Velocity editing feature

3. To change all MIDI velocity values to an exact number, choose the Set All Velocities To parameter, and type the value (1 to 127) you want to use.

4. To add or subtract a certain amount from each MIDI velocity in your selected data, choose the Change Velocities By option and type the value (–127 to +127) you want to use.

5. To scale all MIDI velocity values by a certain percentage, choose the Scale Velocities To option and type the value (1 to 900 percent) that you want to use.

6. The next two options also enable you to scale MIDI velocities, but from one value to another. If you choose the first Change Gradually From option, you can scale MIDI velocities by exact values (1 to 127). If you choose the second Change Gradually From option, you can scale MIDI velocities by a percentage (1 to 900 percent).

7. If you choose the Limit Range From option, all the MIDI velocities in your selected data are changed to fit within the range of velocity values (1 to 127) you specify.

8. In addition to choosing one of the previous options, you can choose the Velocity effect's Randomize By option, which works in tandem with the others. By activating this option, you can add or subtract a random offset

to each MIDI velocity in your selected data. You can enter a maximum value (1 to 127) to be used, and you can give priority over whether the random offset will be lower or higher (–10 to +10) than the maximum value that you specify.

9. Click the Audition button to test the current parameter settings. Make further adjustments if necessary.

10. If you want to use the current settings at a later time, save them as a preset.

11. Click OK.

SONAR processes the data by applying the effect according to the parameter settings you specified.

Session Drummer

Even though the Session Drummer is listed along with all the other MIDI effects, technically it is not an effect because it doesn't process existing data. Instead, it actually generates new MIDI data. You can think of the Session Drummer like a drum machine, a programmable MIDI instrument used to create drum parts. With the Session Drummer, you can compose your own MIDI drum Tracks by combining existing rhythmic patterns into songs. You can even create your own patterns for use with the Session Drummer.

Using the Session Drummer consists of a number of multi-step processes, so I'll provide you with step-by-step procedures for each part of the process.

Opening and Setting Up

The best way to use the Session Drummer is in real-time, because you can use it to compose a drum Track while listening to the existing tracks in your project. You can get started by following these steps:

1. Create a new project or open an existing one.

2. In the Track view, create a new MIDI track.

3. Set the Out and Ch parameters for the new track. The channel (Ch) should probably be set to 10, because that is the standard channel for General MIDI drums on most sound cards and synthesizers. Click OK.

4. Add the Session Drummer effect to the Fx field of the new track by right-clicking in the Fx field and choose MIDI Effects > Cakewalk FX > Session Drummer.

5. The Session Drummer window opens (see Figure 11.42).

Figure 11.42
The Session Drummer window allows you to compose your own MIDI drum tracks by combining existing rhythmic patterns

6.   You'll see three different sections within the window: Style, Pattern, and Song. Just below the Style section is a row of buttons. These buttons control the different Session Drummer features. Click the Plugin Settings button (the one with the picture of the yellow sprocket shown on it) to open the Settings dialog box (see Figure 11.43). Don't worry; I'll go over all the other Session Drummer features shortly.

Figure 11.43
In the Settings dialog box, you can set the Session Drummer's Drum Map, Output Port, MIDI Channel, and Content Folder parameters

7. All the drum patterns and styles included with SONAR are programmed to work with General MIDI. So, if you're using a General MIDI compatible synthesizer, you should be all set. If not, you can change the Drum Map parameter so that each drum instrument is mapped to a different MIDI pitch. To do so, click the name of the drum instrument you want to change in the From column of the Drum Map. Then, to raise or lower the pitch for that instrument, press the plus or minus keys on the numeric keypad of your computer's keyboard, respectively.

8. Set the Output Port and MIDI Channel parameters to the same settings you used for the Out and Ch parameters you entered earlier.

9. All the drum styles and patterns included with SONAR are contained in special MIDI files. These files are initially located in the C:\Program Files\Cakewalk\SONAR 2\Drum Styles folder on your hard drive. If you want to change the location of the files, enter a new location in the Content Folder parameter. Be sure to remember to move any existing files from the old folder to the new folder.

10. Click OK to close the Settings dialog box.

TIP

If you want to use these same settings again in the future, you can save them as a preset. The Presets parameter in the Session Drummer window saves only the parameter values from the Settings dialog box. Saving your Session Drummer songs requires a different procedure, which I'll talk about later.

Creating a Song

As I mentioned earlier, the Session Drummer window is divided into three sections: Style, Pattern, and Song. The Style section lists all the available drum style files currently in the Content Folder. Each file contains a number of different drum patterns. When you select a style from the list in the Style section, all the patterns contained in that style are listed in the Pattern section. By selecting patterns from the Pattern section, you can piece together a song. A song is an entire percussion performance that spans a certain number of measures, depending on how many patterns it contains and the length of each pattern used. The basic procedure for creating a song is as follows (I'm assuming you've already gone through the setup procedure, and the Session Drummer window is open and waiting to be used):

1. Select a style from the Style section.

2. In the Pattern section, you'll see all the patterns within the selected style. The name of each pattern and its length in measures are shown. To hear what a pattern sounds like, click it to select it and then start your Project playing. You can keep the Project playing while you select different patterns. After you find a pattern you like, double-click it (or click the Add

Pattern To Song button, the one with the picture of a plus sign shown on it) to add the pattern to the Song section.

3. In the Song section, the name, length, and the time (in measures, beats, ticks) of when the pattern will be played within the project is shown. You'll also see a Loop Count parameter for the pattern. It tells the Session Drummer how many times to play that pattern before moving on to the next pattern in the song. Set the Loop Count by double-clicking on it and typing a number.

4. Go back to Step 2 to add more patterns to the song.

5. If you want to remove a pattern from the song, select the pattern from the list in the Song section, and click the Remove Pattern From Song button (the one with the picture of a minus sign shown on it). You can also remove all the patterns from the song by clicking on the Clear Song button (the one with the picture of a red X shown on it).

6. If you want to change the order of a pattern within the song, select the pattern. Then click the Move Down button (the one with the picture of a downward-pointing arrow shown on it) to move the pattern toward the end of the song. Alternatively, click the Move Up button (the one with the picture of an upward-pointing arrow shown on it) to move the pattern toward the beginning of the song.

7. To listen to the song, select the first pattern in the list and then start your project playing.

Saving and Loading Song Files

After you've finished creating your song, you can save it as a special Session Drummer Song file. This file type has an .SDX extension, and the files are stored in the same disk location as the styles. To save your song, follow these steps:

1. Click the Save Song To File button (the one with the picture of a floppy disk shown on it) to open the Save As dialog box.

2. Type a name for the file and use an .SDX extension.

3. Click Save.

To load your song for use in Session Drummer at a later date, do the following:

1. Click the Load Song From File button (the one with the picture of a yellow folder shown on it) to open the Open dialog box.

2. Select the file you want to load.

3. Click Open.

CHAPTER 11

CAUTION
If you don't save your song, you'll lose it when you close the current project.

Applying the Song to Your Project

When you save a song, only the information that makes up the song is saved. In other words, only the names of each pattern, their locations in the song, and their number of loops are saved. The actual MIDI data is not saved. To save the MIDI data that is generated from a song into a track (I'm assuming you've already gone through the setup procedure, you've created a song, and the Session Drummer window is still open), follow these steps:

1. Go to the Track view and select the track that you set up previously by clicking on its number.

2. Choose Process > Apply MIDI Effects.

3. In the Apply MIDI Effects dialog box, activate the Delete The Effects From The Track Inserts option.

4. Click OK.

SONAR places the song data into the selected track. No matter where the Now time is currently set, the song data is always placed at the beginning of the project.

Creating Your Own Session Drummer Styles

Styles are stored as standard MIDI files. Therefore, you can easily create your own styles for use in Session Drummer. If you open one of the existing style files as a project in SONAR (see Figure 11.44), you'll notice that a style is made up of nothing more than a single track containing MIDI data composed specifically to be played by General MIDI drum sounds. The track is separated into sections with markers. Each marker designates a different drum pattern. The name of the style file is what shows up in the Style section of the Session Drummer, and the names of the markers are what show up in the Pattern section.

Figure 11.44

You can create your own Session Drummer Styles by recording your own drum patterns and placing them together as a single track

After you've recorded your own drum patterns, you can easily create your own Session Drummer style by following these steps:

1. Open the project that contains the existing drum patterns that you recorded.

2. Create a new project and set a tempo for the project.

3. In the Track view of the original project, copy one of the drum patterns by using Edit > Copy.

4. Create 10 new MIDI tracks in the new project.

5. In the Track view of the new project, paste the drum pattern at the very beginning of Track 10. Track 10 is the standard track used for MIDI drum parts.

6. Set the Now time to the beginning of the Project.

7. Choose Insert > Marker to open the Marker dialog box. Type a name. This is the name of the pattern, and it will appear in the Pattern section of the Session Drummer. Click OK.

8. If you want to add more patterns, be sure to paste each new pattern at the end of the previous one. Each pattern should start at the beginning of a measure and should be at least one measure long.

9. Save the Project as a style by choosing File > Save As to open the Save As dialog box. Type a name for the file. This is the name that will appear in the Style section of the Session Drummer. Also, be sure to choose MIDI Format 0 for the Save As Type parameter. And be sure to save the file to the same directory that you set in the Content Folder parameter of the Session Drummer Settings. Click Save.

The next time you open the Session Drummer, your new style should be listed in the Style section.

CHAPTER 11

Session Drummer Song Example

To give you a quick idea of the results you can get from the session, I've put together this short demonstration:

1. Choose File > Open, select the file called 2-Part Invention #13 in A minor.cwp, and click Open to open the sample project.

2. Close the File Info window, along with the Staff and Big Time views. You don't need them.

3. In the Track view, create a new MIDI track (Track 3).

4. Set the Out and Ch parameters for Track 3. You should probably set the Channel to 10. Click OK.

5. Add the Session Drummer Effect to the Fx field of Track 3 by right-clicking in the Fx field and choosing MIDI Effects > Cakewalk FX > Session Drummer.

6. The Session Drummer window opens.

7. Select the style named Alternative 080 - Straight 16ths.

8. Add the following patterns to the song in the order listed:

    ▶   Crash/Kick/SN/Hat/Tamb—1 Loop

    ▶   SN/Tom fill1—2 Loops

    ▶   var1/Crash/Kick/SN/Hat/Tamb—1 Loop

    ▶   SN/Tom fill2—2 Loops

    ▶   Crash/Kick/SN/Hat—1 Loop

    ▶   SN/Tom fill3—2 Loops

    ▶   var1/Crash/Kick/SN/Hat—1 Loop

    ▶   SN fill1—2 Loops

    ▶   var2/Crash/Kick/SN/Hat—1 Loop

    ▶   SN fill3—2 Loops

9. At this point, you can save the song and apply it to the track if you'd like, but because this is just a demonstration, it's up to you.

10. Before you play the project, change the tempo to 100. The original tempo sounds too slow.

11. Play the project.

Sounds like one of those rearranged classical recordings like the ones on the CD called "BachBusters" by Don Dorsey, doesn't it? Have fun!

12

Mixing It Down

After you've recorded, edited, and added effects to your MIDI and audio data, it's time to mix down your project. It is called the *mixdown process* because you are taking all the MIDI and audio tracks in your project and mixing them together into a single stereo audio track. From there, you can put your music on CD, distribute it over the Internet, or record it onto tape. SONAR provides a number of different features that make the mixdown process as simple and intuitive as possible. Here's what I'll be covering in this chapter:

▶ Using the Console view and Track view for mixing

▶ Using the module and track managers

▶ Taking a snapshot

▶ Recording and editing automation

▶ Grouping

▶ Working with envelopes

The Console View

For mixing down the MIDI and audio tracks in your project, you can use either the Console view or the Track view. I've already covered many of the Track view features in earlier chapters. So, in this chapter, I'll tell you about the Console view and also let you know how the Track view fits into the mixdown process.

The Console view enables you to adjust the main parameters for each track in your project via on-screen buttons, knobs, sliders, and faders (vertical sliders). Similar in appearance to a hardware-based mixing board found in most recording studios, the Console view displays tracks as a collection of modules, each with its own set of adjustable controls.

More precisely, the Console view consists of four major sections: the toolbar (located at the top of the view, containing some of the view's related controls); the MIDI and audio track modules (located in the main part of the view, displaying the controls for each MIDI and audio track in the project); the aux buses (located to the right of the MIDI and audio track modules, containing additional mixing controls, which I'll explain later); and the Mains (located to the right of the aux buses, also containing additional mixing controls, which I'll explain later).

Opening the Console View

To open the Console view, simply choose View > Console. The Console view then opens, displaying modules for every track in the current project. To see how it works, follow these steps:

1. Choose File > Open. In the Open dialog box that appears, select the file named Don't Matter Audio and Midi Demo.cwb and click Open to open that sample project file.

2. Choose View > Console to open the Console view.

The Console view should look similar to the one shown in Figure 12.1.

Figure 12.1
When you open the Console view, it automatically displays a module for every track in the current project

You'll also notice that one of the modules has a dotted outline around it. This dotted line indicates that the track corresponding to that module is currently the selected or focused track in the Track view.

The MIDI Track Modules

Each MIDI track module contains a number of different controls that enable you to manipulate many of its corresponding track parameters (see Figure 12.2).

Figure 12.2
A MIDI track module contains controls for adjusting the parameters of its corresponding track

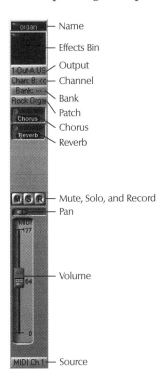

— Name
— Effects Bin
— Output
— Channel
— Bank
— Patch
— Chorus
— Reverb

— Mute, Solo, and Record
— Pan

— Volume

— Source

As matter of fact, all the controls are the equivalent of the track parameters shown in the track pane of the Track view (all of which I have described in previous chapters). This means that if you change the value of a control in the Console view, the equivalent track parameter is also changed in the Track view. From top to bottom, the controls in a MIDI track module correspond to the controls described in the following sections:

Name

The Name control displays the name of the track represented by the MIDI track module. It is the equivalent of the Name parameter in the Track view. You can change the name by clicking on the control, typing some new text, and pressing the Enter key on your computer keyboard.

Effects Bin

You can use the Effects bin control to assign effects to the track represented by the MIDI track module. These effects are applied only in real-time. This control works in exactly the same way as the Fx field in the Track view (which I described in Chapter 11).

Output

Using the Output control, you can set the MIDI output of the track represented by the MIDI track module. It is the equivalent of the Out parameter in the Track view. You can change the output by clicking on the control and selecting a new MIDI port from the pop-up menu.

Channel

The Channel control enables you to set the MIDI channel of the track represented by the MIDI track module. It is the equivalent of the Ch parameter in the Track view. You can change the channel by clicking on the control and selecting a new MIDI channel from the pop-up menu.

Bank

You can use the Bank control to set the MIDI patch bank of the track represented by the MIDI track module. It is the equivalent of the Bnk parameter in the Track view. You can change the bank by clicking on the control and selecting a new MIDI patch bank from the pop-up menu.

Patch

You can use the Patch control to set the MIDI patch of the track represented by the MIDI track module. It is the equivalent of the Pch parameter in the Track view. You can change the patch by clicking on the control and selecting a new MIDI patch from the pop-up menu.

Chorus and Reverb

Some MIDI instruments have built-in chorus and reverb effects. Some special MIDI controller messages even enable you to change the settings for these effects. Using the chorus and reverb controls, you can adjust the appropriate MIDI controller messages so that you can apply the chorus and reverb effects to your MIDI instrument. To adjust either control, simply click and drag the corresponding slider left or right. As you drag the slider, the Value parameter in the toolbar at the top of the Console view displays the current value of the control you are adjusting. If you drag the slider left, the value gets lower. If you drag the slider right, the value gets higher. Both the Chorus and Reverb controls can be adjusted from 0 to 127. The Chr and Rev parameters in the Track view are the equivalents of the Chorus and Reverb controls, respectively.

TIP

When you're adjusting sliders, knobs, or faders in the Console view or parameters in the Track view, a quick way to return them to their original positions is to double-click them. When you do, the control snaps back to its default value. You can also change the default value for a control. To do so, set the control to the value you want to use as its default. Then right-click the control and choose Set Snap-To = Current from the pop-up menu.

Mute, Solo, and Record Arm

The Mute, Solo, and Record Arm controls enable you to turn the Mute, Solo, and Record Arm (for recording) options on or off for the track represented by the MIDI track module. They are the equivalents of the Mute, Solo, and Record options in the Track view (which I described in Chapter 6). You can toggle these options on and off by clicking on them.

TIP

The Record Arm control is available in the Console view because you can actually use the view during recording instead of the Track view if you'd like. You can even create new tracks in the Console view. To do so, simply right-click in any blank space (such as just below the Aux Buses), and choose Add Track > Audio or Add Track > MIDI from the pop-up menu. A new MIDI or audio track module is added, representing the new track. You'll notice that the new track is added to the Track view as well.

Pan

You can use the Pan control to set the MIDI panning of the track represented by the MIDI track module. It is the equivalent of the Pan parameter in the Track view. You can change the pan by clicking and dragging the slider left or right. As you drag the slider, the Value parameter in the toolbar at the top of the Console view displays the current value of the control. The value can range from 0 (all the way left) to 127 (all the way right). A value of 64 is dead center.

NOTE

In the Track view, the Pan parameter values range from 100 percent left to Center to 100 percent right, instead of the 0 to 64 to 127 in the Console view. But even though the values are shown differently, they are equivalent to each other—meaning a value of 0 in the Console view (which equals all the way left) is equal to a value of 100 percent left in the Track view (which also equals all the way left).

Volume

Using the Volume control, you can set the MIDI volume of the track represented by the MIDI track module. It is the equivalent of the Vol parameter in the Track view. You can change the volume by clicking and dragging the fader (vertical slider) up or down. As you drag the fader, the Value parameter in the toolbar at the top of the Console view displays the current value of the control. The value can range from 0 (lowest volume level) to 127 (highest volume level).

Source

The Source control enables you to set the MIDI input of the track represented by the MIDI track module. It is the equivalent of the In parameter in the Track view. You can change the source by clicking on the control and selecting a new source from the pop-up menu.

The Audio Track Modules

Like the MIDI track modules, the audio track modules contain a number of different controls that you can use to manipulate their corresponding track parameters (see Figure 12.3).

Figure 12.3
The audio track modules are very similar to the MIDI track modules in terms of the controls they provide

Name
Effects Bin
Aux Sends
Phase
Preferred Interleave
Mute, Solo, and Record
Pan
Volume
Output
Input

As a matter of fact, almost all the controls are the same as those on the MIDI track modules. Included are the Name, Effects Bin, Mute, Solo, Record Arm, Pan, Volume, and Source controls. They all work in exactly the same manner as they do on the MIDI track modules, except, of course, they are controlling audio data instead of MIDI data. The one difference is with the Volume control. Instead of displaying its value as a MIDI volume controller number, its value is shown as decibels (dB).

Other than that, only four completely different types of controls are available on the audio track modules: Phase, Preferred Interleave, Output, and Aux Sends.

Phase

Sometimes phase cancellation can occur between the audio data of two different tracks. Phase cancellation occurs when one audio waveform increases in volume and the other decreases in volume at exactly the same time with the same amount. Because of this phenomenon, they cancel each other out, making the mixed audio sound "hollow." The Phase control allows you to invert the audio waveform of the data in an audio track around the zero axis. This can sometimes help eliminate phase cancellation. To invert the data in an audio track, just click the Phase control in the Console view. The Phase control is the equivalent of the Phase parameter in the Track view.

Preferred Interleave

There may be times when you want to hear a stereo track play in mono (via one channel) or hear a mono track play in stereo (if stereo effects are applied). Using the Preferred Interleave control in the Console view or the Preferred Interleave parameter in the Track view, you can determine how the data in a track will be played. By default, all Preferred Interleave parameters for each track are set to Auto. The Auto setting means that SONAR will automatically determine how a track will play according to the data it contains. If a track contains mono data, it will play in mono. If a track contains stereo data, it will play in stereo. If you click the Preferred Interleave control or parameter, it will cycle through the options. A value of A means Auto. A single left speaker symbol means Mono. And a double speaker symbol means Stereo.

Output

The Output control (located directly below the Volume control and directly above the Source control) enables you to route the data from the track represented by the audio track module to one of the mains (which I'll explain later). This control is the equivalent of the Out parameter in the Track view. You can change the Output by clicking on the control and selecting a new main from the pop-up menu.

Aux Sends

The Aux Send controls (located directly below the Effects bin in the Console view or directly below the Fx field in the Track view) enable you to route (send) the audio data from the track represented by the audio track module to one of the aux buses (which I'll explain later). You can have up to sixteen aux sends for each audio track module, although, by default, there are only two (I'll show you how to change this number later). Each aux send has a number (1 to 16), which corresponds to the number of the aux bus to which its data will be sent. Each aux send also has three controls within it: an on/off button, a Send Level slider, and a Pre/Post Fader button. The on/off buttons are located in the bottom-right corner of each aux send. To toggle an aux send on or off, just click its on/off button. The Send Level slider controls the volume (or level) of the audio data that will be sent to the aux bus. To adjust the slider, simply drag it left or right. As you drag the slider, the Value parameter in the toolbar at the top of the Console view displays the current value of the send level. If you drag the slider left, the value gets lower. If you drag the slider right, the value gets higher. The send level can be adjusted from –INF (infinity, the lowest level setting) to +6 dB (the highest level setting). The Pre/Post Fader button is located to the left of the on/off button. The Pre/Post Fader button determines from what point in the audio track module the audio data will be taken and sent to the aux bus. You can toggle the Pre/Post Fader button by clicking on it. Initially, the button is set to Pre (you can see this because the button says Pre on it). When you click the button, it changes its name to Post. When you click it again, it changes its name back to Pre.

CHAPTER 12

NOTE

As SONAR plays a project, it reads the data for each audio track from your hard drive. It then routes the data through the appropriate sections of the Console view, until it is finally sent to your sound card, and then to your speakers so you can hear it. The routing works as follows: The data for an audio Track is read from your hard drive and routed through the corresponding audio track module. Within the module, the data first passes through the Effects bin (where any assigned effects are applied). The data is then sent through the Volume control (where its level can be adjusted), then the Pan control, and finally to the Output control. From here, it is sent out of the module and into the assigned main (which I'll talk about shortly). During this routing process, the data can be sent to an aux send either before or after it reaches the Volume control. If the Pre/Post Fader button is set to Pre, the data is routed to the aux bus after it goes through the Effects bin, but before it reaches the Volume control. This means that the Volume control will have no effect on the level of the signal being sent to the aux bus. If the Pre/Post Fader button is set to Post, the data is routed to the aux bus after it goes through the Volume control. This means that the Volume control does affect the level of the signal being sent to the aux bus. For a graphical view of how audio signals are routed in SONAR, take a look at the diagram on page 384 in the SONAR user's guide.

The on/off buttons are the equivalents of the A1 through A16 (depending on the number of aux sends available) parameters in the Track view. The Send Level sliders are the equivalents of the Snd parameters in the Track view. And the Pre/Post Fader buttons are the equivalents of the Pre/Post Fader parameters in the Track view.

NOTE

The aux sends shown in the Track view also provide Pan parameters. These Pan parameters are not provided in the Console view. So, if you want to apply panning to the audio data being sent to an aux bus, you'll need to adjust the parameters in the Track view, because there's no way to do it in the Console view.

The Aux Buses

The aux buses provide additional mixing control of your audio signals. Like the audio track modules, each aux bus contains Name, Effects Bin, and Output controls (see Figure 12.4).

Figure 12.4
Shown here in the Console view, the aux buses provide some of the same controls as the audio track modules

You can also access the aux buses in Track view by clicking on the Show/Hide Mains And Aux Buses button located at the bottom of the Track view (see Figure 12.5).

Figure 12.5
Access the aux buses in the Track view by clicking the Show/Hide Mains And Aux Buses button

In addition to the Name, Effects Bin, and Output, each aux bus provides four other controls: Send Level, Send Balance, Return Level, and Return Balance.

Send Level

Although the name might be misleading, the Send Level control enables you to set the input level of the audio data coming into the aux bus. You can change the send level by clicking and holding down on the knob and then dragging up or down. As you drag your mouse, the Value parameter in the toolbar at the top of the Console view displays the current value of the control. If you drag up, the value gets higher. If you drag down, the value gets lower. The value can range from –INF to +6 dB. The Send Level control is the equivalent of the Snd parameter in the Track view.

Send Balance

Each aux bus works in stereo, so SONAR provides balance controls. Using the Send Balance controls, you can set the panning of the audio data coming into the aux bus. You can change the send balance by clicking and dragging the slider left or right. As you drag the slider, the Value parameter in the toolbar at the top of the Console view displays the current value of the control. The value can range from 0 (all the way left) to 127 (all the way right). A value of 64 is dead center. The Send Balance control is the equivalent of the Snd Bal parameter in the Track view.

Return Level

The Return Level control works just like the Send Level control, except that it enables you to adjust the output level of the audio data going out of the aux bus. You can change the return level by clicking and holding down on the knob and then dragging up or down. As you drag your mouse, the Value parameter in the toolbar at the top of the Console view displays the current value of the control. If you drag up, the value gets higher. If you drag down, the value gets lower. The value can range from –INF to +6 dB. The Return Level control is the equivalent of the Rtn parameter in the Track view.

Return Balance

The Return Balance control works just like the Send Balance control, except that it enables you to adjust the panning of the audio data going out of the aux bus. You can change the return balance by clicking and dragging the slider left or right. As you drag the slider, the

CHAPTER 12

Value parameter in the toolbar at the top of the Console view displays the current value of the control. The value can range from 0 (all the way left) to 127 (all the way right). A value of 64 is dead center. The Return Balance control is the equivalent of the Rtn Bal parameter in the Track view.

What's It Good For?

One good use for the aux buses is to add the same effects to a number of different tracks. For example, say you have four audio tracks (1, 2, 3, and 4) containing the background vocals for your project, and you want to add some nice chorus to them. Without using an aux bus, you would have to set up a Chorus effect (each with identical parameter settings) in the Effects bins of each of the audio track modules for tracks 1, 2, 3, and 4. Not only is this approach cumbersome and tedious, it also puts extra strain on your computer because it has to process each of the four effects at the same time.

Using an aux bus, however, the process becomes much more streamlined. You can use Aux Bus 1 for this example. First, you activate Aux Send 1 in each of the four audio track modules (1, 2, 3, and 4). Then you set the send levels for each of the aux sends. In the Effects bin of Aux Bus 1, you set up the Chorus effect. Only one effect needs to be set up, because all four tracks are being sent to the aux bus. You then set the Send Level and Send Balance controls, along with the Return Level and Return Balance controls. Finally, you set the Pre/Post Fader buttons to Pre or Post. If you set the buttons to Pre, the data in each audio track module is sent to the aux bus before it's routed through each Volume control. This means that you can control the level of the effect (with the send level) and the level of the original data (with the Volume control) independently. If you set the Pre/Post Fader buttons to Post, the level of the effect goes up and down with the level of the original data via the Volume control.

The Mains

For every individual output on your sound card, a main is displayed in the Console view (see Figure 12.6).

Figure 12.6
A main looks similar
to an audio track
module

Name

Effects Bin

Preferred Interleave

Pan

Volume

Output

So, if your sound card has only one output, only one main is displayed, and all the audio data from the audio track modules is sent to it. If your sound card has more than one output, more than one main is shown, and you can choose to which main the data from each audio track module and aux bus is sent.

TIP
Even if you have only one output on your sound card, you can have more than one main. By using more than one main, you can create subgroups of different mixes for your project. For example, you could send all your vocal tracks to one main, and all your drum tracks to another main. This would allow you to process each group of tracks with different effects. Also, if you have a sound card with only one output, but that output is stereo, you can set up one main to control the left channel and another main to control the right channel. To set up additional main modules, choose Options > Audio to open the Audio Options dialog box. Click the General tab. Then enter the number of mains you would like to set up in the Number Of Virtual Mains parameter. You can have up to 64 mains.

A main provides seven different controls. From top to bottom, the Name control initially displays a letter designating the sound card output assigned to the main. You can change it to something more recognizable if you'd like. Next is the Effects bin. Because the outputs from all the modules and buses are routed through the main, adding effects to its Effects bin applies those effects to your entire final stereo signal. A good use for this control is to apply reverb to your entire mix. After the Effects bin comes the Main Meter, which shows the output level of your final stereo signal as SONAR plays the project. Levels are shown in decibels. Right-click the Main Meter to change the decibel range that will be displayed. Next is the Preferred Interleave control, which works as I described earlier. Then comes the Main Balance control, which lets you set the panning for the main. The Volume control lets you adjust the output level of your final stereo signal, which is sent to your sound card output. And last is the Output control, which allows you to assign a main to a sound card output of your choice.

TIP

Although the controls in Tracks, Aux Buses, and Mains are presented in a certain order, you have the option of changing that order if you'd like. There is a hidden feature in SONAR that lets you arrange the controls of Tracks, Aux Buses, and Mains in the Track view. Here is how it works:

1. Using the Windows Notepad, open the Cakewalk.ini file located on your hard drive at C:\Program Files\Cakewalk\SONAR 2\cakewalk.ini

2. Add the following lines (exactly as shown) to the file:

   [MIDI Widgets]
   W0=Volume
   W1=Pan
   W2=Trim
   W3=Input
   W4=Output
   W5=Channel
   W6=Bank
   W7=Patch
   W8=Key
   W9=Time
   W10=FX
   W11=Chorus
   W12=Reverb

   [Audio Widgets]
   W0=Volume
   W1=Pan
   W2=Trim
   W3=Input
   W4=Output
   W5=FX
   W6=Aux
   W7=Phase
   W8=Interleave

Continued

```
[Aux Widgets]
W0=Send
W1=Return
W2=Output
W3=FX

[Mains Widgets]
W0=Volume
W1=Balance
W2=Interleave
W3=Output
W4=FX
```

3. By changing the numbers next to each letter W, you can change the order in which the controls appear.

4. Save the file after you've made your changes.

The next time you open a project, the controls will appear using the new arrangement. Unfortunately, this only works in the Track view and not in the Console view.

Configuring the Console and Track Views

Earlier, I mentioned that the number of aux buses shown in the Console view can be changed. Along with these changes, you can customize how the Console view looks and works in many other ways. These methods are described in the following sections.

Number of Aux Buses

Choose Options > Audio to open the Audio Options dialog box and click the General tab (see Figure 12.7).

Figure 12.7
You can adjust the
number of aux buses in
the Audio Options
dialog box

To designate the number of aux buses you want to be displayed in the Console view, just type a number in the Number Of Aux Buses parameter. Up to sixteen aux buses can be displayed.

TIP
If you know you won't need any aux buses during mixdown, you can enter a value of 0 in the Number Of Aux Buses parameter. This setting helps keeps the Console view neat and compact.

When you adjust the number of aux buses, it also affects the number of aux buses displayed in the Track view.

The Track Managers

SONAR provides track managers for the both the Console view and the Track view, which allow you to hide modules, aux buses, and mains. What may seem a bit confusing, however, is that the track managers in the Console view and Track view work independently of one another. Meaning, if you hide a track in the Track view, its corresponding track module in the Console view is NOT hidden. Instead, you would have to hide the track module using the track manager in the Console view. In a way, this may seem a bit awkward at first, but it provides you with the flexibility to have the Track view and Console view set up differently.

The track managers work as follows:

1. To open the Track view track manager, make sure the Track view is the active window and then press the M key on your computer keyboard.

2. To open the Console view track manager, make sure the Console view is the active window and then press the M key on your computer keyboard.

3. The Track Manager dialog box opens (see Figure 12.08). The track managers are identical, so the remaining instructions apply to both.

Figure 12.8
The track managers are identical

4. To hide an individual component, click to remove the check mark next to that component in the list. Then click OK.

5. To hide a group of components (such as all the MIDI track modules, all the audio track modules, all the aux buses, or all the mains), click the appropriate button—Toggle Audio, Toggle MIDI, Toggle Aux Bus, Toggle Mains—to select the appropriate group. Then press the spacebar on your computer keyboard to remove the check marks. Finally, click OK.

Of course, you can also make the components appear again by doing the opposite of the preceding procedures. These changes to the Console view and Track view are in appearance only. They don't affect what you hear during playback. For example, if you hide an audio track module that outputs data during playback, you still hear that data even if you hide the module. Hiding components of the Console view or Track view can come in handy when you want to work only on a certain group of tracks at a time and you don't want to be distracted or overwhelmed by the number of controls being displayed.

CHAPTER 12

NOTE

The Track view actually provides some additional features when it comes to managing tracks, which are not available in the Console view. I covered these features in chapter 7.

Changing the Meters

You can also change how the meters in the Console and Track views behave. While recording your audio tracks, you'll notice that the meters on the tracks that have their Arm controls activated will light up. These meters show the input level for the tracks (which I described in Chapter 6). To toggle these meters on or off, simply click the Record Meters button in the toolbar at the top of Console view. You can do the same thing with the meters that are active during playback by clicking on the Playback Meters button. And of course, you can also control the main meters by clicking on the Main Bus Meters button.

In the Track view, you click the downward arrow next to the Show/Hide All Meters button to access the meter options (see Figure 12.09).

Figure 12.9
Access meter options in the Track view with the Show/Hide All Meters downward arrow

The Console view provides one additional button: By clicking on the Peaks Only button, you can control whether the meters will show the entire output level or just if the output level peaks (meaning it hits 0 dB).

NOTE

Like the track managers, the meters in the Console view and Track view work independently of one another. For instance, if you turn off the record meters in the Track view, this does NOT turn off the record meters in the Console view, and vice-versa.

TIP

If you ever need to lighten the load on your computer during recording or play-back, you might want to try turning off some or all of the meters. The meters can take up quite a bit of your computer's processing power and affect SONAR's performance.

In addition to being able to turn the meters on and off, you can set various options to deter-mine how the meters will work. If you click the downward arrow next to one of the meter buttons in the Console view (or use the Show/Hide All Meters downward arrow in the Track view), you'll see a pop-up menu with a number of options available. These options let you set how the meters will display the audio signal, how to measure the audio signal, the range of measurement, and various cosmetic options such as whether or not the decibel markings are shown. For detailed descriptions of each option, take a look at page 393 in the SONAR user's guide.

Taking Snapshots

SONAR provides a number of different methods of mixdown, one of which is called snapshots. Using snapshots, you can take a "picture" of all the current control values in the Console and Track views and then store those values in your project at a specified Now time. For example, if your project is a pop song with a number of different sections (such as the intro, verse, chorus, and so on), you might want to change the mix each time a new section is reached by the Now time during playback. You can easily do so by creat-ing a different snapshot at the beginning of each section of the song. During playback, as the Now time passes a point in the project where a snapshot is stored, the values for all the recorded controls are automatically changed to reflect the snapshot.

NOTE

For automation purposes, the controls in the Console view and the parameters in the Track view work together rather than independently. This means that if you automate a control in the Console view, its corresponding parameter in the Track view is also automated and vice-versa.

To create a snapshot, just follow these steps:

1. Set the Now time to the point in the project where you want the snapshot to be stored.

2. Adjust the controls in the Console or Track view to values at which you want them to be set during that part of the project.

3. For all the controls you adjusted, right-click each one and choose Arm For Automation from the pop-up menu.

TIP

Instead of having to arm each control one-by-one, you can also arm all the controls in a track by first selecting the track (click the track number to select the track) and then choosing Track > Arm For Automation. You can also arm the controls in multiple tracks at once. Just select all the tracks whose controls you want to arm (use CTRL-click to select more than one track) and, again, choose Track > Arm For Automation.

NOTE

You'll notice that not all the controls/parameters can be automated. If a control/parameter cannot be automated, the Arm For Automation option in the pop-up menu will be grayed out. Also, after a parameter in the Track view is armed for automation, it will have a red outline displayed around it.

4. Make sure the Automation toolbar is visible by choosing View > Toolbars, activating the Automation option, and clicking Close. The Automation toolbar is displayed (see Figure 12.10).

Figure 12.10
Use the Automation toolbar to take snapshots

5. Click the Snapshot button (the one with the picture of a camera shown on it) in the Automation toolbar.

6. Repeat steps 1 through 5 until you've created all the snapshots you need for your project.

7. When you're finished, click the Disarm All Automation Controls button (the first button to the right of the Snapshot button) in the Automation toolbar to disarm all of the previously armed controls/parameters.

When you play your project, you'll notice the snapshots take effect as the Now time passes each snapshot point.

TIP

If you want to disable automation temporarily without changing or deleting any of the snapshots in your project, click the Enable/Disable Automation Playback button (the second button to the right of the Snapshot button) in the Automation toolbar.

Snapshot control values for each of the MIDI and audio track modules, as well as the aux bus and mains, are stored as nodes on individual envelopes in the individual tracks represented by those modules. These envelope nodes can be edited, allowing you to change your recorded snapshot data. I'll talk more about envelopes later in the chapter.

Automating the Mix

Snapshots are great if you need quick control in value changing at certain points in your project, but most of the time, you'll want the controls to change smoothly over time as the project plays. To achieve this effect, you need to use SONAR's Record Automation feature. Using Record Automation, you can record the movements of any of the controls in the Console or Track views. You do so in real-time as your project plays.

You can record the values of the controls in the Console and Track views into your project by activating the Record Automation feature and manipulating the controls with your mouse as the project plays. This feature works as follows:

1. Make sure the Automation toolbar is visible by choosing View > Toolbars, then activate the Automation option and click Close.

2. For the controls or parameters that you want to automate, right-click each one and choose Arm For Automation from the pop-up menu.

TIP

Instead of having to arm each control one by one, you can also arm all the controls in a track by first selecting the track (click the track number to select the track) and then choosing Track > Arm For Automation. You can also arm the controls in multiple tracks at once. Just select all the tracks whose controls you want to arm (use CTRL-click to select more than one track) and, again, choose Track > Arm For Automation.

NOTE

You may notice that the Automation toolbar contains a dropdown menu that is supposed to allow you to choose an Automation Record Mode. You may also notice that the Transport menu has a listing for Automation Record Options. These features were accidentally left over from SONAR version 1. SONAR 2 only provides Touch mode automation, so you don't need to concern yourself with setting the automation recording mode. When you record automation, any existing data of the same kind is overwritten.

3. Set the Now time to just before the point in the project where you want to start recording control changes.

4. Choose Transport > Record Automation to start the project playing and to start recording automation data.

5. When the Now time gets to the point in the project where you want to begin recording control changes, adjust the controls or parameters with your mouse.

6. When you're finished, choose Transport > Stop to stop playback of the project.

7. Because you're manipulating on-screen controls with your mouse, you can make only one change at a time. What if you want to have two different controls change at the same time? For every control that you want to have change in the same time frame, you must repeat steps 2 through 6.

TIP

Instead of starting and stopping playback each time you want to record additional control changes, try setting up a loop so that SONAR will play the project (or section of the project) over and over again. I described loop recording in Chapter 6.

8. After you've finished recording all the control changes you need for your mix, click the Disarm All Automation Controls button (the first button to the right of the Snapshot button) in the Automation toolbar to disarm all of the previously armed controls/parameters.

When you play your project, you'll notice the automation taking effect as the Now time passes the sections where you recorded data.

Just as with snapshots, the control values for each of the MIDI and audio track modules, as well as the aux bus and mains, are stored as envelopes in the individual tracks represented by those modules. These envelopes can be edited, allowing you to change your recorded automation data.

Grouping

As I mentioned earlier, to change more than one control or parameter at once while you're recording automation data, you have to play through your project several times. To make things easier, you can connect a number of controls or parameters together so that, if you move one, the others will move with it. You do so by using SONAR's Grouping feature. With the Grouping feature, you can create groups of buttons, knobs, sliders, and faders whose movements are linked to one another.

Creating Groups

You can create up to twenty-four different groups, each of which is designated by a letter of the alphabet (A through X) and a color. The number of controls that can belong to a group is unlimited. To create a group, follow these steps:

1. Right-click a control in the Console view or a parameter in the Track View and choose Group > A-X. Depending on what letter you choose, that control takes on the associated color.

2. Right-click another control and choose Group > A-X. This time, choose the same letter as you did for the first control. This other control then takes on the same color.

3. Continue to add as many other controls to the group as you'd like. You can even create other groups. The same control, however, cannot belong to more than one group.

Now, if you move the first control, the second control will move too, and vice versa. The values of both of these controls are also recorded if you have them grouped while recording automation data.

Ungrouping

To remove a control from a group, right-click the control and then select Ungroup from the pop-up menu. The color of the control turns back to normal.

Group Properties

In addition to simple groups, in which you link different controls together so that they move identically, you can create some advanced control groups by manipulating the properties of a group. To change the properties of a group, right-click one of the controls in the group and select Group Properties from the pop-up menu to open the Group Properties dialog box (see Figure 12.11).

Figure 12.11
You can use the Group Properties dialog box to change the properties of a group

By changing the properties of a group, you can change the way the controls in the group are related to one another in terms of the way they move. Controls in groups can be related absolutely, relatively, or via a custom definition.

Absolute

To make it so the controls in a group are related absolutely, select the Absolute option (which is the default setting when you create a new group) in the Group Properties dialog box and click OK. Controls in a group that are related absolutely have the same range of motion. This means that if you move one control in the group, the others move by the same amount. This is true even if one control starts at one value and another control starts at a different value. For example, suppose you have two Volume controls on two different MIDI track modules linked together, and one of the Volume controls has a value of 10 and the other has a value of 20. If you move the first control up by 10, the other control moves up by 10 too. Now the first control has a value of 20, and the second control has a value of 30.

Relative

To make it so the controls in a group are linked relatively, select the Relative option in the Group Properties dialog box and click OK. Controls in a group that are linked relatively do not have the same range of motion. This means that if you move one control in the group, the others can move by different amounts. For example, suppose you have two Pan controls linked together, and one has a value of 0 (all the way left) and the other has a value of 64 (centered in the middle). If you move the first control so that it has a value of 64 (centered in the middle), the other moves so that it has a value of 127 (all the way right). Now if you move the first control to a value of 127 (all the way right), the second control remains at 127 (all the way right). The second control remains in this position because it can't go any higher, so it stays at that value, while the first control continues to be raised in value. I know this concept is a bit confusing, but if you try it for a while, you'll begin to understand it.

Custom

To make it so the controls in a group are related according to your own custom definition, select the Custom option in the Group Properties dialog box. All the controls in the group are listed in the dialog box (see Figure 12.12).

Figure 12.12
You can create complex relationships between controls in a group by using the Custom option

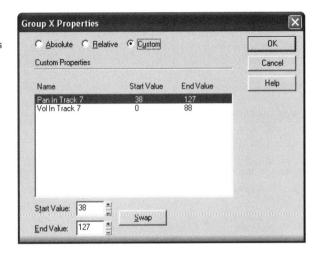

Along with the names of each control, the Start and End values are also listed. By changing the Start and End values of each control, you can define some complex ranges of motion. For example, one good use of the Custom option is to create a "crossfade" motion between two Volume controls. Suppose you have one Volume control in a group with a Start Value of 0 and an End Value of 127, and you have another Volume control in the same group with a Start Value of 127 and an End Value of 0. As you move the first control up in value, the second control comes down, and vice versa. You can also set up more complex relationships simply by assigning different Start and End values to each control in a group.

To change the Start or End Value of a control in the list in the Group Properties dialog box, select the control and then type a value for either the Start Value or End Value parameters located at the bottom of the box. If you want to exchange the current Start and End values, click the Swap button. After you've finished creating your custom definition, click OK.

TIP
You can also change the Start and End values of a control without having to open the Group Properties dialog box. Just set the control to the value that you want to set as the Start or End, right-click the control, and select either Set Start = Current or Set End = Current.

Remote Control

Even with grouping, you still might find it cumbersome having to adjust on-screen controls with your mouse. To remedy this situation, SONAR provides a Remote Control feature. With the Remote Control feature, you can use an external MIDI device to control the movements of the on-screen controls in the Console view or parameters in the Track view. For example, if you have a MIDI keyboard, you can use a key on the keyboard to manipulate one of the button controls. Or if you have a pitch bend wheel on your keyboard, you can use it to manipulate one of the knob, slider, or fader controls.

By assigning different types of MIDI controller messages to the controls in the Console view or parameters in the Track view, you'll no longer have to use your mouse to change the value of the controls. You can use the actual button and keys or levers and sliders on your MIDI instrument or device. To activate the Remote Control feature for a control or parameter, just do the following:

1. Right-click the control and select Remote Control from the pop-up menu to open the Remote Control dialog box (see Figure 12.13).

Figure 12.13
You can use the
Remote Control dialog
box to assign MIDI
controller messages to
controls in the Console
view so that they can
be changed via an
external MIDI device

2. If you want to use a key on your MIDI keyboard to manipulate this control, select either the Note On option or the Note On/Off option. Then enter the pitch of the key that you want to use. If you choose Note On, the value of the control is toggled on or off (for a button control) or to minimum value or maximum value (for knobs and sliders) each time you press the key. If you select the Note On/Off option, the value of the control is toggled on when you press the key and off when you let go of the key.

3. If you want to use a lever or slider on your MIDI keyboard to manipulate this control, select the Controller option. Then enter the value of the MIDI controller that you want to use. You can use this option to manipulate only knob, slider, and fader controls.

4. If you want to use the pitch bend wheel on your MIDI keyboard to manipulate this control, select the Wheel option.

5. If you want to use the special registered parameter number or non-registered parameter number MIDI messages to manipulate this control, choose either the RPN or NRPN option. Then enter the number of the parameter that you want to use.

6. If you want to use a Sysx message to manipulate this control, choose a Byte option. If the message contains a single byte of data that changes, while the rest of the bytes in the message remain static, choose the Single Byte option. If the changing data contains two bytes with the first being the high byte, choose the High Byte First option. If the changing data contains two bytes with the first being the low byte, choose the Low Byte First option. Then enter into the Starts With parameter the bytes in the Sysx message that come before the changing data. And enter into the Ends With parameter the bytes in the Sysx message that come after the changing data.

7. Set the MIDI channel that your MIDI keyboard or device is using.

8. Click OK.

TIP

Instead of having to figure out how the parameters for Remote Control need to be set, you can use the Learn feature to have it done automatically for you. First, move a control on your external MIDI device. Right-click the control or parameter in SONAR that you want to manipulate and choose Remote Control from the pop-up menu. Then click the Learn button. The Remote Control parameters are set up for you automatically. Click OK.

Now you can manipulate the control from your MIDI keyboard or device, and you can do this while recording automation as well.

TIP

SONAR 2 provides special support for external devices designed specifically for remote control purposes such as the CM Labs MotorMix, the Tascam US-428, the Roland U-8, and the Peavey StudioMix. For more information on how to use each of these devices, look in the SONAR Help file under the topic "Working with External Devices."

Envelopes

In addition to the Snapshot and Record Automation features, SONAR provides one more method of automating its controls or parameters. I'm talking about the Envelope feature. Using this feature, you can "draw" control changes into individual clips or entire tracks within the Track view. In the following sections, I'll cover how to create and edit control changes using the Envelope feature.

Creating and Editing Envelopes

Earlier I mentioned that whenever you use the Snapshot or Record Automation features, SONAR stores the automation data as envelopes in the Track view. Well, you can also create (as well as edit) envelopes manually using the Envelope tool and your mouse.

Audio Envelopes

SONAR allows you to create envelopes for both audio and MIDI tracks, as well as the aux bus and main tracks in the Track view. Since the aux buses and mains deal with audio data, you automate them using audio envelopes. MIDI and audio envelopes are basically the same, but they have enough differences to require separate step-by-step procedures. To create and/or edit an audio envelope, do the following:

1. Activate the Envelope tool by clicking on the Envelope tool button in the Track view (see Figure 12.14).

Figure 12.14
Use the Envelope tool
to create a new
envelope

2. If you want to create an envelope for an individual clip, right-click that clip and choose Envelopes > Clip > (name of the parameter you want to automate). For individual clips, you can automate the gain (volume) or panning.

3. If you want to create an envelope for an entire track (including the aux bus and main tracks), right-click that track in the clips pane and choose Envelopes > Create Track Envelope > (name of the parameter you want to automate). For tracks, you can automate the Mute, Volume, Pan, and Aux Bus Send Level/Pan controls. The aux bus and main tracks provide different parameters for automation (see the list in the pop-up menu).

NOTE

If you create an envelope for a clip inside of a track that already has an envelope for the same parameter, the clip envelope will be merged into the track envelope.

4. Initially, the envelope is shown as a straight, dotted line that runs from left to right in the clip or track. If it's a clip envelope, it will stop at the end of the clip. If it's a track envelope, it will continue past the right side of the Track view (see Figure 12.15). The vertical position of the envelope inside the clip or track indicates the current value for its associated parameter. For example, if you're automating the Vol (volume) parameter and its current value is 0, the envelope will be shown at the very bottom of the clip or track. If the Vol parameter value is 127, the envelope will be shown at the very top of the clip or track. And other values will be shown somewhere between the top and bottom of the clip or track.

Figure 12.15
A straight line in a clip or track represents a new envelope

TIP
You can show and hide envelopes for easier editing purposes. If you don't see your new envelope, click the downward arrow next to the Envelope tool button and choose one of the options (such as Show All Envelopes) from the pop-up menu.

5. At the beginning of the envelope is a small square (called a *node*). To change the value of the envelope, click and drag the node up or down. As you drag the node, you will see the value of the parameter represented by the envelope displayed alongside your mouse cursor.

6. To make things more interesting, you can add more nodes to the envelope either by double-clicking anywhere on the envelope or by right-clicking on the envelope and selecting Add Node from the pop-up menu. You can add as many nodes as you need, which enables you to create some very complex parameter value changes. And in addition to dragging them up or down, you can also drag nodes left or right (to change their time/location within the project), so you can create any envelope shape you'd like (see Figure 12.16). You can also change the time and value of a node more precisely by right-clicking on it, choosing Properties from the pop-up menu, and then entering the new values in the Edit Node dialog box.

CHAPTER 12

Figure 12.16

You can create
complex envelopes by
adding more nodes

7. To make things even more interesting, you can change the shape of the line segments between two nodes. Right-click a line segment and choose one of the following options from the pop-up menu: Jump, Linear, Fast Curve, or Slow Curve. If you want abrupt changes in the parameter values, choose Jump. For straight changes in the values, choose Linear. For fast but smooth changes in the values, choose Fast Curve. For slow and smooth changes in the values, choose Slow Curve. Depending on the option you choose, the shape of the line segment will change respectively.

8. If you need to delete a node, right-click it and select Delete Node from the pop-up menu. And to delete all nodes, just right-click the envelope and select Clear All from the pop-up menu.

9. If you need to reset a node to its original position, right-click it and select Reset Node from the pop-up menu.

10. If you want to delete an entire envelope, right-click it and select Delete Envelope from the pop-up menu.

11. If you want to change an envelope assignment so that it controls a different parameter, right-click the envelope and choose Assign Envelope > (name of the new parameter to automate).

MIDI Envelopes

To create and/or edit a MIDI envelope, do the following:

1. Activate the Envelope tool by clicking on the Envelope tool button in the Track view.

2. If you want to create an envelope for an individual clip, right-click that clip and choose Envelopes > Clip > (name of the parameter you want to automate). For individual MIDI clips, you can automate the velocity.

3. If you want to create an envelope for an entire track, right-click that track in the Clips pane and choose Envelopes > Create Track Envelope > (name of the parameter you want to automate). For MIDI tracks, you can automate the Mute, Volume, Pan, Chorus, and Reverb controls. In addition, you can automate any other MIDI controller messages by choosing the Envelopes > Create Track Envelope > MIDI option, which opens the MIDI

Envelope dialog box (see Figure 12.17). In the dialog box, choose the type of controller, the value of that controller, and the MIDI channel you want to use for the controller. Then click OK to create the new envelope.

Figure 12.17
For MIDI tracks, you can create envelopes for any kind of MIDI controller messages

TIP

If you think the parameters in the MIDI Envelope dialog box look familiar, you're right. They are the same parameters found in the Controller pane at the bottom of the Piano Roll view, which are used to choose MIDI controllers for editing in the Controller pane. If a track contains MIDI controller messages and you create an envelope for that track with the same controller, they will contradict one another. In this case, you should select the track and choose Edit > Convert MIDI To Shapes. You'll see the Convert MIDI To Shapes dialog box, which is exactly the same as the MIDI Envelope dialog box. Choose the controller you want to convert and click OK. The controller messages in that track will be converted to envelopes.

4. Initially, the envelope is shown as a straight line that runs from left to right in the clip or track. If it's a clip envelope, it will stop at the end of the clip. If it's a track envelope, it will continue past the right side of the Track view. The vertical position of the envelope inside the clip or track indicates the current value for its associated parameter. For example, if you're automating the Vol (volume) parameter and its current value is 0, the envelope will be shown at the very bottom of the clip or track. If the Vol parameter value is 127, the envelope will be shown at the very top of the clip or track. And other values will be shown somewhere between the top and bottom of the clip or track.

5. At the beginning of the envelope is a small square (called a *node*). To change the value of the envelope, click and drag the node up or down. As you drag the node, you will see the value of the parameter represented by the envelope displayed alongside your mouse cursor.

6. To make things more interesting, you can add more nodes to the envelope either by double-clicking anywhere on the envelope or by right-clicking on the envelope and selecting Add Node from the pop-up menu. You can add as many nodes as you need, which enables you to create some very complex parameter value changes. And in addition to dragging them up or down, you can also drag nodes left or right (to change their time/location within the project), so you can create any envelope shape you'd like. You can also change the time and value of a node more precisely by right-clicking on it,

choosing Properties from the pop-up menu, and then entering the new values in the Edit Node dialog box.

7. To make things even more interesting, you can change the shape of the line segments between two nodes. Right-click a line segment and choose one of the following options from the pop-up menu: Jump, Linear, Fast Curve, or Slow Curve. If you want abrupt changes in the parameter values, choose Jump. For straight changes in the values, choose Linear. For fast but smooth changes in the values, choose Fast Curve. For slow and smooth changes in the values, choose Slow Curve. Depending on the option you choose, the shape of the line segment will change respectively.

8. If you need to delete a node, right-click it and select Delete Node from the pop-up menu. And to delete all nodes, just right-click the envelope and select Clear All from the pop-up menu.

9. If you need to reset a node to its original position, right-click it and select Reset Node from the pop-up menu.

10. If you want to delete an entire envelope, right-click it and select Delete Envelope from the pop-up menu.

11. If you want to change an envelope assignment so that it controls a different parameter, right-click the envelope and choose Assign Envelope > (name of the new parameter to automate).

Now, when you play your project, the parameter values that you edited will follow the shape of the envelopes.

TIP

If you want to temporarily turn off all envelopes in your tracks to hear how your project sounds without the automation, click the Enable/Disable Automation Playback button in the Automation toolbar.

TIP

Normally during playback, if you have an envelope assigned to a track parameter, you cannot change that parameter because the envelope is controlling it. But SONAR provides a special mode in which you can add an offset to envelope values by changing parameters during playback. This mode is called Offset mode and can be activated by clicking the Envelope/Offset Mode button in the Track view toolbar (see Figure 12.18). This button toggles between Envelope mode and Offset mode. Also be aware that when you return to Envelope mode, you last parameter offset settings are still in effect. So if you change a parameter in Offset mode and leave it, the parameter will still be offset even if you return to Envelope mode. A good use for this feature is if you have an envelope that's just about perfect, but you want to make an adjustment to the entire envelope without having to change all the nodes in the envelope.

Figure 12.18
Use the Envelope/
Offset Mode button
to toggle between
Envelope and
Offset modes

Additional Envelope Editing

Even though I've covered most of the editing procedures for envelopes in the previous sections, there are some additional ways in which you can edit envelopes.

Deleting Envelopes

Earlier I mentioned that to delete an envelope, you just need to right-click the envelope and choose Delete Envelope from the pop-up menu. But if you want to delete more than one envelope or only part of an envelope, the procedure is a bit different:

1. Make sure the Select tool is activated by clicking on the Select tool button in the Track view (see Figure 12.19).

Figure 12.19
For normal data
selection, use the
Select tool

2. Select the data containing the envelope data you want to delete. This can be a single clip, an entire track, multiple tracks, or even part of a clip or track. To refresh your memory on how to select data in the Track view, go back to Chapter 7.

3. Choose Edit > Delete to open the Delete dialog box.

4. Depending on the data you selected in Step 2, either the Track/Bus Automation option or the Clip Automation option will be available (or maybe even both). Activate either one or both options.

CAUTION
If you don't want to delete any other data along with the envelope data, make sure to deactivate all other options in the Delete dialog box.

CHAPTER 12

5. Click OK.

SONAR deletes your selected envelope/automation data.

Copying and Pasting Envelopes

You can also copy and paste an envelope (or part of an envelope) from one track to another. Why would you want to do that? Well, you might want the volume of one instrument in your project to follow the volume of another instrument. You can do this by copying and pasting the volume envelope from the first instrument track to the other. Here is how it works:

1. Make sure the Select tool is activated by clicking on the Select tool button in the Track view.

2. Select the data containing the envelope data you want to delete. This can be a single clip, an entire track, multiple tracks, or even part of a clip or track. To refresh your memory on how to select data in the Track view, go back to Chapter 7.

TIP

If you are selecting clips in the Clips pane and you want the track envelope data for the track in which the clips reside to be selected, be sure to choose Edit > Select > Select Track Envelopes With Selected Clips.

3. Choose Edit > Copy to open the Copy dialog box.

4. Depending on the data you selected in Step 2, either the Track/Bus Automation option or the Clip Automation option will be available (or maybe even both). Activate either one or both options.

CAUTION

If you don't want to copy any other data along with the envelope data, make sure to deactivate all other options in the Copy dialog box.

5. Click OK.

6. Select the track(s) and change the Now time to the position in the project at which you want to paste the envelope data.

7. Choose Edit > Paste to open the Paste dialog box. Then click the Advanced button to expand the Paste dialog box to its full size.

8. Make sure the Blend Old and New option is activated in the What To Do with Existing Material section.

9. Make sure the Track/Bus Automation and/or Clip Automation options are activated in the What To Paste section.

10. Click OK.

SONAR copies your selected envelope data and pastes it at the new location in the project.

Automating Effects and DXi's

In addition to automating track parameters, SONAR lets you automate individual audio effect and DXi parameters. I talked about effects in Chapter 11, and about DXis in Chapter 10. The procedures for automating audio effects and DXis are essentially the same as for track parameters, but arming the parameters is a bit different.

Automating Effects Parameters

To automate effects parameters, you can follow the same procedures outlined in the "Taking Snapshots" and "Automating the Mix" sections of this chapter, which I discussed earlier. But when you get to the part of the procedure where you need to arm the parameter that you want to automate, follow these steps instead:

1. Right-click in the Fx field of the audio track to which you want to apply the real-time effect and choose Audio Effects > Cakewalk > (the name of the effect you want to use). You can choose from the five following effects: FxChorus, FxDelay, FxEq, FxFlange, and FxReverb. If you have SONAR XL, you can also automate the Sonic Timeworks effects by choosing Audio Effects > Timeworks > (the name of the effect you want to use).

NOTE

At the time of this writing, only five of the effects included with SONAR can be automated: FxChorus, FxDelay, FxEq, FxFlange, and FxReverb. For SONAL XL users, there are two additional effects: CompressorX (Sonar XL) and Equalizer (Sonar XL). This is because the technology for automating effects parameters is very new and most manufacturers have not yet updated their plug-ins to take advantage of it. In addition, only audio effects can be automated, not MIDI effects.

2. After the window for the effect appears, right-click the name of the effect in the Fx field and choose Arm Parameter.

3. In the dialog box that appears, put a check mark next to each of the parameters in the Param Armed list that you would like to automate.

4. Click OK.

Now just follow the procedures in the "Taking Snapshots" or "Automating the Mix" sections of this chapter to record automation for your effect parameters.

As with track parameters, you can also use envelopes to automate effects parameters. The procedure is basically the same as outlined in the audio envelopes section of this chapter, which I discussed earlier. But only track envelopes can be used to automate effects parameters, and the procedure for initially creating the envelope is a bit different. To create an envelope to automate an effect parameter, do the following:

1. Right-click in the Fx Field of the audio track to which you want to apply the real-time effect and choose Audio Effects > Cakewalk > (the name of

the effect you want to use). You can choose from the five following effects: FxChorus, FxDelay, FxEq, FxFlange, and FxReverb. If you have SONAR XL, you can also automate the Sonic Timeworks effects by choosing Audio Effects > Timeworks > (the name of the effect you want to use).

2. After the window for the effect appears, close it. Then right-click in the Clips pane of the track to which you applied the effect and choose Envelopes > Create Track Envelope > (the name of the effect to be automated).

3. In the dialog box that appears, put a check mark next to each of the parameters in the Envelope Exists list that you would like to automate.

4. Click OK.

Now just follow the procedures in the "Audio Envelopes" section of this chapter to finish creating the envelopes for your effect parameters.

Automating DXi Parameters

Unlike effects, some DXi's can be automated only by using envelopes. It depends on the DXi. In addition, the procedure for recording DXi parameter movements is different from what I described earlier. So, I'll go through each procedure step-by-step.

Recording Parameter Movements

If you would like to record automation for a DXi by directly manipulating its onscreen controls, do the following:

1. If you haven't done so already, set up a DXi in the Track view of your project. I went over this procedure in chapter 10. Be sure to keep the DXi's window open.

2. Arm the MIDI track for recording to which you want to record the automation data.

TIP

Normally, SONAR will only allow you to record DXi automation to the MIDI track that has its output assigned to the DXi. If you want to use any MIDI track to record your DXi automation data, choose Options > Global > MIDI. Then activate the Echo DXi Input To All MIDI Tracks option.

3. Choose Transport > Record Options to set the recording mode. I explained this feature in chapter 6. It works the same way here. More than likely, you'll want to keep the recording mode set to Sound On Sound. This will allow you to record new data to the track without overwriting any of the existing data.

4. Set up the DXi to enable automation recording. This procedure is different for every DXi so you will have to refer to the DXi's documentation for instructions.

NOTE

Although automation set up for each DXi is different, SONAR ships with a number of DXi's, so I can at least show you how to work with those particular products. Here's how to set up each of the DXi's included with SONAR:

Alien Connection's ReValver SE

This DXi can only be automated using envelopes, so please refer to the next section of this chapter to learn how to automate this DXi.

Cyclone

This DXi doesn't provide any kind of automation. It cannot be automated via recording its control movements, and it cannot be automated via envelopes.

DreamStation DXi2

This DXi doesn't require any setup procedure. Just follow the step-by-step instructions to record automation. As you move the DreamStation's onscreen controls, they will be recorded.

EDIROL VSC

To activate automation for the Edirol Virtual Sound Canvas, click its Setup button to open the VSC Settings dialog box. Then click the Misc tab and activate the Record VSC Panel Operations option.

LiveSynth Pro SE

This DXi doesn't provide any kind of automation. It cannot be automated via recording its control movements, and it cannot be automated via envelopes.

DR-008 DXi2 (SONAR XL)

SONAR XL users have access to an additional DXi called the DR-008. This DXi can only be automated using envelopes, so please refer to the next section of this chapter to learn how to automate this DXi.

5. Set the Now Time to the point in the project at which you want to start recording automation.

6. Choose Transport > Record (or press the R key on your computer keyboard) to start recording.

7. Move the DXi's control(s) to record their movements.

8. Choose Transport > Stop (or press the Spacebar on your computer keyboard) to stop recording.

9. If you want to record more automation, repeat steps 5 through 8.

TIP

When you record automation data from a DXi, it is saved to the MIDI track as MIDI controller data. There's nothing wrong with this. You can easily edit the data using the Controller pane in the Piano Roll view. But if you would rather edit the data as envelopes in the Track view, use the Edit > Convert MIDI To Shapes feature to convert the MIDI controller data to envelopes.

Using Envelopes

You'll find that using envelopes to automate DXi parameters is more accurate, since you can actually "draw" the control movements. To use envelopes to automate DXi parameters, do the following:

1. Set up a DXi in the Track view of your project. I went over this procedure in Chapter 10.

2. In the MIDI track that drives the DXi, right-click in the Clips pane and choose Envelopes > Create Track Envelope > MIDI to open the MIDI Envelope dialog box.

3. In the Type drop-down list, choose the Control, RPN, or NRPN options.

4. The Value drop-down list will show all of the parameters that the DXi offers for automation. Choose a parameter from the list.

5. In the Channel drop-down list, choose the MIDI channel of the current patch (program) being used in the DXi.

6. Click OK.

Now follow the procedures in the "MIDI Envelopes" section of this chapter to automate the DXi parameters.

A Mixdown Exercise

Of course, what would a chapter on mixing be without a sample mixdown session, right? Follow along as I show you how to use some of the features I described earlier in the chapter by mixing one of the sample projects included with SONAR:

1. Select File > Open, choose the Don't Matter Audio and MIDI Demo.cwb file, and click Open to open that sample project.

2. Close the File Info window and the Staff view. You don't need them right now.

3. In the Track View, select Tracks 1, 8, and 9. Then choose Track > Delete to delete those tracks. They are MIDI tracks, and you don't need them for this exercise.

4. Choose View > Console to open the Console view.

NOTE
You can also use the Track view for this mixing exercise. Remember that all the parameters in the Console view are also available in the Track view.

5. Because Tracks 1 and 2 and Tracks 5 and 6 are stereo pairs, their Volume controls should be grouped together so that the drums and horns volume can be adjusted easily. Go ahead and group Tracks 1 and 2 together using Group A; then group Tracks 5 and 6 together using Group B.

6. Set up a flanging effect on the guitar by adding the FxFlange to the Effects bin in Track 4. Choose the Preset called Classic Flange; then change the Wet Mix parameter to 0.40. The original setting adds a bit too much of the effect to the guitar. Remember, subtlety is the key to applying good-sounding effects.

7. Set up a delay effect on the horns by activating the Aux Send 1 controls on Tracks 5 and 6. Then set both Send Levels to 0 dB and set both Pre Fader Enable buttons to Pre. In the Effects bin of Aux Bus 1, add the FxDelay effect. Open the effect and choose the Preset called 1 Delay – Middle, Medium. Change the Coarse parameter of the Delay to 500 ms, and change the Mix Level to 0.23. On Aux Bus 1, set the Send Level to 0 dB, the Return Level to –3 dB, and both the Send and Return Balances to 64. Now adjust the Volume controls for Tracks 5 and 6 to –5 dB.

8. Set up a reverb effect for the entire mix by activating the Aux Send 2 controls on all the tracks except Track 3 (reverb isn't usually applied to bass instruments). Then set the Send Levels for the drums (Tracks 1 and 2) to –8 dB; for the guitar (Track 4) to –8 dB; and for the horns (Tracks 5 and 6) to –10 dB. Set all the Pre Fader Enable buttons to Pre. In the Effects bin of Aux Bus 2, add the FxReverb effect. Choose the Preset called Drum Room – Small, Warm. On Aux Bus 2, set the Send Level to 0 dB, the Return Level to 0 dB, and both the Send and Return Balances to 64. Now adjust the Volume controls for the drums to 1 dB; for the guitar to –2 dB; and set the bass to –2 dB. Your Console view should now look similar to the one shown in Figure 12.20.

CHAPTER 12

Figure 12.20
The initial settings for
the mixdown exercise
should look something
like the Console view
shown here

TIP

You could use the Effects bin in a main to apply reverb to all the tracks, but then you don't have the flexibility of leaving the effect off the bass and also having varying degrees of the effect on the other instruments via the Send Levels. Using the aux bus provides you with more choices in creating the mix.

9. Play the project. Sounds pretty good, no? But I think it could be a little more interesting. Set the Pan controls for the drums to 64. Set the Now time to 1:01:000 (the beginning of the project). Be sure to arm the Pan controls for automation. Now take a snapshot of all the initial mix settings. Set the Now time to 1:04:000. Set the Pan controls to 0 for Track 1 (Drums Left) and 127 for Track 2 (Drums Right). Take another snapshot. Right in the beginning of the song, the drums play in the very center of the stereo field. Then a few beats in, they quickly spread to the far left and right. This arrangement gives the mix a really powerful introduction.

10. Add a bit of movement to the guitar by first setting the Now time to 1:01:000 (the beginning of the project). Then arm the Pan control for the guitar track for automation. Choose Transport > Record Automation. Play the project. As the music plays, move the Pan control for the guitar slowly back and forth between the values 30 and 98. Don't worry if you go a little past one of the values; just try to move the control slowly so that the position of the guitar doesn't change too quickly. When the project stops playing, deactivate Record Automation and activate the Enable/Disable Automation Playback feature. During playback, the guitar moves subtly from left to right and vice versa through the stereo field.

TIP

You could also automate the Pan parameter of the Guitar track by "drawing" an envelope in the Track view. This would give you precise control of the guitar movement through the stereo field.

11. Play the project again from the beginning. Isn't that cool?

Feel free to add more changes or expand upon the mix a bit by applying other effects or maybe an envelope or two. Mixing music is an art form, but with a little practice, you'll find it's really not all that difficult. As always, don't be afraid to try new things. Just play with the mix, and if you like what you hear, great! If not, change it.

The Next Steps

After you've finished mixing all the data in your tracks together at just the right settings, it's time to create a final stereo track, which you can use to burn your project onto CD or get it ready for distribution in a multimedia project or on the Internet. Instead of including the information on how to do that here in this chapter, I've decided to break things up a bit. The next few chapters deal with some other important features found in SONAR, such as music notation and using StudioWare and CAL. If you would prefer to read these chapters later, you can skip to Chapter 18 to learn how to finish the mixing process and burn your music to a compact disc. For information on converting your project to a compatible format for multimedia or the Internet, read Appendix C, "Producing for Multimedia and the Web."

13

Making Sheet Music

In Chapter 7, I described how you can edit the data in your MIDI tracks graphically by using the Piano Roll View. SONAR also provides tools so that you can edit your MIDI data as standard music notation and guitar tablature. As a matter of fact, you can compose new music while working with notation by graphically adding, editing, and deleting notes. You can also add many of the symbols used in music notation, such as chord symbols, expression markings, and lyrics. And when you're ready, you can print your music as sheet music, complete with title, copyright notice, page numbers, and more by using the printer attached to your computer. To give you an idea on how to use all these wonderful features, in this chapter, I'll cover the following:

▶ Using the Staff View
▶ Editing music as notes and tablature
▶ Applying musical symbols
▶ Handling percussion
▶ Using the Lyrics View
▶ Printing your music

The Staff View

SONAR provides three different tools for editing MIDI data: the Event List View, the Piano Roll View, and the Staff View. For precise numerical editing, the Event List View can't be beat. For precise graphical editing of both MIDI note and controller data, the Piano Roll View is the tool you'll want to use. (I described the Event and Piano Roll Views in Chapter 7.) Many musicians, however, are used to composing and editing in standard music notation. The Staff View comes into play at this point.

Using the Staff View (see Figure 13.1), you can add, edit, and delete MIDI note data within your MIDI tracks. Looking similar to sheet music on a piece of paper, the Staff View represents notes as standard music notation and guitar tablature on musical staves with clefs, key signatures, time signatures, and many of the other symbols you might expect to see on a sheet of music.

Figure 13.1
Working in the Staff View is just like composing music on paper, but a lot easier

More precisely, the Staff View consists of three major sections: the Toolbars (located at the top of the View, containing all the View's related controls), the Staff pane (located in the center of the View, displaying the notes in the currently selected track[s]), and the Fretboard pane (located at the bottom of the View, displaying the notes currently being played as they would appear on a six-string guitar neck that uses standard tuning).

You'll also notice that the Staff View has scroll bars. They work just as they do in the other Views. In addition, this View has a Snap To Grid function, which is represented by the Grid button in the first Toolbar. Other similarities are the Marker area and the Time Ruler, which are located just above the Staff pane. The Staff View also has zoom tools, but they are located in the first Toolbar rather than in the lower-right corner of the View. There is a reason for this placement—when you're zooming in the Staff View, the notation grows larger both horizontally and vertically in equal proportions, so you don't need multiple zoom tools.

You can open the Staff View in two different ways:

▶ In the Track View, select the MIDI track(s) you want to edit and then choose View > Staff (or press Alt+7 on your computer keyboard). You can also click the Staff View button in the Views toolbar.

▶ In the Track View, right-click a track or Clip and choose View > Staff from the pop-up menu.

Whatever method you choose, SONAR then opens the Staff View and displays the data from the track(s) that you've selected.

Changing the Layout

If you select more than one track to be displayed at once, the Staff View shows the data from each track on a separate stave.

TIP

Just like the other Views, the Staff View provides a Pick Tracks button in the first Toolbar. You can use it to change the tracks being displayed.

SONAR picks the clef (treble or bass) for each stave automatically by looking at the range of notes contained in the data. If a track has notes that fall into both clefs, it shows the data on two connected staves, one with a treble clef and one with a bass clef.

NOTE

Up to twenty-four staves of notation can be displayed in the Staff View at once. This does not necessarily mean twenty-four tracks can be displayed, though. If the data from each track is shown on a single stave, then twenty-four tracks can be displayed at once. If, however, the data from each track is shown on a pair of staves (as previously mentioned), only twelve tracks can be displayed at once. Of course, you can also have some tracks shown with one stave and some shown with two, so the number of tracks will vary.

You can override these automatic stave settings, though, if you'd like, by adjusting the Staff View Layout parameters. To adjust the way the data from your MIDI tracks is displayed in the Staff View, just do the following:

1. Right-click anywhere within the Staff pane and select Layout from the pop-up menu to open the Staff View Layout dialog box (see Figure 13.2).

Figure 13.2
You can use the Staff
View Layout dialog box
to change the way your
data is displayed in the
Staff View

2. From the list, select the name of the track that you want to change.

3. In the Staff Properties section, set the Clef parameter to the type of clef
    you want to use for that track. If you choose the Treble/Bass option, the
    track is displayed on two staves. To determine which notes will be shown
    on which stave, enter a note value for the Split parameter. Notes that are at
    or above the pitch that you enter are shown on the treble clef staff, and
    notes below are shown on the bass clef staff.

4. Click Close.

The track is now shown with the stave settings you specified.

Percussion Tracks

If you open a MIDI track in the Staff View that has its Channel parameter set to 10 and you
had previously set up your sound card ports to use the General MIDI Drums instrument
definition (which you learned about in Chapter 3), the Staff View automatically displays
that track as percussion notation in a percussion staff. It displays the track this way
because, when you're using General MIDI, it is standard practice to put all percussion
instruments on MIDI channel 10. If you want to override this automatic setting, you can
do so as explained previously.

You can also change a number of other settings to customize the way your percussion
staves appear. If you select your percussion track in the Staff View Layout dialog box, a
new button (called Percussion Settings) becomes active. If you click this button, the
Percussion Notation Key dialog box appears (see Figure 13.3).

Figure 13.3
You can use the
Percussion Notation
Key dialog box to
further adjust how
your percussion
tracks appear

By manipulating the parameters in this dialog box, you can change the noteheads and articulation symbols used to display your percussion notes. You can also change which percussion sounds correspond to the different positions on the percussion staff. You do so as follows:

1. In the MIDI Note section, select the name of the instrument you want to change.

2. If you want to change the position on the percussion staff where that instrument will be shown, select the appropriate pitch in the Display As section. Then click the Bind button to assign that staff position to the selected instrument.

3. If you don't want an instrument to have a specific staff position assignment, select the instrument and click either the Unbind button or the Default note button. To remove all instrument assignments, click the Zap All button.

NOTE
Any instruments that don't have a specific assigned staff position automatically use the default position, shown at the bottom of the Display As section. This means that those instruments are shown at that pitch position on the percussion staff. You can change the default position by typing in a new pitch value.

4. After you've bound an instrument to a position on the staff, you can designate the Notehead Type and Articulation Symbol it will use. Just select the appropriate options in those sections of the dialog box. When setting the Notehead Type, you can also opt to have the notehead circled or not by setting the Notehead Circled parameter.

5. If you want to use these settings again later, save them as a Preset.

6. Click OK to close the Percussion Notation Key dialog box.

7. Click Close to close the Staff View Layout dialog box.

Now the data in your percussion tracks is shown using the settings you specified.

TIP

SONAR displays ghost strokes (percussion notes played very softly for ornamentation) using the standard method of parentheses around the percussion notehead. It determines ghost strokes by testing to see whether the note velocity is lower than 32. This number is a fixed value that can't be changed. You can, however, change the note velocities of your data and then use the Vel+ track parameter to trick SONAR into using a different determining value. For example, to stop notes from being shown as ghost notes, simply raise their velocity values. Then, so that the sound of the data isn't changed, set the Vel+ parameter so that it lowers the velocities to their original values during playback. Do the opposite to have notes shown as ghost notes.

Showing Pedal Events and Chord Grids

You also can control whether or not the Staff View will display Pedal Events or Guitar Chord Grids (I'll talk more about both of these symbols later). To do so, in the Display section of the Staff View Layout dialog box, set the Show Pedal Events and Show Chord Grids options.

Changing Text Fonts

You can also change how any of the text used in your data will be displayed. For example, you can change track names, measure numbers, lyric text, expression text, chord text, triplet numbers, and tablature fret numbers. To do so, just follow these steps:

1. Right-click anywhere within the Staff pane and select Layout from the pop-up menu to open the Staff View Layout dialog box.

2. In the Display section, choose the type of text you want to change by picking its designation from the Set Font drop-down list. For example, if you want to change how the track names look in your sheet music, select Track names from the list.

3. Click the Set Font button to open the Font dialog box (see Figure 13.4).

Figure 13.4
Using the Font dialog box, you can set how you want the text in your sheet music to appear

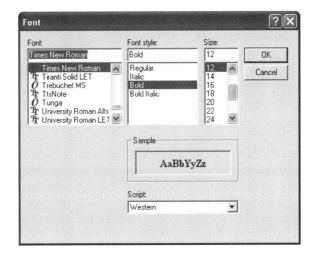

4. In the Font section, choose the font you want to use.

5. In the Font style section, choose a style for your text, such as Bold or Italic.

6. In the Size section, choose the size of the text you want to use.

NOTE
As you are changing these parameters, you can see a preview of how the text will look in the Sample section.

7. Click OK to close the Font dialog box.

8. Click Close to close the Staff View Layout dialog box.

Your text is now displayed according to the settings you specified.

Rhythmic Appearance

When converting your MIDI data into music notation, SONAR has to make some educated guesses about how to display the rhythmic values of the notes. It does this because, when you record your musical performance in real-time, instead of playing notes with perfect timing, you'll more than likely play some of them either a little ahead or a little behind the beat. You may also hold some notes a little longer than they should be held. Most often, these slight timing "errors" are desirable because they give your music a more "human" feel.

SONAR doesn't understand these slight rhythmic variations, however; it knows only exact note timing and durations. So, when it displays your data in the Staff View, the data may not always look like it's supposed to. That's why SONAR provides a number of parameters you can adjust to give it a better idea of how the music should be displayed.

Beaming Rests

When you're notating music with very complex rhythms, it's standard practice to lengthen the beams on beamed groups of notes to also include rests. Lengthening the beams makes it much easier for the person reading the music to pick out the right rhythms. For rhythmically simple music, however, it's usually best not to beam rests. In case you need this feature, though, you can turn it on and off by opening the Staff View Layout dialog box and setting the Beam Rests option in the Display section.

Setting the Display Resolution

For SONAR to make an educated guess as to how the rhythms in your music should be displayed, you have to give it a point of reference, which is called the Display Resolution. By setting this parameter, you are telling SONAR what is the smallest rhythmic note value used in your music. For example, if the smallest rhythmic value that can be found in your music is a sixteenth note, then you would set a sixteenth note value to be used for the Display Resolution. SONAR then rounds any start times and note durations to the nearest sixteenth note so that your music looks more like it should. This setting changes only the appearance of the music, not how it sounds. To set the Display Resolution, select a rhythmic value from the Display Resolution drop-down list located in the first Toolbar (see Figure 13.5).

Figure 13.5
You can set the Display Resolution so that SONAR can make a better guess as to how your data should be displayed

Filling and Trimming Durations

In addition to the Display Resolution parameter, SONAR provides two other options you can set to help it better understand how to display your music. The Fill Durations option rounds note durations up to the next beat or note (whichever comes first). For example, instead of showing two quarter notes tied together in the same measure, SONAR simply shows a single half note.

The Trim Durations option rounds note durations down so that they do not overlap one another. For example, if you have a note with a duration that extends past the start of the next note, the first note's duration is shortened so that you don't end up with something like a half note tied to a quarter note with an eighth note sitting in between the two.

Neither of these options changes the music in any way, just how it's displayed. The results vary depending on the music you are trying to display as notation, so you'll have to try either or both of these options to see whether they help "clean up" the rhythmic notation values. To turn the options on or off, just click the Fill Durations and Trim Durations buttons (located in the first Toolbar to the immediate left of the Display Resolution parameter).

Dealing with Notes

As you know, when you open a MIDI track in the Staff View, the notes in that track are displayed in the Staff pane as standard music notation. In addition to simply displaying the notes, the Staff View also enables you to edit and delete them, as well as add new ones.

You can add new notes to a track or edit the existing ones by using the tools represented by the first four buttons in the first Toolbar (going from left to right on the left side of the Staff View).

Selecting

The first button in the Toolbar represents the Select tool. Using this tool, you can select the notes for further manipulation, such as deleting, copying, moving, and so on. Essentially, you select notes the same way you would in the Piano Roll View. To select a single note, click on it. To select more than one note, hold down the Ctrl key on your computer keyboard while clicking on the notes you want to select. You know the rest. For more information, check out Chapter 7.

NOTE
When you select a note that is tied to another note, both notes are selected automatically because they are essentially the same MIDI note with its duration shown as two tied notes rather than one note with a larger rhythmic value.

Editing

After you've made a selection, you can copy, cut, paste, move, and delete the notes the same way you would in the Piano Roll View. You can also edit notes individually by using the Draw tool. The second button in the Toolbar represents the Draw tool. Using this tool, you can add (which I'll talk about shortly) and edit the notes in the Staff pane.

To move a note to a different location within a staff, simply click its note head and drag it left or right. This action moves the note to a different horizontal location within the staff and along the Time Ruler.

NOTE
If you have the Snap To Grid featured activated, the note snaps to the nearest note value set in the Snap To Grid dialog box.

To change the pitch of a note, simply click on its note head and drag it up or down within the same staff or into another staff. As you move the note, SONAR plays the different pitches so that you can hear what they sound like.

TIP

By default, SONAR uses note pitches that match the current diatonic key signature of the music. This means that as you drag a note to a new pitch, it automatically remains in the correct musical key. If you don't want the note to stay within the key, however, click the right mouse button after you've begun to drag the note to a new pitch. This way, you can change the pitch of the note chromatically in half steps.

Of course, you sometimes might want to make more precise changes to a note or change its duration. You can do so by using the Note Properties dialog box. With the Draw tool, just right-click a note to open the Note Properties dialog box (see Figure 13.6).

Figure 13.6
Using the Note Properties dialog box, you can make precise changes to a note in the Staff View

In the Note Properties dialog box, you can make precise changes to the Time, Pitch, Velocity, Duration, and MIDI Channel of an individual note by typing in numerical values. You can also specify the fret and string upon which the note will be played in the Fretboard pane (which I'll talk about later).

Drawing (or Adding)

In addition to editing, the Draw tool enables you to add notes to a staff by literally drawing them in. To do so, follow these steps:

1. Select the Draw tool by clicking its Toolbar button.

2. Select a duration for the new note(s). If you look at the second Toolbar (just below the first one), you'll notice a number of buttons with note values shown on them. Clicking on these buttons determines the duration for your new note(s). For example, if you click the Quarter Note button, the duration is set to a quarter note. This Toolbar also contains two additional buttons: one representing a dotted note and another representing a triplet. If you want your notes to be dotted or part of a triplet, click one of these buttons as well.

NOTE

When you create a triplet, SONAR places all three notes on the staff with the same pitch. Triplets have to be created with a full set of three notes without rests or ties. After you add the triplet, you can change the pitches of the notes to whatever you desire.

3. Click anywhere on a staff in the Staff pane to place the new note(s) at the start time(s) and pitch(es) you want.

TIP

It's a good idea to turn off the Fill Durations and Trim Durations options when you're entering new notes in the Staff pane. While you add notes, SONAR tries to change the way they are displayed, so you might find this confusing when you're trying to read the music.

Erasing

Even though you can select and delete notes (as described earlier), the Staff View includes an Erase tool for added convenience. To use it, just select the Erase tool and then click any note(s) in the Staff pane that you want to delete. You can also click and drag the Erase tool over a number of notes to erase them all at once. By the way, the Erase tool is represented by the button in the Toolbar with the picture of an eraser shown on it, located right next to the Draw tool.

TIP

If you want to delete one note in a pair of tied notes, you need to realize that tied notes are actually a single note event that has a long duration. To delete one note that is tied to the other, change the duration of the first note by making it shorter. The tied note will then be removed, while leaving the original note intact.

Scrub and Step Play

When you're editing the data in a track, the procedure usually involves making your edits and then playing back the Project to hear how the changes sound. But playing back very small sections can be a bit difficult, especially when you're working with a fast tempo. To remedy this situation, you can use the Scrub tool and the Step Play feature in the Staff View.

Scrub

Using the Scrub tool, you can drag over the notes in the Staff View to hear what they sound like. To use it, simply select the Scrub tool by clicking on its button in the first Toolbar (the one with the small yellow speaker shown on it, located right next to the Erase tool). Then click and drag over the notes in the Staff pane. Dragging left to right plays the data forward (what would normally happen during playback), and dragging right to left enables you to hear the data played in reverse. This feature can be useful for testing very short (one or two measure) sections.

Step Play

The Step Play feature enables you to step through (play) the notes in the Staff View note by note. To use it, follow these steps:

1. Set the Now Time to the point in the music where you want to begin stepping through the notes. You can do so by simply clicking in the Time Ruler.

2. To step forward through the notes, click the Play Next button in the first Toolbar (the third-to-last button, going from left to right). You can also press Ctrl plus the right-arrow keys on your computer keyboard.

3. To step backward through the notes, click the Play Previous button in the first Toolbar (the fourth-to-last button, going from left to right). You can also press Ctrl plus the left-arrow keys on your computer keyboard.

SONAR then moves the Now Time cursor one set of notes at a time either to the right or left and plays the notes it lands on.

TIP

Instead of using the Scrub tool or the Step Play feature, you might want to try another useful technique for hearing what your changes sound like. Did you know that you can edit the data in your Project as it's being played back? Of course, it's a bit difficult to edit anything while SONAR is scrolling the display as the Project plays. What I like to do is work on a small section of a Project at a time. I set up a section of the Project to loop over and over, and as SONAR is playing the data, I make any changes I think might be needed. Because the data is being played back while I edit, I can instantly hear what the changes sound like. Using this approach is much easier than having to keep going back and forth, making changes, and manually starting and stopping playback. I described looping in Chapter 6.

Dealing with Symbols and Lyrics

In addition to notes, SONAR lets you add other markings to your notated music, including chord symbols, guitar chord grids, expression marks, and pedal marks. These markings, however, are only ornamental in nature; they have nothing to do with the data in your MIDI tracks. They also do not affect your music in any way, although there is one exception (pedal marks), which I'll explain later.

Essentially, SONAR provides these features so that you can create sheet music with a more professional look, but you have to enter the marks manually. The procedures are basically the same as when you're working with notes. You use the Draw tool to add the markings, and you can also select, copy, cut, paste, delete, and move them. To give you an idea of how to utilize them, I'll go through them one at a time.

Chord Symbols and Grids

Most sheet music sold to the public includes chord symbols with just simple chord names or with both names and guitar grids. SONAR gives you the flexibility to enter either one or both.

Adding and Editing

To add a chord symbol to your music, do the following:

1. Select the Draw tool.

2. Select the Chord tool by clicking the Chord button on the second Toolbar (the one with the letter *C* shown on it).

3. Position your mouse pointer above the staff to which you want to add the symbol.

NOTE

You can add chord symbols only in certain positions within your music. If a track is displayed as a single staff, you can place symbols above that staff. If a track is shown using a pair of staves (treble and bass clefs), you can place symbols above the top (treble clef) staff only.

Also, chord symbols in music are usually lined up with the notes on the staff. SONAR allows you to place chord symbols in the same horizontal location above a note along the staff only (although there is an exception, which I'll explain later). As you move your mouse pointer along the top of the staff, the pointer changes to look like a pencil when you find a "legal" position to place a chord symbol.

4. Left-click to place the symbol above the staff. SONAR adds a copy of the most recently added chord (the default is C).

5. To change the name of the chord symbol, right-click it to open the Chord Properties dialog box (see Figure 13.7).

Figure 13.7
You can change the name (and other assets) of a chord symbol by using the Chord Properties dialog box

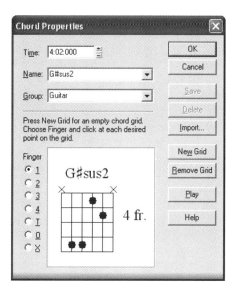

6. Select the types of chords you want to choose from by selecting a group from the Group parameter drop-down list. SONAR includes only a single group of chords, called Guitar. You can, however, create your own groups and chord symbols, which I'll talk about shortly.

7. For the Name parameter, select a new name from the drop-down list. You'll notice that multiple chords in the list have the same name. They're named the same because some chords have guitar chord grids associated with them, and some don't. If a chord includes a grid, the grid is shown in the Grid section of the dialog box. You'll also find multiple chords with grids having the same name. This is to accommodate the different fingerings that can be used to play each chord on a guitar.

TIP

The list of chords is very long, and sometimes it can be tedious trying to scroll through it all just to find the chord you want. For a quicker way to navigate through the list, type the name of the chord you want to find in the Name parameter. Then click the up- or down-arrow keys (depending on which way you want to move through the list) on your computer keyboard.

8. Earlier, I mentioned that SONAR allows you to place chords only at certain horizontal locations along the top of a staff. Although this is true when you are initially adding a chord, you can change the position of the chord by changing its start time. Just enter a new time (measures, beats, ticks) in the Time parameter of the Chord Properties dialog box. This way, chord symbols can be placed anywhere along the top of a staff. They don't have to line up with the notes.

9. Click OK.

SONAR changes the name and position of the chord symbol and adds a grid to it according to the new properties you specified.

The Chord Library

SONAR includes a large number of predefined chord symbols, which it stores as a Chord Library in a file named CHORDS.LIW. (This file is located on your hard drive in the folder named C:\Program Files\Cakewalk\SONAR 2.) You can edit these chords or even add your own by using the Chord Properties dialog box.

To add a chord into a new or existing group, do the following:

1. Right-click a chord symbol to open the Chord Properties dialog box.

2. To add a chord to an existing group, select the group from the Group parameter drop-down list. To add a chord to a new group, type the name of the new group in the Group parameter.

3. Type the name of the new chord in the Name parameter.

4. To add a grid to the new chord, click the New Grid button. An empty grid is displayed in the Grid area (see Figure 13.8).

Figure 13.8
You can add a grid to a chord symbol by clicking on the New Grid button

5. To place a dot on the grid, first choose a finger number from the Finger options and then click the appropriate string and fret location on the grid. To assign an open string, select O for the finger number. To assign a muted string, select X for the finger number.

6. To insert a fret designation for the grid, click just to the right of the grid in the Grid section to open the Chord Fret Number dialog box. Then type a fret number and click OK.

7. To hear what the chord sounds like, click the Play button.

8. When you're satisfied with the new chord, click the Save button to save it to the Chord Library.

9. Click OK.

To edit a chord or group in the Chord Library, follow these steps:

1. Right-click a chord symbol to open the Chord Properties dialog box.

2. To delete a group, select the group in the Group parameter drop-down list and click the Delete button.

3. To edit a chord in an existing group, select the group from the Group parameter drop-down list.

4. To delete a chord, select the chord from the Name parameter drop-down list and click the Delete button.

5. To edit a chord, select the chord from the Name parameter drop-down list and then type a new name.

6. If the chord has an accompanying chord grid, you can either delete it or edit it. To delete it, click the Remove Grid button.

7. To edit the grid, change the finger assignment for a dot by clicking on the dot repeatedly to cycle through the Finger options.

8. To hear what the chord sounds like, click the Play button.

9. When you're satisfied with the edited chord, click the Save button to save it to the Chord Library.

10. Click OK.

TIP

You can also import new chord definitions into the Chord Library by clicking on the Import button and selecting an .LIW file.

Expression Marks

Expression marks in music designate any kind of text that provides instructions on how the music should be played during different passages. These marks include tempo designations (such as *Allegro*), musical characteristics (such as *Play with feeling*), and dynamics instructions (such as *cresc.*, *ppp*, or *fff*). Essentially, expression marks are just simple text added to the sheet music.

Adding an Expression Mark

To add an expression mark to your music, do the following:

1. Select the Draw tool.

2. Select the Expression tool by clicking on the Expression button in the second Toolbar (the one with the letter *f* shown on it).

3. Position your mouse pointer below the staff to which you want to add the mark.

NOTE

As with chord symbols, you can place expression marks only in certain positions within your music. If a track is displayed as a single staff, you can place the marks below that staff. If a track is shown using a pair of staves (treble and bass clefs), you can place marks below the top (treble clef) staff only.

Also, as with chord symbols, marks are initially lined up with the notes in the staff (although you can change the way they're lined up by editing the marks and altering their start times). As you move your mouse pointer below the staff, the pointer changes to look like a pencil when you find a "legal" position to place a mark.

4. Left-click to place the mark below the staff. SONAR opens an insertion box.

5. Type the text that you want to use for the mark (see Figure 13.9).

Figure 13.9
Expression marks are
just simple text that
you type into the
Staff pane

TIP
To leave a dangling hyphen at the end of an expression mark, type a space and a single hyphen after the text in the insertion box. Dangling hyphens are often used with expression marks in sheet music to show that the expression should be continued over a range of notes or measures until the next expression mark appears.

6. Press the Enter key on your computer keyboard.

TIP
You can also press the Tab or Shift+Tab keys on your computer keyboard to move to the next or previous expression mark location, respectively.

SONAR then adds the expression mark to your music.

Editing an Expression Mark

To edit an expression mark, do the following:

1. Right-click the expression mark to open the Expression Text Properties dialog box (see Figure 13.10).

Figure 13.10
Using the Expression
Text Properties dialog
box, you can edit
expression marks

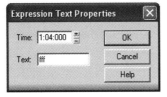

2. To change the position of the expression mark, enter a new start time (measures, beats, ticks) in the Time parameter.
3. To change the text of the expression mark, enter the new text in the Text parameter.
4. Click OK.

The expression mark is then displayed in the new position showing the new text according to your settings.

TIP
You can also edit the text of an expression mark by clicking on it with the Draw tool to reopen the insertion box.

Hairpin Symbols

In addition to showing crescendos and decrescendos as text via expression marks, they can also be shown graphically via hairpin symbols. These symbols look like large "greater than" and "less than" signs (see Figure 13.11).

Figure 13.11
Crescendos and decrescendos can also be designated via hairpin symbols

Adding a Hairpin Symbol

To add a hairpin symbol to your music, follow these steps:

1. Select the Draw tool.

2. Select the Hairpin tool by clicking on the Hairpin button in the second Toolbar (the one with the "less than" sign shown on it).

3. Position your mouse pointer below the staff to which you want to add the symbol.

NOTE

As with expression marks, if a track is displayed as a single staff, you can place the symbol below that staff. If a track is shown using a pair of staves (treble and bass clefs), you can place the symbol below the top (treble clef) staff only.

4. Click to place the symbol below the staff.

SONAR then adds a copy of the most recently added hairpin symbol. To change the symbol, you can edit it by using the Hairpin Properties dialog box.

Editing a Hairpin Symbol

To edit a hairpin symbol, do the following:

1. Right-click the hairpin symbol to open the Hairpin Properties dialog box (see Figure 13.12).

Figure 13.12
Using the Hairpin
Properties dialog box,
you can edit hairpin
symbols

2. To change the position of the hairpin symbol, enter a new start time (measures, beats, ticks) in the Time parameter.

TIP
You can also change the position of the hairpin symbol by dragging it.

3. To change the type of the hairpin symbol, choose either the Crescendo option or the Diminuendo (same as decrescendo) option.
4. To change the length of the hairpin symbol, enter a new value (beats, ticks) in the Duration parameter.
5. Click OK.

The hairpin symbol is displayed in the new position, with the new type and duration according to your settings.

Pedal Marks

Earlier, I mentioned that there was one exception to the fact that markings do not affect the data in your MIDI tracks. That exception is pedal marks. On a sheet of music, pedal marks usually designate when the performer is supposed to press and let go of the sustain pedal on a piano. In SONAR, they mean essentially the same thing, but they refer to the sustain pedal attached to your MIDI keyboard (if it has one). More precisely, pedal marks in the Staff View designate MIDI controller number 64 (Pedal-sustain) messages in your MIDI tracks (which can also be edited in the Controller pane of the Piano Roll View). So, whenever you add or edit pedal marks in the Staff View, you are also editing the MIDI controller number 64 messages in that track.

Adding a Pedal Mark

To add a pedal mark to your music, follow these steps:

1. Select the Draw tool.

2. Select the Pedal tool by clicking on the Pedal button in the second Toolbar (the one with the letter *P* shown on it).

3. Position your mouse pointer below the staff to which you want to add the mark.

NOTE

Similar to expression marks, if a track is displayed as a single staff, you can place the symbol below that staff. If, however, a track is shown using a pair of staves (treble and bass clefs), you can place the symbol below the bottom (bass clef) staff only.

4. Click to place the mark below the staff.

SONAR adds a pair of pedal marks (pedal down, which looks like an asterisk, and pedal up, which looks like a *P*) to your music. To edit the marks, you can use the Pedal Properties dialog box.

Editing a Pedal Mark

To edit a pedal mark, do the following:

1. Right-click the pedal mark (either a pedal down mark or a pedal up mark; you can't edit them both at once) to open the Pedal Properties dialog box (see Figure 13.13).

Figure 13.13
You can use the Pedal Properties dialog box to edit pedal marks

2. To change the position of the pedal mark, enter a new start time (measures, beats, ticks) in the Time parameter.

TIP
You can also change the position of the pedal mark by dragging it.

3. To change the MIDI channel for the pedal mark, type a new channel number in the Channel parameter.

4. To change the type of the pedal mark, enter a new number in the Value parameter. Enter any value from 0 to 63 to make it a pedal up mark. Enter any value from 64 to 127 to make it a pedal down mark.

5. Click OK.

The pedal mark is displayed in the new position, with the new type and MIDI channel appearing according to your settings.

Lyrics

Just like any good notation software, SONAR enables you to add lyrics to your sheet music. Lyrics (like expression marks) are represented by simple text displayed below a staff. You can add lyrics to a track by using the Lyrics tool or the Lyrics View.

The Lyrics Tool

Follow these steps to add lyrics to your music with the Lyrics tool:

1. In the Staff View, select the Draw tool.

2. Select the Lyrics tool by clicking on the Lyric button in the second Toolbar (the one with the letter *L* shown on it).

3. Position your mouse pointer below the staff, underneath the first note to which you want to add lyrics.

CHAPTER 13

NOTE

If a track is displayed as a single staff, you can place the lyrics below that staff. If a track is shown using a pair of staves (treble and bass clefs), you can place marks below the top (treble clef) staff only.

Also, each word or syllable in the lyrics must be aligned with a note. SONAR automatically aligns the lyrics to the notes in the staff.

4. Click to place the lyric below the staff. SONAR opens an insertion box (just like when you add expression marks).

5. Type a word or syllable to be aligned with the current note.

6. To move forward and add a lyric to the next note, enter a space, type a hyphen, or press the Tab key on your computer keyboard. The insertion box moves to the next note waiting for you to enter text.

7. To skip over a note, don't type any text into the insertion box. Either enter a space or type a hyphen.

8. To move back to the previous note, press the Shift+Tab keys on your computer keyboard.

9. When you're finished entering lyrics, press the Enter key on your computer keyboard.

To edit lyrics by using the Lyrics tool, do the following:

1. Select the Draw tool.

2. Select the Lyrics tool.

3. Click the word you want to change.

4. Edit the word.

5. Press the Enter key on your computer keyboard.

The Lyrics View

After you've entered some lyrics in the Staff View, you can display them in a separate window called the Lyrics View. This View is useful for providing a cue for performers while recording vocal tracks because you can make the lyrics appear in any size font that you would like (see Figure 13.14).

Figure 13.14
The Lyrics View is
useful as a cue for
vocal performers

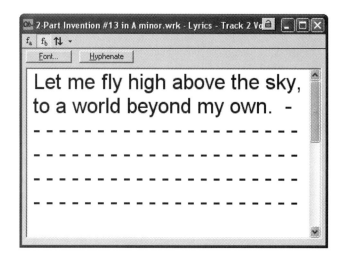

To open the Lyrics View, select a track in the Track View, then select View > Lyric. To change the size of the text, click the fa or fb buttons. They provide two different preset font sizes. You can also use more specific font settings by clicking on the Font button to open the Font dialog box (which I described earlier). In this dialog box, you can change the font, style, and size of the text. The Lyrics View also has a Pick Tracks button that works just as in the other Views.

Of course, you can also add and edit Lyrics in the Lyrics View, but I don't recommend doing so. The process is not very intuitive, because you can't see what notes the words and syllables are being aligned with. If you want to use the Lyrics View for adding and editing, you can do so just as you would enter and edit text in the Windows Notepad. Each word that you type is automatically aligned to a note in the current track, and you can split words into syllables by entering hyphens either manually or automatically by pressing the Hyphenate button. That's all there is to it.

TIP

In addition to typing and editing lyrics in the Lyrics View, you can also select, cut, copy, paste, and delete text. Again, this procedure works just like in the Windows Notepad. What's nice about the Lyrics View is that if you already have some text saved in a text file, you can copy and paste it into this View to quickly add lyrics to a track. When you look at the lyrics in the Staff View, the words are automatically aligned to the notes in the staff. And if you want all or some of the words to be hyphenated automatically, just select all or some of the text in the Lyrics View and then click the Hyphenate button. It's very quick and simple.

The Fretboard and Tablature

For all the guitar players out there, SONAR provides a couple of nice notation-related features just for you. The first one I'll describe is the Fretboard pane.

The Fretboard Pane

The Fretboard pane, located at the bottom of the Staff View, is both a visual aid and an editing tool. During playback, the Fretboard displays the notes at the current Now Time in a selected track as they would be played on a six-string guitar using standard tuning. This makes the Fretboard a cool learning tool when you're trying to learn to play a new piece of music. It also displays notes when you use the Scrub tool or Step Play feature, which makes it even easier to pick out the fingerings. The color of the notes matches the color of the Clip (from the Track View) in which they are stored.

Fretboard Properties

You can configure certain aspects of the Fretboard, such as its background style and the orientation of the strings. You can also turn it on or off.

To toggle the Fretboard on and off, click the Fret View button located in the first Toolbar. It's the second-to-last button, going from left to right.

To change the background style, right-click on the Fretboard and choose one of the following from the pop-up list: Rosewood Hi, Rosewood Lo, Ebony Hi, Ebony Lo, Maple Hi, or Maple Lo. The Hi and Lo designations have to do with the screen resolution you are using on your computer monitor. If you're using a high screen resolution, use one of the styles marked Hi. If you're using a low screen resolution, use one of the styles marked Lo. To be honest, the resolution you choose really doesn't make that much of a difference.

To change the orientation of the strings, right-click the Fretboard and select Mirror Fretboard from the pop-up menu to invert the Fretboard so that the highest-sounding string appears at the bottom. To change it back, just select Mirror Fretboard again.

Adding Notes

In addition to using the Fretboard to display notes, you can add new notes to a track (staff) by clicking on the Fretboard. Just follow these steps:

1. Set the Now Time so that the cursor rests at the point in the staff where you want to add the note(s). You can do so quickly by clicking in the Time Ruler.

2. Select the Draw tool.

3. Select a note duration by clicking one of the appropriate buttons in the second Toolbar.

4. Click on the guitar strings in the Fretboard to enter notes on the staff. You can enter up to six notes (one per string).

5. Make the Now Time cursor move forward by the same amount as the current note duration setting by pressing the Shift and right-arrow keys on your computer keyboard.

6. Repeat steps 3 through 5 to continue adding more notes.

Editing Notes

You can also edit existing notes in a track (staff) by using the Fretboard. You can change only the pitch of the notes, though. To do so, just follow these steps:

1. Set the Now Time so that the cursor rests on top of the note(s) that you want to edit. You can do so quickly by clicking in the Time Ruler. You can also use the Step Play feature.

2. Select the Draw tool.

3. Drag the note(s) along the string(s) to a new fret (thus changing the pitch).

After you let go of the mouse button, SONAR changes the pitch of the note(s) in the staff.

Tablature

As a guitar or bass player, you might be more comfortable reading and working with tablature rather than standard notation. If that's the case, then you're in luck, because SONAR includes a number of features that enable you to display and edit your music as tablature.

Displaying Tablature

To display tablature for a track (staff), follow these steps:

1. Right-click in the Staff pane and select Layout from the pop-up menu to open the Staff View Layout dialog box.

2. Select the name of the track from the list for which you want to display tablature.

3. In the Tablature section, activate the Display Tablature option.

4. Select a tablature style from the Preset drop-down list.

5. Click OK.

SONAR displays a tablature staff below the current staff, complete with tablature for each note in the track (see Figure 13.15).

Figure 13.15
Adding tablature to a
track in the Staff
View is very easy
with SONAR

NOTE

SONAR also offers another feature, called QuickTab, that lets you quickly
generate tablature for a track, but it works only when you're displaying a
single track in the Staff View. So, I recommend you simply use the previously
mentioned method.

Defining a Tablature Style

While you're setting up a track to display tablature, you might not find a preset style that
fits your needs. If that's the case, you can always create your own by doing the following:

1. Right-click in the Staff pane and select Layout from the pop-up menu to
    open the Staff View Layout dialog box.

2. Select the name of the track from the list for which you want to display
    tablature.

3. In the Tablature section, activate the Display Tablature option.

4. Click the Define button to open the Tablature Settings dialog box (see
    Figure 13.16).

Figure 13.16
You can create your own tablature styles by using the Tablature Settings dialog box

5. Under the Tablature tab, set the Method parameter. This parameter determines how the tablature will be displayed. If you select Floating, the notes can be shown anywhere on the Fretboard. If you select Fixed, notes are limited to a specific area on the neck of the guitar. To determine the size and position of that area, you must set the Finger Span parameter and the Lowest Fret parameter. The Finger Span parameter sets the size of the area in a number of frets. The Lowest Fret parameter sets the position of the area on the neck of the guitar by specifying the first fret upon which the area is based. The last tablature method (MIDI Channel) is useful if you record your guitar parts using a MIDI guitar and you use MONO mode so that each string is recorded using its own MIDI channel. If this is your situation, then select the MIDI Channel method and set the 1st Channel parameter to the lowest number channel used by your MIDI guitar.

6. In the Number Of Frets parameter, enter the number of frets that the tablature should be based on.

7. In the String Tuning section, choose an instrument/tuning upon which to base the tablature.

8. Set the Number of Strings parameter to the number of strings the instrument provides.

9. The pitches of each string for the instrument appear in the parameters below the Number of Strings parameter. You can either leave them as is, or you can customize the pitches to your liking.

10. Save your settings as a Preset.

11. Click OK to close the Tablature Settings dialog box.

Your new tablature style should now appear in the Preset drop-down list in the Tablature section of the Staff View Layout dialog box.

Regenerating Tablature

You can use different tablature styles for different sections of the same tablature staff by following these steps:

1. In the Staff pane, select the notes or tablature numbers for which you want to use a different tablature style.

2. Right-click anywhere in the Staff pane and select Regenerate Tablature from the pop-up menu to open the Regenerate Tablature dialog box (see Figure 13.17).

Figure 13.17
You can define different tablature styles for selected notes by using the Regenerate Tablature feature

3. Set the Method, Finger Span, Lowest Fret, and 1st Channel parameters, if applicable. These parameters work the same way as described previously.

4. Click OK.

SONAR changes the tablature style of the selected notes based on your parameter settings.

Adding Notes via Tablature

In addition to just displaying tablature, you can use a tablature staff to add notes to a track by doing the following:

1. Select the Draw tool.

2. Choose a note duration by clicking on the appropriate note duration button in the second Toolbar.

3. Move the mouse pointer over the tablature staff. It changes its shape to a crosshair.

4. Position the crosshair within any measure and over a line in the tablature staff.

5. Click and hold the left mouse button. Now drag your mouse pointer up and down to select a fret number.

6. Release the mouse button to enter the note.

Editing Notes via Tablature

You can also edit notes via a tablature staff. To do so, just follow these steps:

1. Select the Draw tool.

2. To change the fret number of a note, right-click on it and select a new number from the pop-up menu.

3. To move a note to a different string (line) on the tablature staff, click and drag the note while pressing the Alt key on your computer keyboard. Drag the note up or down to move it. If the note is not supposed to play on a certain string, it will not be allowed to move there.

Exporting Tablature to a Text File

One last tablature feature that you might find useful is being able to save the tablature as a text file either for printing or distribution over the Internet. By saving the tablature this way, you can share your tablature with other guitarists even if they don't own SONAR. You use this feature as follows:

1. Select a MIDI track in the track View.

2. In the Staff View, right-click anywhere in the Staff pane and select Export To ASCII TAB. The Save As dialog box opens.

3. Type a name for the file.

4. Click Save.

SONAR saves the data in the MIDI track as tablature in a text file.

TIP
You might want to try quantizing the track before you save it as tablature. Doing so usually produces more accurate results.

Printing Your Music

After all is notated and done, you can print your music to paper if you have a printer connected to your computer. SONAR automatically sets up your music on separate pages, including the song title, composer, and other information, along with the notation. You can print your musical score like this:

1. Select File > Info to open the File Info window and fill out all the information you want to have included on your sheet music. You can use the Title, Subtitle, Instructions, Author, and Copyright parameters. For more information about the File Info window, see Chapter 4.

2. With the Staff View open, select File > Print Preview. SONAR goes into Print Preview mode (see Figure 13.18) and displays your music on virtual pages, letting you see how it will look before you print it.

Figure 13.18
You can see how your music will look on paper before you print it by using the Print Preview mode

3. To zoom the display in or out, click the Zoom In or Zoom Out buttons.

4. Depending on the length of your song, SONAR usually shows two pages at once on the screen. If you would rather view only one page at a time, click the One Page button.

5. If your song takes up more than two pages, you can navigate through them by using the Next Page and Prev Page buttons.

6. Before you print your music, you need to select a size for your score. To do so, click the Configure button to open the Staff View Print Configure dialog box.

7. From the single drop-down list, choose the size you want to use. SONAR provides nine different sizes to choose from. They are standard music-engraving sizes used by professional music publishers. Each size is used for a different purpose. Size 0 (Commercial or Public) is usually used for wire-bound manuscripts. Size 1 (Giant or English) is usually used for school band music books or instructional books. Sizes 2 or 3 (Regular, Common, or Ordinary) are usually used for printing classical music. Size 4 (Peter) is usually used for folios or organ music. Size 5 (Large Middle) is usually used for ensemble music. Size 6 (Small Middle) is usually used for condensed sheet music. Size 7 (Cadenza) is usually used for pocket music editions. And Size 8 (Pearl) is usually used for thematic advertisement.

8. Click OK. The music is redrawn using the new size.

9. Click the Print button.

When the standard Windows Print dialog box opens, you can set up your printer and print your music.

TIP

Here's one final tip. If you like to compose your music from scratch using the Staff View, you can use one of the included templates listed in the New Project File dialog box when creating your new Project. For example, if you want to compose for a string quartet, select the Classical String Quartet template.

The templates come with all the track parameters preset, but you might need to change a few of them to match your studio setup. After that, select all the tracks in the Track View and then select View > Staff to open them in the Staff View.

Everything is set up with the proper clefs, staff names, and more. The only settings you might need to adjust are the meter and key. Other than that, you have a blank slate ready and waiting to be filled with the music notation for your latest masterpiece.

14

Studio Control with StudioWare and Sysx

Most of today's modern appliances are computer controlled. Need to cook a meal? Push a few buttons on the stove, and it automatically sets the right time and temperature for your recipe. Need to wash your clothes? Yada, yada, yada.... It's the same thing with modern recording studio gear—most everything is computer controlled, and the gear supports MIDI, too. I'm not just talking about MIDI instruments (such as synthesizer keyboards), but audio processing equipment and mixing boards as well.

Why would these products include support for MIDI? Because, like MIDI instruments, they have internal parameters that can be changed and stored. Because these products provide support for MIDI, their parameters become accessible to other MIDI devices, such as your computer. This means it is now possible to control just about every piece of equipment in your studio via your computer, provided the equipment supports MIDI and you have the right software. Lucky for you, you don't need to buy any additional software, because SONAR has some built-in features for controlling and storing the parameters for any outboard MIDI gear. All you have to do is connect your MIDI devices to your computer (just as you would any MIDI instrument), and they can "talk" to each other—which brings me to the topics I'm going to discuss in this chapter. They include the following:

▶ Working with System Exclusive data

▶ Learning how to use the Sysx View

▶ Introducing StudioWare

▶ Taking Snapshots with StudioWare

▶ Recording control movements in StudioWare

System Exclusive

MIDI devices (other than MIDI instruments) don't usually provide standard musical functions, so their internal parameters are not compatible with standard MIDI messages, such as Note On messages, for instance. Instead, they have to communicate using special MIDI messages called *System Exclusive*. I talked a little about System Exclusive messages in Chapter 3. System Exclusive messages give you access to any special functions that a manufacturer includes in a MIDI instrument or device.

Not only do you have access to these functions, but by utilizing System Exclusive messages, you can send all the data from the MIDI instruments and devices in your studio to SONAR to be stored in your Projects. Why is this capability important? Because you can set up all your equipment with specific settings for a Project, store the data in the Project, and then send the data back to the devices at the beginning of your next recording session. This means that the next time you open the Project, you can have all the equipment in your studio set up automatically, without your having to touch a single knob. Cool, no?

The Sysx View

SONAR gives you access to System Exclusive data via the Sysx View (see Figure 14.1). Using the Sysx View, you can store up to 8,192 banks, each of which can contain any number of System Exclusive messages (limited only by the amount of memory in your computer system). So, for example, you could dedicate a different bank to store the data for each separate piece of equipment in your studio. You could also store different sets of Patch data for a single MIDI instrument in separate banks. Then, during different times in your Project, you could send specific Patch data to change the sounds in the instrument for that part of the song (you'll learn more about this topic later).

Figure 14.1
The Sysx View lets you store System Exclusive data within the current Project

Receiving System Exclusive Data

To store System Exclusive data in a bank in the Sysx View, you need to do a *data dump*. Essentially, the MIDI device from which you want to grab data dumps (or sends) it to your computer to be stored in one of the Sysx View banks.

NOTE
Be sure to check SONAR's Global MIDI Options to see whether the Record
System Exclusive data setting is activated. To do so, select Options > Global to
open the Global Options dialog box. Then select the MIDI tab. In the Record
section, click System Exclusive to place a check mark next to it. If this setting
isn't turned on, SONAR will block all incoming System Exclusive data.

To do a data dump, follow these steps:

1. Choose View > Sysx to open the Sysx View and then click a bank to
   highlight it for incoming System Exclusive data.

2. Click the Receive Bank button (the one with the downward-pointing red
   arrow) to open the Receive System Exclusive dialog box (see Figure 14.2).

Figure 14.2
You use the Receive
System Exclusive
dialog box to request a
data dump from your
MIDI device

3. Choose a DRM (Dump Request Macro) from the list. If you don't see your
   MIDI device listed, select the very first option: <You start dump on instru-
   ment>. Click OK. Then start the data dump using the Control Panel on
   your device. (See the device's user guide for more information on how to
   use the Control Panel.)

NOTE
Dump Request Macros (DRMs) are special System Exclusive messages. Some
MIDI devices support them, and some don't. If you have a MIDI device that
supports DRMs, SONAR can send a DRM to the device, asking it to send back its
parameter data. If you have a MIDI device that doesn't support DRMs, you have
to initiate the data dump manually from the Control Panel on the device.

TIP

Just because your MIDI device isn't listed in the Receive System Exclusive dialog box doesn't mean the device doesn't support DRMs. You'll need to look in its user's guide to see whether it has DRMs available. If so, you can set them up to be used within SONAR. To do so, open the file C:\Program Files\Cakewalk\ SONAR 2\cakewalk.ini using the Windows Notepad. Inside that file, you'll find instructions on how to add new DRMs to the list in the Receive System Exclusive dialog box.

4. If you do see your device listed, select the appropriate DRM and click OK. The DRM may ask you for additional information. For instance, if the DRM requests that the device send the data for a single sound patch, you'll need to input the patch number you want it to send. This process is pretty straightforward; you can just follow the prompts.

5. Whichever method you use to initiate the data dump, SONAR ultimately displays the Sysx Receive dialog box when it's ready to receive the data (see Figure 14.3). The dialog box shows the number of bytes of data being received as the dump takes place.

Figure 14.3
The Sysx Receive dialog box displays a count of the System Exclusive data

6. When the count stops, click Done.

NOTE

If the number of bytes stays at zero for more than a few seconds, then most likely something is wrong. Your MIDI device might not be hooked up properly, or you could have given the wrong answers for the additional DRM questions. Those answers differ depending on the MIDI device, so you'll need to consult its user's guide. In any event, if you have this problem, click Cancel. Then check your connections and try the procedure again.

After the dump is complete, the Sysx View shows the bank you selected with a new name and length (in bytes).

Changing the Name of a Bank

If you want to change the name of a bank, follow these steps:

1. Select the bank.
2. Click the Name button (the one with the lowercase *abc* shown on it) to open the Sysx Bank Name dialog box (see Figure 14.4).

Figure 14.4
In the Sysx Bank Name dialog box, you can change the name of a bank

3. Type a new name.
4. Click OK.

TIP
You can also record System Exclusive data directly to a Track, just as you would any other MIDI data. To do so, just set up your Track parameters, start SONAR recording, and then manually initiate a data dump from your MIDI device. You should be aware of some limitations, though. When you're recording directly to a Track, SONAR stores the data in Sysx Data Events instead of banks. Each Sysx Data Event can hold a single System Exclusive message of only 255 bytes in length. This means that if your MIDI device sends a message longer than 255 bytes, the message will get cut off, and it won't work when you try to send the data back. Plus, you won't get any warning that this has happened. It just won't work. So, essentially, you're better off using the Sysx View and banks to handle System Exclusive data. It's much easier, more efficient, and you can still send data back to a device during playback (I'll talk more about that in the next section).

Sending System Exclusive Data

After you set up your banks in a Project, you can send the data back to your MIDI devices. Before you do, though, you should be sure that each bank being sent is first set to the appropriate MIDI output. Just as each Track in the Track View can be set to send data to a particular MIDI output on your MIDI interface, each bank in the Sysx View can be set to a specific output as well. To do so, follow these steps:

1. Select the bank.
2. Click the Output button (the one with the picture of a MIDI connection shown on it) to open the Sysx Bank Output dialog box (see Figure 14.5).

Figure 14.5
In the Sysx Bank
Output dialog box,
you can change the
MIDI output assigned
to a bank

3. Type a new Output number. Remember that the data in this bank will be sent only to this MIDI output, so be sure the number is the same as the output number your device is connected to.

4. Click OK.

After you assign the right output numbers to each of your banks, you can easily transmit the data to the appropriate MIDI devices in three different ways.

Manually

To send the data in a bank manually, just select the bank and click the Send Bank button (the one with the single, black upward-pointing arrow shown on it). That's all there is to it. No muss, no fuss. You can also send all the data in every bank at once. You don't need to make any selections; just click the Send All Banks button (the one with the three upward-pointing arrows shown on it).

Automatically

Each bank in the Sysx View has an option called Auto. If you activate this option for a bank, that bank will be sent automatically every time you open the Project. For example, if you store all the parameter data from all your MIDI devices in a number of banks using the Sysx View and you set the Auto option on each of those banks, the next time you open your Project, SONAR will send the System Exclusive data to your MIDI devices automatically. Your studio will then be ready to go, with all the correct settings for your Project, without your having to do anything manually. To set the Auto option on a bank, just select the bank and click the Auto Send Bank button (the one with the black, upward-pointing arrow and yellow star shown on it).

During Playback

Although using the Auto option is a very convenient way to send System Exclusive data, sometimes you might want to send a bank at a specific time during the playback of your Project. For this purpose, SONAR provides a special Sysx Bank Event that you can place in any MIDI Track in your Project. Whenever SONAR encounters a Sysx Bank Event, it looks up the Event's associated bank number in the Sysx View and then sends that bank.

To add a Sysx Bank Event to a MIDI Track, you have to do so manually by using the Event View. Here's how:

1. Select a MIDI Track in your Project and choose View > Event List to open the Event List View for that Track (see Figure 14.6).

Figure 14.6
Using the Event List View, you can add Sysx Bank Events to your MIDI Tracks

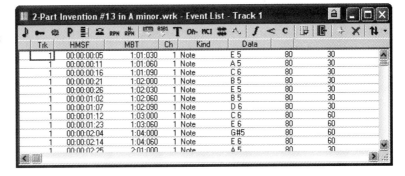

2. Move the Now Time cursor to the point within the list where you want to insert the new Sysx Bank Event.

3. Click the Insert Event button (the one with the yellow star shown on it) to insert a new Event. Initially, the Event will take on the characteristics of the Event at which the Now Time cursor was placed.

4. To change the Event to a Sysx Bank Event, move the Now Time cursor over to the Kind column and press the Enter key on your computer keyboard to open the Kind of Event dialog box (see Figure 14.7).

Figure 14.7
In the Kind of Event dialog box, you can change the type of the current Event

5. Select the Sysx Bank option in the Special section and click OK.

6. Move the Now Time cursor over to the Data column and press the Enter key on your computer keyboard. The number in the Data column becomes highlighted. Here, you enter the number of the bank you want to be sent.

7. Type a bank number and press the Enter key on your computer keyboard.

Now, when SONAR encounters that Sysx Bank Event during playback, it will send the appropriate System Exclusive data to your MIDI device.

CAUTION

MIDI is meant to transmit only one piece of data at a time. Of course, it transmits the data so fast that it sounds as if all the data in the Tracks are playing simultaneously. But MIDI does have its limits, and if you try to transmit huge amounts of data in a short amount of time, playback will be interrupted. This happens quite often with System Exclusive data. So, if you're going to send banks of data during playback, try to send only one bank at a time throughout your Project and also try to keep each bank short in length. In addition, try to insert each bank event where there is a break between notes. You'll have to do a little experimenting, but if you keep each bank between 100 and 255 bytes, you shouldn't have any problems.

Editing Bank Data

The Sysx View provides a feature that allows you to edit the data in a bank. To edit this data, select a bank, and click the Edit Data button (the one with a hand pointing to a piece of paper shown on it). Clicking on this button opens the Edit System Exclusive Bytes dialog box (see Figure 14.8).

Figure 14.8
In the Edit System Exclusive Bytes dialog box, you can edit the data in a bank

Edit System Exclusive Bytes

F0 41 10 42 12 40 00 7F 00 41 F7

OK

Cancel

Help

Tip: Remember to start with 'F0' and end with 'F7'

In the dialog box, you'll see a list of numbers. Each number represents one byte of System Exclusive data in hexadecimal format. You can change the numbers just as you would with text in a word processor. If the bank contains more than one System Exclusive message, the beginning of each message is designated by the number F0 and the end of each message is designated by the number F7. This way, System Exclusive data stays compatible with standard data in the MIDI language.

Whenever a MIDI device sees the number F0, it automatically knows that this number designates the beginning of a System Exclusive message. But that's as far as it goes in terms of identifying the data. All the bytes in a System Exclusive message that fall between the F0 and F7 are different, depending on which MIDI device they are associated with, so there's really not much else I can explain about this feature. If you want to learn more about the System Exclusive messages your MIDI device supports, consult the user's manual for that device.

If you ever want to delete a bank in the Sysx View, just select the bank and click the Clear Bank button (the one with the big red X on it). SONAR will ask whether you really want to delete. Be careful, because you cannot undo this procedure. When a bank is deleted, you cannot get it back without doing a data dump all over again.

Sharing with Friends

Even though all the data in the banks of the Sysx View are stored along with the data in your current Project, you can also load and save banks individually in a special System Exclusive data file format. This file format is the same one used by the public-domain System Exclusive data dump software utility called MIDIEX. MIDIEX is such a popular program that its file format became a standard for storing System Exclusive data on disk. What's great about the file format is that SONAR and many other sequencers support it, so you can easily share your System Exclusive data with your friends. Of course, being able to share won't matter much if you don't own the same MIDI devices, but if you do, you can easily share sound patch data for your MIDI instruments, and so on.

Saving

To save the data in a bank, follow these steps:

1. Select the bank.
2. Click the Save Bank To File button (the one with the floppy disk shown on it) to open the Save As dialog box.
3. Type a name for the file. The file should have an .SYX extension; SONAR should append this extension to the name automatically.
4. Click Save.

Loading

To load data into a bank, follow these steps:

1. Select a bank.

2. Click the Load Bank From File button (the one with the yellow folder shown on it).

3. If the bank you selected already has some data in it, SONAR will ask whether you want to append the data from the file to the existing data. Click Yes to append the data, or click No to replace the data. SONAR then displays the Open dialog box.

4. Select an .SYX file to load and click Open.

The data from the file is loaded into the bank you selected, and the bank is named after the file. You can change the name of the bank, as you learned earlier.

TIP

There's no easy method for copying a bank either within the same Project or from one Project to another, but you can copy using the Save Bank and Load Bank features. Just save a bank to an .SYX file from the current Project. If you want to have a copy of that bank in the current Project, just load it into another bank. If you want to have a copy of that bank in another Project, open the other Project and then load the bank into the Sysx View of that Project.

Intro to StudioWare

Being able to store all the parameter settings for your MIDI gear within a Project is great. You can have your whole studio set up in a matter of seconds. To set those parameters initially, you still have to fiddle with the knobs and controls on the MIDI gear itself. Because some MIDI devices have a limited number of controls, the only way to change their parameters is to wade through an endless maze of menus on a small (and sometimes cryptic) LCD screen. SONAR provides a feature, called StudioWare, that lets you adjust all the parameters in your MIDI devices without ever having to leave your computer. And, more importantly, it lets you access those less-than-accessible parameters in a very intuitive and easy manner.

Using StudioWare, you can create on-screen Control Panels that let you adjust the parameters in any of your MIDI devices remotely from your computer. Basically, you can have virtual buttons, knobs, and faders on your computer screen that represent each of the adjustable parameters in your MIDI devices. When you move a knob or fader on your computer screen, it changes the value of an assigned parameter in a MIDI device. So now, not only can you store MIDI device parameters, but you also can adjust them. Using the Sysx View and StudioWare, you may never have to touch your MIDI gear again (except maybe to turn it on). Plus, the adjustments you make to any on-screen controls can be recorded and then played back in real-time, which means you can automate parameter changes for a MIDI device as well.

The StudioWare View

Creating your own StudioWare Panels may sound like a complicated task—and yes, it can be. You need to have a good understanding of MIDI and System Exclusive data, but that doesn't mean you can't get any use out of StudioWare. Besides, some basic Panels are easy enough for anyone to put together, as I'll discuss in Chapter 15.

Getting started with StudioWare is actually very easy. As a matter of fact, for a really quick demonstration, you can have SONAR automatically create a Panel for you from the Track setup in your Project. To see what I mean, do the following:

1. Select File > Open and load one of the sample Projects included with SONAR. For this example, use the Don't Matter Audio and Midi Demo.cwb Project.

2. After the file loads, take a look at the Track View (see Figure 14.9). Notice that Tracks 2, 3, 4, 5, 6, and 7 are audio Tracks, and Tracks 8 and 9 are MIDI Tracks. Highlight all of them. (Forget about Track 1. It's blank.)

Figure 14.9
The Track View for Don't Matter Audio and Midi Demo.bun shows both audio and MIDI Tracks

3. Select View > StudioWare to open the StudioWare View (see Figure 14.10).

Figure 14.10
The StudioWare View
houses the virtual on-
screen Control Panels

As you can see in Figure 14.10, StudioWare has created a Control Panel representing all the Tracks you selected in the Track View. Each Track has its own set of controls, and yes, they really work. If you don't believe me, go ahead and start playing the Project. Then try changing one of the volume faders (by clicking and dragging it)—say, for the guitar Track. See? Of course, you might be saying to yourself, "This View looks similar to the Console View, so why would I need it?" You're absolutely right. It mimics the same controls that are in the Console View, and you really don't need it. It's just a cool demonstration trick. StudioWare's real power lies in mimicking the Control Panels of your external MIDI devices.

Unfortunately, there's no quick trick for creating those types of Panels, but SONAR does include a number of predesigned Panels that you can use within your own Projects. If you can't find a Panel for your MIDI device, Cakewalk also provides a nice library of additional StudioWare Panels on its Web site; you can download these Panels for free. And you can even find other places on the Internet where you can download free Panels written by other users (see Appendix D, "SONAR Resources on the Web").

Opening a StudioWare Panel

A StudioWare Panel is either stored as part of a Project file or as a separate StudioWare file with the extension .CakewalkStudioWare. If a Project file contains a Panel, the Panel is automatically opened when you open the Project. To open a StudioWare file, just do the following:

1. Select File > Open to display the Open dialog box.
2. Select StudioWare from the Files of Type drop-down list to display only StudioWare files.
3. Choose a file.
4. Click Open.

SONAR then displays the StudioWare View containing the Panel from the file you just opened. Because all Panels are different, I can't really explain how each one works. Usually, a Panel mimics the controls of a MIDI device, so if you own the corresponding MIDI device, you shouldn't have any trouble figuring out how to use its StudioWare counterpart.

After you've opened a Panel, you can adjust the controls, take a Snapshot, or record your control movements, and so on. Adjusting the controls is straightforward. The buttons, knobs, and faders in a StudioWare Panel work the same way they do in the Console View (which you learned about in Chapter 12.).

Taking a Snapshot

The Snapshot function works almost the same way as with the Console View, too, but there are a few differences. Instead of recording the control data in separate Tracks, the control data from a StudioWare Panel is recorded into a single Track. Most StudioWare Panels include a knob control that allows you to set which Track the control data will be recorded into. As an example, take a look at the General MIDI.CakewalkStudioWare Panel. You'll see a knob labeled Track. Adjusting that knob changes the Track number for the Panel. If you open some of the other sample Panels, you'll notice the same type of Track control. It might look a little different, but it functions in the same way. By the way, if a Panel doesn't have a Track control knob, either the Panel wasn't designed to record data to a Track (some of them don't), or the Panel will automatically record its data to Track 1. So, when you're working with this kind of Panel, it's a good idea to leave Track 1 dedicated to recording control data.

To take a Snapshot of the controls in a StudioWare panel, do the following:

1. Set the Now Time to the point in the project where you want the Snapshot to be stored.

2. Adjust the controls in the StudioWare panel to the values at which you want them to be set during that part of the project.

3. Click the Snapshot button (the one with the picture of a camera shown on it) in the toolbar at the top of the StudioWave View (see Figure 14.11).

Figure 14.11
Click the Snapshot button to take a Snapshot in the StudioWare View

Snapshot button

4. Repeat steps 1 through 3 until you've created all the Snapshots that you need for your Project.

Recording Control Movements

Recording the movements of the controls on a StudioWare Panel is also similar to the same procedure in the Console View, but, as with taking a Snapshot, there are a few differences. The first difference is the Track number procedure I described in the preceding section.

The second difference is in grouping controls together. Just as you can do in the Console View, you can group multiple controls together in a StudioWare Panel so that you can easily change more than one control simultaneously. The differences here are in how controls are grouped and in how single controls in a group are adjusted.

For grouping controls, instead of right-clicking on a control and assigning it to a colored group, you simply select an initial control, hold down the Ctrl key on your computer keyboard, and click one or more additional controls in the Panel. Those controls are then grouped. Grouping controls in a StudioWare Panel is much less sophisticated. They don't have any grouping properties like there are in the Console View either.

For adjusting a single control that belongs to a group, just hold down the Shift key on your computer keyboard and then adjust the control. In the Console View, the procedure is the same, except that you hold down the Ctrl key.

All these techniques work with any StudioWare Panel, even the ones you design yourself, which you'll learn about in Chapter 15.There are also differences in the actual recording of the control movements. The procedure for recording control movements in the StudioWare View are as follows:

1. Turn on the Record Widget Movements function by clicking on the Record Widget Movements button (the button with the big red dot shown on it), located just to the right of the Snapshot button at the top of the StudioWare View (see Figure 14.12).

Figure 14.12
Click the Record Widget Movements button to activate the Record Widget Movements function

Record Widget Movements button

2. Set the Now Time to just before the point in the project where you want to start recording control changes.

3. Start the project playing.

4. When the Now time gets to the point in the project where you want to begin recording control changes, adjust the controls in the StudioWare Panel with your mouse.

5. When you're finished, stop playback of the project.

6. Because you're manipulating on-screen controls with your mouse, you can make only one change at a time. What if you want to have two different controls change at the same time? For every control that you want to have change in the same timeframe, you must repeat steps 2 through 5.

TIP

Instead of starting and stopping playback each time you want to record additional control changes, try setting up a loop so that SONAR will just play the project (or section of the project) over and over again. I described looping in Chapter 6.

7. After you've finished recording all the control changes that you need, be sure to turn off the Record Widget Movements function.

TIP

If you want the controls in your StudioWare Panel to move according to the changes you recorded, activate the Update Widget Values function by clicking on the Update Widget Values button (the button with the picture of a slider on it), located just to the right of the Record Widget Movements button at the top of the StudioWare View.

15

Advanced StudioWare Techniques

Chapter 14 ended with an introduction to StudioWare–what it is, what it does, and how you can use it to control your outboard MIDI devices from your computer with on-screen Panels. That chapter also briefly touched on the topic of creating your own StudioWare Panels. Initially, you might think that StudioWare should be left to the real techno-oriented musicians among us, but that's not true. Anyone can get some good use out of SONAR's StudioWare features. This chapter further describes StudioWare, covering the following topics:

▶ The basics of designing your own Panels

▶ Widgets

▶ Widget properties and how to use

▶ A step-by-step Panel: Custom SONAR toolbars

Designing Basics

Designing your own StudioWare Panels can get very involved, so Cakewalk has tried to make the process as intuitive as possible. Instead of making you wade through all kinds of complex computer programming code, SONAR lets you essentially drag and drop your way to creating a Panel.

If you take a look at the StudioWare View (see Figure 15.1), you'll notice a button labeled Design at the top of the window.

Figure 15.1
The Design button puts
StudioWare into
Design mode

Clicking on that button puts StudioWare into Design mode and, at the same time, reveals ten new buttons along the top of the window (see Figure 15.2).

Figure 15.2
In Design mode, ten
new buttons become
available in the
StudioWare View

The first new button (the one with the grid shown on it) controls the Snap To Grid feature. It is similar to the Snap To Grid feature found in other areas of SONAR, which you learned about in Chapter 5. Instead of musical intervals, though, the grid is based on the pixels (dots) that make up your computer screen display. Clicking on the Snap To Grid button toggles that feature on or off. And if you click the button while holding down the Shift key on your computer keyboard, the Snap To Grid dialog box is displayed. In this dialog, you can set the size of the grid.

Clicking on the second button (the one with the mouse arrow shown on it) activates the Select tool. This tool allows you to select, move, and set the size of the Widgets. The other eight buttons represent the Widgets—the elements that make up a StudioWare Panel. (I'll describe the Widgets in more detail later in this chapter.) Clicking on any of these buttons activates their associated Widgets, allowing you to visually design a Panel by placing objects (Widgets) within the StudioWare View.

In other words, you can create a StudioWare Panel by selecting different Widgets and placing them within the StudioWare View with your mouse; for example, you can use the Button Widget to add buttons to your Panel. Then you can assign functions to each Widget, making them perform different tasks. After you've finished your design, you can save the Panel and then later use it within any of your Projects. Using Widgets isn't really complicated, although assigning functions to Widgets can get a bit confusing; I'll go over that topic later.

The basic procedure for designing a new StudioWare Panel is as follows:

1. Either create a new Project or open an existing one. StudioWare Panels can be designed or used only while a Project is open.
2. Select View > StudioWare to open the StudioWare View (see Figure 15.3). You can also open the StudioWare View by selecting File > New and choosing StudioWare Panel from the New Project File dialog box.

Figure 15.3
This new StudioWare
Panel contains the
default set of controls

3. Click the Design button to put StudioWare into Design mode.

4. As you can see in Figure 15.3, whenever you create a new Panel, SONAR automatically adds a set of controls for each Track that's currently selected in the Track View. If no Tracks are selected, just one set of controls is added for Track 1. But because you want to create your own Panel from scratch, you should remove those default controls. To do so, click each of the controls (Widgets) one by one and press the Delete key on your computer keyboard.

TIP

You also can get rid of all the Widgets simultaneously by clicking at the top of the set of controls, where you see the Track name—for example, Track 1. Clicking here selects the Cluster Widget (I'll explain this term in a moment), which contains all the other Widgets. Then just press the Delete key on your computer keyboard to remove everything.

5. The StudioWare View should now look like the View shown in Figure 15.4. That vertical gray rectangle at the left is the blank slate that serves as the initial building block for your Panel. This blank Panel is actually a permanent Cluster Widget. You can't erase it. It will hold any other Widgets you plan to add to the Panel. Click the Cluster Widget to select it and then drag the sides or corners with your mouse to change its size, thus setting the size of your Panel.

Figure 15.4
The permanent Cluster Widget holds all the other Widgets in your Panel

6. Add new Widgets to your Panel by clicking on one of the eight Widget buttons at the top of the window to select it. Then click somewhere within the permanent Cluster Widget to place the new Widget on your Panel (see Figure 15.5). You can add as many Widgets as you need (limited only by the amount of memory in your computer).

Figure 15.5
You just point and click to add a Widget to your Panel

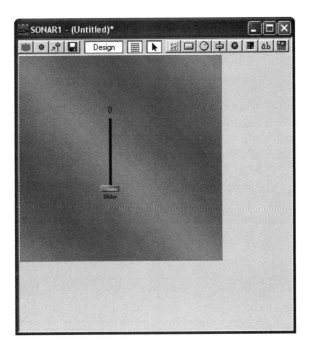

7. To change the position of a Widget, select it and drag it to a new location within the Panel. To change the size of a Widget, select it and drag the highlighted sides or corners, just as you would a window. You can also copy, cut, and paste Widgets as you would with anything else by using SONAR's Edit > Copy, Edit > Cut, and Edit > Paste menu commands.

8. Assign properties to each of the Widgets in your Panel. To do so, double-click a Widget to open the Widget Properties dialog box (see Figure 15.6). Adjust the relevant parameters and click OK. (I'll explain Widget properties in the next section of this chapter.)

Figure 15.6
Using the Widget Properties dialog box, you can assign functions to each of the Widgets in your Panel

9. After you finish making additions or changes to your new Panel, you should save it. You either can save it along with the current Project (you learned how to save Projects in Chapter 4) or as a separate CakewalkStudioWare file. To save it as a file, click the Save button (the one with the floppy disk shown on it) to open the Save StudioWare dialog box (see Figure 15.7). There, type a name for the Panel and click OK.

Figure 15.7
You can save your new
Panel by using the Save
StudioWare dialog box

TIP

If you want to share your Panel with friends, but you don't want them to be able to make any design changes to it, type a password in addition to a name in the Save StudioWare dialog box. The next time you open the StudioWare Panel and click the Design button, you will first be asked to enter the password. Don't forget your password, because you cannot make changes to your Panel without it!

If you're sometimes forgetful—like Yours Truly—try encoding the password into the name of the Panel. For example, you could use every other letter in the name of the Panel as your password. So, for a Panel named Special Proteus Panel, the password would be *seil poes pnl.* It's doubtful that anyone will ever guess it, but you'll still have a quick and easy way to remember it.

Widgets and Their Properties

Graphically designing a StudioWare Panel is one thing, but assigning properties to the Widgets to make the Panel work as you want it to is quite another. The basics are relatively easy to understand, and if you know the MIDI language well enough, you should get the hang of creating Panels fairly quickly. Teaching how to create StudioWare Panels could easily take up a whole book on its own, so, instead, I'll just get you started by providing some basic information about each of the Widgets—what they are, how to change their properties, and how to use them.

Cluster Widget

The Cluster Widget is a special Widget that has but one purpose: to hold other Widgets. Using it, you can design different sections of controls in your Panel, just like what can be found in many real Control Panels on MIDI devices. For example, you could use one Cluster Widget to hold all the pitch-related controls for your device and another Cluster Widget to hold all the volume-related controls. You can also put Cluster Widgets inside each other so that you can divide your Panel into additional subsections.

Name Change

Because a Cluster Widget doesn't provide any function other than acting as a "container" for other Widgets, its only alterable property is its name. To change the name of a Cluster Widget, do the following:

1. Double-click the Cluster Widget to open the Widget Properties dialog box.
2. In the field marked Label, type a name for the Cluster Widget.
3. Make sure the Show Label option is activated.
4. Click OK.

By the way, you can change the name of other Widgets in your Panel using this same procedure.

Hidden Panel Sections

A Cluster Widget is good for one more thing: creating hidden sections of a Panel. Why would you want to hide a part of your Panel? Well, perhaps part of the Panel should be accessible to the user only when certain conditions are met within another part of the Panel. For example, you may have a very sophisticated MIDI device with a large number of alterable parameters—too many to fit nicely within the visible area of your Panel. So, to keep things tidy, you could simply create a number of master buttons that, when clicked, would reveal their associated set of controls. Or you might just want to add a cool informational window containing author and copyright information about your Panel. You do so as follows:

1. Click the Cluster Widget button (the one with the dual faders shown on it) and then click anywhere within the Panel to add a new Cluster Widget to the Panel.
2. Resize the Cluster Widget so that it can fit the text of your name and per-haps a copyright notice.
3. Click the Text/Numeric Widget button (the one with the lowercase *ab* shown on it) and then click inside the new Cluster Widget to add a new Text/Numeric Widget.

4. Double-click the Text/Numeric Widget to open the Widget Properties dialog box. Then, in the Label field, type Created by *Insert Your Name Here* and click OK. You might have to resize the Text/Numeric Widget so that your text will show correctly. At this point, your Panel should look similar to Figure 15.8.

Figure 15.8
Creating a hidden
Cluster Widget is a
fairly easy task,
although it does
involve quite a
few steps

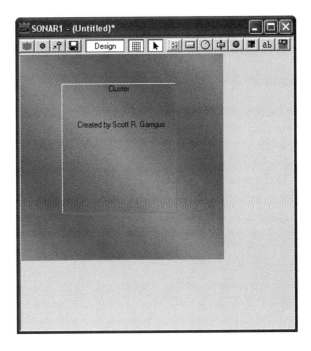

5. Add another Text/Numeric Widget and label it Copyright 2002 All Rights Reserved.

6. Change the name of the Cluster Widget to About this Panel..., but don't close the Widget Properties dialog box just yet. In the field named Alias, type HideAbout to assign a variable to the Cluster Widget.

NOTE

An *alias* is a variable that allows you to assign a numeric value to a Widget. In other words, an alias lets a Widget hold a number that can vary according to input from other Widgets in the Panel or from a user adjusting the Widget's on-screen control. This programmable nature allows for some very sophisticated and complex Panels.

In the case of a Cluster Widget, the value of its alias determines whether it will be visible. As soon as the alias surpasses a minimum value (that you set), the Cluster Widget becomes visible. As long as the alias remains less than the minimum value, however, the Cluster Widget stays invisible.

7. Under the Range section of the Widget Properties dialog box, type a Minimum value of 126 and an Initial value of 126. Also, make sure the Maximum value is 127.

8. Click OK. The Cluster Widget will disappear. Don't worry; it's still there. You just can't see it.

9. To control the appearance of the Cluster Widget, you need to add a button to the Panel. Click the Button Widget button (yeah, the one with a button shown on it) and then click inside the Panel (preferably somewhere other than where the Cluster Widget is located).

10. Double-click the Button Widget and, in the Widget Properties dialog box, type HideAbout in the Alias field (or assign the value using the Alias drop-down list). Then make sure the Maximum value in the Range section is set to 127. Next, click OK. (You can also give a name to the button, but I'll talk more about Button Widgets later.)

11. Remember to click the Design button to exit Design mode.

Now try clicking on the button in your Panel. The first time you click the button, the About this Panel… Cluster Widget should appear. You see this Panel because, when you click the button, it changes the value of the "HideAbout" Alias to 127 (which is higher than the Minimum value). This makes the Cluster Widget become visible. Click the button again, and the Cluster should disappear. This time, the button changes the value of the "HideAbout" Alias back to 0 (which is lower than the Minimum value), thus making the Cluster invisible again. What a neat trick, huh?

Text/Numeric Widget

The Text/Numeric Widget is similar to the Cluster Widget in that it has a very simple nature; it enables you to add text to your Panels. That's pretty much it. Text is useful for providing simple instructions on how to use the Panel or for identification purposes, as I mentioned earlier. To change the text content of a Text/Numeric Widget, just type some text in the Label field of the Widget Properties dialog box.

The Text/Numeric Widget *does* have one advanced use, though. You can use it to display the numerical values of other Widgets in the Panel. You simply assign the same Alias to the Text/Numeric Widget as another Widget, such as a Button, Knob, or Slider. Then, when the value of the Alias is changed by clicking on the Button or moving the Knob or Slider, for example, the Text/Numeric Widget will display the numerical value of the Alias. You can set up a working example as follows:

1. If you don't already have a Project open, do so now and set up a blank Panel in the StudioWare View.

2. Click the Slider Widget button (the one with the single vertical fader shown on it) and then click somewhere inside the blank Panel to add the Slider Widget to it.

3. Double-click the Slider Widget to open the Widget Properties dialog box.

4. Type SlideValue as the Alias and click OK. Don't worry about any of the other properties. The default values are fine.

5. Click the Text/Numeric Widget button (the one with the lowercase *ab* shown on it) and then click somewhere inside the Panel to add the Text/Numeric Widget to it.

6. Double-click the Text/Numeric Widget to open the Widget Properties dialog box.

7. Type SlideValue as the Alias and type The Slider Value Is %d as the Label.

TIP

In addition to the alias, StudioWare provides some special default variables that allow you to display the value of an alias via the Text/Numeric Widget. By placing %d in the Label property of a Text/Numeric Widget, you can show the value of that Widget's alias as a decimal number. You can also display the value of an alias in hexadecimal form by using %x instead of %d. In addition, you can even specify the number of decimal digits that you want to see displayed by using the special variable %04d. In this case, if the alias were equal to 42, it would be displayed with four decimal places, like this: 0042.

8. Click OK and turn off Design mode by clicking on the Design button. Your finished Panel should look something like the one shown in Figure 15.9.

Figure 15.9
You can use the Text/Numeric Widget like this to display the value of its Alias

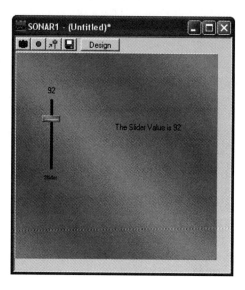

Now try dragging the slider control up and down. See how the text changes to reflect the value of the slider? When you move the slider up and down, it changes the value of its Alias property (in this case "SlideValue"). Because the Text/Numeric Widget also has "SlideValue" as an alias, it is linked to the Slider Widget. Plus, the special %d variable allows the value of the alias to be displayed in the Label property of the Text/Numeric Widget.

Image Widget and Widget Appearance

To improve the look of your Panels, you can use StudioWare to assign images to any of the Widgets or place graphics directly in a Panel using the Image Widget. Actually, because StudioWare enables you to assign images to any of the other Widgets, you probably won't use the Image Widget very much. Perhaps if you want to add a logo to your Panel, you might use the Image Widget, but then, you could also do so by simply assigning an image to a Cluster Widget. To see what you can do with images, take a look at some of the sample Panels included with SONAR—in particular, the Line 6 POD.CakewalkStudioWare and the Roland JV-2080 Patch.CakewalkStudioWare files. They use images extensively to make the Panels look very cool. By the way, these samples also use the hidden Cluster Widget technique I described earlier. Try clicking on some of the buttons, and you'll see what I mean.

Adding an Image Widget

If you ever need to use the Image Widget, follow these steps:

1. If you don't already have a Project open, do so now and set up a blank Panel in the StudioWare View.

2. Click the Image Widget button (the one with the picture shown on it) and then click somewhere inside the blank Panel to add the Image Widget to it.

3. Right-click the Image Widget and select Foreground Bitmap from the pop-up menu to open the Widget Bitmap file selector.

TIP

When you select Foreground Bitmap, the image you choose will be stretched to fill the Image Widget. If you want to add a tiled background instead (the same thing you can do to the Windows Desktop), select Background Bitmap from the pop-menu.

4. Select a file and then click Open. The image file has to be in the Windows Bitmap (.BMP) image file format, or you won't be able to open it.

TIP

If you want to put the Image Widget back to its original state (just a blank gray box), click either the Default or the None buttons in the Widget Bitmap file selector.

Your new Image Widget is then filled with the image you selected. As an example, take a look at Figure 15.10.

Figure 15.10
This Image Widget
filled with a picture
of Yours Truly

TIP

To assign the same image to multiple widgets, select all the widgets before assigning an image.

Changing Widget Appearance

Earlier, I mentioned that you can also simply assign an image to any of the Widgets instead of having to use the Image Widget. You do so in the same way you add an image to an Image Widget, but with one small difference: The Foreground Bitmap and Background Bitmap options fill different parts of the Widget with their images. For example, if you assign a Background Bitmap to a Meter Widget, the image fills the dark part of the meter display. If you assign a Foreground Bitmap, the image fills the lit part of the meter display. The Background and Foreground options work differently with each Widget. To find out how, do a little experimenting.

NOTE

You must consider two exceptions when assigning images to Widgets. First, the feature doesn't work at all with Text/Numeric Widgets, for obvious reasons. Second, a Cluster Widget can accept only a Background Bitmap, and the image always fills the entire Widget. Also, when creating custom images, be aware that the color of the top left pixel determines which color should be treated as transparent.

Instead of assigning an image to a Widget, you can change its color. The procedure is the same as when you assign an image, except that you select either Foreground Color or Background Color from the pop-up menu and choose a color from the standard Windows Color Chooser dialog box.

NOTE
If you have previously assigned an image to a widget, you must first set the image to None before you will see a custom color.

Indicator Widgets

In addition to the Text/Numeric Widget, two other Widgets provide feedback on Alias values. They are the LED and Meter Widgets. Instead of textual or numeric feedback, though, the LED and Meter Widgets provide graphical indications of Alias values.

The LED Widget

The LED Widget works similarly to the Cluster Widget in that it reacts whenever its alias becomes greater than the specified Minimum value. Instead of appearing or disappearing, however, the LED Widget turns its "virtual light" on and off. You can use this Widget for many different purposes; for example, you can use it to indicate when a button is pressed or not. Here's an example:

1. If you don't already have a Project open, do so now and set up a blank Panel in the StudioWare View.
2. Click the Button Widget button (the one with the button shown on it) and then click somewhere inside the blank Panel to add the Button Widget to it.
3. Double-click the Button Widget to open the Widget Properties dialog box.
4. Type LEDTest as an Alias and click OK.
5. Click the LED Widget button (the one with the red "light" shown on it) and then click somewhere inside the Panel to add the LED Widget to it.
6. Double-click the LED Widget to open the Widget Properties dialog box.
7. Type LEDTest as an Alias and enter 126 for the Minimum and Initial values in the Range section. Then click OK.
8. Turn off Design mode by clicking on the Design button. Your finished Panel should look something like the one shown in Figure 15.11.

Figure 15.11
This Panel example
shows how to use an
LED Widget

Now try clicking on the button in your Panel. The first time you click the button, the LED should light up (with the color red). It lights up because, when you click the button, it changes the value of the "LEDtest" Alias to 127 (which is higher than the Minimum value). This makes the LED Widget light up. Click the button again, and the LED should turn off. This time, the button changes the value of the "LEDtest" Alias back to 0 (which is lower than the Minimum value), thus turning off the LED.

The Meter Widget

Instead of just a simple on/off indication, the Meter Widget can display a whole range of values. This Widget works well for graphically showing the value of the Knob or Slider Widgets (which I'll talk about in a moment). Essentially, it works the same way as a Text/Numeric Widget in that, if you assign the same Alias to a Knob or Slider Widget and the Meter Widget, they are linked together and the Meter Widget provides a graphical representation of the value of the alias. As an example, try the following steps:

1. If you don't already have a Project open, do so now and set up a blank Panel in the StudioWare View.

2. Click the Slider Widget button (the one with the single vertical fader shown on it), and then click somewhere inside the blank Panel to add the Slider Widget to it.

3. Double-click the Slider Widget to open the Widget Properties dialog box.

4. Type SlideValue as the Alias, and click OK. Don't worry about any of the other properties. The default values are fine.

5. Click the Meter Widget button (the one with the double bar meter shown on it) and then click somewhere inside the Panel to add the Meter Widget to it.

6. Double-click the Meter Widget to open the Widget Properties dialog box.

7. Type SlideValue as the Alias.

8. Click OK, and turn off Design mode by clicking on the Design button. Your finished Panel should look something like the one shown in Figure 15.12.

Figure 15.12
This example shows how to use the Meter Widget to graphically display the value of its alias

Now try dragging the slider control up and down. See how the meter changes to reflect the value of the slider? When you move the slider up and down, it changes the value of its Alias property (in this case "SlideValue"). Because the Meter Widget also has "Slide-Value" as an alias, it is linked to the Slider Widget. So, when you move the slider up and down, the meter changes along with it.

Button Widget

As I've already demonstrated in a few of the previous examples, you can use the Button Widget to make Cluster Widgets appear or disappear and to turn LED Widgets on or off. You also can use it to send MIDI data (either to be recorded into a Track or directly out to a MIDI Port), run CAL Programs (see chapters 16 and 17 for more information about CAL), and even activate functions within SONAR. You do so by using the other property settings in the Widget Properties dialog box.

More Widget Properties

If you open the Widget Properties dialog box (see Figure 15.13), you'll notice a number of other properties that you can apply to the Widgets. These properties, which provide additional functionality to the Button, Knob, and Slider Widgets, are the real power behind StudioWare Panels.

Figure 15.13
The additional
property settings in the
Widget Properties
dialog box really give
StudioWare Panels
their power

Automate in Track and Direct to Port Properties

As you learned in Chapter 14, the movements of the controls on a Panel can either be
recorded to a Track or sent directly out a MIDI Port to be received by a MIDI device. What
determines whether a Widget's movements will be recorded or sent to a MIDI Port are the
Automate in Track and the Direct to Port properties.

Setting these properties is actually very simple. If you want the movements of a Widget to
be recorded to a Track, you activate the Automate in Track property and select a Track
number from its drop-down list. If you want the movements of a Widget to be sent directly
out a MIDI Port, you activate the Direct to Port property and select a Port number from its
drop-down list.

TIP

You can also use aliases with the Automate In Track and Direct To Port properties. This capability is useful if you want to be able to change the Track or Port
number via another Widget on the Panel. For example, you can set up a Knob
Widget to act as a Track number control. To do so, just assign the Knob Widget
an alias and then assign the same alias to the Automate in Track property of
another Widget. While you're using the panel, any adjustments you make to the
Knob affect which Track is used to record the data from the other Widget. Take a
look at the sample Panel called General MIDI.CakewalkStudioWare for a working
demonstration. The Track Knob in that Panel affects which Track the data from
all the other controls in the Panel will be recorded on.

Primary Action Property

Of course, a Widget also needs to be told what kind of data it's supposed to send, and that's where the Primary Action property comes in. The Primary Action property determines a Widget's main function. Its function can be sending MIDI data (note, controller, patch change, pitch wheel, Aftertouch, System Exclusive, and so on), running CAL programs, activating SONAR functions, or controlling Track parameters, for example.

To set the Primary Action for a Widget, you simply select the type of Action from the Primary Action Kind drop-down list. For each Action, you must set additional associated parameters. For example, if you select Note from the list, you can set the MIDI Channel, pitch, and velocity at which the note will be played when the Widget is manipulated. I'm not going to go over all the Primary Actions available. If you know your MIDI, then most of them are self-explanatory. The SONAR Help file provides some basic reference information about Actions in the Working with External Devices > Working with StudioWare > Functional Settings section, but, as I mentioned earlier, it would take a whole book to show you how to really delve into StudioWare Panel creation. Of course, I won't leave you without anything to ponder. To set up a Button Widget to send a Sysx Bank from the Sysx View, follow these steps:

1. Click the Button Widget button and then click somewhere inside your Panel to add the Button Widget to it.

2. Double-click the Button Widget to open the Widget Properties dialog box.

3. Select Sysx Bank from the Primary Action Kind drop-down list.

4. Type the number of the Sysx Bank you want to send in the Bank parameter box that appears.

5. Click OK and then click the Design button to exit Design mode.

Now, when you click the button, the Sysx Bank that you specified is sent. See how easy that is?

Return Action Property

Another property you should know about is the Return Action property. It is the same as the Primary Action property in that you can set it to execute the same types of Actions. Instead of carrying out its function when a Widget is first activated, however, it carries out the function in a secondary manner. In other words, if you set up a Return Action for the preceding button example, when you first click the button, the Primary Action is initiated. When you click the button a second time (to return it to its original up position), the Return Action is initiated. To see what I mean, assign a Return Action to the button example I just talked about and then test it.

Adjustable Widgets

Like Button Widgets, the Knob and Slider Widgets can be used to send MIDI data, manipulate Track parameters, and so on. But instead of just a single value, the Knob and Slider Widgets can send a whole range of values. Being able to send several values is great for sending MIDI controller data such as pitch change messages.

You can assign Primary and Return Actions to Knob and Slider Widgets in the same way you would with a Button Widget, but to ensure the value of the Widget is used when sending a range of data, you need to use an alias. You simply assign an alias to the Knob or Slider; then you type that same alias name into any of the Primary Action Kind parameters. For example, to set up a Knob Widget that sends MIDI volume controller data, you can do the following:

1. Click the Knob Widget button (the one with the little knob shown on it) and then click somewhere inside your Panel to add the Knob Widget to it.
2. Double-click the Knob Widget to open the Widget Properties dialog box.
3. Type VolumeKnob as an Alias.
4. Select Controller from the Primary Action Kind drop-down list.
5. For Channel, type the MIDI channel you want to use (1 to 16).
6. Select 7-Volume from the Number drop-down list.
7. Type the name of the Alias (VolumeKnob) into the Value parameter.
8. Click OK and then click the Design button to exit Design mode.

Now, when you move the knob, it sends MIDI volume controller data to the MIDI channel you assigned.

Other Properties

Several other Widget properties can come in handy when you're designing your Panels. They include overlapping and precise sizing and positioning.

Widget Overlapping

When you place Widgets on your Panels, you can put them on top of one another. The last Widget that you place will overlap any others that are underneath it. If you ever get into a situation in which you want a Widget that's underneath to be on top instead, just right-click it and select Bring to Top from the pop-up menu. Selecting this option brings that Widget to the foreground on top of any of the other Widgets. There is also a function for the opposite (Send to Bottom), which you access in the same manner.

Precise Sizing and Positioning

In the Widget Properties dialog box, you'll find a section called Placement. In that section, you can choose properties to specify the exact size and position of a Widget right down to the pixel. This capability can be useful if you're trying to make things look really nice on your Panel, and you want to make sure all the Button Widgets are the same size and so on.

The X and Y parameters specify the location of the top-left corner of the Widget. Using these parameters, you can place the Widget at any precise location within your Panel. The Width and Height parameters do exactly what you would expect: They specify the exact width and height of the Widget in pixels.

Custom Toolbars

If you invest enough time in learning how to use StudioWare, I guarantee you'll find that it makes many tasks a whole lot easier to deal with. The possibilities are numerous, so I really can't show them all to you. Of course, I couldn't end the chapter without at least giving you one nice example to try out.

Remember back in Chapter 3, when I mentioned that SONAR doesn't include any way for you to create your own custom Toolbars? Well, I wasn't exactly telling the whole truth, because, by utilizing StudioWare, you can create Panels that will function like your very own custom Toolbars. And creating these kinds of Panels is very easy, too. One of my personal favorites is a custom Toolbar for SONAR's audio editing functions (which you can find by choosing Process > Audio). You create it as follows:

1. If you don't already have a Project open, do so now and set up a blank Panel in the StudioWare View. Double-click the blank panel to open the Widget Properties dialog box. Type Process > Audio for the Label and activate the Show Label option. Then click OK.

2. Click the Button Widget button and then click somewhere inside the blank Panel to add the Button Widget to it.

3. Double-click the Button Widget to open the Widget Properties dialog box.

4. Type Normalize for the Label.

5. Select Binding from the Primary Action drop-down list.

6. Select Process > Audio > Normalize from the Verb drop-down list.

TIP

If you want to have a button activate your own custom editing functions that you created with CAL (see chapter 16 and 17), select CAL Program as the Primary Action. Then, in the Program field, type (do(include "ProgramName.CAL")), where ProgramName.CAL is the name of the program you want to run.

7. Activate the Spring-loaded option in the Range section and click OK.

NOTE

The Spring-loaded option in the Widget Properties dialog box makes the widget automatically snap back to its initial value after you move it. This capability is especially handy for creating single-click buttons. Normally, when you click a button, it stays pressed until you click it again to bring it back up to its original position. With the Spring-loaded option activated, the button "springs" back up, ready to be pressed again.

8. Repeat steps 2 through 7 until you have created buttons for all the Process > Audio commands available.

9. Click the Design button to exit Design mode and then save your new Panel (or custom Toolbar) as ProcessAudioToolbar.CakewalkStudioWare.

Now you can open the Panel and use it within any Project as a custom Toolbar. To make things even easier, you might want to save the Panel again, but this time save it inside your Project so that it will be loaded automatically every time you open the Project.

TIP

You can also assign key bindings to the panels that you create. See Chapter 3 for more information about key bindings.

You're Not Alone

If you're still a little fuzzy about some of the information described in this chapter, don't worry. In time, you'll learn to master the full potential of StudioWare. And if you need some help along the way, you might turn to some of the other users out there who are still learning the software, just like you. There are plenty of places on the Internet where you can get in touch with your fellow users. Check out Appendix D. You may even find that you're satisfied with simply downloading existing Panels that others have created. Either way, StudioWare will make your recording sessions easier and more productive.

16

CAL 101

One advantage that SONAR has over any other music sequencing product I've worked with is that it enables you to extend its functionality. If you find yourself in a situation in which you need to edit your MIDI or audio data in some way that is not possible with any of the current SONAR features—not a common occurrence, but it can happen—you can create a new editing function to take care of the task by using CAL. What is CAL, and how do you use it? Well, that's exactly what you'll learn in this chapter. This chapter covers the following:

- ▶ The definition of CAL
- ▶ How to run an existing CAL program
- ▶ Prewritten CAL programs
- ▶ Viewing CAL programs

What Is CAL?

CAL, which stands for Cakewalk Application Language, is a computer programming language that exists within the SONAR environment. You can use it to extend the functionality of SONAR by creating your own custom MIDI and audio data editing commands via CAL *programs* (also called *scripts*). A CAL program is a set of instructions written in the Cakewalk Application Language that tells SONAR how to perform a certain task. For example, if you want to change the volume of every other MIDI note in Track 1 to a certain value automatically, you can write a CAL program to do just that. And for future use, you can save CAL programs to disk as files with a .CAL extension.

NOTE

A *programming language* is a set of commands, symbols, and rules that are used to "teach" a computer how to perform tasks. By combining these language elements in different ways, you can "teach" a computer to perform any number of tasks, such as record and play music. The combination of elements for a certain task or set of tasks is called a computer *program*. For example, SONAR is a computer program, albeit a very complex one.

A number of different kinds of programming languages are in use, including BASIC, FORTRAN, C, LISP, and more. Each has unique characteristics. If you are familiar with C and LISP, you'll feel right at home with CAL; CAL derives many of its characteristics from these two languages.

You might be saying to yourself, "Um, well, that's nice, but I know nothing about computer programming, so what good is CAL going to do me?" Not to worry. Yes, CAL is a very complex feature of SONAR. If you really want to take full advantage of it, you have to learn how to use the language, but that doesn't mean CAL isn't accessible if you're a beginning user.

Included with SONAR are a number of prewritten CAL programs that you can use within your own Projects. Cakewalk also provides a nice library of additional CAL programs on its Web site that you can download for free. And you can even find other places on the Internet where you can download free CAL programs that have been written by other users (see Appendix D). Let's talk about how you can use the existing CAL programs included with SONAR and any others that you might download from the Internet.

Running a CAL Program

Because all CAL programs are different, I can't explain how to use them in one all-encompassing way. When you run a CAL program, it usually asks you for some kind of input, depending on what the program is supposed to do and how it is supposed to manipulate your music data. But you can still follow this basic procedure to run a CAL program:

1. Select the Track or Tracks (or data within the Tracks) in the Track View that you want to be edited by the CAL program. This first step is not always necessary. It depends on the task that the CAL program is supposed to perform. It also depends on whether the CAL program was written to process only selected data in a Project or all the Tracks in a Project. The only way to determine the function of a CAL program is to view it with the Windows Notepad, which you'll learn about later in this chapter.

2. Select Process > Run CAL to display the Open dialog box.

3. Choose the CAL program that you want to run and click Open.

That's all there is to it. Some CAL programs immediately carry out their tasks, whereas others first display additional dialog boxes if you need to input any values. The best way to begin using CAL (and to see how it works) is to try out some of the sample programs included with SONAR.

TIP
You can run CAL programs while a Project is being played back. This means you can hear the results of the editing that the CAL program applies to your data at the same time your music is being played. If you don't like what the CAL program does, just choose Edit > Undo to remove any changes the program makes to your data. If you then decide that you actually like the changes, instead of running the CAL program again, just select Edit > Redo to put the changes back in place.

The CAL Files

To give you a better understanding of how CAL works and also how you can benefit from it, I'll describe the prewritten CAL programs included with SONAR in the following sections. I'll give you a brief description of what each program does and how to use it.

Dominant 7th Chord.CAL

The Dominant 7th Chord.CAL program builds dominant seventh chords by adding three notes with the same time, velocity, and duration to each selected MIDI note in a Track. In other words, if you select a note within a Track, and you run Dominant 7th Chord.CAL, the program treats the selected note as the root of a dominant seventh chord and adds a minor third, a perfect fifth, and a minor seventh on top of it, thus creating a dominant seventh chord automatically.

Of course, if you know how to compose music, you probably won't get much use out of this CAL program. However, you might find it useful while working in the Staff View. While you're editing a MIDI data Track in the Staff View, try highlighting a note and then running Dominant 7th Chord.CAL. It's cool to see those additional notes just appear as if by magic. This program can save you some time while you're inputting notes by hand, too.

Other Chord.CAL Programs

SONAR includes a number of other chord-building CAL programs that work the same way as Dominant 7th Chord.CAL, except they build different kinds of chords:

▶ **Major 7th Chord.CAL**—This builds major seventh chords by adding the major third, perfect fifth, and major seventh intervals to the selected root note or notes.

▶ **Major Chord.CAL**—This builds major chords by adding the major third and perfect fifth intervals to the selected root note or notes.

▶ **Minor 7th Chord.CAL**—This builds minor seventh chords by adding the minor third, perfect fifth, and minor seventh intervals to the selected root note or notes.

▶ **Minor Chord.CAL**—This builds minor chords by adding the minor third and perfect fifth intervals to the selected root note notes.

Random Time.CAL

If you overindulge yourself while using SONAR's quantizing features (see Chapter 8), your music can sometimes come out sounding like computer music, with a robotic or machine-like feel to it. In some cases, this sound can be desirable, but when you're working on a jazz or rhythm and blues piece, you don't want the drums (or any of the other instruments for that matter) to sound like a robot played them. In that case, Random Time.CAL may be of some help.

This CAL program takes the start times of each selected Event in a Track and adds a random number of ticks to them. To give you some control over this randomization, the program first asks you for a number of ticks to base its changes on. It then adds a random number to each Event time that is between plus or minus one-half the number of ticks that you input. For instance, if you tell the program to use six ticks, each Event time will have one of the following numbers—chosen at random—added to it: –3, –2, –1, 0, 1, 2, or 3. Using this program is a great way to add a little bit of "human" feel back into those robotic-sounding Tracks. To use Random Time.CAL, just follow these steps:

1. Select the Track or Tracks in the Track View that you want to process. You can also just select a single Clip within a Track, or you can select a specific range of Events within one of the other Views, such as the Piano Roll View or the Staff View.

2. Choose Process > Run CAL to display the Open dialog box.

3. Choose the Random Time.CAL file and click Open. The Random Time.CAL Program then displays a CAL dialog box (see Figure 16.1).

Figure 16.1
The Random Time.CAL Program asks for number of ticks upon which to base its Event time processing

4. Enter the number of ticks you want to use and click OK.

You'll probably need to experiment a little with the number of ticks that you use, because too large a number can make your music sound "sloppy" or too far off the beat.

Scale Velocity.CAL

The Scale Velocity.CAL program is included with SONAR just to serve as a programming example; other than that, you don't really need it. SONAR already includes a Scale Velocity editing function, which provides even more features than Scale Velocity.CAL. For more information about Scale Velocity, see Chapter 8.

Split Channel to Tracks.CAL

If you ever need to share your music data with someone who owns a sequencing program other than SONAR, you can save your Project as a Standard MIDI File (SMF). Standard MIDI Files are supported by most computer music software products on the market; thus, they allow musicians to work together on the same song without having to own the same software. But not all Standard MIDI Files are created equal. Actually, several types of files are available; one in particular is called Type 0. A Type 0 MIDI file stores all its data—which is all the MIDI data from all sixteen MIDI Channels—on one Track. Type 0 files are sometimes used for video game composing, but hardly ever when composing for any other medium. Still, you might run across a Type 0 MIDI file, and if you open the file in SONAR, all the data shows up on one Track in the Track View. Editing the data is, therefore, kind of difficult, so Split Channel to Tracks.CAL is a useful tool in this situation.

Split Channel to Tracks.CAL takes the selected Track and separates the data from it by MIDI Channel into sixteen new Tracks. For example, if the Track contains data on MIDI Channels 1, 4, 5, and 6, Split Channel to Tracks.CAL creates sixteen new Tracks (from the initial Track), with the first Track containing data from Channel 1, the fourth Track containing data from Channel 4, and so on. The remaining Tracks that don't have corresponding Channel data are just blank. You use it like this:

1. Select a Track in the Track View.

2. If you want to split only a portion of the Track, set the From and Thru markers to the appropriate time values.

3. Choose Process > Run CAL to open the Open dialog box.

4. Choose the Split Channel to Tracks.CAL file and click Open. The Split Channel to Tracks.CAL Program then displays a CAL dialog box (see Figure 16.2).

Figure 16.2
The Split Channel to
Tracks.CAL Program
asks for the number
of the Track to start
with when creating the
new Tracks

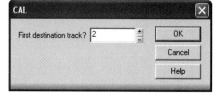

5. Enter the number of the first Track that you want Split Channel to
    Tracks.CAL to use when it creates the new Tracks and click OK.

CAUTION
Be sure to enter the number of the last track in your Project plus one, so that the
newly created tracks don't overwrite any existing ones. For example, if the number of the last track in your Project is 16, then enter 17.

After it's finished processing the original Track, Split Channel to Tracks.CAL creates
sixteen new Tracks starting with the Track number you selected, each containing data
from the sixteen corresponding MIDI Channels. Now you can access and edit the music
data more easily.

Split Note to Tracks.CAL

The Split Note to Tracks.CAL Program is similar to Split Channel to Tracks.CAL, except
that, instead of separating the MIDI data from a selected Track by channel, it separates the
data by note. For example, if you select a Track that contains notes with values of C4, A2,
and G3, Split Note to Tracks.CAL separates that Track into three new Tracks, each containing all notes with only one of the available note values. So, in this example, a new
Track containing only notes with a value of C4 would be created, another new Track
containing only A2 notes would be created, and another new Track containing only G3
notes would be created.

This Program can be useful if you're working with a single drum track that contains the
data for a number of different drum instruments. In MIDI, different drum instruments are
represented by different note values because drums can't play melodies. So, if you want
to edit a single drum instrument at a time, having each instrument on its own Track
would be easier. In that case, Split Note to Tracks.CAL can be put to good use. To apply
Split Note to Tracks.CAL to your music data, follow these steps:

1. Choose Process > Run CAL to open the Open dialog box.

2. Choose the Split Note to Tracks.CAL file and click Open.

3. The Split Note to Tracks.CAL Program asks for the number of your Source Track (see Figure 16.3). It is the Track that you want to split into new Tracks. Enter a Track number and click OK.

NOTE

You'll notice this program is different from the other CAL programs in which you had to first select a Track in the Track View. It's different because the person who wrote this CAL Program did it differently from the rest. Why? I have no idea.

Figure 16.3
Here, you can enter the Source Track for the Split Note to Tracks.CAL Program

4. The program then asks you for the number of the First Destination Track (see Figure 16.4). It is the number of the first new Track that will be created. Enter a number and click OK.

Figure 16.4
Here, you can enter the First Destination Track for the Split Note to Tracks.CAL Program

CAUTION

Be sure to enter the number of the last track in your Project plus one, so that the newly created tracks don't overwrite any existing ones. For example, if the number of the last track in your Project is 16, then enter 17.

5. The program then asks you for the number of the Destination Channel (see Figure 16.5). It is the MIDI channel that you want all the new Tracks to be set to. Unless you want to change the channel, you should simply select the same channel that the Source Track is using. Enter a number from 1 to 16 and click OK.

Figure 16.5
Here, you can enter the
Destination Channel
for the Split Note to
Tracks.CAL Program

6.   The program finally asks you for the number of the Destination Port (see Figure 16.6). It is the MIDI output that you want all the new Tracks to be set to. Again, you should simply select the same output that the Source Track is using. Enter a number from 1 to 16 and click OK.

Figure 16.6
Here, you can enter the
Destination Port for the
Split Note to
Tracks.CAL Program

After you answer the last question, Split Note to Tracks.CAL processes the original Track and creates a number of new Tracks (depending on how many different note values are present in the original Track), each containing all the notes for each corresponding note value.

Thin Controller Data.CAL

You use MIDI Controller data to add expressive qualities to your MIDI music Tracks. For example, you can make a certain passage of music get gradually louder or softer (crescendo or decrescendo) by adding MIDI Controller number 7 (Volume) to your MIDI Tracks. Sometimes, though, an overabundance of MIDI data can overload your MIDI instruments and cause anomalies such as stuck notes and delays in playback. If you have this problem, you can try thinning out the MIDI Controller data in your Tracks by using Thin Controller Data.CAL. This program allows you to decrease the amount of data being sent to your MIDI instruments by deleting only a select number of Controller Events—enough to reduce the amount of data without adversely affecting the music performance. It works like this:

1.   Select the Track or Tracks in the Track View that you want to process. You can also just select a single Clip within a Track, or you can select a specific range of Events within one of the other Views, such as the Piano Roll View or the Staff View.

2. Choose Process > Run CAL to display the Open dialog box.

3. Choose the Thin Controller Data.CAL file and click Open.

4. The Thin Controller Data.CAL Program asks you for the number of the MIDI Controller that you want to process (see Figure 16.7). For example, if you want to remove some of the volume data from a Track, use MIDI Controller number 7. Enter a number from 0 to 127 and click OK.

Figure 16.7
Here, you can enter the Controller number for the Thin Controller Data.CAL Program

5. The program then asks you for the thinning factor (see Figure 16.8). For example, if you enter a value of 4, the program deletes every fourth volume Event it finds in the selected Track or Tracks. Enter a number from 1 to 100 and click OK.

Figure 16.8
Here, you can enter the thinning factor for the Thin Controller Data.CAL Program

After you answer the last question, Thin Controller Data.CAL processes the selected Track or Tracks and deletes all the MIDI Controller Events that correspond to the MIDI Controller number and the thinning factor you entered. If this procedure doesn't clear up your MIDI playback problems, you can try thinning the data some more, but be careful not to thin it too much; otherwise, your crescendos and decrescendos (or other Controller-influenced music passages) will start to sound choppy rather than smooth.

CHAPTER 16

Other Thin.CAL Programs

Also included with SONAR are two other Controller-thinning CAL Programs. These programs work almost the same way as Thin Controller Data.CAL, but each is targeted toward one specific type of Controller. Thin Channel Aftertouch.CAL thins out Channel Aftertouch MIDI Controller data, and Thin Pitch Wheel.CAL thins out Pitch Wheel (or Pitch Bend) MIDI Controller data. To run these programs, you use the same procedure as you do with Thin Controller Data.CAL, but with one exception. The programs don't ask you to input the number of a MIDI Controller, because they are each already targeted toward a specific Controller. Other than that, they work in the same manner.

Viewing CAL Programs

Unless a CAL program comes with some written instructions, you won't know what it is designed to do to the data in your Project. This is especially true if you download CAL programs from the Internet. Many come with documentation, but many don't. Most programs, however, do come with a brief description (as well as instructions on use) within their source code.

NOTE

Source code (or *program code*) is the text of the programming language commands used for a particular program. You create a program by first writing its source code. A computer can then run the program by reading the source code and executing the commands in the appropriate manner, thus carrying out the intended task.

To read the source code of a CAL program, you need to use the Windows Notepad (or some other plain text editor). As an example, take a look at the source code for Major Chord.CAL:

1. Choose Start > Programs > Accessories > Notepad to open the Windows Notepad.

2. Choose File > Open and select the Major Chord.CAL file from the SONAR directory on your hard drive (or some other directory where your CAL files are stored). Click Open. Windows Notepad then opens Major Chord.CAL and displays its source code (see Figure 16.9).

Figure 16.9
You can use the Windows Notepad to examine and edit the source code of a CAL Program

```
Major Chord.cal - Notepad
File  Edit  Format  View  Help

;; Major Chord.cal
;;
;; Treats each note as the root of a major chord, and creates that chord:
;; For each note event, adds two note events with same time, vel, and dur
;; but a major third and a perfect fifth higher.
;;
(do
        (include "need20.cal")   ; Require version 2.0 or higher of CAL

        (forEachEvent
                (if (== Event.Kind NOTE)
                (do
                        (insert Event.Time Event.Chan NOTE (+ Note.Key 4) Note.Vel Note.Dur)
                        (insert Event.Time Event.Chan NOTE (+ Note.Key 7) Note.Vel Note.Dur)
                )
                )
        )
)
```

CHAPTER 16

As you can see in Figure 16.9, the Windows Notepad allows you to see the source code of Major Chord.CAL and also allows you to read the brief description included there. You can do the same thing with any other CAL program to find out how it can be used and what task it's supposed to perform. But that's not all.

Using the Windows Notepad, you also can edit the source code for a CAL program, as well as create a CAL program from scratch. Since CAL programs are just plain text, you can use the same editing techniques as you do with any other text such as cut, copy, and paste text-editing procedures. I'll cover creating your own CAL programs in Chapter 17.

17

Advanced CAL Techniques

In Chapter 16, you learned about the Cakewalk Application Language—what it is, what it does, and how you can run prewritten CAL programs to tackle some of the editing tasks that the built-in SONAR functions can't. I briefly touched on the topic of creating your own CAL programs. This chapter continues the CAL discussion and covers the following:

▶ Cakewalk Application Language

▶ Anatomy of a CAL program

▶ CAL functions reference

Intro to CAL Programming

Unfortunately, there is no easy way to create your own CAL programs. To tap the full power of its functionality, you need to learn how to create programs from scratch using the Cakewalk Application Language. The problem is that teaching a course in CAL programming would take up a whole book in and of itself. So instead, I'll just get you started by providing a brief introduction to the language. And the best way to do that is to walk you through the code of one of the CAL programs that comes included with SONAR.

To get started, open the Scale Velocity.CAL program using Windows Notepad (see Figure 17.1). The first thing you'll see is a bunch of lines that start with semicolons and contain some text describing the CAL program. These lines are called *comments*. Whenever you insert a semicolon into the code of a CAL program, SONAR ignores that part of the code when you run the program. This way, you can mark the code with descriptive notes. When you come back to the program at a later date, you will understand what certain parts of the program are supposed to accomplish.

Figure 17.1
The code for the Scale
Velocity.CAL program
provides a nice exam-
ple for an explanation
of the Cakewalk
Application Language

```
Scale Velocity.cal - Notepad
File  Edit  Format  View  Help
;; Scale Velocity.cal
;;
;; This is a sample CAL program that implements an editing command to
;; scale note velocities by a certain percentage.
;;
;; Demonstrates:
;;
;;     (forEachEvent)
;;     Getting input from the user
;;     Arithmetic operators
;;     Event kind and parameter variables
;;
(do
        (include "need20.cal")  ; Require version 2.0 or higher of CAL

        (int percent 100)
        (getInt percent "Percentage?" 1 1000)

        (forEachEvent
                (if (== Event.Kind NOTE)
                (do
                        (*= Note.Vel percent)
                        (/= Note.Vel 100)
                )
                )
        )
)
```

A little further down, you'll notice the first line of the actual code used when the program
is run. The line reads (do. All CAL programs start with this code. The parenthesis designates the start of a function, and the do code designates the start of a group of code. As a
matter of fact, a CAL program is just one big function with a number of other functions
within it. You'll notice that for every left parenthesis, you'll have a corresponding right
parenthesis. CAL programs use parentheses to show where a function begins and ends.

Include

The next line in Scale Velocity.CAL reads (include "need20.cal"). This is the Include
function. This function allows you to run a CAL program within a CAL program. You might
want to do so for a number of reasons. For instance, if you're creating a very large program,
you might want to break it down into different parts to make it easier to work with. Then
you could have one master program that runs all the different parts. You can also combine
CAL programs. For example, you could combine the Thin Channel Aftertouch.CAL, Thin
Controller Data.CAL, and Thin Pitch Wheel.CAL programs that come with SONAR by using
the Include function in a new CAL program. Then, when you run the new program, it
would run each of the included programs, one right after the other, so that you could thin
all the types of MIDI controller data from your project in one fell swoop.

In Scale Velocity.CAL, the Include function is used to run the need20.cal Program. This
program simply checks the version of CAL and makes sure that it is version 2.0 or higher.
Some CAL programs check the version to avoid an error in case a very old version of CAL
is being used.

Variables

After the <u>Include</u> function, the code for Scale Velocity.CAL shows (<u>int percent 100</u>). This is a <u>Variable</u> function. In CAL programs, you can define variables to hold any values you might need while the program is running. In this instance, the variable <u>percent</u> is defined as an integer and is given a value of <u>100</u>. Variables can be used to store both number and text information. After you define a variable, you can refer to its value later in your code by simply using the variable name. That's what you see in the next line of code in Scale Velocity.CAL.

User Input

This next line reads (<u>getInt percent "Percentage?" 1 1000</u>). Here, the program asks for input from the user. In English, this line of code translates to "Get an integer between 1 and 1000 from the user by having the user type a value into the displayed dialog box. Then store the value into the variable named <u>percent</u>." So, basically, when SONAR reaches this line of code in the program, it pauses and displays a dialog box (see Figure 17.2). Then it waits for the user to input a value and click the OK button. It then assigns whatever the inputted value was to the variable <u>percent</u>. And then it continues running the rest of the program.

Figure 17.2
A CAL program gets input from the user by displaying dialog boxes

ForEachEvent

The main part of the Scale Velocity.CAL program begins with the line of code that reads (<u>forEachEvent</u>. <u>ForEachEvent</u> is known as an *iterating* function. In this type of function, a certain portion of code is run (or cycled through) a specific number of times. In this case, for every Event in the selected Track(s), the code enclosed within the <u>forEachEvent</u> function is cycled through one time. So, in Scale Velocity.CAL, for every Event in the selected Track(s), this block of code is run through once:

```
(if (== Event.Kind NOTE)
        (do
                (*= Note.Vel percent)
                (/= Note.Vel 100)
        )
)
```

What does this code do? Let's talk about it.

Conditions

Within the <u>forEachEvent</u> function in Scale Velocity.CAL, every Event in the selected Track(s) is tested using the <u>if</u> function. This function is known as a *conditional* function. Depending on whether certain conditions are met, the code enclosed within the <u>if</u> function may or may not be run. In Scale Velocity.CAL, every Event is tested to see whether it is a MIDI Note Event. This test is performed with the line of code that reads (= = <u>Event</u>.Kind NOTE). In English, this line translates to "Check to see whether the current Event being tested is a MIDI Note Event." If the current Event is a MIDI Note Event, then the next block of code is run. If the current Event is not a MIDI Note Event, then the next block of code is skipped, and the <u>forEachEvent</u> function moves on to the next Event in the selected Track(s) until it reaches the last selected Event; then the CAL program stops running.

Arithmetic

The final part of Scale Velocity.CAL is just some simple arithmetic code. If the current Event is a MIDI Note Event, the Velocity value of the Note is multiplied by the value of the <u>percent</u> variable, and the resulting value is assigned as the Note Velocity. Then the new Velocity value of the Note is divided by the number 100, and this resulting value is then assigned to be the final value of the Note Velocity. This way, the program scales the velocities of the notes in the selected Track(s).

Master Presets

One of the most effective uses I've found for CAL is in creating what I like to call *Master Presets*. As I mentioned in Chapter 8, SONAR lets you save the settings for some of its editing functions as presets. This way, you can easily use the same editing parameters you created by simply calling them up by name, instead of having to figure out the settings every time you use a function. Presets are a real time-saver, but unfortunately, you can save presets for each of the individual functions only. What if you want to combine a few of the functions to create a certain editing process? For example, say you like to shorten your MIDI Tracks before you quantize them. To do so, you first need to select the Tracks, use the Length function, and then use the Quantize function to process your Tracks. For each of the editing functions, you have to make the appropriate settings adjustments. If you create a CAL program to automatically run through the process for you, though, all you need to do is select your Tracks and run the CAL program.

To show you what I mean, I've cooked up a sample Master Preset that you can run as a CAL program and use in your Projects. You need to do the following:

1. Open the Windows Notepad.
2. Type in the first few lines of code, as shown in Figure 17.3.

Figure 17.3
These are the first few lines of code in our new Master Preset

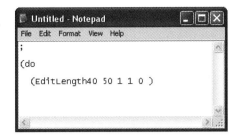

3. Examine the code. The first line is just a blank comment. The second line designates the beginning of the program. The third line tells SONAR to activate the Length function using the parameters as shown in Figure 17.4. In the source code, the command EditLength40 tells SONAR to activate the Length function. The number 50 corresponds to the Percent parameter in the Length dialog box. The numbers 1, 1, and 0 correspond to the Start Times, Durations, and Stretch Audio options, respectively. A 1 indicates that option is activated. A 0 indicates that option is not activated.

Figure 17.4
The first part of the CAL program shortens the selected MIDI Tracks by 50 percent with the Length editing function

TIP
You may be wondering how to apply commands in CAL to the editing functions in SONAR and how to determine their corresponding parameters. To find out, take a look at the CAL Reference section of the SONAR Help file.

4. Now type in the last two lines of code as shown in Figure 17.5.

Figure 17.5
The final source code should look like this after you edit it

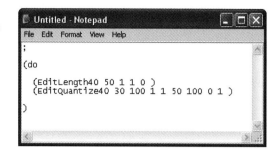

5. Examine the code. The command EditQuantize40 tells SONAR to activate the Quantize function using the parameters as shown in Figure 17.6. The numbers following that command designate the following parameter settings: Resolution, Strength percent, Start Times (on/off), Note Durations (on/off), Swing percent, Window percent, Offset, and Notes/Lyrics/Audio option (on/off).

Figure 17.6
The second part of the CAL program quantizes the notes in the selected MIDI Tracks with the Quantize editing function

6. Save the new program with a file extension of .CAL.

Now, when you run this CAL program, it performs all the editing functions for you automatically with the same exact settings that you used. It's too bad that CAL doesn't support SONAR's MIDI or audio effects functions. I really wish that it did, because then you could create Master Presets to process your audio Tracks, too. That capability would make CAL a hundred times more powerful than it already is. I hope that Cakewalk will add this functionality in a future version. In the meantime, you can still find plenty of uses for CAL.

CAL References

So, are you totally confused yet? If you've had some previous programming experience, you should have no trouble in picking up the Cakewalk Application Language. If you're familiar with the C or Lisp computer programming languages, CAL is just a stone's throw away in terms of functionality.

Really, the best way to learn about CAL is to study the code of existing CAL programs. As I mentioned earlier, you can also read the reference material included in the SONAR Help file. A couple of references cover all the CAL functions and data types, describing what they are and how they work. You can find the references in the CAL Reference section of the Help file.

If, even after this discussion, you still find yourself lost in all this technical jargon, you can utilize CAL by using prewritten programs. As I mentioned before, this part of SONAR has a lot of power, and it would be a shame if you let it go to waste. CAL can save you time and even let you manipulate your music data in ways you may never have thought of. Don't be afraid to experiment. Just be sure to back up your data, in case things get a bit messed up in the process.

TIP

For more information about programming with CAL, check out some of the Web sites I've listed in Appendix D, "SONAR Resources on the Web."

18

Take Your SONAR Project to CD

Congratulations! You've made it to the final chapter of the book. Your Project has been recorded, edited, mixed, and now you can share it with the rest of the world. To be able to share it, you need to create your very own CD. So, in this chapter, I'll cover the basics of creating a custom audio CD, including the following:

▶ Preparing your Project for CD audio

▶ Using the popular Easy CD Creator software

▶ Using the built-in Windows XP CD burning functions

Preparing a Project for CD Audio

A Project can't be laid down as audio Tracks on a CD as is. Instead, you have to convert all your MIDI Tracks in a Project to audio Tracks. Then you have to export those audio Tracks to a .WAV file so that your CD recording software can write the file to your CD. To do so, you need to follow a number of steps.

Convert Your MIDI Tracks

As I explained in chapter 2, Sound Blaster (and other similar consumer-level) sound cards really shouldn't be used for serious music making. But if you happen to have one of these cards that provides a built-in synthesizer, the first step is to convert any MIDI Tracks that use your sound card's built-in synthesizer for playback to audio Tracks as follows:

1. Insert a new audio Track and assign the input for the Track to your sound card's stereo input. For instance, if you have a Sound Blaster Live card, set the Track to the Stereo SB Live Wave In input.

2. Mute all the Tracks in your Project except the one you just created and the MIDI Tracks you're going to convert.

3. Open your sound card's mixer controls (see Figure 18.1) by double-clicking on the small speaker icon in the Windows Taskbar.

Figure 18.1
This window shows the sound card mixer controls for the Sound Blaster Live

4. Select Options > Properties and click Recording in the Adjust Volume For section of the resulting Properties dialog box. Then click the OK button to bring up the recording mixer controls, as shown in Figure 18.2.

Figure 18.2
This window shows the recording mixer controls for the Sound Blaster Live sound card

5. Activate the recording source for your sound card's synth by clicking on the appropriate Select option (see Figure 18.3).

Figure 18.3
You need to activate
your sound card's
synth before you can
record its output

6. Click the Record button on the toolbar in SONAR, and your MIDI Tracks are recorded to the stereo audio Track.

Next, you need to convert any MIDI Tracks that use external MIDI instruments for playback to audio Tracks, as shown in the following steps. If you don't have any MIDI Tracks of this kind, you can skip this section.

1. Insert a new audio Track and assign the input for the Track to your sound card's stereo input. For instance, if you have a Sound Blaster Live card, set the Track to the Stereo SB Live Wave In input.

2. Mute all the Tracks in your Project except the one you just created and the MIDI Tracks you're going to convert.

3. Open your sound card's mixer controls by double-clicking on the small speaker icon in the Windows Taskbar.

4. Select Options > Properties, and click Recording in the Adjust Volume For section of the resulting Properties dialog box. Then click the OK button to bring up the recording mixer controls.

5. Activate the recording source for your sound card's line input(s) by clicking on the appropriate Select option (see Figure 18.4).

Figure 18.4
You need to activate your sound card's line input(s) before you can record any external MIDI instruments

6. Be sure the audio outputs from your external MIDI instrument are connected to the line input(s) of your sound card. If you have more than one MIDI instrument and you're using a mixing board, connect the stereo output(s) of your mixing board to the line input(s) of your sound card.

7. Click the Rewind button on the toolbar in SONAR so that recording will begin at the beginning of the song. Then click the Record button on the toolbar in SONAR, and your MIDI Tracks are recorded to the stereo audio Track.

After you're finished, you should have two new audio Tracks representing your sound card's built-in synthesizer and your external MIDI instruments.

Convert Your DXi Tracks

You also need to convert any MIDI Tracks that use DXi's for playback. To do so, just follow these steps:

1. Mute all the Tracks in your project except the MIDI and audio Tracks pertaining to your DXi's.

2. Choose Edit > Bounce To Tracks to open the Bounce To Tracks dialog box. I talked about the Bounce To Tracks function in Chapter 7.

3. Choose New Track in the drop-down list for the Destination parameter.

4. Choose Mix To Single Track Stereo Event(s) in the drop-down list for the Format parameter.

5. In the Source Bus(es) section, choose the output of your sound card you would like SONAR to use when recording your DXi's.

6. In the Mix Enables section, make sure all the options are activated.

7. Click OK.

SONAR creates a new stereo audio Track containing all the music from your DXi's.

Convert Your Audio Tracks

After all your MIDI Tracks are converted to audio Tracks, you need to mix and export all your audio Tracks down to a .WAV file. SONAR provides a very convenient feature expressly for this purpose, called Export Audio. This feature takes any number of original audio Tracks—preserving their volume, pan, and effects settings—and mixes them into a single stereo .WAV file. Here's how to use it:

1. Mute all the MIDI Tracks in your Project and any audio Tracks that you don't want included in the new Track(s).

2. Choose File > Export Audio to open the Export Audio dialog box, as shown in Figure 18.5.

Figure 18.5
You use the Export Audio dialog box to mix and export your Tracks

3. From the Look In list, select the folder you want to save the .WAV file to. Then type a name for the file in the File Name field.

4. Choose the type from the Files of Type drop-down list. In this case, use the Wave option.

5. Select the Format you want to use. You can mix your audio Tracks to a single stereo file, two mono files (that, when combined, create a stereo file), or a single mono file. You can also set the bit depth using the Bit Depth parameter. I explained bit depth in Chapter 6.

6. Choose the sound card(s) you want to use to process your audio Tracks from the Source Bus(es) field.

7. Leave the Each Source To Separate Submix option deactivated.

8. Leave all the Mix Enables options activated to ensure that your new .WAV file will sound exactly the same when played back as the original audio Tracks.

9. Click the Export button, and SONAR mixes all your audio Tracks down to a new .WAV file.

When you're done, you should have a .WAV file that you can use along with your CD recording software to create an audio CD.

Using Easy CD Creator

When it comes to CD recording software, almost 90 percent of the drives on the market include a "lite" version of Easy CD Creator from Roxio. Also, an upgrade offer is usually included for the full version of the software. Because of its popularity, I'll discuss how to use Easy CD Creator to burn your own CDs. If you have some other CD recording software, the process should be similar.

NOTE

Because a laser is used to heat up the blank CD and write the information to it, recording a CD is also referred to as *burning* a CD.

You can just follow these basic steps to create an audio CD:

1. Start Easy CD Creator.

2. Choose File > New CD Project > Music CD to create an untitled music CD project (see Figure 18.6).

Figure 18.6
You can create a music CD using Easy CD Creator's main interface

3. In the Select Source Files drop-down list, choose the drive containing the WAV files you want to burn to CD.

4. In the file list below the Select Source Files drop-down list, select the WAV file(s) you want to burn to CD.

5. To preview the file(s), click the Preview button.

6. Click the Add button to add the selected file(s) to your music CD project. The file(s) are added to the music CD project list in the bottom half of the Easy CD Creator window (see Figure 18.7).

CHAPTER 18

Figure 18.7
The files for your
music CD project are
listed in the bottom
half of the Easy CD
Creator window

7. To remove a file from the project list, select it and click the Remove button.

8. Repeat steps 3 through 7 until you've finished adding all your files to the project.

TIP

You don't have to fill the entire CD at this point. As long as you don't finalize the CD, you can add to it over time until it is filled.

9. Add a title to your project by typing the name of the CD in the New CD Title field.

10. Add an artist to your project by typing the name of the artist in the Artist Name field.

11. Click the Record button to open the Record CD Setup dialog box. Click the Options button to reveal the entire dialog box (see Figure 18.8).

Figure 18.8
Record your project
to CD using the Record
CD Setup dialog box

12. Choose your CDR drive using the Select CD-R Drive drop-down list.

13. Choose the write speed for your drive using the Write Speed drop-down list.

14. Choose the number of copies you want to make by typing a number into the Number Of Copies parameter.

15. Decide whether you want to add more files to the CD later. If you want to add more files later, choose the Track-At-Once and Don't Finalize Session options in the Record Method section. If you don't want to add more files later, choose the Track-At-Once and Finalize CD options.

TIP

If you plan on having your audio CD duplicated professionally, you should have all your songs gathered together and burn them to the CD all at once using the Disc-At-Once option. This option writes and closes a CD in one move, without turning the writing laser on and off between tracks. If you use the Track-At-Once option to burn your CD, the writing laser is turned on and off between tracks and multiple sessions to create "links" between them. These "links" will show up as errors when the duplication service tries to create a master copy from your CD-R.

16.   When you're creating a CD, it helps to first have your system do a test. Testing ensures the best quality and improves your chances for a successful burn. Although testing nearly doubles the time required to create a CD, Roxio recommends testing at least the first few times you use the program. After that, you can probably skip it. Choose the Test and Record CD option in the Record Options section.

17.   To burn your CD, click the Start Recording button.

TIP

To avoid glitches in the burning process—especially for audio CDs—you should leave your computer alone until the process is complete. If it gets bogged down while burning, you could end up with a ruined CD. Of course, you can just go ahead and burn another one, but then you'll be wasting both your time and money.

Burn CDs with Windows XP

If you are running SONAR under Windows XP, then you don't need any third-party CD burning software because Windows XP provides built-in burning capabilities. By utilizing the new version of the Windows Media Player (included with Windows XP), you can burn audio CDs (and data CDs, which I'll talk about in Appendix B) by following a few simple steps:

1.   In Windows XP, click Start > Windows Media Player to open the Windows Media Player.

2.   If the Player is not displayed in full mode (as a normal window with a menu bar), then click the Show Menu Bar button (see Figure 18.9).

Figure 18.9
Click the Show Menu
Bar button to display
Windows Media Player
in a full window

Show Menu Bar button

3. Click the Media Library button (located on the left side of the Player
    window) to display the Media Library (see Figure 18.10).

Figure 18.10
Access the Media
Library using the
Media Library button

4. In the list on the left side of the Media Library, select All Audio.

5. Choose File > Add To Media Library > Add File to display the Open dialog box.

6. In the Look In drop-down list, choose the location of the WAV files you want to burn to CD.

7. In the file list below the Look In drop-down list, select the WAV file(s) you want to burn to CD. To select multiple files, hold the CTRL key on your computer keyboard as you select files with your mouse.

8. When you are finished selecting files, click Open. Your selected files will then be displayed as a list on the right side of the Media Library.

9. If you want to remove a file from the list, right-click the file and choose Delete From Library.

10. To change the title of a file, right-click the file and choose Properties to open the Properties dialog box (see Figure 18.11). In addition to the title, you can also specify the file's artist, author, album, and genre. Click OK.

Figure 18.11
Use the Properties dialog box to specify a Title, Artist, and other attributes for your file(s)

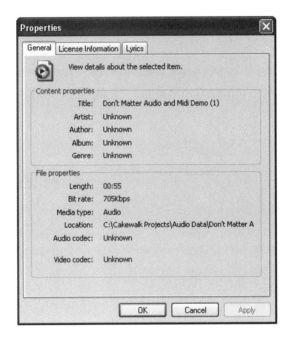

11. Click the Copy To CD Or Device button (located on the left side of the Player window) to display the CD Copier (see Figure 18.12).

Figure 18.12
Use the CD Copier to
burn your audio to CD

12. Insert a blank CD-R disc into your CD-R drive. The CD Copier recognizes
the blank disc and displays the following message: 'Copy "All Audio" to
"CD Drive"'.

13. To burn your CD, click the Copy Music button (located on the top right of
the CD Copier).

TIP

To avoid glitches in the burning process—especially for audio CDs—you should
leave your computer alone until the process is complete.

Appendix A

Sample Project Outline: From Recording to Mixdown

Throughout this book, you've learned about everything you need to know to create a Project from start to finish in SONAR. This information includes how to set up a Project, record your Tracks, edit your MIDI and audio data, mix your Tracks down to stereo, and burn the final recording to CD. But just to give you a brief overview of the whole process, I've put together this outline of all the steps you need to take to record a song using SONAR.

Set Up Your Project

1. Create a new Project. If you use a Template other than Normal to automatically set the parameters for your Project, you can skip the rest of this section. Otherwise, move on to Step 2.

2. Add a Title and other descriptive information to your Project using the File Info window.

3. Set the types of MIDI data to be recorded in the Global Options dialog box under the MIDI tab.

4. Set the Clock, Metronome, MIDI Input, and MIDI Out parameters in the Project Options dialog box.

5. Set the tempo for the Project by using the Tempo toolbar.

6. Set the Meter and Key for the Project by using the Meter/Key View.

7. Set the bit depth and sampling rate (if you're going to record audio) for the Project on the General tab in the Audio Options dialog box.

For more information, refer to Chapter 4, "Working with Projects."

Record Your Tracks

1. Create a new Track and set it up, typing in a Name and choosing an Input and Output in the Track View.

2. Enter initial values for the Volume and Pan parameters, if you need them.

3. If the Track is for audio, you can skip this step; otherwise, for a MIDI Track, choose values for the Channel, Bank, and Patch parameters.

4. Set the Record Mode using the Record Options dialog box.

5. Arm the Track and set your input signal level.

6. Click the Record button and start your performance.

7. If you need to add data to only a certain part of the Track, use the Auto Punch Record Mode and set the Punch In and Punch Out Times. You can also use the Loop toolbar to set loop points and have SONAR loop a certain section of the song for recording in only that section.

8. Repeat steps 1 through 7 for every Track you need to complete your song.

9. Save your Project as a Work (.CWP) file if it contains only MIDI data; otherwise, if it contains audio data, save it as a Bundle (.CWB) file.

For more information, refer to Chapter 6, "Recording and Playback."

Edit Your Data

1. Use the Track View to make any arrangement changes to your song. For example, you can move clips from one part of the song to another part. You can also mute any Tracks that you don't want to use in the final mix. Also, adjust the Key+, Vel+, and Tme+ parameters at this time.

2. If you need to do any precise editing to your MIDI Tracks, use the Piano Roll and Event Views. You use these Views for tasks such as changing the pitch and velocity of different notes or correcting the timing of your performance using quantizing. You can also use the Staff View for certain tasks if you feel more comfortable using standard music notation. If you want to add any permanent MIDI Effects to your data, do so at this time. Otherwise, you can add Effects in real-time during mixdown.

3. For precise editing of your audio Tracks, use the Track View. Cut, copy, or paste sections of audio and make adjustments to the volume if you need to. Add any EQ or permanent Effects at this point, too. Otherwise, you can wait to add Effects in real-time during mixdown, if your computer system can handle it.

4. Save your Project as a Work (.CWP) file if it contains only MIDI data; otherwise, if it contains audio data, save it as a Bundle (.CWB) file.

For more information, refer to Chapter 7, "Editing Basics," and Chapter 8, "Exploring the Editing Tools."

Mix Down Your Project

1. Using the Track View or the Console View, set initial values for the volume and panning for each Track in the Project.
2. Set the chorus and reverb settings for the MIDI Tracks.
3. Set the Aux Send settings for the audio Tracks.
4. Add any real-time effects you want to use for the individual MIDI and/or audio Tracks.
5. Add any real-time effects you want to use on the Aux Buses.
6. Add any real-time effects you want to use on the Mains.
7. Take a Snapshot of the current setup in case you want to come back to it later.
8. Perform a test run of the mix by playing the song and adjusting the parameters during playback.
9. Record your mix movements using the Record Automation feature. If you find that you need to make two different value changes at once during a mix, just make multiple Record Automation passes. You can also use Envelopes for automation if you prefer that method.
10. Save your Project as a Work (.CWP) file if it contains only MIDI data; otherwise, if it contains audio data, save it as a Bundle (.CWB) file.

For more information, refer to Chapter 11, "Exploring Effects," and Chapter 12, "Mixing it Down."

Burn to CD

1. Export your project to a stereo audio WAVE (.WAV) file.
2. Use Easy CD Creator or Windows XP to record your WAVE file to CD.

For more information, refer to Chapter 18, "Take Your SONAR Project to CD."

Appendix B
Backing Up Your Project Files

At the end of every recording session, I back up my Project files. It doesn't matter whether I'm running late or whether I'm so tired that I can barely keep my eyes open. I always back up my files. Why? Because there once was a time I didn't really think much of making backups. I would do it occasionally—just to be safe—but I never thought I'd run into any trouble. Then one day I went to boot up my PC, and *poof*! My hard drive crashed, taking a lot of important files with it, including a Project that I spent weeks working on. Believe me, after that experience, I never took file backups for granted again, and you shouldn't either.

Backing up your files really isn't difficult, and it doesn't take up very much extra time. This is especially true if your Project includes only MIDI data. Work (.CWP) files containing only MIDI data are usually very small, and you can make backups of them by simply copying them to a floppy disk, just like you would any other small files. Bundle (.CWB) files—project files that contain audio data—on the other hand, need to be handled a little differently because of their large size. Most Bundle files do not fit on a floppy disk, but if you have an Iomega Zip disk drive (or similar "super floppy" drive), you might be able to make a quick backup copy that way.

Back Up with Easy CD Creator

If you have a bunch of files to back up, you need a much larger storage format such as a CD-recordable drive. In Chapter 18, "Take Your SONAR Project to CD," you learned about using Easy CD Creator to create an audio CD from your SONAR Project. Well, in case you didn't know it, you can also use Easy CD Creator along with your CD-R drive to back up data files. The procedure is similar to creating an audio CD, and you can use the Easy CD Creator Wizard to step through the process like this:

1. Start Easy CD Creator.
2. Choose File > New CD Project > Data CD to create an untitled data CD project.

3. In the Select Source Files drop-down list, choose the drive containing the file(s) you want to burn to CD.

4. In the file list below the Select Source Files drop-down list, select the file(s) you want to burn to CD.

CAUTION

If you use video in your Project, not only do you have to back up the Work or Bundle file for the Project, but the individual video file, too. SONAR does not save video data along with Project data, not even in a Bundle file. For more information about SONAR's video features, read Appendix C, "Producing for Multimedia and the Web."

5. Click the Add button to add the selected file(s) to your data CD project. The file(s) are added to the data CD project list in the bottom half of the Easy CD Creator window (see Figure B.1).

Figure B.1
When you're creating a data CD, you can select any file or files from any of the storage drives connected to your computer system

6. To remove a file from the project list, select it and click the Remove button.

7. Repeat steps 3 through 6 until you've finished adding all your files to the project.

8. Click the Record button to open the Record CD Setup dialog box. Click the Options button to reveal the entire dialog box.

9. Choose your CD-R drive using the Select CD-R Drive drop-down list.

10. Choose the write speed for your drive using the Write Speed drop-down list.

11. Choose the number of copies you want to make by typing a number into the Number Of Copies parameter.

12. Decide whether you want to add more files to the CD later. If you want to add more files later, choose the Track-At-Once and Don't Finalize Session options in the Record Method section. If you don't want to add more files later, choose the Track-At-Once and Finalize CD options.

13. When you're creating a CD, it helps to first have your system do a test. Testing ensures the best quality and improves your chances for a successful burn, although testing nearly doubles the time required to create a CD, Roxio recommends testing at least the first few times you use the program. After that, you can probably skip it. Choose the Test and Record CD option in the Record Options section.

14. To burn your CD, click the Start Recording button.

Back Up with Windows XP

As I mentioned in chapter 18, Windows XP provides built-in CD burning capabilities—not just for audio CDs, but for data CDs as well. If you are using Windows XP, you can back up your Project files to CD using the following procedure:

1. Insert a blank CD-R or CD-RW disc into your CD recording drive. If Windows XP opens a CD Drive window, just click Cancel.

2. In Windows XP, choose Start > My Computer to open My Computer (see Figure B.2).

Figure B.2
Use My Computer in Windows XP to select your Project files

3. Double-click the hard disk drive icon and navigate to the location of your Project file(s). Then select the file(s) that you want to back up.

4. On the left side of the window, you'll see a section called File and Folder Tasks (see Figure B.3). Click the option called Copy This File (for single files) or Copy The Selected Items (for multiple files).

Figure B.3
Choose the appropriate option in the File and Folder Tasks section

5. In the Copy Items dialog box, select your CD recording drive and click the Copy button.

6. A balloon message will pop-up in the Windows XP task bar saying, "You have files waiting to be written to the CD." Click the balloon to open a new window for your CD recording drive (see Figure B.4). The right side of the window lists the files to be burned.

Figure B.4
The CD Drive window
lists the files to be
burned

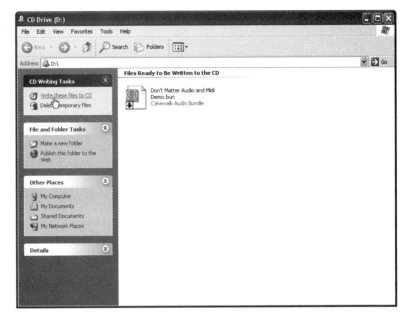

7. On the left side of the window, you'll see a section called CD Writing
    Tasks. Click the option called Write These Files To CD to open the CD
    Writing Wizard (see Figure B.5).

Figure B.5
Use the CD Writing
Wizard to burn your
files to CD

8. Enter a name for the CD in the CD Name field, and click Next. Windows XP
    then burns your file to the CD.

9. Follow the remaining prompts and click Finish when you are done.

TIP

Sometimes you may find that you have a Project file that is actually too big to fit on a single CD. Project files containing audio (Bundle files) can get quite large, especially if they contain many audio tracks, or if you are using a high bit depth (like 24-bit) or a high sampling rate (like 96 kHz). In this case, it would seem that you have no way of storing your file on a data CD. Well, if you use a file splitting utility, you can get around this limitation.

A file splitting utility will take your file and divide it into smaller files that can then be burned to multiple CDs. These smaller files represent different sections of your one large file. If you ever need to access the file again, you can copy the smaller files from the CDs to your hard drive, and then use the utility to combine them into the large file.

Take a look at the following Internet site for a list of some of the available file splitting utilities:

http://download.cnet.com/downloads/1,10150,0-10001-103-0-1-7,00.html?tag=srch&qt=file+split&cn=&ca=10001

Now, don't you feel better already? You can rest easy knowing that all your hard recording work won't be lost even if your computer does decide to give up on you one of these days. Believe me, it's not a fun experience.

Appendix C

Producing for Multimedia and the Web

In addition to regular music production, SONAR includes a number of features to help you in creating music for multimedia and the Internet. You can import a video file into a SONAR Project and then compose music to it. You can also export video files along with your synchronized music. And you can export your music files to a number of popular Internet audio file formats, including RealAudio, Windows Media Format, and MP3. In essence, these capabilities round out SONAR's full set of features, allowing you to use the program for most—if not all—of your music production needs.

Importing Video Files

If you're ever asked to compose music for film, video games, or some other visually based task, SONAR's File > Import Video File command will come in very handy. Using this command, you can include an AVI, MPEG, or QuickTime video in your Project and edit the existing audio Track or Tracks or add new ones.

NOTE

AVI, MPEG, and QuickTime are special digital video file formats specifically designed for working with video on computers. Each format uses its own unique compression scheme to achieve video quality as good as possible in a file size as small as possible. AVI (Audio Video Interleaved) is a Windows-based format, which means that any computer running Windows can play AVI files. Quick-Time is a Mac-based format, which means that any Macintosh computer can play QuickTime files. With special player software, a computer running Windows can play QuickTime files, too, which is why the format is supported by SONAR. MPEG (Motion Pictures Expert Group) is a more advanced format that sometimes requires special hardware for playback. Therefore, MPEG video files are usually of much better quality than AVI or QuickTime, and they are also smaller in size.

To add a video file to your Project, follow these steps:

1. Select File > Import Video File to open the Import Video File dialog box (see Figure C.1).

Figure C.1
Here, you can select a video file to add to your Project

2. Choose the type of video file (AVI, MPEG, or QuickTime) you want to add from the Files Of Type drop-down list and select a file.

3. If the video file contains audio data, you can import that data, too, by activating the Import Audio Stream option at the bottom of the box. If the audio is in stereo, you can import it as a single stereo audio Track or a pair of audio Tracks containing the left and right channels of the stereo signal by deactivating or activating the Stereo Split option, respectively.

4. Click Open.

SONAR then loads the video file and displays the first video frame along with the current Now Time in the Video View (see Figure C.2). If you imported audio along with the video, the new audio Track or Tracks are inserted into the Project above the currently selected Track.

Figure C.2
The Video View displays the video along with the current Now Time

Initially, when you play the Project, the video starts playing back at the beginning, but you can change where the video starts by adjusting the Start Time, as well as the Trim-in Time and Trim-out Time. Using these parameters, you can adjust when within the Project the video will start and end playback. To change these parameters, follow these steps:

1. Right-click within the Video View and select Video Properties from the pop-up menu to open the Video Properties dialog box.

2. Under the Video Settings tab, input the new values for Start Time, Trim-In Time, and Trim-Out Time. The Start Time uses measures, beats, and frames for its value; and the Trim-in and Trim-out Times use hours, minutes, seconds, and frames just as with SMPTE Time Code.

3. Click OK.

The video now starts and stops playing back within the Project at the times you specified. You also can adjust a number of other parameters for the Video View, and you access all of them via the right-click pop-up menu. For instance, if you want to remove the video from your Project, just select the Delete command. If you want to temporarily disable video playback, select the Animate command. You can even change the size of the video display by using the Stretch Options command.

TIP

If you choose Full Screen under the Stretch Options command, the video display covers the entire computer screen and you cannot access SONAR with the mouse (although keyboard commands still work). To get back to the normal display, just press the Esc (Escape) key on your computer keyboard.

Exporting Video Files

After you've imported a video file into your Project, and either edited its existing audio or added new audio Tracks to it, you can export the file so that other people can see and hear your work. Follow these steps to export the file:

1. Select File > Export Video To AVI to open the Export Video To AVI dialog box (see Figure C.3).

Figure C.3
You can use the Export Video To AVI dialog box to export video files

Export Video to AVI	? ☒

Save in: ☐ Animals   ▼ ← ⬆ ⬜ ▦▾

AK01.AVI	AK09.AVI	AK18.AVI
AK02.AVI	AK11.AVI	AK20.AVI
AK03.AVI	AK12.AVI	AK21.AVI
AK04.AVI	AK15.AVI	AK23.AVI
AK06.AVI	AK16.AVI	AK25.AVI
AK08.AVI	AK17.AVI	

File name: [   ]   [Save]

Save as type: [Video For Windows ▼]   [Cancel]

[Help]

Video Codec   [Default Codec ▼]   [Props...]

Audio Codec   [Default Codec ▼]   [Props...]

Keyframe Rate   [-1   ⬍] Frames   [Mix Options...]

Data Rate   [-1   ⬍] K/Sec

Quality (0-100)   ├───── -1

Change AVI Settings ☐

2. Type a name for the file in the File Name area. You don't need to select a file type because SONAR allows you to save your video to the AVI format only. You can't save to MPEG or QuickTime.

3. Click Save, and the video file is saved with its original parameter settings. If you want to dabble with the method of compression used in the file, along with other video-related parameters, you can set them in the lower half of the dialog box.

TIP

For more information about multimedia and video-related parameters, you should consult a dedicated book on the subject. I've found *Multimedia: Making It Work, Fifth Edition* (McGraw-Hill Professional Publishing, 2001) by Tay Vaughn to be very informative.

When you save your video file, any audio Tracks in your Project are mixed down and saved along with the video.

Exporting Audio Files

In addition to exporting your audio Tracks as WAVE (.WAV) files for the purpose of burning to CD (as you learned in Chapter 18, "Take Your SONAR Project to CD"), you can also export them as RealAudio, Windows Media Format, and MP3 files for distribution over the Internet.

NOTE

Just as AVI, MPEG, and QuickTime are special digital video file formats, RealAudio, Windows Media, and MP3 are special audio file formats specifically designed for distributing audio over the Internet. Each format uses its own unique compression scheme to achieve the best possible sound quality in the smallest possible file size. All three formats are very popular, and all three support streaming audio as well. This means that you can listen to the audio as you download it rather than having to wait for the whole audio file to be downloaded before you can play it. In terms of quality, the order from highest to lowest goes like this: Windows Media, MP3, RealAudio.

However, this order depends on who's listening, because everyone has his or her own opinions on the subject. For more information about RealAudio, visit **www.real.com/devzone/**. For more information about Windows Media, visit **www.microsoft.com/windows/windowsmedia/**. For more information about MP3, visit **http://help.mp3.com/help/**.

Preparing Audio for the Internet

Since the RealAudio, MP3, and Windows Media formats all use compression to reduce the size of audio data so that it's easier to download over the Internet, they can sometimes affect the sound of your audio. You can compensate for these unwanted changes in quality, though, by following a few simple processing procedures before you convert your files.

TIP

Instead of processing your existing tracks, it would be a good idea to mix down all your tracks to a single stereo audio track using the procedures outlined in Chapter 18. This way you can keep all your original tracks intact and just process the single stereo track for exporting as RealAudio, MP3, or Windows Media.

TIP

Before processing your audio data, you should remove any DC offset that may be present in the data. What is DC offset? Well, depending on the quality of your sound card, your audio may not be recorded as accurately as it should. Many times (especially with less expensive sound cards, such as the Sound Blaster), an electrical mismatch may occur between a sound card and the input device. When this happens, an excess of current is added to the incoming signal and the resulting audio waveform is offset from the zero axis (a line running horizontally through the center of a waveform that represents no sound or zero amplitude). This is known as DC offset.

Unfortunately, SONAR doesn't provide a DC offset removal function. But you can download a free DirectX effects plug-in to use for this purpose. The plug-in is called DCOffset, and it can be downloaded from **http://www.analogx.com/ contents/download/audio/dcoffset.htm**

Apply Equalization

Equalize your audio while keeping in mind that most of the high-end and extreme low-end content might be lost when you export the audio to one of the compressed file formats. It may take some experimentation, but cutting the low frequencies (below 60 Hz) and the high frequencies (above 10 kHz) is a good place to start. This will help in reducing any of the anomalies that can occur during the file format compression. To compensate for the frequencies being cut, you can boost some of the low frequencies that are still intact, around 200 Hz. You can also boost the important content in your audio, such as vocals, if there are any. Here's how it's done:

1. Select the stereo audio track that you created from bouncing down all the other existing tracks (mentioned earlier).

2. Choose Process > Audio Effects > Cakewalk > FxEq to open the FxEq dialog box.

3. Choose the None preset to assign all the parameter settings to their default values.

4. Activate the Lo Shelf option. Set its Center Frequency (Coarse) to around 60 Hz. Then, set its gain to –15 dB (the lowest setting). Doing this will cut out most frequencies below 60 Hz, as I mentioned earlier.

5. Activate the Hi Shelf option. Set its Center Frequency (Coarse) to around 10,000 Hz. Then, set its gain to –15 dB (the lowest setting). Doing this will cut out most frequencies above 10 kHz, as I mentioned earlier.

6. Set the Gain on the first parametric band to +3.0 dB. Then, set its Center Frequency (Coarse) to around 200 Hz. Also, set its Bandwidth (Coarse) to 1.00. You can experiment with how much the frequencies are boosted, but I wouldn't go any higher than +6.0 dB.

7. Set the Gain on the second parametric band to +3.0 dB. Then, set its Center Frequency (Coarse) to around 2,500 Hz. Also, set its Bandwidth (Coarse) to 1.00. This will boost the mid-range frequencies around 2,500 Hz. You can experiment with how much the frequencies are boosted, but I wouldn't go any higher than +6.0 dB.

8. Leave all the other parameters set to their defaults. When you're finished, the FxEq dialog box should look similar to Figure C.4.

Figure C.4
Use the FxEq function to equalize your audio in a single process

9.   Click the Audition button to preview your audio before making any changes. If you hear any clipping or distortion, try lowering the gain on one or both of the parametric bands.

10. Click OK.

Apply Dynamic Processing

In addition to altering the frequency content of your audio, converting to RealAudio, MP3, or Windows Media can reduce the dynamic (amplitude) range, making your audio sound flat or dull. Adding a bit of dynamic processing before conversion will give you some control over you final signal levels, rather than leaving them to chance. To accomplish this, you need to use SONAR's FX Compressor/Gate effect:

1.   Select the stereo audio track that you created from bouncing down all the other existing tracks (mentioned earlier).

2.   Choose Process > Audio Effects > Cakewalk > FX Compressor/Gate to open the FX Compressor/Gate dialog box.

3.   Choose the Flat preset to assign all the parameter settings to their default values.

4.   Set the Attack Time parameter to 1 ms (milliseconds).

5.   Set the Compressor Ratio parameter to 2.0:1. You can experiment with the Compressor Ratio if you'd like. A good ratio range is between 2.0:1 and 4.0:1, but it may vary with some audio material, so you'll have to use your own judgement. But be careful, because too much dynamic processing can sometimes add unwanted artifacts and make your audio sound dull and lifeless.

6.   Set the Release Time parameter to 500 ms.

7.   Set the Compressor Thr (threshold) parameter to –18 dB.

8. Leave all the other parameters set to their defaults. When you're finished, the FX Compressor/Gate dialog box should look similar to Figure C.5.

Figure C.5
Use the FX
Compressor/Gate
effect to apply
dynamic processing
to your audio

9. Click the Audition button to preview your audio before making any changes.

10. Click OK.

Normalize

The last step is to normalize your audio. As I talked about in Chapter 8, normalization raises the amplitude of an audio signal as high as it can go without causing clipping or distortion. This guarantees that your file will use the maximum amount of digital resolution and amplitude available. It also ensures that you'll be using the highest possible volume when exporting your audio for the Internet, which helps in masking low-level noise and possible compression artifacts. But keep in mind that normalization is not always necessary, so you may want to try exporting your audio with normalization and without normalization. To normalize your audio:

1. Select the stereo audio track that you created from bouncing down all the other existing tracks (mentioned earlier).

2. Choose Process > Audio > Normalize.

Now, your audio is ready to be exported to RealAudio, MP3, or Windows Media.

Exporting to RealAudio

Do the following to mix and save your audio Tracks as a RealAudio file:

1. Select the Track or Tracks you want to export in the Track View.

2. Choose File > Export Audio to open the Export Audio dialog box (see Figure C.6).

Figure C.6
You can use the Export Audio dialog box to export to RealAudio

3. From the Look In list, select the folder you want to save the RealAudio file into. Then type a name for the file in the File Name box.

4. Choose a file type from the File Of Types list. In this case, use the RealAudio option.

5. Select the Format you want to use. You can mix your audio Tracks to a single stereo file, two mono files (that, when combined, create a stereo file), or a single mono file.

6. Choose the sound card or cards you want to use to process your audio Tracks from the Source Bus(es) list.

7. Leave all the Mix Enables options activated to ensure that your new RealAudio file will include the same effects and mix automation that you used on the original audio Tracks.

8. Click Export to open the RealAudio Settings dialog box (see Figure C.7).

Figure C.7
In the RealAudio Settings dialog box, you can adjust specific parameters for the RealAudio file

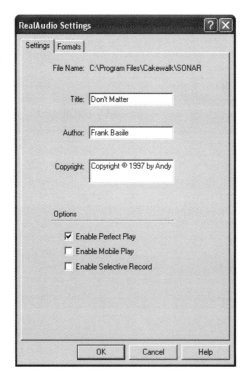

9. Under the Settings tab, you can enter Title, Author, and Copyright information for the RealAudio file.

10. Choose from the three Options at the bottom of the dialog: Enable Perfect Play, Enable Mobile Play, and Enable Selective Record. Enable Perfect Play requires the listeners to download the entire RealAudio file before hearing it rather than being able to stream the file. This option ensures uninterrupted playback, but your listeners will also have to wait for the download. Enable Mobile Play gives listeners a choice between downloading and streaming a file. Enable Selective Record lets listeners save the file to their hard drive for later use. If you don't want people to be able to keep a copy of the file, make sure Enable Mobile Play and Enable Selective Record are not activated.

11. Under the Formats tab (see Figure C.8), you can select the modem speeds that you want your RealAudio file to be optimized for. It's really best to just select them all so that your listeners can hear the best quality at their own specific modem speed. For example, someone using a 56 Kbps modem will hear a better version of your file than someone listening with a 28 Kbps modem. Otherwise, everyone would hear just the same low-quality file.

Figure C.8
You can set modem speeds on the Formats tab of the RealAudio Settings dialog box

12. If you want your file to be compatible with the older 5.0 version of RealAudio, select the Include A RA 5.0 Compatible Stream option. This option makes your file a little bigger, but it's worth the extra size just in case someone using the old RealAudio Player software tries to listen to your file.

13. If you want to optimize the RealAudio file for certain types of content, select the type of music that you've recorded in your Project in the Content Type section. Most of the time, you'll probably use the Stereo Music option.

14. Click OK, and your audio is saved as a RealAudio file with an .RM extension.

Exporting to Windows Media

To mix and save your audio Tracks as a Windows Media file, just follow these steps:

1. Select the Track or Tracks you want to export in the Track View.

2. Choose File > Export Audio to open the Export Audio dialog box.

3. From the Look In list, select the folder you want to save the Windows Media file into. Then type a name for the file in the File Name box.

4. Choose the type of file from the File Of Types list. In this case, use the Windows Media option.

5. Select the Format you want to use. You can mix your audio Tracks to a single stereo file, two mono files (that, when combined, create a stereo file), or a single mono file.

6. Choose the sound card or cards you want to use to process your audio Tracks from the Source Bus(es) list.

7. Leave all the Mix Enables options activated to ensure that your new Windows Media file will include the same effects and mix automation that you used on the original audio Tracks.

8. Click Export to open the Microsoft Audio Encode Options dialog box (see Figure C.9).

Figure C.9
In the Microsoft Audio Encode Options dialog box, you can adjust specific parameters for the Windows Media file

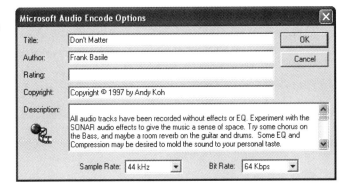

9. Enter Title, Author, Rating, Copyright, and Description information for the Windows Media file.

10. Choose from the two other settings: Sample Rate and Bit Rate. You learned about sampling rates in Chapter 1, "Understanding MIDI and Digital Audio." Sample Rate lets you set the sampling rate for the Windows Media file. The higher the rate, the better the file will sound, but the bigger the file size will be. Bit Rate lets you target the modem speed for the Windows Media file. For example, if you want the file to be able to play over a 28.8 Kbps modem, select the 22 Kbps bit rate. This bit rate will play over any modem speed 28.8 Kbps and higher. If you want to produce a higher quality file, you can select a higher bit rate, but the file won't play on a 28.8 Kbps modem. A bit rate of 48 Kbps or lower should play on a 56 Kbps modem, but you are better off with a 40 Kbps or lower setting because the Internet can be slow at times.

11. Click OK, and your audio is saved as a Windows Media file with a .WMA extension.

Exporting to MP3

To mix and save your audio Tracks as an MP3 file, follow these steps:

1. Select the Track or Tracks you want to export in the Track View.

2. Choose File > Export Audio to open the Export Audio dialog box.

3. From the Look In list, select the folder you want to save the MP3 file into. Then type a name for the file in the File Name box.

4. Choose the type of file from the File Of Types list. In this case, use the MP3 option.

5. Select the Format you want to use. You can mix your audio Tracks to a single stereo file, two mono files (that, when combined, create a stereo file), or a single mono file.

6. Choose the sound card or cards you want to use to process your audio Tracks from the Source Bus(es) list.

7. Leave all the Mix Enables options activated to ensure that your new MP3 file will include the same effects and mix automation that you used on the original audio Tracks.

8. Click Export to open the Cakewalk MP3 Encoder dialog box (see Figure C.10).

Figure C.10
In the Cakewalk MP3 Encoder dialog box, you can adjust specific parameters for the MP3 file

9. Similar to Windows Media, you can select a Sampling Rate, Bit Rate, and Stereo Mode. One difference is Joint Stereo mode, which lets you create smaller MP3 files by comparing the left and right audio signals and eliminating any material that is the same in both channels. Using this option usually degrades the audio quality, though, so I advise against choosing it unless you really need smaller MP3 files.

10. Use the Optimize Encoding setting to adjust how long it takes to encode your MP3 file. If you set the slider toward the left, encoding will go faster; to the right, encoding will go slower. But the more time spent on encoding, the better the quality of the file. So, I recommend you leave the slider set all the way to the right. Encoding a file doesn't take very long anyway.

11. If you want to include some information about the file, select the Include ID3 Info option. To enter the information, click Set ID3 Info to open the ID3 Info dialog box. Here, you can enter Title, Artist, Album, Year, Track Number, Comment, and Genre information. Click OK when you're done.

12. Click Encode, and your audio is saved as an MP3 file with an .MP3 extension.

TIP

If you want to include the music from the MIDI Tracks of your Project in your RealAudio, Windows Media, or MP3 files, read the "Convert Your MIDI Tracks" section of Chapter 18, "Take Your SONAR Project to CD."

Appendix D

SONAR Resources on the Web

Although I've made every effort to include as much information as possible about SONAR within this book, someone will always have that one question that goes unanswered. And, as I mentioned earlier in the book, some of the topics could fill up tomes all on their own. But that doesn't mean I'm going to leave you out in the cold with nowhere to turn.

I spent some time searching the Internet and found that it provides a number of resources you can use to locate any additional information you might need. I've tried to be sure to list all the quality sites that are available, but I may have missed a few. If you know of a great Cakewalk-related Web site that's not on this list, please drop me a note at **www.garrigus.com** so that I can be sure to include the site in the next edition of this book.

DigiFreq

http://www.digifreq.com/digifreq/

This is one of the first sites you should visit. I have created a site called DigiFreq that provides free news, reviews, tips, and techniques for music technology users. There is a Discussion area, where you can post your questions and get them answered directly by me. There is also a Live Chat area, where I hold scheduled chat sessions. You can also get a free subscription to the DigiFreq monthly music technology newsletter, which includes articles, tips, and all kinds of information about music technology, including SONAR. Plus, as a subscriber you are eligible to win free music products each month, and you also have access to all the newsletter back issues. Be sure to stop by to sign up for the free newsletter and to meet all of the other SONAR 2 Power readers out there!

Cakewalk Technical Support Homepage

http://www.cakewalk.com/Support/

The Cakewalk Technical Support Homepage is also one of the first places you should look for answers. Cakewalk provides a large selection of materials, including answers to the most frequently asked questions (FAQs), product updates, and technical documents. You also can find lessons, tips, and tricks, as well as additional helpful publications and resources. And, of course, you can get in touch with Cakewalk's Tech Support people if you need to.

Official Cakewalk Newsgroups

http://www.cakewalk.com/Support/newsgroups.html

Another place you can look for help is the Official Cakewalk Newsgroups. The Cakewalk newsgroups not only provide you with direct access to Cakewalk Technical Support, but also to other users. You can find specific topics on SONAR, digital audio, and MIDI FX, as well as dedicated groups for general information and beginners.

AudioForums.com

http://www.audioforums.com/

AudioForums.com is yet another Web site where you can find discussions about Cakewalk products. You won't find anything overly special about this site, but you can find some good information here, so I thought I should include it. This site also includes discussion areas for audio-related topics such as PC Audio Hardware, Mac Audio Hardware, Studio Gear, and more.

Cakewalk Users Guild

http://www.milan.net/cakewalk/

Unfortunately, what could be one of the best unofficial Cakewalk resources on the Web—the Cakewalk Users Guild—isn't updated on a regular basis. But this site still contains plenty of useful information. You can find answers to frequently asked questions (FAQs), file downloads, Projects by other users for download, and so on.

Li'l Chips Cakewalk Area

http://www.lilchips.com/store/index.asp

The Li'l Chips Cakewalk Area provides free Instrument Definition files and free StudioWare panels for download. Most of them pertain to Roland MIDI products, but you still can find a nice collection that could be useful to you.

Synth Zone

http://www.synthzone.com/

Although not a dedicated Cakewalk site, the Synth Zone is an excellent MIDI, synthesizer, and electronic music production resource guide. You can find links to a ton of information, such as patches and associated software, for just about any synthesizer product from just about any manufacturer. You can also find links to discussion groups, classifieds ads and auctions, music and audio software downloads, and more.

Harmony Central

http://www.harmony-central.com/

Another excellent non-dedicated Cakewalk site, Harmony Central is one of the best Internet resources for musicians. Updated on a daily basis, the site provides industry news and separate "departments" for Guitar, Bass, Effects, Software, Recording, MIDI, Keyboard and Synths, Drums and Percussion, Computers and Music, and a Bands Page. Sifting through all the information on this site will take awhile, but it's definitely worth the time and effort.

ProRec

http://www.prorec.com/

An additional non-dedicated Cakewalk site, ProRec is one of the best audio recording resources for musicians. Updated regularly, the site provides industry news, articles, and reviews. Like Harmony Central, sifting through all the information on this site will take a while, but it's definitely worth the time and effort.

Index

INDEX

X

Y

Z

Electronic Musician

Mail in the attached card today to receive your

3 free issues

of **Electronic Musician**!

Courtesy of **Muska & Lipman**
and **Electronic Musician**.